NEW YORK REVIEW BOOKS
CLASSICS

SHAKESP

MICHEL EYQUEM DE MO.   1s
born in Aquitaine, not far from Bordeaux, in the chateau of
his wealthy aristocratic family. Educated by his father in
Latin and Greek from an early age, Montaigne attended
boarding school in Bordeaux before studying law in Toulouse.
He then embarked on a distinguished public career, serving
as a counselor of court in Périgueux and Bordeaux, becoming
a courtier to Charles the IX, and receiving the collar of the
Order of Saint Michael. After the death of his father in 1568,
Montaigne succeeded to the title of Lord of Montaigne, and
in 1571 he retired from public life in order to devote himself
to reading and writing, publishing the first two volumes of
his essays in 1580 and a third in 1588. From 1581 to 1585, he
was the elected mayor of Bordeaux, confronting ongoing
strife between Catholics and Protestants as well as an outbreak
of the plague. Married to Françoise de Cassaigne, Montaigne
was the father of six daughters, only one of whom survived
into adulthood. He continued to write new essays and to add
new material to the existing ones until the end of his life. The
complete essays appeared posthumously in 1595.

JOHN FLORIO (1553–1625) was born in London, the son of
Michelangelo Florio, a Tuscan convert to Protestantism who
had moved to England because of his religious beliefs and
who served as a language tutor to several highborn English
families. Raised in Italian-speaking Switzerland and Germany,
where his father fled after the Catholic Queen Mary I came to
the English throne, John Florio returned to England during
the reign of Queen Elizabeth I and followed in his father's
footsteps as an instructor of languages, teaching French and

Italian at Magdalen College, Oxford, and, under King James I, working as a private tutor to the Crown Prince and the Queen Consort. Florio's works include *First Fruits, which yield Familiar Speech, Merry Proverbs, Witty Sentences, and Golden Sayings*; *A Perfect Induction to the Italian and English Tongues*; *Second Fruits, to be gathered of Twelve Trees, of divers but delightsome Tastes to the Tongues of Italian and English men*; *Garden of Recreation, yielding six thousand Italian Proverbs*; an Italian–English dictionary, *A World of Words* (the second edition of which was entitled *Queen Anna's New World of Words*); and his celebrated translation of Montaigne's *Essays*.

STEPHEN GREENBLATT is the author of, among other books, *Will in the World: How Shakespeare Became Shakespeare* and *The Swerve: How the World Became Modern* (winner of the National Book Award, the James Russell Lowell Award, and the Pulitzer Prize). He is the John Cogan University Professor of the Humanities at Harvard.

PETER G. PLATT is a professor and chair of English at Barnard College. He is the author of *Shakespeare and the Culture of Paradox* (2009) and *Reason Diminished: Shakespeare and the Marvelous* (1997), and the editor of *Wonders, Marvels, and Monsters in Early Modern Culture* (1999). He has written articles about Shakespeare, Renaissance poetics and rhetoric, and John Florio. He is currently writing a book about Shakespeare and Montaigne.

SHAKESPEARE'S MONTAIGNE

The Florio Translation of the *Essays*

MICHEL DE MONTAIGNE

Translated from the French by
JOHN FLORIO

Edited and with an introduction by
STEPHEN GREENBLATT

Edited, modernized, and annotated by
PETER G. PLATT

NEW YORK REVIEW BOOKS

New York

THIS IS A NEW YORK REVIEW BOOK
PUBLISHED BY THE NEW YORK REVIEW OF BOOKS
435 Hudson Street, New York, NY 10014
www.nyrb.com

Library of Congress Cataloging-in-Publication Data
Montaigne, Michel de, 1533–1592.
 [Essais. Selections. English]
 Shakespeare's Montaigne / by Michel de Montaigne ; translated by John Florio ;
edited by Stephen Greenblatt and Peter Platt.
    pages cm. — (New York Review Books Classics)
 Includes bibliographical references.
 ISBN 978-1-59017-722-8 (paperback)
 I. Florio, John, 1553?–1625, translator. II. Greenblatt, Stephen, 1943– III. Platt,
Peter. IV. Title.
 PQ1642.E6G74 2014
 844'.3—dc23
                        2013043477

ISBN 978-1-59017-722-8
Available as an electronic book; ISBN 978-1-59017-734-1

Printed in the United States of America on acid-free paper.
10 9 8 7 6 5 4 3 2 1

CONTENTS

fruites wilde, which nature of hir selfe, and of hir ordinarie progresse hath produced : where-as indeede, they are those which our selves have altered by our artificiall devises, and diverted from their common order, we should rather terme savage. In those are the true and most profitable vertues, and naturall proprieties most livelie and vigorous, which in these we have bastardized, applying them to the pleasure of our corrupted taste. And if notwithstanding, in divers fruites of those countries that were never tilled, we shall finde, that in respect of ours they are most excellent, and as delicate vnto our taste; there is no reason, arte should gaine the point of honour of our great and puissant mother Nature . We have so much by our inventions, surcharged the beauties and riches of hir workes, that we have altogether o-ver-choaked hir : yet where-ever hir puritie shineth, she makes our vaine, and frivolus enter-prises wonderfully ashamed.

>   *Et veniunt hederæ sponte sua melius,*
> *Surgit & in solis formosior arbutus antris,*
>   *Et volucres nulla dulcius arte canunt.*
>   Ivies spring better of their owne accord,
>   Vn-hanted plots much fairer trees afford,
>   Birdes by no arte much sweeter notes record.

Al our endevours or wit, cannot so much as reach to represent the neast of the least bird-let, it's contexture, beavtie, profit and vse, no nor the webbe of a seelie spider. *All things* (saith *Plato*) *are produced, either by nature, by fortune, or by arte. The greatest and fairest by one or o-ther of the two first, the least and imperfect by the last.* Those nations seeme therefore so barba-rous vnto mee, because they have received very-little fashion from humane wit, and are yet neere their originall naturalitie. The lawes of nature do yet commaund them, which are but little bastardized by ours. And that with such puritie, as I am sometimes grieved the know-lege of it came no sooner to light, at what time ther were men, that better than we could have judged of-it. I am sorie, *Licurgus* and *Plato* had-it not: for me seemeth that what in those na-tions wee see by experience, doth not onelie exceede all the pictures wherewith licentious Poesie hath prowdly imbellished the golden age, & al hir quaint inventions to faine a happy condition of man, but also the conception & desire of Philosophie. They could not imagine a genuitie so pure and simple, as we see it by experience; nor ever beleeve our societie might be maintained with so little arte and humane combination . It is a nation, would I answere *Plato*, that hath no kinde of traffike, no knowledge of Letters , no intelligence of numbers, no name of magistrate, nor of politike superioritie; no vse of service, of riches, or of povertys no contracts, no successions, no dividences, no occupation but idle; no respect of kinred, but common, no apparrell but naturall, no manuring of lands, no vse of wine, corne, or mettle. The very words that import lying, falshood, treason, dissimulation, covetousnes, envie, detra-ction, and pardon, were never heard-of amongst- them. How dissonant would hee finde his imaginary common-wealth from this perfection?

>   *Hos natura modos primùm dedit.*
>   Nature at first vprise,
>   These manners did devise.

Furthermore, they live in a country of so exceeding pleasant and temperate situation, that as my testimonies have tolde me, it is very rare to see a sicke-body amongst-them; and they have further assured me, they never saw any man there, either shaking with the palsie, tooth-lesse, with eyes dropping, or crooked and stooping through age. They are seated alongst the sea-coast, encompassed toward the land with huge and steepie mountaines , having be-tweene both, a hundred leagues or there abouts of open and champaine ground. They have great abundance of fish and flesh, that have no resemblance at all with ours, and eate them without any sawces, or skill of Cookerie , but plaine boiled or broyled. The first man that brought a horse thither, although he had in many other voyages conversed with them, bred so great a horror in the land, that before they could take notice of him , they slew him with arrowes. Their buildings are very long, and able to containe two or three hundred soules, covered with barkes of great trees, fastned in the ground at one end , enterlaced and joyned close together by the toppes, after the manner of some of our Granges; the covering wher-of hangs downe to the ground, and steadeth them as a flancke. They have a kinde of wood so hard, that ryving and cleaving the same, they make blades, swords, and grid-yrons, to broile

their

A page from "Of the Cannibals," as it appeared in the 1603 edition of John Florio's translation of Michel de Montaigne's *Essayes*, including the passage quoted virtually verbatim in *The Tempest.*

Shakespeare's Montaigne

I

WHEN, near the end of his career, Shakespeare wrote *The Tempest*, the tragicomic romance that seems at least in retrospect to signal his impending retirement to Stratford, he had in his mind and quite possibly on his desk a book of Montaigne's *Essays*. One of those essays, "Of the Cannibals," has long been recognized as a source upon which Shakespeare was clearly drawing.

The playwright had long had some degree of acquaintance with French culture and language. For some time in and around 1604 he rented rooms in a house on Silver Street in London that belonged to a family of French Huguenots—Protestant refugees from religious persecution in their own country. Shakespeare probably already knew some French before he moved to Silver Street: He seems to have read in their original language several of the French sources he used in his plays, and *Henry V* (1599) includes a comical scene in which the French princess, instructed by her waiting gentlewoman, tries to learn the English words for the parts of the body: "La main, *de hand*; les doigts, *de fingres*. Je pense que je suis la bonne écolière; j'ai gagné deux mots d'anglais vitement." The scene ends with a flurry of dirty puns that depends on a familiarity with French obscenities.

Yet close attention to the allusions in *The Tempest* and elsewhere makes clear that Shakespeare read Montaigne not in French but in an English translation. That translation, published in a handsome folio edition in London in 1603, was by John Florio. For Shakespeare—and not for Shakespeare alone but for virtually all of his

English contemporaries—Montaigne was Florio's Montaigne. The essays selected here, in their rich Elizabethan idiom and wildly inventive turns of phrase, constitute the way Montaigne spoke to Renaissance England.

Shakespeare quite possibly knew Florio, who was twelve years his senior, personally. English-born, the son of Italian Protestant refugees, Florio was on friendly terms with such writers as Ben Jonson and Samuel Daniel. In the early 1590s, he was a tutor to the Earl of Southampton, the wealthy nobleman to whom Shakespeare dedicated two poems in 1593 and 1594. But it is not simply a likely personal connection that accounts for the fact that Shakespeare read Montaigne in Florio's translation. The translation seemed to address English readers of Shakespeare's time with unusual directness and intensity.

It is not that the translation was impeccably accurate. Montaigne's French is often difficult and occasionally obscure, and there were many occasions in which the translator was venturing no more than an educated guess. But Florio was an exceptionally gifted linguist, steeped in Italian and French and at the same time in love with the resources of the English language. He had the great good fortune to be working at the moment when that language was at its most vital. The brilliance of his achievement was so generally acknowledged that even those English readers with very good command of French—John Donne, Walter Ralegh, Francis Bacon, and Robert Burton, to name a few—chose to encounter Montaigne through Florio's English. To read the *Essays* in Florio's translation is to read them, as it were, over the shoulders of some of England's greatest writers.

2

In 1580 when Shakespeare was an unknown sixteen-year-old with very dim prospects, Montaigne, then at the ripe age of forty-seven, published the first two books of his essays. Nine years earlier, he had made the decision to withdraw from the public sphere and to retire to his estate for a life devoted to reading and thinking. Montaigne was independently wealthy. In the fifteenth century his paternal great-grandfather had made a fortune as a merchant and had bought the château near Bordeaux where Montaigne was born in 1533, thereby transforming himself and his descendants into the hereditary lords of Montaigne. His father, Pierre Eyquem, had as a young man been a soldier in the French wars in Italy and had served as the mayor of Bordeaux. His mother, Antoinette de Louppes (Lopez) of Toulouse, was descended from a wealthy family of Spanish Jewish origin that had converted to Catholicism. Michel Eyquem—the man we know as Montaigne—was their third son, but the death of his two elder brothers meant that he became the head of the family and the heir to the title.

But if from an economic perspective Montaigne's decision to retire was not particularly fraught, nonetheless it was for him personally a momentous and difficult one. Though still fairly young, he had been active in public affairs for years. At the age of twenty-one, he had been made a counselor, first in Périgueux and then in the Bordeaux parliament, and he had been leading a vigorous political and social life both in his own region and in the royal court in Paris. By the 1550s France was in the grip of profound tensions between Catholics and Protestants that would eventually erupt into full-scale massacre and civil war, and there were strong incentives for people of goodwill to dedicate their energies to an attempt to avert the looming disaster. One eloquent expression of the intellectual, moral, and political ferment that Montaigne and his generation experienced is the daring treatise against tyranny written by his closest friend, Étienne de La Boétie, a fellow counselor at Bordeaux. The treatise, which captured Montaigne's admiring attention and sparked the friendship that arose between them, evokes a moment in which thoughtful men and women were asking the most basic questions about the social order, the oppressive force of custom, the nature of obedience, and the ineradicable longing for liberty.

In his great essay "Of Friendship," Montaigne bears witness to the intensity of the bond between himself and La Boétie—"We were co-partners in all things"—and to the almost unbearable grief brought about by his friend's untimely death in 1563. Nothing in his subsequent life, including his marriage in 1565, came close to the emotional depth of this relationship, and he mourned its loss with far more passionate grief than he expressed at the death of five of the six children born to him by his wife.

La Boétie's death, followed by the death in 1568 of his father, played an important role in enabling Montaigne to reach his decision to retire in 1571. Yet even in the wake of this decision, he remained far more involved in the public realm than the tone of his essays suggests. He tried unsuccessfully, after the Saint Bartholomew's Day massacre in 1572, to mediate between the Catholic Henri de Guise and the Protestant Henri de Navarre; he served two two-year terms as the mayor of Bordeaux; he acted as an informal, confidential adviser to successive kings and to important men and women in the court. He took part in the siege by Catholic forces of the Protestant stronghold of La Fère; he was arrested in Paris in 1588 on orders of the Catholic League and then quickly released; constantly attempting to moderate murderous religious passions, he was distrusted and attacked by zealots on both sides. And in the midst of these public affairs, he continued to manage his large, complex estate with its extensive landholdings; he tried to protect his family and dependents from the periodic outbreaks of bubonic plague (which during one of his terms of office killed nearly half the inhabitants of Bordeaux); he visited the mineral baths of Germany, Switzerland, and Italy in the hope of some relief from the excruciating pain of the kidney stones by which he was afflicted. His was not an untroubled life of solitary meditation.

Yet at its vital center was the resolution he inscribed in Latin on the wall of a little study next to the library in his house: "In the year of Christ 1571, at the age of thirty-eight, on the last day of February, his birthday, Michel de Montaigne, long weary of the service of the court and public employments, while still entire, retired to the bosom of the learned virgins, where in calm and freedom from all cares he will spend what little remains of his life, now more than half run out. If the fates permit, he will complete this abode, this sweet ancestral retreat; and he has consecrated to it his freedom, tranquility, and leisure."[1] Though as these words suggest he embarked on some home improvements, the real fruit of this retirement was not the projected completion of his ancestral abode—for when is a house ever truly completed?—but rather the writing of the essays in which Montaigne continues to live.

The essays—some of the earliest of which are less than a page in length—may have begun as little more than random jottings. Renaissance gentlemen made a practice of writing down in what were called commonplace books interesting thoughts or felicitous turns of phrase that they encountered in the course of their reading. A passionate reader from his youth, Montaigne had assembled in a room on the third floor of a tower in his château an unusually large collection of books, centered on classics in the Latin language in which he was perfectly fluent. In his essay "Of Three Commerces or Societies," Montaigne gives us a glimpse of his time in this room:

> At home I betake me somewhat the oftener to my library, whence all at once I command and survey all my household. It is seated in the chief entry of my house; thence I behold under me my garden, my base court, my yard, and look even into most rooms of my house. There, without order, without method, and by piecemeals I turn over and ransack now one book, and now another. Sometimes I muse and rave; and walking up and down, I indite and enregister these my humors, these my conceits.

"Without order, without method, and by piecemeals"—Montaigne's account of his ransacking of books is not, as it would be among many of his contemporaries, a piece of calculated modesty, meant to hide his systematic labor; it gets at something real, not only

---

1. Quoted in *The Complete Essays of Montaigne*, trans. Donald M. Frame (Stanford University Press, 1957), ix–x.

in the way he read but in the way he thought and wrote. The genius of the essays is bound up with his realization that he should trust the apparently random motions of his mind, not forcing them into coherent order but "enregistering" them as they passed. He allowed himself to "try out" his mind's faculties—the French word *"essai"* means a trial—by recording whatever struck him and made him "muse and rave." And in doing so, he came to realize he could capture and transmit crucial elements of his lived life.

Montaigne's essays are not an autobiography in any familiar sense. While they are full of personal details, they do not attempt to narrate what several of Shakespeare's characters call "the story of my life." Montaigne seems to have been allergic to sequential order and suspicious of biographical coherence. He eschewed the desire to construct an ennobling image of himself, for he knew perfectly well that such ideal pictures are at best partial and, still more often, fraudulent. He would not present himself as the fixed embodiment of this or that quality, for he experienced existence as a succession of inconsistent and disjointed thoughts and impulses. He could not narrate his life as a story of heroic virtue or indeed as a story of anything else, for precisely by virtue of being alive his existence was ongoing, incomplete, unfinished. "It is myself I portray," he tells the reader, and therefore he wishes his imperfections and his natural form to be "read to the life." What this means, as we learn when we encounter Montaigne's writing, is that he is constantly in motion.

To be sure, as he notes in his great essay "Of Repenting," "There is no man (if he listen to himself) that doth not discover in himself a peculiar form of his, a swaying form, which wrestleth against the institution and against the tempest of passions which are contrary unto him." But for Montaigne, this "swaying form"—*une forme maistresse*—does not cancel out or even diminish the ceaseless vicissitudes to which he and everyone else is subject. These vicissitudes are no mere accidents, set against an enduring substance; they are, Montaigne concludes, what it means to exist:

I cannot settle my object. It goeth so unquietly and staggering, with a natural drunkenness. I take it in this plight, as it is at the instant I amuse myself about it. I describe not the essence but the passage. Not a passage from age to age, or, as the people reckon, from seven years to seven, but from day to day, from minute to minute. My history must be fitted to the present.

Il faut accommoder mon histoire à l'heure. A history that must "be fitted to the present" is a history that must of necessity abjure the highest form of literary ambition that the Renaissance inherited from the ancient world, namely, the epic. Where the epic is governed by an overarching design, the essay embraces contingency; where the epic invokes gods and heroes, the essays deal with a private individual in a world without supernatural intervention; where the epic appeals for inspiration to the Muses, the essays eschew not only divine aid but even the more modest shaping power of human art. In the design of their lives, the great figures of epic—Achilles, Odysseus, Aeneas—are forever wedded to their passions and to their fates. The essays by contrast steadfastly resist the narrative design of all life stories.

Hence, Montaigne writes in the essay "Of the Inconstancy of Our Actions," "even good authors do ill and take a wrong course, willfully to opinionate themselves about framing a constant and solid contexture of us." Humans are in reality programmatically inconsistent: "We float and waver between diverse opinions: we will nothing freely, nothing absolutely, nothing constantly."

All the same, Montaigne was, of course, engaged in giving an account of himself. No one has ever done it more magnificently. But his "object," as he puts it, would not stay still, and his account was deliberately composed without a shape:

If I speak diversely of myself, it is because I look diversely upon myself.... Shamefaced, bashful, insolent, chaste, luxurious, peevish, prattling, silent, fond, doting, labourious, nice, delicate, ingenious, slow, dull, froward, humorous, debonaire, wise, ignorant, false in words, true-speaking, both liberal, covetous, and prodigal. All these I perceive in some measure or other to be in mine, according as I stir or turn myself.

This sounds at first like a matter of perspective: The angle at which one regards an object, even so intimately familiar an object as oneself, would necessarily change the terms of a depiction. But it is not only a matter of the shifting position of the beholder; rather it is the inner life of the self, as well as the position of the viewer, that is constantly in motion.

However the essays originated, whether as random notes, casual musings, or collections of quotations he found interesting, they evolved into what we may call a life-form. His goal, Montaigne writes in his preface to the reader, is to enable people who care about him to recover, after he is gone, some "lineaments" of his "conditions and humours" and thereby to keep the knowledge they have had of him "more whole, and more lively" (*plus entière and plus vive*).[2] The essays are driven by Montaigne's determination to preserve the recollection of himself entire and hence to remain, as he puts it, alive. But the only way for him to do so is to be true to the restless and irregular movements of his mind and, as far as possible, completely candid.

There are, he acknowledges, some limits to his candor. His was a profoundly intolerant age that allowed at least in print little room for refusing the ferocious seriousness, the sense of all-or-nothing, that characterized both Catholic and Protestant polemicists. On all questions of belief the voices of authority thundered that salvation was at stake and that one's fate both in this world and in the life to come lay in the orthodoxy of one's response. There was little willingness to accept the legitimacy of multiple structures of belief, patterns of behavior, or systems of rule. Instead there was a pervasive

---

2. The phrase may be close to the rhetorical device called hendiadys; that is, it may mean something like "completely alive." But "complete" also suggests the range and diversity of the traits Montaigne is determined to record. This goal is linked to his determination to record his defects "to the life" (*au vif*) and to depict what he calls his "natural form."

sense of a massive, irreconcilable alternative: God or the Devil, Christ or Antichrist. No one in Montaigne's repressive, conflict-ridden world would have grasped, let alone honored, the concept of freedom of speech. "I speak truth," Montaigne writes in "Of Repenting," "not my belly-full, but as much as I dare."

Quite apart from political and religious censorship, deep-rooted social codes of shame and embarrassment, then as now, proved extremely difficult to break. Yet Montaigne tried valiantly: "I am resoluted," he writes in the sexually frank essay "Upon Some Verses of *Virgil*," "to dare speak whatsoever I dare do." The rich sense of intimacy that the essays have produced in his own time and in the centuries that have followed make good on Montaigne's claim in his "The Author to the Reader," with a longing glance at depictions of the New World natives, that had he lived "among those nations which yet are said to live under the sweet liberty of Nature's first and uncorrupted laws, I assure thee I would most willingly have portrayed myself fully and naked."

The force of this desire in a public figure—and the lord of Montaigne was inescapably a public figure, however much he vaunted his privacy—would have seemed all the more remarkable in the Renaissance, obsessed as it was with the fetishism of dress. In the sixteenth century the particular clothes one wore carried a significant measure of one's identity. To forgo that mode of securing a place in the world was to repudiate much of what at the time constituted the very notion of a "person"—a term that derives from the Latin word for a mask. Montaigne longed to strip away the mask and display what lay hidden beneath. It is not that he thought that whatever he would thus show the world was heroic or beautiful; he did not imagine himself as the idealized nude of a classical statue. But he was determined to leave a vivid trace of his actual self, in all its particularity, and he argued—against virtually all the moral philosophers of his age and of centuries past—that this particularity was what actually mattered. "Authors communicate themselves unto the world by some special and strange mark; I the first by my general disposition, as *Michel de Montaigne*, not as a grammarian, or a poet, or lawyer."

Did this mean that he therefore abandoned the hope of reaching beyond the tiny circle of his family and friends? Not at all. *"Every man,"* he wrote, *"beareth the whole stamp of human condition."*

What Montaigne meant by this celebrated phrase had nothing to do with finding a universal essence beneath the accidents of individuality. Pagan philosophers, particularly Plato and his followers, had dreamed of employing dialectical reasoning to pass through Becoming to a realm of pure Being. And Christianity inherited from Judaism a faith in the transcendent Being of God, beyond the accidents of the physical universe. Even the Incarnation did not substantially modify this faith: The Word may have become flesh, but it did not remain flesh. The Son returned to heaven, to reside for eternity at the side of the Father, and the faithful await their own freedom through death from the entrapment of the body and of nature. All this Montaigne knew very well. Yet his essays sweep aside two millennia of nausea at the mutability of the existential world.

There were in Montaigne's time, as in our own, certain familiar psychological, social, or spiritual patterns through which lives could be readily understood: the prodigal son, the faithful servant, the warrior, the pilgrim, the courtier, the Stoic sage, the wise judge, the libertine, the repentant sinner, and so forth. It was almost impossible not to fall into one or another of these patterns, and yet Montaigne somehow manages to elude them all. The conviction that life's inevitable sufferings were a valuable lesson was virtually inescapable, but not for Montaigne: "Crosses and afflictions make me do nothing but curse them; they are for people that cannot be awaked but by the whip." So too the confession of sins, along with the desire to make amends, was part of the essential spiritual structure of virtually everyone, but not Montaigne: "Were I to live again, it should be as I have already lived." In place of a striving for reformation or transcendence, the essays cheerfully embrace imperfection, indeterminacy, and ceaseless change.

That change is recorded powerfully, even unnervingly, in the publication history of the essays. In 1580 Montaigne personally saw to the publication of the first two books. In a world in which the elite often avoided appearing in print—preferring the more socially genteel form of manuscript circulation—such direct, unembarrassed involvement was already unusual. Montaigne did not even pretend, as wellborn authors often did, that the work had been made public without his permission. There is no reason, he jauntily warned the readers, "thou shouldst employ thy time about so frivolous and vain a subject," but he made clear that he was responsible for what had been printed. A few months after its publication, he presented a copy to the king, Henri III. So, too, in 1587, he went to Paris to arrange a new edition published the next year, this time with the thirteen new chapters of Book III and with some six hundred alterations to Books I and II. What is peculiar about these alterations is that they are all additions. That is, they are not corrections or substitutions, not attempts to stabilize and fix the text, but sentences or paragraphs inserted into the existing essays. In other words, when he returned to the essays he had already written, he found that he had many new opinions or further quotations he wished to cite, often in direct contradiction to views he had earlier expressed, but instead of canceling those views, he simply added more.

He was by no means finished. In the years that followed he continued to reread and rethink what he published, jotting down innumerable further thoughts in the margins of his copy of the 1588 edition or on slips of paper. He evidently carried on this work more or less constantly during times in which he was traveling with the royal court or struggling with excruciating episodes of kidney stones or working behind the scenes to keep his region of Bordeaux loyal to Henri de Navarre or corresponding with friends. In 1592, Montaigne, who had managed to survive a number of illnesses, contracted a throat infection from which, on September 13, he died peacefully in his bed. The book in which he had recorded his new material—amounting to about one-fourth of the entire length of the essays—went to Marie de Gournay, a devoted admirer whom Montaigne had made his literary executrix. De Gournay carefully transcribed all that Montaigne had added and published a new edition of the essays, the first complete edition, in 1595.

De Gournay did not signal the presence of new material, any more than Montaigne had done. Whatever was added simply appeared in the great flow of the essays, whose impression of unbroken improvisation was intensified by the fact that they were originally printed without paragraph breaks. Only in 1919, with the first systematic modern edition of the essays, were the distinct levels of the text sorted out and labeled, so that it was possible to track what was originally published in 1580, what was newly inserted in 1588, and what was added yet again after 1588.

It is fascinating by this means to track Montaigne's revisions and rethinking, but readers should be aware that he had no interest in making this tracking possible. On the contrary, he clearly took pleasure in the strange effect of an open-ended text in which the passage of time was present yet unmarked, and in which it would be almost impossible to distinguish with any certainty between early opinions and those which had come to contradict them. The effect for Montaigne's original readers, including Shakespeare, would have been a single self that contained multitudes, a personal stage in which strikingly different voices, past and present, jostled for attention.

Against the grain of Montaigne's own confounding of the distinctions, scholars who study the successive levels have identified shifts in his basic orientation. The early essays share many of the preoccupations of Stoicism, with its central desire to free the core of the self from vulnerability and terror. Appalling things may happen in the course of a life, and everyone without exception must confront death, but pagan moralists like Plutarch and Seneca taught themselves to face the worst and to find freedom from fear in the soul's calm acceptance of necessity. "The premeditation of death," Montaigne wrote in his 1580 essay "That to Philosophize Is to Learn How to Die," "is a fore-thinking of liberty. He who hath learned to die, hath unlearned to serve."

This was not only the teaching of pagans; it was, Montaigne recognized, also linked to one of the central strains of his own religion: "Our religion hath had no surer human foundation than the contempt of life." Therefore, he acknowledged, he fully shared in his culture's widespread fascination with accounts of the ways people met their ends and with what was called the *ars moriendi*, the "art of dying." "There is nothing I desire more to be informed of than of the death of men: that is to say, what words, what countenance, and what face they show at their death." But there were cracks in the Stoics' armor. Montaigne could never forget that even his beloved friend de La Boétie, who so ardently pursued the perfect liberty proferred by Stoicism, had on his deathbed writhed with sudden violence and, raising his voice, made a final, desperate appeal to his friend: "My brother, my brother, do *you* refuse me a place?" Montaigne gently reminded La Boétie that "since he was breathing and speaking and had a body, consequently he had his place." Yet his dying friend's strange words haunted Montaigne and seemed to undermine the Stoical arguments of the early essays, even as he piled them up.

Already by 1576 Montaigne had read the work of one of the great classical skeptics, Sextus Empiricus, and the philosophical doubts he encountered in this work, resonating deep in him, helped shape the longest and probably the most influential of his essays, "An Apology of *Raymond Sebond*." This essay began as a gesture of filial piety toward his father—"the best father that ever was"—who, shortly before his death, had asked his son to translate the Spanish theologian Sebond's treatise *Natural Theology* into French. Sebond's old book, which attempted to establish all of the articles of the Christian faith on the foundation of human reason, had come under sharp criticism. The "Apology" begins as a response to this criticism, but it soon veers in a direction that could only further undermine, indeed devastate, the theological confidence that Sebond hoped to instill.

Montaigne expresses disgust at man's absurd presumption: "Is it possible to imagine anything so ridiculous as this miserable and wretched creature, which is not so much as master of himself, exposed and subject to offences of all things, and yet dareth call himself master and emperour of the universe?" In their insufferable vanity, humans imagine themselves to be superior to all creatures on earth, but in fact almost every one of man's vaunted talents is shared with the other animals, many of whom are clearly better endowed than we are. If at least the imagination is a distinctly human attribute, it is nothing to brag about; rather, it is one of the sources of our misery and folly. We think we occupy the center of the stage, but, as Montaigne famously asks, "When I am playing with my cat, who knows whether she have more sport in dallying with me than I have in gaming with her?"

Sebond had thought to found faith itself on our reason, but in fact our reason gets us nowhere. There are no underlying laws, no secure first principles on which the mind can construct stable knowledge, or if there are such laws and principles the human intellect cannot take hold of them. Both the universe and the mind of man are in flux, and as a result we cannot hope to know anything: "We have no communication with being." All the great intellectual schemes that humans have devised tumble in ruins, and the best we can do is to follow the course of the ancient skeptic Pyrrho, as described by Sextus Empiricus, "ever to waver, to doubt, and to inquire, never to be assured of anything, nor to take any warrant of himself."

"Never to be assured of anything": Montaigne recognizes that the declarative structure of French (or English) makes it very difficult for skeptics to reach a state of absolute doubt, since "when they say 'I doubt,' you have them fast by the sleeve to make them avow that at least you are assured and know that they doubt." The best you can do is to switch from an affirmation to a question: *Que sais-je?*, What do I know?—or, as Florio renders it, "What can I tell?"

Yet even in this expression of his most thoroughgoing skepticism, Montaigne allows a glimpse of something less corrosive than relentless, perpetually renewed doubt. He praises the day-laborer—someone he might have contemplated from the windows of his tower—who does not spend his life in tormenting anticipation of woes to come but simply "follows his natural appetites." This reflection leads him in turn to reflect on the stories reaching France about the natives of Brazil who are said to die not through disease but only through age. Though some impute this good health "to the clearness and calmness of their air," Montaigne attributes it to "the calmness and clearness of their minds, void and free from all passions, cares, toiling, and unpleasant labours, as a people that pass their life in a wonderful kind of simplicity and ignorance without letters, or laws, and without kings or any religion."

There are traces in this primitivist fantasy of the earlier Stoical ideal—"void and free from all passions"—and many marks of radical skepticism: "without letters, or laws, and without kings or any religion." But there are also notes that look forward to the celebration of freedom, pleasure, and natural simplicity that characterizes Montaigne's later essays.

The fullest expression of this celebration comes in the magnificent "Of Experience" where Montaigne reflects on "the miserable condition of so many men" who are constrained by the law and cannot move freely in the world. In his tower, surrounded by his beloved books, the essayist may have found much of what he most needed for his pleasure, but he was not one of those meditative souls who could declare himself happy even in confinement. "I am so besotted unto liberty," he wrote, "that should any man forbid me the access unto any one corner of the Indies, I should in some sort live much discontented."

Still, it is not in gadding about and observing the varied ways of the world that Montaigne found the greatest fascination. It was in himself, in the ordinary, seemingly trivial features of his everyday existence:

> I am not over-much or greedily desirous of sallets or of fruits, except melons. My father hated all manner of sauces; I love them all.... I have heretofore found radish-roots to be very good for me, then very hurtful, and now again very well agreeing with my stomach. In diverse other things I feel my appetite to change and my stomach to diversify from time to time. I have altered my course of drinking, sometimes from white to claret wine, and then from claret to white again.

Why share such details? Because for Montaigne everything in a life is significant and because a preference for radishes has the same weight as the most exalted metaphysical reflection. "What egregious fools are we?" he writes, thinking of all the times we lament that we "have done nothing this day" (a lament that is, I assume, familiar to all of us). "What," Montaigne exclaims, "have you not lived?" Living is "not only the fundamental but the noblest of your occupations."

Montaigne has shifted in these later essays from the Stoical pursuit of invulnerability in the face of pain and death to the goal that characterized the Stoics' great philosophical opponents, the Epicureans: the pursuit of pleasure. The true meaning of this pursuit is not a feverish search for more and more extravagant delights; such a search seemed to him ridiculous and ultimately destructive. Rather, he wrote, "the most usual and common form of life is the best." The key is to value ordinary existence and not to succumb to those ascetic moralists—and there were many in Montaigne's world—who preached contempt for the flesh and for the whole transient, mortal world. "And of all the infirmities we have the most savage is to despise our being."

Against any such desire to escape from the human condition, Montaigne urged the simple cherishing of life. This cherishing he summed up in a sentence that Florio translates with perfect directness: "*It is an absolute perfection and as it were divine for a man to know how to enjoy his being loyally.*"

3

The progression I have just described, from Stoicism to skepticism to an Epicurean embrace of loyalty to one's being, can be teased out of the different layers of Montaigne's evolving text. But, as I have already remarked, the progression would have been much less visible to early readers, whether they knew the essays from de Gourney's 1588 edition or from Florio's translation. And in truth its significance can be exaggerated. For it is clear from the quotations assembled in "That to Philosophize Is to Learn How to Die" that Montaigne has already been passionately reading and absorbing the Epicurean philosopher Lucretius. When in a passage from the earliest version of that early essay Montaigne writes "Let death seize upon me whilst I am setting my cabbages, careless of her dart, but more of my unperfect garden," we are encountering a wish we might well encounter in the last of his writings. So too the deep skepticism he articulates in "An Apology of *Raymond Sebond*" does not appear for the first time there or disappear thereafter; it simply takes its place alongside a more fully articulated desire to enjoy and cherish his life.

It is important to grasp this constant interplay of different perspectives, in part because it is true to Montaigne's cheerfully professed taste for contradicting himself and in part because it is an aspect of the text that Shakespeare and his contemporaries would have experienced. Shakespeare's friend and rival Ben Jonson complained of those who read widely and write down, without any concern for consistency, whatever strikes them. "By which meanes," he observes, "it happens, that what they have discredited, and impugned in one worke, they have before, or after, extolled the same in another." What they reveal in doing so is not an interesting change in viewpoint but simply their own predominant quality, namely folly. "Such are all the *Essayists*," Jonson writes, disclosing the object of his particular contempt, "even their Master *Mountaigne*."[3] Shakespeare would certainly have noted the same feature in Montaigne's writing. We do not know if it bothered him, as it did Jonson; what we do know is that he repeatedly made forays into the essays to seize upon things he thought he could use.

Two instances of such forays have been particularly noted by scholars. In his essay "Of the Affection of Fathers to Their Children," Montaigne, sharply criticizing aged parents who expect their grown children to be grateful to them and who cling avidly to

---

3. Ben Jonson, "Timber, or Discoveries upon Men and Matter," Note 6, in *Ben Jonson*, eds. C. H. Herford, Percy and Evelyn Simpson (Oxford: Clarendon Press, 1947), VIII: 585–86.

their possessions, gives powerful voice to the resentment of the young:

> It is mere injustice to see an old, crazed, sinew-shrunken, and nigh-dead father sitting alone in a chimney-corner to enjoy so many goods as would suffice for the preferment and entertainment of many children, and in the meanwhile, for want of means, to suffer them to lose their best days and years without thrusting them into public service and knowledge of men.

This geriatric avarice can make children despair, driving them "to seek by some way how unlawful soever to provide for their necessaries." Far from producing dutiful obedience, a parental policy of clinging to wealth and treating the younger generation sternly only "maketh fathers irksome unto children, and which is worse, ridiculous." How could it not have this effect? For, as Montaigne coolly notes, children in fact "have youth and strength in their hands, and consequently the breath and favour of the world, and do with mockery and contempt receive these churlish, fierce, and tyrannical countenances from a man that hath no lusty blood left him."

Shakespeare was evidently struck by these passages, for he worked them into his depiction of the bastard Edmund in *King Lear*, simmering with resentment, frustration, mockery, contempt, and a determination "to seek, by some way how unlawful soever" to provide for himself. Specifically, Shakespeare takes Montaigne's words, in Florio's translation, and fashions them into the forged letter that Edmund fobs off as his brother Edgar's. "I hope," Edmund declares with a fraudulent show of concern on his brother's behalf, that he wrote this letter "but as an essay or taste of my virtue." It is difficult not to see in that word "essay" a playful allusion to Montaigne, for what follows is simply a variation on themes from "Of the Affection of Fathers to Their Children":

> This policy and reverence of age makes the world bitter to the best of our times, keeps our fortunes from us till our oldness

cannot relish them. I begin to find an idle and fond bondage in the oppression of aged tyranny; who sways, not as it hath power, but as it is suffered.

Credulous old Gloucester swallows the bait and cries treason.

I have already alluded at the beginning of this introduction to the second and the most frequently cited instance of Shakespeare's borrowing from Montaigne. As early as 1784, the editor Edward Capell noted that in *The Tempest* Shakespeare's imagination was caught by a passage in Florio's translation of Montaigne's "Of the Cannibals." The people recently discovered in the New World, Montaigne writes,

> hath no kind of traffic, no knowledge of letters, no intelligence of numbers, no name of magistrate, nor of politic superiority; no use of service, of riches, or of poverty; no contracts, no successions, no dividences, no occupation but idle; no respect of kindred, but common; no apparel, but natural; no manuring of lands, no use of wine, corn, or metal. The very words that import lying, falsehood, treason, dissimulations, covetousness, envy, detraction, and pardon were never heard of amongst them.

Out of this utopian vision of noble savages in the state of nature Shakespeare crafts the words he gives to the good councillor Gonzalo who is daydreaming about what he would do were he in charge of colonizing the island on which he and the others have been shipwrecked:

> no kind of traffic
> Would I admit, no name of magistrate;
> Letters should not be known; riches, poverty,
> And use of service, none; contract, succession,
> Bourn, bound of land, tilth, vineyard, none;
> No use of metal, corn, or wine, or oil;
> No occupation, all men idle, all;

And women too—but innocent and pure;
No sovereignty—
. . . . . .
All things in common nature should produce
Without sweat or endeavour. Treason, felony,
Sword, pike, knife, gun, or need of any engine,
Would I not have; but nature should bring forth
Of it own kind of foison, all abundance,
To feed my innocent people. (II.i.148–64)

The borrowing extends beyond certain expressions—kind of traffic, name of magistrate, use of service, and the like—to a vision of a whole society organized on principles directly counter to those in place in the familiar, grim realm of contemporary European reality. That is, here as in the case of *King Lear*, Shakespeare is mining Florio's Montaigne not simply for turns of phrase but for key concepts central to the play in question.

But though Gonzalo is a kind and sympathetic character, there is no getting around the fact that his vision of the ideal "commonwealth" is mocked for its incoherence and absurdity. And if the mockers are the cynical and treacherous Sebastian and Antonio, it remains the case that the "natural" social order borrowed from Montaigne for Gonzalo's speech is grossly at odds with anything actually represented on Shakespeare's ocean island. Indeed the island's possessor before the arrival of the Europeans—Caliban, whose name is a kind of anagram for cannibal—is utterly unlike the proud, dignified, self-possessed cannibals of Montaigne's essay. Together with the very mixed bag of Europeans, Shakespeare's native seems designed to reveal Montaigne's vision as hopelessly naïve. Shakespeare's borrowing here, in short, is an act not of homage but of aggression.

So too with the borrowing in *King Lear*: indeed Shakespeare's aggression is still greater, since in that play the words are taken over not by a sweet but unworldly idealist but rather by a cunning and ruthless villain. It is not that Shakespeare necessarily viewed Montaigne's views on the relations between parents and children as themselves wicked; rather the play suggests that they may be exploited by people far nastier than anything the essay allows itself to imagine.

The best solution, Montaigne thought, was for the old and infirm to distribute most of their possessions to their children:

> A father over-burdened with years and crazed through sickness and, by reason of weakness and want of health barred from the common society of men, doth both wrong himself injure his idly and to no use to hoard up and keep close a great heap of riches and deal of pelf. He is in state good enough if he be wise to have a desire to put off his clothes to go to bed—I will not say to his shirt, but to a good warm night gown. As for other pomp and trash whereof he hath no longer use or need, he ought willingly to distribute and bestow them amongst those to whom by natural degree they ought to belong.

This is the argument that the wicked Edmund attributes to his brother Edgar, in order to incense his father: "I have heard him oft maintain it to be fit that, sons at perfect age, and fathers declining, the father should be as ward to the son, and the son manage his revenue" (I.ii.66–70).

Why should arguments that seem so reasonable and even ethically responsible to Montaigne appear in *King Lear* as the center of something horrible? Here, as in *The Tempest*, it is as if Shakespeare thought Montaigne had a very inadequately developed sense of depravity and evil. What if the children do not want to leave the father with "a good warm night gown"? What if they want everything? Montaigne's answer is that, though he would give his children "the full possession of my house and enjoying of my goods," it would be on this "limited condition," that "if they should give me occasion, I might repent myself of my gift and revoke my deed." Everything in *Lear* is designed to show that this idea is tragically foolish. "O, sir, you are old," the reptilian Regan tells her father,

Nature in you stands on the very verge
Of her confine. You should be ruled and led
By some discretion that discerns your state
Better than you yourself. (II.iv.139–43)

There is no repenting of the gift, no revoking of the deed.

It should not entirely surprise us that there is a distinct edge in
Shakespeare's use of Montaigne. There was a huge gap between
them, a gap not linguistic (thanks in part to Florio) but social, cultural, and aesthetic. Montaigne was the friend of kings and princes,
a nobleman directly involved in the key political and religious strug-
gles of his age; Shakespeare, the son of a provincial glover, was a
popular entertainer, permanently stained by a trade everyone re-
garded as vaguely shameful. Montaigne was a master of the Latin
language, with access to all the rich resources of Renaissance humanism; Shakespeare had, as Jonson put it, "small Latin and less
Greek." Montaigne retired to his tower to write; Shakespeare spent
most of his career in London where he wrote for money. Montaigne
had a proud and powerful sense of his name and social position;
Shakespeare participated in a collective 'enterprise, one over whose
results he had only limited control. Montaigne decided to print his
essays and, in doing so, to put himself on display. Shakespeare, who
had an indifferent or ambivalent relationship to print, seems to have
cultivated a certain anonymity. Montaigne was the master of prose
essays with no set shape and no clear narrative arc, works meant to
be read and mused upon in private; Shakespeare fashioned plays,
many of them in verse, intended for public performance. Montaigne
desired to strip away all costumes and reveal the naked body beneath; Shakespeare wrote for an all-male theater that relied upon
costumes to conjure up the social and sexual realities. Montaigne
created a single great character, himself; Shakespeare created innumerable characters, each with a distinct claim to attention.

But if Montaigne and Shakespeare were diametrical opposites in
these and other ways, and if the places in which their works most
explicitly touch—that is, *King Lear* and *The Tempest*—eloquently

demonstrate this opposition, nonetheless there is a whole world that they share. Scholars have seen Montaigne's fingerprints on many other works by Shakespeare, whether in the echoing of words or ideas. When Hamlet exclaims to his mother, "Ecstasy? My pulse as yours doth temperately keep time," (III.iv.130–31), Shakespeare may have picked up a hint from Montaigne's "during his ecstasy, he seemed to have neither pulse nor breath" from "Of the Force of Imagination." And Polonius's "This above all: to thine own self be true" may owe something to "That above all, he be instructed to yield, yea to quit his weapons unto truth" from "Of the Institution of Education of Children." More broadly, there is something strikingly Montaigne-like in Hamlet's intertwining of Stoicism—

> Give me that man
> That is not passion's slave, and I will wear him
> In my heart's core— (III.ii.64–66)

with philosophical skepticism—

> And yet to me what is this quintessence of dust?— (II.ii.297–98)

and inner acceptance—

> If it be now, 'tis not to come. If it be not to come, it will be now. If it be not now, yet it will come. The readiness is all. (V.ii.158–60).

Perhaps, perhaps. But apart from the passages in *King Lear* and *The Tempest*, the attempts to establish the direct influence of Montaigne on Shakespeare have never seemed fully and decisively convincing. The problem is only in part one of dating: Though Florio's Montaigne was published in 1603, at least three years after the probable composition and performance of *Hamlet*, Shakespeare could have seen a manuscript of Florio's translation which, licensed for publication and referred to by Cornwallis in 1600, was evidently in circulation well before the first printing. The more intractable problem has to do with a shared historical moment, a shared grappling with pressing questions of faith, consciousness, and identity, and even, thanks to Florio, a shared language. Did Shakespeare really need Montaigne to think about the relation between imagination, ecstasy, and the beating of the pulse?

But what is a problem for the scholarly attempt to establish a clear line of influence is from the perspective of the common reader a source of deep pleasure. Two of the greatest writers of the Renaissance—two of the greatest writers the world has ever known—were at work almost at the same time, reflecting on the human condition and inventing the stylistic means to register their subtlest perceptions in language. And though, as we have noted, they came from sharply differing worlds and worked in distinct genres, they share many of the same features. Both Montaigne and Shakespeare were masters of the disarming gesture, the creation of collusion and intimacy: essays that profess to be "frivolous and vain" ("The Author to the Reader"); plays with titles like *As You Like It* and *Much Ado About Nothing*. Both were skilled at seizing upon anything that came their way in the course of wide-ranging reading or observation; both prized the illumination of a brilliant perception over systematic thought; both were masters of quotation and transformation; both were supremely adaptable and variable. Both believed that there was a profound link between language and identity, between what you say and how you say it and what you are. Both were fascinated with ethical meanings in a world that possessed an apparently infinite range of human behaviors. Both perceived and embraced the oscillations and contradictions within individuals, the equivocations and ironies and discontinuities even in those who claimed to be single-minded and single-hearted in pursuit of coherent goals.

Montaigne and Shakespeare created works that have for centuries remained tantalizing, equivocal, and elusive, inviting ceaseless speculations and re-creations. In a world that craved fixity and order, each managed to come to terms with strict limits to authorial control, with the unpredictability and instability of texts, with a proliferation of unlimited, uncontrolled meanings. Each turned uncertainty into art. And in accepting open-endedness, each great writer found a way to be "loyal," as Montaigne put it, to life. "As for me, then," Montaigne wrote in his last essay, "Of Experience," "I love my life and cherish it, such as it hath pleased God to grant it us." Philosophical disputes, pious complaints, and ascetic ambitions to rise above the flesh seemed to him absurd and ungrateful. "I cheerfully and thankfully and with a good heart accept what nature hath created for me, and am therewith well pleased and am proud of it." And, as if in tribute to Montaigne, Shakespeare too, in the closing speech of what was probably his final work, *The Two Noble Kinsmen*, gave voice through his character Theseus to strikingly similar sentiments:

> O you heavenly charmers,
> What things you make of us! For what we lack
> We laugh, for what we have, are sorry; still
> Are children in some kind. Let us be thankful
> For that which is, and with you leave dispute
> That are above our question. Let's go off
> And bear us like the time. (V.vi.131–37)

—STEPHEN GREENBLATT

"I am an Englishman in Italian"
John Florio and the Translation of Montaigne

In 1876 Friedrich Nietzsche wonderfully called Shakespeare Montaigne's "best reader," and the Montaigne that Shakespeare read would have been the translation of John Florio, published in London by Edward Blount in 1603. In addition to being a translator, the remarkable Florio was a language tutor to powerful nobles and to Queen Anne of Denmark, James I's wife, whom he also served as groom of the privy chamber from 1604 until her death in 1619. His conversation and grammar books provided the English-speaking world access to the Italian language, and he was the compiler of the first lengthy Italian-English dictionaries. But his greatest achievement was "Englishing" Montaigne, whose essays had been available only in French and in bits of English translation before Florio's monumental work appeared. Appreciation of the Florio Montaigne —Shakespeare's Montaigne—is incomplete without at least some familiarity with its polymath translator.

Born in London in 1553, John Florio was the son of Michael Angelo Florio, an Italian religious reformer and a former Franciscan who fled Italy for London in 1550. (Florio's mother was an Englishwoman whose identity has never been uncovered.) Doing what his son would do later, Michael Angelo was the Italian tutor to powerful nobility: Henry Herbert, second Earl of Pembroke, and Lady Jane Grey—he dedicated Italian grammar books to both. It is possible he tutored the young Queen Elizabeth, too, for he dedicated his translation of Agricola to her in 1563. Supported by William Cecil, Michael Angelo also preached at a church for Italian Protestants in London.

The first contemporary biographical reference to John Florio came in John Aubrey's brief life: "John Florio was borne in London in the beginning of king Edward VI, his father and mother flying from the Valtolin ('tis about Piedmont or Savoy) to London for religion: Waldenses." But the political and religious climate changed with the ascension in 1554 of Mary Tudor, who issued a royal edict calling for the removal of foreigners. In March of that year, Michael Angelo and his family fled England, first for a year in Strasbourg and then for a permanent settlement in Soglio—a town in Switzerland near the Italian border that was home to many Italian religious refugees. Since John seems to have been sent to Tübingen to study when he was about ten, it is possible that, as Frances Yates said in her seminal *John Florio*, Florio, "from whom several have supposed that Shakespeare learnt much of what he knew about Italy and Italian towns, may never have set foot in Italy itself at all." By 1576, Florio was back in England, his father having died in Soglio, probably in the early 1570s.

Florio's first publication, *Firste Fruites*, appeared in 1578 with a dedication to Robert Dudley, the Earl of Leicester, who possibly helped get Florio situated at Oxford, where he matriculated at Magdalen College in 1581 and became a tutor in foreign languages to Emmanuel Barnes, brother of the poet Barnabe Barnes. During his time at Oxford, Florio befriended Samuel Daniel, whose sister he probably married in about 1580 and who would write prefatory poems to both the 1603 and 1613 editions of the Montaigne translation, as well the 1611 edition of the dictionary; Matthew Gwinne, who would be so helpful to Florio in tracing the classical references in the Montaigne project; and Richard Hakluyt, who paid him to translate into English Giovanni Battista Ramusio's Italian translation of Jacques Cartier's account of his first two voyages, *A Short and Brief Narration of the Two navigations and Discoveries to the North-West Parts called New France* (1580).

Florio's intellectual connections expanded when he worked at the French embassy in London's Butcher Row from 1583 to 1585, serving the French ambassador, Michel de Castelnau, Lord of Mauvissière, in the capacity of translator and language tutor to Castelnau's six-year-old daughter, Katherine-Marie. Yates and the historian John Bossy, among others, have suggested that Florio was probably a spy for Sir Francis Walsingham.[1] More certainly, during these years at the embassy Florio befriended the controversial philosopher Giordano Bruno.

In England to lecture on Copernicanism and his theory of multiple worlds at Oxford, Bruno—or "the Nolan," as he called himself after his hometown of Nola, near Naples—stayed at the French embassy at about the same time that Florio did. In one of his books published in England during this period—*The Ash Wednesday Supper* (*Cena de le ceneri*, 1584)—Bruno describes through a thinly veiled fiction the negative reception his ideas received in England. Of interest for the study of Florio, in the second dialogue Bruno tells the story of being escorted by "Messrs. Florio and Gwinne" to dine at Sir Fulke Greville's house (probably in Whitehall). Along the way the men get lost, muddy, and grumpy, but the journey is partly lightened by Florio's singing. As Theophil, the primary narrator, tells us, "Mister Florio (as if reminiscing of his loves) sang *Dove senza me dolce mia vita* [Where, without me, my sweet life]. The Nolan chimed in with *Il Saracen dolente, oh femenil ingegno* [Wherever the grieving Saracen went...oh feminine valor]." When they finally get to the dinner—where Sir Philip Sidney as well as Greville is believed to have been present—Florio tries to be deferential but ends up, initially, taking the seat of highest honor. Eventually things get properly sorted out: "Mister Florio sat across from the cavalier, who sat at the head of the table [usually thought to have been Sidney]; Sir Fulke to the right of Mister Florio; I and the Nolan to the left of Mister Florio...."

---

1. In his *Oxford Dictionary of National Biography* entry, Desmond O'Connor endorses the views of Yates and Bossy. Ingrid Rowland, in *Giordano Bruno: Philosopher/Heretic* (University of Chicago Press, 2009), has challenged these claims, as has the great Bruno scholar Hilary Gatti.

Florio was publicly connected to Bruno in *The Ash Wednesday Supper* (and arguably in Bruno's *Cause, Principle, and Unity* [*De la causa, principio, et uno*, 1584], where he may be the character Elitropio). And in his own writings Florio did nothing to distance himself from the heterodox Bruno. Bruno (Nolano) is named as one of the participants of the first dialogue in *Second Frutes*, and his ideas are everywhere in this book's twelfth and final dialogue. Finally, Florio celebrated Bruno's remarks on translation in "To the Courteous Reader" of his Montaigne's *Essayes*: "Yea, but my old fellow *Nolano* told me and taught publicly that from translation all science had its offspring" (sig. A5).

Before getting to that translation, however, we need to examine briefly Florio's earlier forays into translating, into bridging the gap between English and the Continental languages: his conversation manuals (*Firste Fruites* and *Second Frutes*) and his Italian-English dictionaries. Michael Wyatt, in his important *The Italian Encounter with Tudor England: A Cultural Politics of Translation*, has claimed that Florio was ideally suited to make these translations, "situated as he is *in* and *between* both linguistic cultures." The language books were grammar and conversation books, but they were also, as Warren Boucher has pointed out in turn, "guides to the art of the humanist courtier."

Scholars have detected more crankiness, anti-Englishness, and moralism in *Firste Fruites*—especially Florio's attack on the English language—and, indeed, in *Second Frutes* Florio seems more at home in England. But in this later work he still notes that "critics" are "crickets; no goodly bird of a man mark them," and he recognizes a fundamental xenophobia in his adopted country: He is "*an Englishman in Italian*" but knows that "*they have a knife at command to cut my throat*," immediately afterward quoting Roger Ascham's demonizing words from his *The scholemaster* (1570), "Un Inglese Italianato, é un Diavolo incarnato."

Towards the end of his address "To the Reader" in *Second Frutes*, Florio promises that he "will shortly send into the world an exquisite

Italian and English Dictionary," and he did so in 1598 with *A Worlde of Wordes*, which he expanded in 1611 into *Queen Anna's New World of Words*. The first had about 46,000 definitions, the latter about 74,000. These dictionaries attempt to make the world richer, more polyvocal, more linguistically ambidextrous: "Lame are we in *Plato's* censure, if we be not ambidexters, using both hands alike. Right-hand, or left-hand as peers with mutual parity, without disparagement may it please you Honors to join hand in hand."

In his epistle "To the Reader" of the 1598 edition, Florio celebrates English—which he had earlier denigrated in *Firste Fruites*—as a language providing "pleasure to them [English-gentlemen], to see so great a tongue [Italian] out-vied by their mother-speech, as by the many-fold Englishes of many words in this is manifest" (sig. b1r-v). Florio himself should get a great deal of credit for manifesting the potency of English: He was "a source for some 3,843 English words in the second edition of the OED. Of these Florio is responsible for the earliest appearances of 1,149 words, 173 are unique citations (*hapax legomena* or *h.l.*) so far found nowhere else…."[2] Florio both cataloged and added to the richness of English in the age of Shakespeare.

The man who had his mind filled with a "world of words" was clearly the right person to translate Montaigne's essays into English. He was not the first to attempt to do so, however, as he tells us in the epistle "To the Courteous Reader": "Seven or eight of great wit and

---

2. See Wyatt, in *The Italian Encounter with Tudor England* (Cambridge University Press, 2005), 230, who is drawing on the work of John Willinsky, *An Empire of Words: The Reign of the OED* (Princeton University Press, 1994). Dewitt Starnes, in his important "John Florio Reconsidered," *Texas Studies in Literature and Language* 6 (Winter 1965), sought to minimize the contribution of Florio by emphasizing the number of times Florio pilfered definitions from earlier dictionary-makers. However, responding to this essay, David Frantz's "Florio's Use of Contemporary Italian Literature in *A Worlde of Wordes*," *Dictionaries: Journal of the Dictionary Society of North America* 1 (1979), claimed that "What emerges is a fairly clear picture of Florio's use of his sources; where Florio could draw on earlier dictionaries, he did so in precisely the manner suggested by Starnes. Where Florio could not draw on earlier dictionaries, as he could not extensively if he wanted to make contemporary Italian literature available, he went to the works themselves" (52–53).

worth have assayed but found these Essayes no attempt for French apprentices or Littletonians."[3] Florio's own translation was entered in the Stationers' Register on June 4, 1600.

Florio accounts for the origins of this translation in the "Epistle Dedicatorie," telling Lucy, Countess of Bedford, and her mother, Lady Anne Harrington,

> For (that I may discharge me of all this, and charge you with your own; pardon Madame my plainness) when I with one chapter found myself over-charged, whereto the charge or choice of an Honorable person, and by me not-to-be-denied Benefactor (Noble and virtuous Sir Edward Wotton) had engaged me, (which I finished in your own house) your Honor having deigned to read it, without pity of my failing, my fainting, my labouring, my languishing, my gasping for some breath (O could so Honorable, be so pitiless? Madame, now do I flatter you?) Yet commanded me on: (and let me die outright, ere I do not that command.)

It was a painful birth, and Florio admits to having help in his "labouring" from Gwinne, who "so scholar-like did ... undertake what Latin prose; Greek, Latin, Italian or French Poesie should cross my way," and from Theodore Diodati, who helped him navigate the "inextricable labyrinth" of Montaigne's difficult passages, "dissolved these knots" of text, and "in these dark-uncouth ways" provided "a clear reluent light" (sigs. A2v, A3r).

Florio's Montaigne does not always find this clear light, but it is often beautiful and never dull. Florio uses his copious sense of English to amplify Montaigne's French. He also takes very seriously his

---

3. Florio, "To the Reader," in *The Essayes ... of ... Montaigne* (London, 1603). "Littletonians" alludes to Claudius Hollyband's *French Littleton*, which was a book of grammar and dialogues published in 1566. Yates notes that there was a Stationers' Register entry on October 20, 1595, by Edward Aggras, which "sounds as though it were a translation but it has not survived" (Yates, *John Florio* [Cambridge University Press, 1934], 214).

task of "Englishing" Montaigne. When, for example, Montaigne argued that we cannot understand animals any more than we can "les Basques et les Troglodytes," Florio gave us "no more do we the Cornish, the Welsh, or Irish." Florio's Protestant sympathies also led to his altering Montaigne's text to cleanse it of Catholic perspectives, so "des erreurs de Wiclef"—the errors of John Wycliffe, fourteenth-century English Protestant reformer—became "*Wycliff's* opinions." And unlike in his dictionary, where Florio did not shy away from ribald and sexually explicit slang, his version of Montaigne is often a much more chaste one than Montaigne's own work. Florio could also just get it wrong, the most famous error perhaps being his translation of the French "*poisson*" (fish) as "poison": "For he to whom fasting should procure health and a merry heart, or he to whom poison should be more healthy than meat." Usually, though, one emerges from reading Florio's *Essayes* in wonder at its successful translation of Montaigne into the Elizabethan-Jacobean world and, more than occasionally, overwhelmed by its beauty. Here is a passage from "An Apology of *Raymond Sebond*":

> And when we others do foolishly fear a kind of death, when as we have already passed and daily pass so many others. For not only (as *Heraclitus* said) the death of fire is a generation of air, and the death of air a generation of water; but also we may most evidently see it in ourselves. The flower of age dyeth, fadeth, and fleeteth, when age comes upon us, and youth endeth in the flower of a full-grown man's age; childhood in youth; and the first age dyeth in infancy. And yesterday endeth in this day, and today shall die in tomorrow. *And nothing remaineth or ever continueth in one state.*

And it was a translation that instantly mattered to and had an effect on its earliest readers. Ben Jonson, John Marston, Shakespeare, and John Webster drew on the *Essayes* and quoted from them almost immediately, and Robert Burton would engage with them intensively in his *Anatomy of Melancholy* (1621). Sir Francis

Bacon—usually thought of as the father of the English essay—greatly expanded his *Essayes* in between 1597 and 1612 (from ten to thirty-eight), culminating in the fifty-eight essays of 1625. Florio's Montaigne, somewhat paradoxically, can be said to have shown Bacon just what the essay in English could be. Shakespeare's complicated relationship to Florio will be discussed below, but Jonson seems to have been unequivocally positive about Florio. Jonson sincerely recognizes his intellectual help in a presentation copy of *Volpone*, which he inscribed: "To his loving Father, & worthy friend Mr. John Florio: The ayde of his muses. Ben: Jonson seales this testimony of Freindship [*sic*], & Love." Jonson's signature is also found in a copy of Florio's translation of the *Essayes* in the British Museum.[4]

Shakespeare certainly read Montaigne, whether or not one agrees with Nietzsche that he was Montaigne's best reader. And beyond dispute is Shakespeare's use of Florio's translation of "Of the Cannibals" in act two of *The Tempest*. And it is difficult to imagine that Shakespeare and Florio did not know each other, since Henry Wriothesley, the Earl of Southampton, was a patron of both men in the early 1590s. In two recent essays in *The Guardian*, Saul Frampton has gone so far as to suggest that Florio had an active hand both in the editing of Shakespeare's First Folio and in the publication of the sonnets. As F. O. Matthiessen put it in his *Translation: An Elizabethan Art* (1931), "Shakespeare and Florio were constantly talking with the same people, hearing the same theories, breathing the same air."

This proximity has proved compelling for scholars since the late eighteenth century, when Warburton suggested that Florio was the "original" for the tutor Holofernes in *Love's Labour's Lost*. There is much to be said for the claim. Both of Florio's language manuals contain the proverb on Venice quoted by the schoolmaster: *Venetia, chi non ti vede, non ti pretia*—though Holofernes leaves out the

---

4. Trying to show off her knowledge of the latest intellectual fashion, Lady Politick Would-be refers to "Montaignie," in *Volpone* (1607) as someone whom authors steal from.

darker part of the proverb: *"ma chi to vede, ben gli costa."* And like Florio, the tutor can be said to "have been at a great feast of languages and stolen the scraps."[5] It is hard not to imagine, too, that Shakespeare had Florio's dictionary in mind or at hand—albeit before publication—when one compares Holofernes's copious riffing with entries from Florio's *Worlde of Wordes*:

Holofernes:
The deer was, as you know—*sanguis*—in blood, ripe as the pomewater who now hangeth like a jewel in the ear of *caelo*, the sky, the welkin, the heaven and anon falleth like a crab on the face of *terra*, the soil, the land, the earth.
Florio:
Cielo, *heaven, the sky, the firmament or welkin....*
Térra, ... *earth, country, province, region, land, soil....*

So is Shakespeare poking gentle fun at a friend, or is there something more serious at stake?

Yates was among the first to suggest that Shakespeare and Florio were not friendly. And Florio does seem to be attacking Shakespeare in the letter "To the Reader" of *Worlde of Wordes*. Whether H.S.— that "tooth-less dog that hateth where he cannot hurt, and would fain bite, when he hath no teeth"[6]—is Shakespeare or, as Yates argued, Hugh Sanford, it is much more likely that Shakespeare is being criticized later in the same section:

---

5. See Moth in Shakespeare, *Love's Labour's Lost*, 5.1.34–35. Much labor has been spent—and some would say lost—in speculation about whether the title of Shakespeare's play comes from another part of *Firste Fruites*: "We need not speak so much of love, all books are full of love, with so many authors, that it were labour lost to speak of Love" (sig. 71r). Further evidence that the word "labour" might be connected with Florio comes in the twelve prefatory poems to *Firste Fruites*, where a form of "labour" appears seven times. (Variations of "toyle" appear three times, and "trauaile" appears once.)
6. Florio, *Worlde of Wordes*, "To the Reader," (sig. a5v).

They hurt not God (sayeth Seneca*) but their own souls, that overthrow his altars: Nor harm they good men, but themselves, that turn their sacrifice of praises into blasphemy. They that rave, and rage, and rail against heaven, I say not (sayeth he) they are guilty of sacrilege, but at least they lose their labour. Let* Aristophanes *and his comedians make plays, and scour their mouths on* Socrates; *those very mouths they make to vilify, shall be the means to amplify his virtue.*

Both the seeming allusion to *Love's Labour's Lost* and the reference to the vilifying frivolity of Aristophanes and his players suggest an attack on the playwright.

In addition, Yates argued, a further tension could have come if Southampton considered Florio an informant to Robert Cecil—interestingly, the son of the patron of Florio's father—one who was in the house both to monitor Southampton's connections to the Essex circle and to make sure that the young earl was being raised as a Protestant and not a Catholic. If Southampton viewed Florio in this way, the earl might have enjoyed Shakespeare's parody. Yates also argued for a complicated scenario pitting Shakespeare, Southampton, Essex, and the scholar John Eliot against the so-called "school of night"—a group including Sir Walter Raleigh, the "wizard" Earl of Northumberland, the traveler and scientist Thomas Hariot, and the poet and translator George Chapman—which met to discuss heterodox ideas, including Copernicanism and the theories of Bruno. The satire directed against Berowne and the young men in *Love's Labour's Lost*, then, would be a critique of this school of night.

Alternatively, as Arthur Acheson suggested early in the twentieth century, perhaps Florio is represented by Armado, the often-mocked alien pedant, who nonetheless evokes tremendous sympathy at the play's end as he tries to bring order out of chaos and death. To read either Holofernes or Armado as unequivocally satirized, however, is to oversimplify those characters, whether either or both or neither is a surrogate for Florio. Thus, it is famously difficult to register a Shakespearean response to the translator of Montaigne's *Essayes*.[7]

Florio's final years seem to have been ones of poverty and sadness. When Queen Anne died in 1619, so, too, did Florio's source of livelihood. Although he continued to work on the revisions of his dictionary and of his Montaigne,[8] and probably was the translator of the first English Boccaccio, published in 1620, Florio spent much time in his final years trying to chase down money that he believed was owed to him.

When Florio died of the plague in 1625, he was survived by his second wife, Rose Spicer, whom he had married in 1617, and his daughter Aurelia, almost certainly the sole surviving child from his marriage to Daniel's sister. They are remembered in his will in poignant ways: "I give and bequeath unto my daughter Aurelia Molins the wedding ring wherewith I married her mother being aggrieved at my very heart, that by reason of my poverty, I am not able to leave her anything else." All "goods, cattles, chattels, jewels, plate, debts Leases, money, or money-worth, household-stuff, utensils, English books, movables, or immovables" go to Rose, "most heartily grieving and ever-sorrowing, that I cannot give or leave her more, in requital of her tender love, loving care, painful diligence, and continual labour, to me, and of me, in all my fortunes, and many sicknesses."

There is a sad irony about the end of Florio's life. Whereas his literary legacy was one of fecundity and copiousness, his personal and economic bequest was one of paucity and poverty. Another di-

---

7. In his *Courtier's Library,* John Donne without question sends up Florio—especially his tendency to have copious prefatory matter and dedications in his works: "*The Ocean of Court.* . . . Collected and reduced into a corpus and dedicated to their individual writers by John Florio, an Anglo-Italian: the chapter headings of those included in Book I. are contained in the first seventy pages; the diplomas of Kings with their titles and the attestations of licensers in the next one hundred and seven pages; poems in praise of the author in Books I–XCVII, which follow." See *The Courtier's Library, or Catalogus Librorum Aulicorum incomparabilium et non vendibilium,* edited by Evelyn Mary Simpson (London: Nonesuch Press, 1930).
8. The third edition of the dictionary appeared in 1659, the fourth in 1688. The third edition of the *Essayes* was published in 1632.

vide can be seen to be a part of "Resolute John Florio," too. There was the narrow, petty, vengeful man who seems to have agreed with Stephano, a character from one of his own *Second Frutes* dialogues, that one

> Be circumspect how you offend scholars, for know,
> A serpent's tooth bites not so ill,
> As doth a scholar's angry quill.
> And if you wrong him in his goods,
> He will deprive thee of thy good name,
> And longer bleeds a wound made with a quill,
> Then any made with sword or lance.

But this Florio coexisted with a much more generous one who, like Bruno, could envision infinite worlds—in Florio's case, worlds of words that like "the Universe, contains all things, digested in best equipaged order, embellished with innumerable ornaments by the universal creator."

—PETER G. PLATT

Acknowledgments

THE EDITORS would like to acknowledge the following people for their help and inspiration: Rebecca Cook, Peter Connor, Brian Cummings, Nancy Fee, Saul Frampton, Will Hamlin, Anselm Haverkamp, Karla Nielsen, Bill Sharpe, Alan Stewart, Ramie Targoff, Phillip Usher, and William Worthen.

The illustration of a page from John Florio's translation of "Of the Cannibals" that appears on page viii was provided by the Rare Book and Manuscript Library at Columbia University, shelfmark B842M76 J3.

Note on the Text

THE BASE text for the present volume is the 1603 edition of Florio's translation of *The Essayes or Morall, Politike and Millitarie Discourses of Lo[rd]: Michaell de Montaigne* (Printed at London: By Val. Sims for Edward Blount dwelling in Paules churchyard, 1603; STC 18041). This is the version of the essays known to Shakespeare and his contemporaries in England. To facilitate the comprehension and pleasure of modern readers, we have lightly modernized spelling, punctuation, and paragraphing. But we have done our best to preserve the beautiful—and at times deeply quirky—nature of Florio's translation and have supplemented the text, when necessary, with glosses that explicate difficult words and concepts.

SHAKESPEARE'S MONTAIGNE

To My Dear Friend[1] M. *John Florio*,
concerning *his translation of* Montaigne

Books, the amass of humors,[2] swollen with ease,
The grief of peace, the malady of rest,
So stuff the world, fallen into this disease,
As it receives more than it can digest.
And do so overcharge, as they confound
The appetite of skill with idle store.
There being no end of words, nor any bound
Set to conceit,[3] the Ocean *without shore.*
    As if man labor'd with himself to be
As infinite in words as in intents,
And draw his manifold incertainty
In ev'ry figure, passion represents;
That these innumerable visages,
And strange shapes of opinions and discourse
Shadowed in leaves,[4] may be the witnesses
Rather of our defects, than of our force.
And this proud frame of our presumption,
This Babel *of our skill, this* Tower *of wit,*
Seems only checked with the confusion
Of our mistakings that dissolveth it.
And well may make us of our knowledge doubt,
Seeing what uncertainties we build upon,
To be as weak within book or without;
Or else that truth hath other shapes than one.

But yet although we labor with this store
And with the press of writings seem opprest,
And have too many books, yet want we more,
Feeling great dearth and scarceness of the best;
Which cast in choicer shapes have been produc'd,
To give the best proportions to the mind
To our confusion, and have introduc'd
The likeliest images frailty can find.
And wherein most the skill-desiring soul
Takes her delight, the best of all delight,
And where her motions evenest come to roll
About this doubtful center of the right.[5]

Which to discover this great potentate,
This Prince Montaigne *(if he be not more)*
Hath more adventur'd of his own estate
Than ever man did of himself before.
And hath made such bold sallies out upon
Custom, *the mighty tyrant of the earth,*
In whose Seraglio *of subjection*
We all seem bred-up, from our tender birth;
As I admire his powers, and out of love,
Here at his gate do stand, and glad I stand
So near to him whom I do so much love,
T'applaud his happy settling in our land.
And safe transpassage by his[6] studious care,
Who both of him and us doth merit much,
Having as sumptuously, as he is rare,
Plac'd him in the best lodging of our speech.
And made him now as free,[7] as if born here,
And as well ours as theirs, who may be proud
That he is theirs, though he be everywhere
To have the franchise of his worth allow'd.

It being the portion of a happy pen,
Not to b'invassal'd[8] to one monarchy,
But dwells with all the better world of men

Whose spirits are all of one community.
Whom neither Ocean, *Deserts, Rocks nor Sands*
Can keep from th'intertraffic of the mind,
But that it vents her treasure in all lands,
And doth a most secure commercement[9] find.

   Wrap Excellency *up never so much,*
In hieroglyphics, ciphers, characters,
And let her speak never so strange a speech,
Her Genius *yet finds apt decipherers:*
And never was she born to die obscure,
But guided by the stars of her own grace,
Makes her own fortune, and is ever sure
In man's best hold, to hold the strongest place.

   And let the critic say the worst he can,
He cannot say but that Montaigne *yet,*
Yields most rich pieces and extracts of man,
Though in a troubled frame confus'dly set.[10]
Which yet h'is[11] blest that he hath ever seen,
And therefore as a guest in gratefulness,
For the great good the house yields him within
Might spare to tax th'unapt conveyances.[12]
But this breath hurts not, for both work and frame,[13]
Whilst England English speaks, is of that store
And that choice stuff, as that without the same
The richest library can be but poor.
And they unblest who letters do profess
And have him not, whose own fate beats their want
With more sound blows than Alcibiades
Did his pedant that did Homer *want.[14]*

—SAM: DANIEL
1603

To the Courteous Reader
(selections)

SHALL I apologize translation? Why, but some hold (as for their freehold[1]) that such conversion is the subversion of universities.[2] God hold with them and withhold them from impeach or empaire.[3] It were an ill turn the turning of books should be the overturning of libraries. Yea, but my old fellow *Nolano* told me and taught publicly that from translation all science had its offspring. . . .[4]

Why, but scholars should have some privilege of preeminence. So have they: they only are worthy translators. Why, but the vulgar should not know all. No, they cannot for all this, nor even scholars for much more. I would both could and knew much more than either doth or can. Why, but all would not be known of all. No, nor can: much more we know not than we know; all know something, none know all. Would all know all? They must break ere they be so big. God only; men far from God. . . .[5]

What do the best[6] then but glean after others' harvest? Borrow their colors, inherit their possessions? What do they but translate? Perhaps, usurp? At least, collect? If with acknowledgement, it is well; if by stealth, it is too bad. In this, our conscience is our accuser, posterity our judge; in that, our study is our advocate, and you Readers our jury. . . .

If the famous *Ficinus*[7] were so faulty, who may hope to scape scot-free? But for him and us all let me confess, as he here censureth, and let confession make half amends that every language hath its *Genius* and inseparable form, without *Pythagoras* his *Metempsychosis* it can not rightly be translated. The Tuscan altiloquence,[8] the *Venus* of the French, the sharp state of the Spanish, the strong significancy of the

Dutch cannot from here be drawn to life. The sense may keep form; the sentence is disfigured; the fineness, fitness, featness[9] diminished—as much as art's nature is short of nature's art, a picture of a body, a shadow of a substance. Why then belike I have done *Montaigne*, as *Terence* by *Menander*, made of good French no good English?[10] If I have done no worse, and it be no worse taken, it is well. As he, if no poet, yet am I no thief, since I say of whom I had it, rather to imitate his and his authors' negligence than any backbiter's obscure diligence....

So he, most writing of himself, and the worst rather than the best, disclaimeth all memory, authorities, or borrowing of the ancient or modern, whereas in course of his discourse he seems acquainted not only with all, but no other but authors, and could out of question like *Cyrus* or *Cæsar* call any of his army by his name and condition. And I would for us all he had in this whole body done as much, as in most of that of other languages my peerless dear-dearest and never sufficiently commended friend hath done for mine and your ease and intelligence.[11] Why then again, as *Terence*, I have had help. Yea, and thank them for it and think you need not be displeased by them that may please you in a better matter. Why, but Essayes are but men's school-themes pieced together—you might as well say, several texts. All is in the choice and handling. Yea, marry, but *Montaigne*, had he wit, it was but a French wit, ferdillant, legier, and extravagant....[12]

And should or would any dog-toothed Critic or adder-tongued Satirist scoff or find fault that, in the course of his discourses or web of his Essayes or entitling of his chapters, he holdeth a disjointed, broken, and gadding style; and that many times they answer not his titles and have no coherence together, to such I will say little, for they deserve but little. But if they list, else let them choose, I send them to the ninth chapter of the third book, folio *596*, where himself preventeth their carping, and foreseeing their criticism answereth them for me at full.[13]

Yet are there herein errors. If of matter, the author's; if of omission, the printer's. Him I would not amend but send him to you as I found him; this I could not attend. But where I now find faults, let me pray and entreat you for your own sake to correct as you read, to amend as you list. But some errors are mine, and mine are by more than translation. Are they in grammar or orthography? As easy for you to right as me to be wrong. Or in construction, as misattributing him, her, or it to things alive or dead or neuter. You may soon know my meaning and eftsoones[14] use your mending. Or are they in some uncouth terms, as entrain, conscientious, endear, tarnish, comport, efface, facilitate, amusing, debauching, regret, effort, emotion, and such like? If you like them not, take others more commonly set to make such likely French words familiar with our English, which well may bear them. If any be capital in sense mistaking,[15] be I admonished, and they shall be recanted. Howsoever, the falseness of the French prints, the diversities of copies, editions, and volumes (some whereof have more or less than others), and I in *London* having followed some and in the country others; now those in folio, now those in octavo, yet in this last survey reconciled all. Therefore or blame not rashly or condemn not fondly the multitude of them set for your further ease in a table (at the end of the book) which, ere you begin to read, I entreat you to peruse.[16] This Printer's wanting a diligent Corrector, my many employments, and the distance between me and my friends I should confer with may extenuate, if not excuse, even more errors.

In sum, if any think he could do better, let him try; then will he better think of what is done. Seven or eight of great wit and worth have assayed but found these Essayes no attempt for French apprentices or Littletonians.[17] If thus done it may please you as I wish it may, and I hope it shall, I with you shall be pleased; though not, yet still I am the *same resolute*.

—JOHN FLORIO

The Author to the Reader

READER, lo here a well-meaning book. It doth at the first entrance forewarn thee that in contriving the same I have proposed unto myself no other than a familiar and private end. I have no respect or consideration at all, either to thy service or to my glory: my forces are not capable of any such design. I have vowed the same to the particular commodity of my kinsfolk and friends, to the end that, losing me (which they are likely to do ere long), they may therein find some lineaments of my conditions and humours, and by that means reserve more whole, and more lively foster the knowledge and acquaintance they have had of me.

Had my intention been to forestall and purchase the world's opinion and favour, I would surely have adorned myself more quaintly, or kept a more grave and solemn march. I desire therein to be delineated in mine own genuine, simple, and ordinary fashion, without contention, art, or study; for it is myself I portray. My imperfections shall thus be read to the life, and my natural form discerned, so far-forth as public reverence hath permitted me. For if my fortune had been to have lived among those nations which yet are said to live under the sweet liberty of Nature's first and uncorrupted laws, I assure thee I would most willingly have portrayed myself fully and naked.

Thus, gentle Reader, myself am the groundwork of my book; it is then no reason thou shouldst employ thy time about so frivolous and vain a subject. Therefore farewell.

From *Montaigne*,
the first of March, 1580.

THE ESSAYS

That to Philosophize Is to Learn How to Die

CICERO sayeth, that to *Philosophize is no other thing than for a man to prepare himself to death*:[1] which is the reason that study and contemplation doth in some sort withdraw our soul from us, and severally[2] employ it from the body, which is a kind of apprentisage[3] and resemblance of death. Or else it is that all the wisdom and discourse of the world doth in the end resolve upon this point: to teach us not to fear to die. Truly either reason mocks us, or it only aimeth at our contentment, and in fine[4] bends all her travel to make us live well and, as the holy Scripture sayeth, *at our ease.* All the opinions of the world conclude that pleasure is our end, howbeit they take diverse means unto and for it, else would men reject them at their first coming. For who would give ear unto him[5] that for its end would establish our pain and disturbance?

The dissensions of philosophical sects in this case are verbal: *Transcurramus solertissimas nugas*: *Let us run over such over-fine fooleries and subtle trifles.*[6] There is more willfulness and wrangling among them than pertains to a sacred profession. But what person a man undertakes to act, he doth ever therewithal personate[7] his own. Although they say that, in virtue itself, the last scope of our aim is voluptuousness. It pleaseth me to importune their ears still with this word, which so much offends their hearing: And if it imply any chief pleasure or exceeding contentments, it is rather due to the assistance of virtue than to any other supply. Voluptuousness, being more strong, sinewy, sturdy, and manly, is but more seriously voluptuous. And we should give it the name of pleasure, more favorable, sweeter, and more natural; and not term it vigor, from which it hath his denomination. Should this baser sensuality deserve this fair name, it should be by competency and not by privilege. I find it less void of incommodities and crosses than virtue. And besides that her taste is more fleeting, momentary, and fading, she hath her fasts, her eves, and her travels, and both sweat and blood. Furthermore, she hath particularly so many wounding passions and of so several sorts, and so filthy and loathsome a society waiting upon her, that she is equivalent to penitence.[8]

We are in the wrong to think her incommodities[9] serve her as a provocation and seasoning to her sweetness, as in nature one contrary is vivified by another contrary: and to say, when we come to virtue, that like successes and difficulties overwhelm it, and yield it austere and inaccessible. Whereas much more properly than unto voluptuousness, they ennoble, sharpen, animate, and raise that divine and perfect pleasure, which it meditates and procureth us. Truly he is very unworthy her acquaintance, that counter-balanceth her cost to his fruit, and knows neither the graces nor use of it. Those who go about to instruct us, how her pursuit is very hard and laborious, and her jouissance[10] well-pleasing and delightful: what else tell they us, but that she is ever unpleasant and irksome? For, what humane mean did ever attain unto an absolute enjoying of it?[11] The perfectest have been content but to aspire and approach her, without ever possessing her. But they are deceived; seeing that of all the pleasures we know, the pursuit of them is pleasant. The enterprise is perceived by the quality of the thing, which it hath regard unto: for it is a good portion of the effect, and consubstantial. That happiness and felicity, which shineth in virtue, replenisheth her approaches and appurtenances, even unto the first entrance and utmost bar.[12]

Now of all the benefits of virtue, the contempt of death is the chiefest, a mean that furnisheth our life with an easeful tranquility and gives us a pure and amiable taste of it, without which every other voluptuousness is extinguished. Lo, here the reasons why all rules encounter and agree with this article. And albeit they all lead us with a common accord to despise grief, poverty, and other accidental crosses, to which man's life is subject, it is not with an equal care: as well because accidents are not of such a necessity, for most men pass their whole life without feeling any want or poverty, and other-some without feeling any grief or sickness, as *Xenophilus* the musician, who lived an hundred and six years in perfect and continual health: as also if the worst happen, death may at all times, and whensoever it shall please us, cut off all other inconveniences and crosses. But as for death, it is inevitable.

> *Omnes eodem cogimur, omnium*
> *Versatur urna, serius, ocius*
> *Sors exitura, et nos in æter-*
> *Num exitium impositura cymbæ.*
> All to one place are driv'n, of all
> Shak't is the lot-pot,[13] where-hence shall
> Sooner or later drawn lots fall,
> And to death's boat for aye[14] enthrall.[15]

And by consequence, if she make us afeard, it is a continual subject of torment, and which can no way be eased. There is no starting-hole[16] will hide us from her; she will find us wheresoever we are; we may as in a suspected country start and turn here and there: *quæ quasi saxum Tantalo semper impendet*: *Which evermore hangs like the stone over the head of Tantalus.*[17] Our laws do often condemn and send malefactors to be executed in the same place where the crime was committed: to which place, whilst they are going, lead them along the fairest houses or entertain them with the best cheer you can,

> *non Siculæ dapes*
> *Dulcem elaborabunt saporem:*
> *Non avium, citharæque cantus*
> *Somnum reducent.*
> Not all King *Denys* dainty fare,
> Can pleasing taste for them prepare:
> No song of birds, no music's sound
> Can lullaby to sleep profound.[18]

Do you think they can take any pleasure in it? Or be anything delighted? And that the final intent of their voyage being still before their eyes, hath not altered and altogether distracted their taste from all these commodities and allurements?

> *Audit iter, numeratque dies, spatioque viarum*
> *Metitur vitam, torquetur peste futura.*
> He hears his journey, counts his days, so measures he
> His life by his way's length, vex't with the ill shall be.[19]

The end of our cariere[20] is death. It is the necessary object of our aim: if it affright us, how is it possible we should step one foot further without an ague? The remedy of the vulgar sort is not to think on it. But from what brutal stupidity may so gross a blindness come upon him? He must be made to bridle his ass by the tail,

> *Qui capite ipse suo instituit vestigia retro.*
> Who doth a course contrary run
> With his head to his course begun.[21]

It is no marvel if he be so often taken tripping; some do no sooner hear the name of death spoken of, but they are afraid, yea the most part will cross themselves, as if they heard the Devil named. And because mention is made of it in men's wills and testaments, I warrant you there is none will set his hand to them, till the physician hath given his last doom and utterly forsaken him. And God knows, being then between such pain and fear, with what sound judgment they endure him.

For so much as this syllable sounded so unpleasantly in their ears, and this voice seemed so ill-boding and unlucky, the Romans had learned to allay and dilate the same by a Periphrasis.[22] In lieu of saying, he is dead, or he hath ended his days, they would say, he hath lived. So it be life, be it past or no, they are comforted: from whom we have borrowed our phrases *quondam*, *alias*, or *late such a one*.

It may happily be, as the common saying is, the time we live is worth the money we pay for it. I was born between eleven of the clock and noon, the last of February 1533, according to our computation, the year beginning the first of January.[23] It is but a fortnight since I was 39 years old. I want at least as much more.[24] If in the mean time I should trouble my thoughts with a matter so far from me, it were but folly. But what? We see both young and old to leave their life after one self-same condition. No man departs otherwise from it than if he but now came to it. Seeing there is no man so crazed, bedrell,[25] or decrepit, so long as he remembers *Mathusalem*,[26] but thinks he may yet live twenty years.[27]

Moreover, seely[28] creature as thou art, who hath limited the end of thy days? Happily thou presumest upon physicians' reports. Rather consider the effect and experience. By the common course of things, long since thou livest by extraordinary favor. Thou hast already overpassed the ordinary terms of common life. And to prove it, remember but thy acquaintances and tell me how many more of them have died before they came to thy age than have either attained or outgone the same. Yea, and of those that through renoune[29] hath ennobled their life, if thou but register them,[30] I will lay a wager I will find more that have died before they came to five and thirty years than after. It is consonant with reason and piety to take example by the humanity of *Jesus Christ*, who ended his human life at three and thirty years. The greatest man that ever was, being no more than a man, I mean *Alexander* the great, ended his days and died also of that age.

How many several means and ways hath death to surprise us.

> *Quid quisque vitet, nunquam homini satis*
> *Cautum est in horas.*
> A man can never take good heed,
> Hourly what he may shun and speed.[31]

I omit to speak of agues and pleurisies; who would ever have imagined that a Duke of *Brittany* should have been stifled to death in a throng of people, as whilome[32] was a neighbour of mine at *Lyons*, when Pope *Clement* made his entrance there? Hast thou not seen one of our late Kings slain in the midst of his sports? And one of his ancestors die miserably by the chocke[33] of an hog?[34] *Eschilus*,[35] fore-threatened by the fall of an house when he stood most upon his guard, strucken dead by the fall of a Tortoise shell, which fell out of the talons of an eagle flying in the air; and another choked with the kernel of a grape? And an Emperor die by the scratch of a comb, whilst he was combing his head? And *Lepidus* with hitting his foot against a door-sill? And *Aufidius* with stumbling against the coun-cil-chamber door as he was going in thereat? And *Cornelius Gallus*, the Prætor; *Tegiliinus* Captain of the Roman watch; *Lodovico*, son of *Guido Gonzaga*, Marquis of *Mantua*—end their days between women's thighs? And of a far worse example *Speusippus*, the Plato-nian philosopher, and one of our Popes? Poor *Bebius*, a judge, whilst he demurreth the suit of a plaintiff but for eight days, behold his last expired. And *Caius Julius* a physician, whilst he was anointing the eyes of one of his patients, to have his own sight closed forever by death. And if amongst these examples, I may add one of a brother of mine, called Captain *Saint Martin*,[36] a man of three and twenty years of age, who had already given good testimony of his worth and forward valor, playing at tennis, received a blow with a ball that hit him a little above the right ear, without appearance of any contu-sion, bruise, or hurt; and never sitting or resting upon it, died within six hours after of an apoplexy, which the blow of the ball caused in him. These so frequent and ordinary examples, happening and being still before our eyes, how is it possible for man to forgo or forget the remembrance of death? And why should it not continually seem unto us that she is still ready at hand to take us by the throat?

What matter is it, will you say unto me, how and in what manner it is, so long as a man do not trouble and vex himself therewith? I am of this opinion, that howsoever a man may shroud or hide himself from her dart, yea were it under an ox-hide, I am not the man would shrink back. It sufficeth me to live at my ease; and the best recreation I can have, that do I ever take; in other matters, as little vainglorious and exemplary as you list.

——prætulerim delirus inersque videri,
Dum mea delectent mala me, vel denique fallant,
Quam sapere et ringi.
A dotard I had rather seem, and dull,
Sooner my faults may please, make me a gull,
Than to be wise, and beat my vexed scull.[37]

But it is folly to think that way to come unto it. They come, they go, they trot, they dance: but no speech of death. All that is good sport. But if she be once come, and on a sudden and openly surprise either them, their wives, their children, or their friends, what torments, what out-cries, what rage, and what despair doth then overwhelm them? Saw you ever anything so drooping, so changed, and so distracted? A man must look to it, and in better times foresee it. And might that brutish carelessness lodge in the mind of a man of understanding (which I find altogether impossible), she sells us her ware at over-dear a rate. Were she an enemy by man's wit to be avoided, I would advise man to borrow the weapons of cowardliness. But since it may not be, and that be you either a coward or a runaway, an honest or valiant man, she overtakes you,

Nempe et fugacem persequitur virum,
Nec parcit imbellis iuuentæ
Poplitibus, timidoque tergo.
She persecutes the man that flies,
She spares not weak youth to surprise,
But on their hams and back turn'd, plies.[38]

And that no temper of cuirace[39] may shield or defend you,

Ille licet ferro cautus se condat in ære,
Mors tamen inclusum protrahet inde caput.
Though he with iron and brass his head impale,
Yet death his head enclosed thence will hale.[40]

Let us learn to stand and combat her with a resolute mind. And being to take the greatest advantage she hath upon us from her, let us take a clean contrary way from the common; let us remove her strangeness from her; let us converse, frequent, and acquaint ourselves with her; let us have nothing so much in mind as death; let us at all times and seasons, and in the ugliest manner that may be, yea with all faces shapen,[41] and represent the same unto our imagination. At the stumbling of a horse, at the fall of a stone, at the least prick with a pin, let us presently ruminate and say with ourselves: what if it were death it self? And thereupon let us take heart of grace and call our wits together to confront her. Amidst our banquets, feasts, and pleasures, let us ever have this restraint or object before us, that is, the remembrance of our condition, and let not pleasure so much mislead or transport us that we altogether neglect or forget how many ways, our joys, or our feastings, be subject unto death, and by how many hold-fasts she threatens us and them. So did the Egyptians, who in the midst of their banquetings and in the full of their greatest cheer, caused the anatomy of a dead man to be brought before them, as a memorandum and warning to their guests.

> *Omnem crede diem ubi diluxisse supremum,*
> *Grata superveniet, quæ non sperabitur hora.*
> Think every day shines on thee as thy last,
> Welcome it will come, whereof hope was past.[42]

It is uncertain where death looks for us; let us expect her every where: the premeditation of death is a fore-thinking of liberty. He who hath learned to die, hath unlearned to serve. There is no evil in life for him that hath well conceived how the privation of life is no evil. To know how to die doth free us from all subjection and constraint. *Paulus Æmilius* answered one whom that miserable king of *Macedon*, his prisoner, sent to entreat him [that] he would not lead him in triumph: "let him make that request unto himself."

Verily, if nature afford not some help in all things, it is very hard that art and industry should go far before. Of myself, I am not much given to melancholy, but rather to dreaming and sluggishness. There is nothing wherewith I have ever more entertained myself than with the imaginations of death, yea in the most licentious times of my age.

> *Iucundum, cum ætas florida ver aqeret.*
> When my age flourishing
> Did spend its pleasant spring.[43]

Being amongst fair ladies and in earnest play, some have thought me busied or musing with myself how to digest some jealousy or meditating on the uncertainty of some conceived hope, when God he knows I was entertaining myself with the remembrance of some one or other that but few days before was taken with a burning fever and of his sudden end, coming from such a feast or meeting where I was myself, and with his head full of idle conceits, of love, and merry glee; supposing the same, either sickness or end, to be as near me as him.

> *Iam fuerit, nec post, unquam revocare licebit.*
> Now time would be, no more
> You can this time restore.[44]

I did no more trouble myself or frown at such a conceit than at any other. It is impossible we should not apprehend or feel some motions or startings at such imaginations at the first and coming suddenly upon us. But doubtless he that shall manage and meditate upon them with an impartial eye, they will assuredly, in tract of time, become familiar to him. Otherwise, for my part, I should be in continual fear and agony; for no man did ever more distrust his life, nor make less account of his continuance. Neither can health, which hitherto I have so long enjoyed and which so seldom hath been crazed, lengthen my hopes, nor any sickness shorten them of it. At every minute methinks I make an escape. And I uncessantly record unto myself, that whatsoever may be done another day may be effected this day. Truly hazards and dangers do little or nothing approach us at our end; and if we consider how many more there remain besides this accident, which in number more than millions seem to threaten us and hang over us, we shall find that be we sound or sick, lusty or weak, at sea or at land, abroad or at home, fighting or at rest, in the midst of a battle or in our beds, she[45] is ever alike near unto us. *Nemo altero fragilior est, nemo in crastinum sui certior. No man is weaker than other; none surer of himself (to live) till to-morrow.*[46] Whatsoever I have to do before death, all leisure to end the same, seemeth short unto me, yea were it but of one hour.

Somebody, not long since turning over my writing tables, found by chance a memorial of something I would have done after my death. I told him (as indeed it was true) that being but a mile from my house, and in perfect health and lusty, I had made haste to write it because I could not assure myself I should ever come home in safety. As one that am ever hatching of mine own thoughts and place them in myself, I am ever prepared about that which I may be. Nor can death (come when she please) put me in mind of any new thing.

A man should ever, as much as in him lieth, be ready booted to take his journey, and above all things look he have then nothing to do but with himself.

Quid brevi fortes iaculamur ævo
Multa?
To aim why are we ever bold,
At many things in so short hold?[47]

For then we shall have work sufficient without any more accrease.[48] Some man complaineth more that death doth hinder him from the assured course of an hoped-for victory than of death itself; another cries out, he should give place to her before he have married his daughter or directed the course of his children's bringing up; another bewaileth he must forgo his wife's company; another moaneth the loss of his children, the chiefest commodities of his being.

I am now by means of the mercy of God in such a taking that, without regret or grieving at any worldly matter, I am prepared to dislodge whensoever he shall please to call me. I am everywhere free:

my farewell is soon taken of all my friends, except of myself. No man
did ever prepare himself to quit the world more simply and fully, or
more generally spake of all thoughts of it, than I am fully assured I
shall do. The deadest deaths are the best.

> *Miser, o miser (aiunt) omnia ademit,*
> *Una dies infesta mihi tot præmia vitæ:*
> O wretch, O wretch (friends cry), one day,
> All joys of life hath ta'ne[49] away:[50]

And the builder,

> ——*maneant (saith he) opera interrupta, minæque*
> *Murorum ingentes.*
> The works unfinisht lie,
> And walls that threatned hie.[51]

A man should design nothing so long aforehand, or at least with
such an intent, as to passionate himself to see the end of it; we are all
born to be doing.

> *Cum moriar, medium soluar et inter opus.*
> When dying I myself shall spend,
> Ere half my business come to end.[52]

I would have a man to be doing, and to prolong his life's offices, as
much as lieth in him, and let death seize upon me whilst I am setting
my cabbages, careless of her dart, but more of my unperfect garden.
I saw one die who, being at his last gasp, uncessantly complained
against his destiny and that death should so unkindly cut him off in
the midst of an history which he had in hand, and was now come to
the fifteenth or sixteenth of our kings.

> *Illud in his rebus non addunt, nec tibi earum,*
> *Iam desiderium rerum super insidet una.*

Friends add not that in this case, now no more
Shalt thou desire or want things wished before.[53]

A man should rid himself of these vulgar and hurtful humours. Even as churchyards were first placed adjoining unto churches and in the most frequented places of the city, to inure (as *Lycurgus* said) the common people, women, and children not to be scared at the sight of a dead man, and to the end that continual spectacle of bones, sculls, tombs, graves, and burials should forewarn us of our condition and fatal end.

Quin etiam exhilarare viris convivia cæde
Mos olim, et miscere epulis spectacula dira
Certantum ferro, sæpe et super ipsa cadentum
Pocula, respersis non parco sanguine mensis.
Nay more, the manner was to welcome guests,
And with dire shows of slaughter to mix feasts
Of them that fought at sharp, and with boards tainted
Of them with much blood, who o're[54] full cups fainted.[55]

And even as the Egyptians after their feastings and carousings caused a great image of death to be brought in and showed to the guests and by-standers by one that cried aloud, *Drink and be merry, for such shalt thou be when thou art dead*. So have I learned this custom or lesson, to have always death, not only in my imagination but continually in my mouth. And there is nothing I desire more to be informed of than of the death of men: that is to say, what words, what countenance, and what face they showed at their death; and in reading of histories, which I so attentively observe. It appeareth by the shuffling and huddling up of my examples, I affect no subject so particularly as this. Were I a composer of books, I would keep a register, commented of the diverse deaths which, in teaching men to die, should after teach them to live. *Dicearchus* made one of that title, but of another and less profitable end.

Some man will say to me, the effect exceeds the thought so far that there is no sense so sure, or cunning so certain, but a man shall either lose or forget if he come once to that point. Let them say what they list: To premeditate on it giveth no doubt a great advantage. And is it nothing at the least to go so far without dismay or alteration, or without an ague? There belongs more to it: Nature herself lends us her hand and gives us courage. If it be a short and violent death, we have no leisure to fear it; if otherwise, I perceive that according as I engage myself in sickness, I do naturally fall into some disdain and contempt of life. I find that I have more ado to digest this resolution that I shall die when I am in health than I have when I am troubled with a fever. Forsomuch as I have no more such fast hold on the commodities of life whereof I begin to lose the use and pleasure and view death in the face with a less undaunted look, which makes me hope that the further I go from that, and the nearer I approach to this, so much more easily do I enter in composition for their exchange. Even as I have tried in many other occurrences, which *Caesar* affirmed, that often some things seem greater, being far from us, than if they be near at hand. I have found that, being in perfect health, I have much more been frighted with sickness than when I have felt it. The jollity wherein I live, the pleasure and the strength, make the other seem so disproportionable from that, that by imagination I amplify these commodities by one moiety[56] and apprehended them much more heavy and burdensome than I feel them when I have them upon my shoulders. The same I hope will happen to me of death.

Consider we by the ordinary mutations and daily declinations which we suffer how Nature deprives us of the sight of our loss and impairing. What hath an aged man left him of his youth's rigor, and of his forepast life?

Heu senibus vitæ portio quanta manet!
Alas to men in years, how small
A part of life is left in all?[57]

Caesar to a tired and crazed soldier of his guard, who in the open street came to him to beg leave he might cause himself to be put to death, viewing his decrepit behaviour, answered pleasantly: *Dost thou think to be alive then?*[58] Were man all at once to fall into it, I do not think we should be able to bear such a change. But being fair and gently led on by her hand, in a slow and as it were unperceived descent, by little and little, and step by step, she rolls us into that miserable state, and day by day seeks to acquaint us with it. So that when youth fails in us, we feel, nay we perceive, no shaking or transchange at all in ourselves, which in essence and verity is a harder death than that of a languishing and irksome life or that of age. Forsomuch as the leap from an ill being unto a not being is not so dangerous or steepy as it is from a delightful and flourishing being unto a painful and sorrowful condition.

A weak bending and faint stooping body hath less strength to bear and undergo a heavy burden: so hath our soul. She must be roused and raised against the violence and force of this adversary. For, as it is impossible, she should take any rest whilst she feareth, whereof if she be assured (which is a thing exceeding human condition), she may boast that it is impossible unquietness, torment, and fear, much less the least displeasure, should lodge in her.

> *Non vultus instantis tyranni*
> *Mente quatit solida, neque Auster,*
> *Dux inquieti turbidus Adriæ.*
> *Nec fulminantis magna Iovis manus.*
> No urging tyrants threatening face,
> Where mind is found can it displace,
> No troublous wind the rough sea's Master,
> Nor *Jove's* great hand the thunder caster.[59]

She[60] is made mistress of her passions and concupiscence, lady of indulgence, of shame, of poverty, and of all fortune's injuries. Let him that can attain to this advantage: herein consists the true and sovereign liberty that affords us means wherewith to jest and make a scorn of force and justice and to deride imprisonment, gyves,[61] or fetters.

——*in manicis, et*
Compedibus, sævo te sub custode tenebo.
Ipse Deus simul atque volam, me solvet: opinor,
Hoc sentit moriar, mors ultima linea rerum est.
In gyves and fetters I will hamper thee,
Under a jailor that shall cruel be:
Yet, when I will, God me deliver shall,
He thinks, I shall die: death is end of all.[62]

Our religion hath had no surer human foundation than the contempt of life. Discourse of reason doth not only call and summon us unto it. For why should we fear to lose a thing which, being lost, cannot be moaned?[63] But also, since we are threatened by so many kinds of death, there is no more inconvenience to fear them all than to endure one. What matter is it when it cometh, since it is unavoidable? *Socrates* answered one that told him, "The thirty tyrants have condemned thee to death"; *And Nature them*, said he.

What fondness is it to cark[64] and care so much, at that instant and passage from all exemption of pain and care? As our birth brought us the birth of all things, so shall our death the end of all things. Therefore is it as great folly to weep we shall not live a hundred years hence as to wail we lived not a hundred years ago. *Death is the beginning of another life.* So wept we, and so much did it cost us to enter into this life; and so did we spoil us of our ancient vale in entering into it.

Nothing can be grievous that is but once. Is it reason so long to fear, a thing of so short time? Long life or short life is made all one by death. For long or short is not in things that are no more. *Aristotle* sayeth there are certain little beasts alongst the river *Hispanis* that live but one day. She which dieth at 8 o'clock in the morning, dies in her youth, and she that dies at 5 in the afternoon, dies in her decrepitude. Who of us doth not laugh when we shall see this short moment of continuance to be had in consideration of good or ill fortune? The most and the least in ours, if we compare it with eternity, or equal it to the lasting of mountains, rivers, stars, and trees, or any other living creature, is no less ridiculous.

But nature compels us to it.[65] *Depart,* sayeth she, *out of this world, even as you came into it. The same way you came from death, to death return without passion or amazement, from life to death. Your death is but a piece of the world's order and but a parcel of the world's life.*

> ———*inter se mortales mutua vivunt,*
> *Et quasi cursores vitæ lampada tradunt.*
> Mortal men live by mutual intercourse:
> And yield their life-torch, as men in a course.[66]

Shall I not change this goodly contexture of things for you? It is the condition of your creation: death is a part of yourselves; you fly from yourselves. The being you enjoy is equally shared between life and death. The first day of your birth doth as well address you to die as to live.

> *Prima quæ vitam dedit, hora, carpsit.*
> The first hour that to me
> Gave life straight, cropped it then.[67]
> *Nascentes morimur, fluisque ab origine pendet.*
> As we are born we die; the end
> Doth of th'original depend.[68]

All the time you live, you steal it from death: it is at her charge. The continual work of your life is to contrive death; you are in death, during the time you continue in life; for you are after death, when you are no longer living. Or if you had rather have it so, you are dead after life; but during life, you are still dying, and death doth more rudely touch the dying than the dead, and more lively and essentially.

If you have profited by life, you have also been fed thereby; depart then satisfied.

Cur non ut plenus vitæ conviva recedis?
Why like a full-fed guest,
Depart you not to rest?[69]

If you have not known how to make use of it, if it were unprofitable
to you, what need you care to have lost it? To what end would you
enjoy it longer?

——*cur amplius addere quæris*
Rursum quod pereat male, et ingratum occidat omne?
Why seek you more to gain, what must again,
All perish ill, and pass with grief or pain?[70]

Life in itself is neither good nor evil; it is the place of good or evil
according as you prepare it for them.[71]

And if you have lived one day, you have seen all: one day is equal to
all other days. There is no other light, there is no other night. This sun,
this moon, these stars, and this disposition is the very same which
your forefathers enjoyed and which shall also entertain your posterity.

Non alium videre patres, aliumve nepotes
Aspicient.
No other saw our sires of old,
No other shall their sons behold.[72]

And if the worst happen, the distribution and variety of all the acts
of my comedy[73] is performed in one year. If you have observed the
course of my four seasons, they contain the infancy, the youth, the
virility, and the old age of the world. He hath played his part: he
knows no other wiliness belonging to it but to begin again. It will
ever be the same, and no other.

——*Versamur ibidem, atque insumus usque,*
We still in one place turn about,

Still where we are, now in, now out.[74]
Atque in se sua per vestigia volvitur annus.
The year into it self is cast
By those same steps that it hath past.[75]

I am not purposed to devise you other new sports.

Nam tibi præterea quod machinor, inveniamque
Quod placeat, nihil est, eadem sunt omnia semper.
Else nothing, that I can devise or frame,
Can please thee, for all things are still the same.[76]

Make room for others, as others have done for you. *Equality is the chief ground-work of equity. Who can complain to be comprehended where all are contained.* So may you live long enough, you shall never diminish anything from the time you have to die. It is bootless: so long shall you continue in that state which you fear as if you had died being in your swathing-clothes and when you were sucking.

——*licet, quod vis, vivendo vincere secla,*
Mors æterna tamen, nihilominus illa manebit.
Though years you live, as many as you will,
Death is eternal, death remaineth still.[77]

And I will so please you that you shall have no discontent.

In vera nescis nullum fore morte alium te,
Qui possit vivus tibi te lugere peremptum,
Stansque iacentem.
Thou knowst not, there shall be no other thou,
When thou art dead indeed, that can tell how
Alive to wail thee dying, standing to wail thee lying.[78]

Nor shall wish for life, which you so much desire.

Nec sibi enim quisquam tum se vitamque requirit,
Nec desiderium nostri nos afficit ullum.
For then none for himself or life requires:
Nor are we of our selves affected with desires.[79]

Death is less to be feared than nothing, if there were anything less than nothing.

    ——*multo mortem minus ad nos esse putandum,*
Si minus esse potest quam quod nihil esse videmus.
Death is much less to us, we ought esteem,
If less may be, than what doth nothing seem.[80]

Nor alive, nor dead, it doth concern you nothing. Alive, because you are; dead, because you are no more.

Moreover, no man dies before his hour. The time you leave behind was no more yours than that which was before your birth and concerneth you no more.

Respice enim quam nil ad nos anteacta vetustas
Temporis æterni fuerit.
For mark, how all antiquity fore-gone
Of all time ere we were, to us was none.[81]

Wheresoever your life ended, there is it all. The profit of life consists not in the space, but rather in the use. Some man hath lived long that hath had a short life. Follow it whilst you have time. It consists not in number of years, but in your will, that you have lived long enough. Did you think you should never come to the place where you were still going? There is no way but hath an end. And if company may solace you, doth not the whole world walk the same path?

    ——*omnia te vita perfuncta sequentur.*
Life past, all things at last
Shall follow thee as thou hast past.[82]

Do not all things move as you do, or keep your course? Is there anything grows not old together with yourself? A thousand men, a thousand beasts, and a thousand other creatures die in the very instance that you die.

Nam nox nulla diem, neque noctem aurora sequuta est,
Quæ non audierit mistus vagitibus ægris
Ploratus mortis comites et funeris atri.
No night ensued day light: no morning followed night,
Which heard not moaning mixed with sick-men's groaning.
With deaths and funerals joined was that moaning.[83]

To what end recoil you from it, if you cannot go back? You have seen many who have found good in death, ending thereby many many miseries. But have you seen any that hath received hurt thereby? Therefore it is mere simplicity to condemn a thing you never approve, neither by yourself nor any other. Why dost thou complain of me and of destiny? Although thy age be not come to her period, thy life is. A little man is a whole man, as well as a great man. Neither men nor their lives are measured by the Ell.[84]

Chiron refused immortality, being informed of the conditions thereof, even by the God of time and of continuance, *Saturn* his father. Imagine truly how much an ever-during life would be less tolerable and more painful to a man than is the life which I have given him. Had you not death, you would then incessantly curse and cry out against me that I had deprived you of it. I have of purpose and unwittingly blended some bitterness amongst it, that so seeing the commodity of its use, I might hinder you from over greedily embracing or indiscreetly calling for it. To continue in this moderation, that is neither to fly from life nor to run to death (which I require of you), I have tempered both the one and other between sweetness and sourness.

I first taught *Thales*, the chiefest of your sages and wise men, that to live and die were indifferent, which made him answer one very wisely who asked him wherefore he died not: *Because*, sayeth he, *it is indifferent. The water, the earth, the air, the fire, and other members of this my universe are no more the instruments of thy life than of thy death. Why fearest thou thy last day? He[85] is no more guilty and conferreth no more to thy death than any of the others. It is not the last step that causeth weariness; it only declares it. All days march towards death; only the last comes to it.*

Behold here the good precepts of our universal mother Nature.[86] I have oftentimes bethought myself whence it proceedeth that, in times of war, the visage of death (whether we see it in us or in others) seemeth without all comparison much less dreadful and terrible unto us than in our houses or in our beds. Otherwise, it should be an army of physicians and whiners. And she[87] ever being one, there must needs be much more assurance amongst country people and of base condition than in others. I verily believe these fearful looks and astonishing countenances wherewith we encompass it are those that more amaze and terrify us than death. A new form of life: the outcries of mothers; the wailing of women and children; the visitation of dismayed and swooning friends; the assistance of a number of pale-looking, distracted, and whining servants; a dark chamber, tapers burning round about; our couch beset round with physicians and preachers; and to conclude, nothing but horror and astonishment on every side of us. Are we not already dead and buried? The very children are afraid of their friends when they see them masked; and so are we. The mask must as well be taken from things, as from men, which being removed, we shall find nothing hid under it but the very same death that a seely[88] varlet or a simple maid-servant did lately suffer without amazement or fear. Happy is that death which takes all leisure from the preparations of such an equipage.[89]

It Is Folly to Refer Truth or Falsehood to Our Sufficiency

IT IS NOT peradventure without reason that we ascribe the facility of believing and easiness of persuasion unto simplicity and ignorance. For me seemeth to have learnt heretofore that belief was, as it were, an impression conceived in our mind, and according as the same was found either more soft or of less resistance, it was easier to imprint anything therein. *Ut necesse est lancem in libra ponderibus impositis deprimi: sic animum perspicuis cedere. As it is necessary a scale must go down in the balance when weights are put into it, so must a mind yield to things that are manifest.*[1] Forasmuch, therefore, as the mind being most empty and without counterpoise, so much the more easily doth it yield under the burden of the first persuasion. And that's the reason why children, those of the common sort, women, and sick-folks are so subject to be misled and so easy to swallow gudgeons.[2]

Yet on the other side it is a sottish[3] presumption to disdain and condemn that for false which unto us seemeth to bear no show of likelihood or truth; which is an ordinary fault in those who persuade themselves to be of more sufficiency than the vulgar sort. So was I sometimes wont to do; and if I heard anybody speak either of ghosts walking, of foretelling future things, of enchantments, of witchcrafts, or any other thing reported which I could not well conceive or that was beyond my reach,

> *Somnia, terrores magicos, miracula, sagas,*
> *Nocturnos lemures, portentáque Thessala:*
> Dreams, magic terrors, witches, uncouth-wonders,
> Night-walking spirits, *Thessalian* conjur'd-thunders.[4]

I could not but feel a kind of compassion to see the poor and seely[5] people abused with such follies. And now I perceive that I was as much to be moaned myself. Not that experience hath since made me to discern anything beyond my former opinions; and yet was not my curiosity the cause of it.[6] But reason hath taught me that so resolutely to condemn a thing for false and impossible is to assume unto himself the advantage to have the bounds and limits of God's will and of the power of our common mother Nature tied to his sleeve. And that there is no greater folly in the world than to reduce them to the measure of our capacity and bounds of our sufficiency.

If we term those things monsters or miracles to which our reason cannot attain, how many such do daily present themselves unto our sight? Let us consider through what clouds and how blindfold[ed] we are led to the knowledge of most things that pass our hands. Verily, we shall find it is rather custom than science[7] that removeth the strangeness of them from us:

> ——*iam nemo fessus saturúsque videndi,*
> *Suspicere in cœli dignatur lucida templa.*
> Now no man tir'd with glut of contemplation
> Deigns to have heav'ns bright church in admiration.

And that those things, were they newly presented unto us, we should doubtless deem them as much, or more, unlikely and incredible than any other.

> ——*si nunc primum mortalibus adsint*
> *Ex improviso, ceu sint obiecta repentè,*
> *Nil magis his rebus poterat mirabile dici,*
> *Aut minus ante quod auderent fore credere gentes.*
> If now first on a sudden they were here
> 'Mongst mortal men, object to eye or ear,
> Nothing, than these things, would more wondrous be,
> Or that, men durst less think, ever to see.[8]

He who had never seen a river before, the first he saw he thought it to be the *Ocean*. And things that are the greatest in our knowledge we judge them to be the extremest that nature worketh in that kind.

> *Scilicet et fluvius qui non est maximum, ei est*
> *Qui non ante aliquem maiorem vidit, et ingens*
> *Arbor homoque videtur, et omnia de genere omni*
> *Maxima quæ vidit quisque, hæc ingentia fingit.*
> A stream none of the greatest, may so seem
> To him that never saw a greater stream.
> Trees, men seem huge, and all things of all sorts,
> The greatest one hath seen, he huge reports.[9]

Consuetudine oculorum assuescunt animi, neque admirantur, neque requirunt rationes earum rerum, quas semper vident. Minds are acquainted by custom of their eyes, nor do they admire or inquire the reason of those things which they continually behold.[10]

The novelty of things doth more incite us to search out the causes than their greatness. We must judge of this infinite power of nature with more reverence and with more acknowledgement of our own ignorance and weakness. How many things of small likelihood are there, witnessed by men, worthy of credit, whereof if we cannot be persuaded, we should at least leave them in suspense?[11] For to deem them impossible is by rash presumption to presume and know how far possibility reacheth. If a man did well understand what difference there is between impossibility and that which is unwonted, and between that which is against the course of nature[12] and the common opinion of men, in not believing rashly and in not disbelieving easily, the rule of Nothing too-much, commanded by *Chilon*, should be observed.

When we find in *Froysard*[13] that the Earl of *Foix* (being in *Bearne*) had knowledge of the defeature at *Iuberoth* of King *John* of *Castile* the morrow next it happened, and the means he allegeth for it, a man may well laugh at it. And of that which our annals report that Pope *Honorius*, the very same day that King *Philip Augustus* died at *Mantes*, caused his public funeral to be solemnized and commanded them[14] to be celebrated throughout all *Italy*. For the authority of the witnesses hath peradventure no sufficient warrant to restrain us. But what if *Plutarch*, besides diverse examples which he allegeth of antiquity, sayeth to have certainly known that in *Domitian's time the news of the battle, lost by Antonius in Germany many days' journeys thence, was published at Rome and divulged through the world the very same day it succeeded*. And if *Cæsar* holds that it hath many times happened that report hath foregone the accident—shall we not say that those simple people have suffered themselves to be cousoned[15] and seduced by the vulgar sort because they were not as clear-sighted as we? Is there anything more dainty, more unspotted, and more lively than *Pliny's* judgment, whensoever it pleaseth him to make show of it? Is there any farther from vanity? I omit the excellency of his learning and knowledge, whereof I make but small reckoning, in which of those two parts do we exceed him? Yet there is no scholar so meanly learned but will convince him of lying and read a lecture of contradiction against him upon the progress of nature's works.

When we read in *Bouchet* the miracles wrought by the relics of Saint *Hilary*, his credit is not sufficient to bar us the liberty of contradicting him.[16] Yet at random to condemn all such-like histories seemeth to me a notable impudence. That famous man Saint *Augustine* witnesseth to have seen a blind child to recover his sight over the relics of Saint *Gervase* and *Protaise* at *Milan*; and a woman at *Carthage* to have been cured of a canker[17] by the sign of the holy cross, which a woman newly baptized made upon her; and *Hesperius* a familiar friend of his, to have expelled certain spirits that molested his house with a little of the earth of our Savior's sepulcher, which earth being afterward transported into a church, a paralytic man was immediately therewith cured; and a woman going in procession, having as she passed by with a nosegay touched the case wherein Saint *Steven's* bones were, and with the same afterward rubbed her eyes, she recovered her sight, which long before she had utterly lost; and diverse other examples, where he affirmeth to have been an assistant[18] himself.[19] What shall we accuse him of, and two other holy Bishops, *Aurelius* and *Maximinus*, whom he calleth for his witnesses? Shall it be of ignorance, of simplicity, of malice, of facility, or of imposture? Is any living man so impudent that thinks he may be compared to them, whether it be in virtue or piety, in knowledge or judgment, in wisdom or sufficiency? *Qui ut rationem nullam afferrent, ipsa auto-ritate me frangerent: Who though they alleged no reason, yet might subdue me with their very authority.*[20]

It is a dangerous fond-hardiness and of consequence, besides the absurd temerity it draws with it, to despise what we conceive not. For after that, according to your best understanding, you have estab-lished the limits of truth and bounds of falsehood, and that it is found you must necessarily believe things wherein is more strange-ness than in those you deny, you have already bound yourself to abandon them. Now that which methinks brings as much disorder in our consciences, namely in these troubles of religion[21] wherein we are, is the dispensation Catholics make of their belief. They suppose to show themselves very moderate and skillful when they yield their adversaries any of those articles now in question. But besides that, they perceive not what an advantage it is for him that chargeth you, if you but once begin to yield and give him ground, and how much that encourageth him to pursue his point, those articles which they choose for the lightest are oftentimes most important. Either a man must wholly submit himself to the authority of our ecclesiastical policy, or altogether dispense himself from it. It is not for us to de-termine what part of obedience we owe unto it.

And moreover, I may say it because I have made trial of it, having sometimes used this liberty of my choice and particular election, not regarding certain points of the observance of our Church, which seem to bear a face either more vain or more strange. Coming to communicate them with wise men, I have found that those things have a most solid and steady foundation and that it is but foolishness and ignorance makes us receive them with less respect and reverence than the rest. Why remember we not what, and how many, contra-dictions we find and feel even in our own judgment? How many things served us but yesterday as articles of faith, which to day we deem but fables? Glory and curiosity are the scourges of our souls. The latter induceth us to have an oar in every ship, and the former forbids us to leave anything unresolved or undecided.

Of Friendship

CONSIDERING the proceeding of a painter's work I have,[1] a desire hath possessed me to imitate him. He maketh choice of the most convenient place and middle of every wall there to place a picture, laboured with all his skill and sufficiency, and all void places about it he filleth up with antique Boscage[2] or Crotesko[3] works, which are fantastical pictures, having no grace but in the variety and strangeness of them. And what are these my compositions in truth other than antique works and monstrous bodies, patched and huddled up together of diverse members without any certain or well-ordered figure, having neither order, dependency, or proportion, but casual and framed by chance?

> *Definit in piscem mulier formosa superne.*
> A woman fair for parts superior,
> Ends in a fish for parts inferior.[4]

Touching this second point I go as far as my painter, but for the other and better part I am far behind; for my sufficiency reacheth not so far as that I dare undertake a rich, a polished, and, according to true skill, an art-like table.[5] I have advised myself to borrow one of Steven de la Boitie,[6] who with this kind of work shall honour all the world. It is a discourse he entitled *Voluntary Servitude*, but those who have not known him have since very properly baptized the same, *The Against One*. In his first youth he writ, by way of essay, in honour of liberty against tyrants. It hath long since been dispersed amongst men of understanding, not without great and well-deserved commendations; for it is full of wit and containeth as much learning as may be. Yet doth it differ much from the best he can do. And if in the age I knew him in, he would have undergone my design to set his fantasies down in writing, we should doubtless see many rare things and which would very nearly approach the honour of antiquity; for especially touching that part of Nature's gifts, I know none may be compared to him. But it was not long of him[7] that ever this treatise came to man's view, and I believe he never saw it since it first escaped his hands; with certain other notes concerning the Edict of January,[8] famous by reason of our intestine war,[9] which haply in other places find their deserved praise. It is all I could ever recover of his relics (whom when death seized, he by his last will and testament, left with so kind remembrance, heir and executor of his library and writings), besides the little book I since caused to be published.[10]

To which his pamphlet I am particularly most bounden, for so much as it was the instrumental mean of our first acquaintance. For it was showed me long time before I saw him, and gave me the first knowledge of his name, addressing and thus nourishing that unspotted friendship which we (so long as it has pleased God) have so sincerely, so entire and inviolably maintained between us, that truly a man shall not commonly hear of the like, and amongst our modern men no sign of any such is seen. So many parts are required to the erecting of such a one that it may be counted a wonder if fortune once in three ages contract the like.

There is nothing to which Nature hath more addressed us than to society. And *Aristotle* sayeth that *perfect law-givers have had more regardful care of friendship than of justice.*[11] And the utmost drift of its perfection is this. For generally, all those amities[12] nourished by voluptuousness or profit, public or private need, are thereby so much the less fair and so much the less true amities, in that they intermeddle other causes, scope, and fruit with friendship than itself alone. Nor doe those four ancient kinds of friendships—natural, social, hospitable, and venerian[13]—either particularly or conjointly beseem the same.

That from children to parents may rather be termed respect.

Friendship is nourished by communication, which by reason of the over-great disparity cannot be found in them and would happly[14] offend the duties of nature. For neither all the secret thoughts of parents can be communicated unto children, lest it might engender an unbeseeming[15] familiarity between them, nor the admonitions and corrections (which are the chiefest offices of friendship) could be exercised from children to parents. There have nations been found where, by custom, children killed their parents, and others where parents slew their children, thereby to avoid the hindrance of enterbearing[16] one another in after times; for naturally one dependeth from the ruin of another. There have philosophers been found disdaining this natural conjunction: witness *Aristippus* who, being urged with the affection he ought his children as proceeding from his loins, began to spit, saying, *That also that excrement proceeded from him, and that also we engendered worms and lice.*[17] And that other man, whom *Plutarch* would have persuaded to agree with his brother, answered, *I care not a straw the more for him, though he came out of the same womb I did.*[18]

Verily, the name of brother is a glorious name and full of loving kindness, and therefore did he and I term one another sworn brother. But this commixture, dividence,[19] and sharing of goods, this joining wealth to wealth, and that the riches of one shall be the poverty of another, doth exceedingly distemper and distract all brotherly alliance and lovely conjunction. If brothers should conduct the progress of their advancement and thrift in one same path and course, they must necessarily oftentimes hinder and cross one another. Moreover, the correspondency and relation that begetteth these true and mutually perfect amities, why shall it be found in these? The father and the son may very well be of a far-differing complexion, and so may brothers. He is my son, he is my kinsman, but he may be fool, a bad, or a peevish-minded man. And then according as they are friendships which the law and duty of nature doth command us, so much the less of our own voluntary choice and liberty is there required unto it. And our genuine liberty hath no production more properly her own than that of affection and amity. Sure I am that concerning the same I have assayed all that might be, having had the best and most indulgent father that ever was, even to his extremest age, and who from father to son was descended of famous house and touching this rare-seen virtue of brotherly concord very exemplary:

> *et ipse*
> *Notus in fratres ommi paterni.*
> To his brothers known so kind,
> As to bear a father's mind.[20]

To compare the affection toward women unto it although it proceed from our own free choice, a man cannot, nor may it be placed in this rank. Her fire, I confess it—

> *(neque enim est dea nescia nostri*
> *Quæ dulcem curis miscat amaritiem.)*
> (Nor is that Goddess ignorant of me,
> Whose bitter-sweets with my cares mixed be.)[21]

—to be more active, more fervent, and more sharp. But it is a rash and wavering fire, waving and diverse, the fire of an ague subject to fits and stints, and that hath but slender hold-fast of us. In true friendship, it is a general and universal heat, and equally tempered, a constant and settled heat, all pleasure and smoothness, that hath no pricking or stinging in it. Which the more it is in lustful love, the more is it but a raging and mad desire in following that which flies us:

> *Come seque la lepre il cacciatore*
> *Al fredo, al caldo, alla montagna, al lito,*
> *Ne piu l'estima poi che presa vede,*
> *E sol dietro a chi fugge afretta il piede.*
> Ev'n as the huntsman doth the hare pursue,
> In cold, in heat, on mountains, on the shore,
> But cares no more, when he her ta'en espies,
> Speeding his pace only at that which flies.[22]

As soon as it creepeth into the terms of friendship, that is to say, in the agreement of wits, it languisheth and vanisheth away. Enjoying doth lose it, as having a corporal end, and subject to satiety. On the other side, friendship is enjoyed according as it is desired; it is neither bred nor nourished nor increaseth but in jouissance,[23] as being spiritual, and the mind being refined by use and custom. Under this chief amity, these fading affections have sometimes found place in me, lest I should speak of him, who in his verses speaks but too much of it. So are these two passions entered into me in knowledge one of another, but in comparison, never. The first flying a high and keeping a proud pitch,[24] disdainfully beholding the other to pass her points far under it.

Concerning marriage, besides that it is a covenant which hath nothing free but the entrance, the continuance being forced and constrained depending elsewhere than from our will, and a match ordinarily concluded to other ends. A thousand strange knots are therein commonly to be unknit, able to break the web and trouble the whole course of a lively affection; whereas in friendship there is no commerce or business depending on the same but itself. Seeing (to speak truly) that the ordinary sufficiency of women cannot answer this conference and communication, the nurse of this sacred bond; nor seem their minds strong enough to endure the pulling of a knot so hard, so fast, and durable. And truly, if without that, such a genuine and voluntary acquaintance might be contracted, where not only minds had this entire jouissance but also bodies a share of the alliance, and where a man might wholly be engaged, it is certain that friendship would thereby be more complete and full. But this sex could never yet by any example attain unto it and is by ancient schools rejected thence.

And this other Greek licence[25] is justly abhorred by our customs, which notwithstanding, because according to use it had so necessary a disparity of ages and difference of offices between lovers, did no more sufficiently answer the perfect union and agreement which here we require: *Quis est enim iste amor amicitiæ? cur neque deformem adolescentem quisquam amat, neque formosum senem?* For *what love is this of friendship? Why doth no man love either a deformed young man, or a beautiful old man?*[26] For even the picture the Academy[27] makes of it will not (as I suppose) disavow me to say thus in her behalf: That the first fury—inspired by the son of Venus[28] in the lover's heart upon the object of tender youth's flower, to which they allow all insolent and passionate violences, an immoderate heat may produce—was simply grounded upon an external beauty, a false image of corporal generation.[29] For in the spirit it had no power, the sight whereof was yet concealed, which was but in his infancy and before the age of budding. For, if this fury did seize upon a base-minded courage, the means of its pursuit were riches, gifts, favour to the advancement of dignities, and such like vile merchandise, which they reprove. If it fell into a more generous mind, the interpositions were likewise generous: philosophical instructions, documents to reverence religion, to obey the laws, to die for the good of his country; examples of valor, wisdom and justice; the lover endeavoring and studying to make himself acceptable by the good grace and beauty of his mind (that of his body being long since decayed), hoping by this mental society to establish a more firm and permanent bargain.

When this pursuit attained the effect in due season (for by not requiring in a lover, he should bring leisure and discretion in his enterprise, they require it exactly in the beloved; forasmuch as he was to judge of an internal beauty, of a difficile knowledge[30] and abstruse discovery), then by the interposition of a spiritual beauty was the desire of a spiritual conception engendered in the beloved. The latter was here chiefest; the corporal, accidental, and second, altogether contrary to the lover. And therefore do they prefer the beloved and verify that the gods likewise prefer the same, and greatly blame the poet *Æschylus*, who in the love between *Achilles* and *Patroclus* ascribeth the lover's part unto *Achilles*, who was in the first and beardless youth of his adolescence and the fairest of the Græcians.

After this general community, the mistress[31] and worthiest part of it, predominant and exercising her offices (they say the most availful[32] commodity did thereby redound both to the private and public);

that it was the force of countries received the use of it, and the principal defence of equity and liberty: witness the comfortable[33] loves of *Hermodius* and *Aristogeiton*. Therefore name they it sacred and divine, and it concerns not them whether the violence of tyrants or the demisness[34] of the people be against them.[35] To conclude, all that can be alleged in favor of the Academy is to say that it was friendship, a thing which hath no bad reference unto the Stoical definition of love: *Amorem conatunt esse amicitiæ faciendæ ex pulchritudinis specie. That love is an endeavour of making friendship by the show of beauty.*[36]

I return to my description in a more equitable and equal manner. *Omnino amicitiæ, corroboratis iam confirmatisque, ingeniis et ætatibus, judicandæ sunt. Clearly, friendships are to be judged by wits and ages already strengthened and confirmed.*[37]

As for the rest, those we ordinarily call friends and amities are but acquaintances and familiarities, tied together by some occasion or commodities, by means whereof our minds are entertained. In the amity I speak of, they intermix and confound themselves one in the other, with so universal a commixture that they wear out and can no more find the seam that hath conjoined them together. If a man urge me to tell wherefore I loved him, I feel it cannot be expressed but by answering: Because it was he, because it was myself.

There is beyond all my discourse, and besides what I can particularly report of it I know not what inexplicable and fatal power a mean and a mediatrix[38] of this indissoluble union. We sought one another before we had seen one another and by the reports we heard one of another, which wrought greater violence in us than the reason of reports may well bear; I think by some secret ordinance of the heavens. We embraced one another by our names. And at our first meeting, which was by chance at a great feast and solemn meeting of a whole township, we found ourselves so surprised, so known, so acquainted, and so combinedly bound together, that from thence forward nothing was so near unto us as one unto another's. He writ an excellent Latin satire since published by which he excuseth and expoundeth the precipitation of our acquaintance, so suddenly come to her perfection. Sithence it must continue so short a time, and begun so late (for we were both grown men, and he some years older than myself), there was no time to be lost. And it was not to be modeled or directed by the pattern of regular and remiss[39] friendship, wherein so many precautions of a long and preallable[40] conversation are required. This hath no other idea than of itself and can have no reference but to itself. It is not one especial consideration, nor two, nor three, nor four, nor a thousand: it is I wot not what kind of quintessence of all this commixture, which, having seized all my will, induced the same to plunge and lose itself in his; which likewise having seized all his will, brought it to lose and plunge itself in mine, with a mutual greediness, and with a semblable[41] concurrence. I may truly say "lose," reserving nothing unto us that might properly be called our own, nor that was either his or mine.

When *Lelius,* in the presence of the Roman consuls—who, after the condemnation of *Tiberius Gracchus,* pursued all those that had been of his acquaintance—came to inquire of *Caius Blosius* (who was one of his[42] chiefest friends) what he would have done for him, and that he answered, *All things. What, all things?* replied he. *And what if he had willed thee to burn our temples? Blosius* answered, *He would never have commanded such a thing. But what if he had done it?* replied *Lelius.* The other answered, *I would have obeyed him.* If he were so perfect a friend to *Gracchus* as histories report, he needed not offend the consuls with this last and bold confession and should not have departed from the assurance he had of *Gracchus* his mind. But yet those who accuse this answer as seditious understand not well this mystery, and do not presuppose in what terms he stood and that he held *Gracchus* his will in his sleeve, both by power and knowledge. They were rather friends than citizens, rather friends than enemies of their country or friends of ambition and trouble. Having absolutely committed themselves one to another, they perfectly held the reins of one another's inclination; and let this yoke be guided by virtue and conduct of reason (because without them it is altogether impossible to combine and proportion the same). The answer of *Blosius* was such as it should be. If their affections miscarried, according to my meaning, they were neither friends one to other, nor friends to themselves.

As for the rest, this answer sounds no more than mine would do to him that would in such sort inquire of me, "If your will should command you to kill your daughter, would you do it?" and that I should consent unto it. For that heareth no witness of consent to do it, because I am not in doubt of my will and as little of such a friend's will. It is not in the power of the world's discourse to remove me from the certainty I have of his intentions and judgments of mine. No one of its actions might be presented unto me, under what shape soever, but I would presently find the spring and motion of it. Our minds have jumped so unitedly together, they have with so fervent an affection considered of each other, and with like affection so discovered and sounded, even to the very bottom of each other's heart and entrails, that I did not only know his, as well as mine own, but would (verily) rather have trusted him concerning any matter of mine than myself.

Let no man compare any of the other common friendships to this. I have as much knowledge of them as another, yea of the perfectest of their kind, yet will I not persuade any man to confound their rules, for so a man might be deceived. In these other strict friendships a man must march with the bridle of wisdom and precaution in his hand: the bond is not so strictly tied but a man may in some sort distrust the same. *Love him* (said *Chilon*) *as if you should one day hate him again. Hate him as if you should love him again.* This precept, so abominable in this sovereign and mistress[43] amity, is necessary and wholesome in the use of vulgar and customary friendships, toward which a man must employ the saying *Aristotle* was wont so often repeat, *Oh ye friends, there is no perfect friend.*[44]

In this noble commerce, offices and benefits (nurses of other amities) deserve not so much as to be accounted of; this confusion so full of our wills is cause of it. For even as the friendship I bear unto myself admits no accrease[45] by any succour I give myself in any time of need, whatsoever the Stoics allege, and as I acknowledge no thanks unto myself for any service I do unto myself; so the union of such friends, being truly perfect, makes them lose the feeling of such duties, and hate and expel from one another these words of division and difference: benefit, good deed, duty, obligation, acknowledgement, prayer, thanks, and such their like. All things being by effect common between them—wills, thoughts, judgements, goods, wives, children, honour, and life—and their mutual agreement, being no other than one soul in two bodies, according to the fit definition of *Aristotle*, they can neither lend or give ought to each other.[46] See here the reason why lawmakers, to honour marriage with some imaginary resemblance of this divine bond, inhibit donations between husband and wife, meaning thereby to infer that all things should peculiarly be proper to each of them and that they have nothing to divide and share together.

If, in the friendship whereof I speak, one might give unto another, the receiver of the benefit should bind his fellow. For, each seeking more than any other thing to do each other good, he who yields both matter and occasion is the man showeth himself liberal, giving his friend that contentment to effect towards him what he desireth most. When the philosopher Diogenes wanted money, he was wont to say that he *re-demanded the same of his friends, and not that he demanded it.* And to show how that is practised by effect, I will relate an ancient singular example.

Eudamidas the Corinthian had two friends: *Charixenus*, a Sycionian, and *Aretheus*, a Corinthian. Being upon his deathbed and very poor, and his two friends very rich, thus made his last will and testament: *To* Aretheus, *I bequeath the keeping of my mother, and to maintain her when she shall be old. To* Charixenus, *the marrying of my daughter, and to give her as great a dowry as he may; and in case one of them shall chance to die before, I appoint the survivor to substitute his charge and supply his place.* Those that first saw this testament laughed and mocked at the same; but his heirs being advertised thereof were very well pleased and received it with singular contentment. And *Charixenus*, one of them, dying five days after *Eudamidas*, the substitution being declared in favour of *Aretheus*, he carefully and very kindly kept and maintained his mother, and of the five talents that he was worth, he gave two and a half in marriage to one only daughter he had, and the other two and a half to the daughter of *Eudamidas*, whom he married both in one day.

This example is very ample, if one thing were not, which is the multitude of friends. For this perfect amity I speak of is indivisible: each man doth so wholly give himself unto his friend that he hath nothing left him to divide elsewhere; moreover, he is grieved that he is [not] double, triple, or quadruple, and hath not many souls or sundry wills, that he might confer them all upon this subject. Common friendships may be divided; a man may love beauty in one, facility of behaviour in another, and wisdom in another, paternity in this, fraternity in that man, and so forth; but this amity that possesseth the soul and sways it in all sovereignty, it is impossible it should be double. If two at one instant should require help, to which would you run? Should they crave contrary offices of you, what order would you follow? Should one commit a matter to your silence, which if the other knew would greatly profit him, what course would you take? Or how would you discharge yourself? A singular and principal friendship dissolveth all other duties and freeth all other obligations. The secret I have sworn not to reveal to another, I may without perjury impart it unto him, who is no other but myself. It is a great and strange wonder for a man to double himself, and those that talk of tripling know not nor cannot reach into the height of it. *Nothing is extreme that hath his like.* And he who shall presuppose that of two I love the one as well as the other, and that they inter-love one another and love me as much as I love them, he multiplieth in brotherhood a thing most singular and alonely[47] one, and than which one alone is also the rarest to be found in the world.

The remainder of this history agreeth very well with what I said, for *Eudamidas* giveth us a grace and favor to his friends to employ them in his need. He leaveth them as his heirs of his liberality, which consisteth in putting the means into their hands to do him good. And doubtless the force of friendship is much more nobly shown in his deed than in *Aretheus.*

To conclude, they are inimaginable effects to him that hath not tasted them, and which makes me wonderfully to honor the answer of that young soldier to *Cyrus,* who enquiring of him what he would take for a horse with which he had lately gained the prize of a race, and whether he would change him for a kingdom.[48] *No surely, my Liege (said he), yet would I willingly forgo him to gain a true friend, could I but find a man worthy of so precious an alliance.* He said not ill, in saying, *could I but find.* For a man shall easily find men fit for a superficial acquaintance. But in this, wherein men negotiate from the very centre of their hearts and make no spare of anything, it is most requisite all the wards[49] and springs be sincerely wrought and perfectly true.

In confederacies which hold but by one end,[50] men have nothing to provide for but for the imperfections which particularly do interest and concern that end and respect. It is no great matter what religion my physician or lawyer is of; this consideration hath nothing in common with the offices of that friendship they owe me. So do I in the familiar acquaintances that those who serve me contract with me. I am nothing inquisitive whether a lackey be chaste or no but whether he be diligent. I fear not a gaming muleteer,[51] so much as if he be weak, nor a hot-swearing cook as one that is ignorant and un-skillful. I never meddle with saying what a man should do in the world—there are over many others that do it—but what myself do in the world:

Mihi sic usus est: Tibi, ut opus est facto, face.
So is it requisite for me;
Do thou as needful is for thee.[52]

Concerning familiar table-talk, I rather acquaint myself with and follow a merry conceited humour than a wise man; and in bed, I rather prefer beauty than goodness; and in society or conversation of familiar discourse, I respect rather sufficiency though without *Preud'hommie,*[53] and so of all things else.

Even as he that was found riding on an hobby-horse, playing with his children, besought him who thus surprised him not to speak of it until he were a father himself, supposing the tender fondness and fatherly passion which then would possess his mind should make him an impartial judge of such an action; so would I wish to speak to such as had tried what I speak of. But knowing how far such an amity is from the common use and how seld[54] seen and rarely found, I look not to find a competent judge. For even the discourses which stern antiquity hath left us concerning this subject seem to me but faint and forceless in respect of the feeling I have of it. And in that point the effects exceed the very precepts of philosophy.

> *Nil ego contulerim jucundo sanus amico.*
> For me, be I well in my wit.
> Nought, as a merry friend, so fit.[55]

Ancient *Menander* accounted him happy that had but met the shadow of a true friend. Verily, he had reason to say so, especially if he had tasted of any. For truly, if I compare all the rest of my fore-passed life—which, although I have by the mere mercy of God passed at rest and ease and, except the loss of so dear a friend, free from all grievous affliction with an ever-quietness of mind, as one that have taken my natural and original commodities in good payment without searching any others—if, as I say, I compare it all unto the four years I so happily enjoyed the dear society of that worthy man, it is nought but a vapour, nought but a dark and irksome light. Since the time I lost him,

> *quem semper acerbum,*
> *Semper honoratum (sic Dii voluistis) habebo.*
> Which I shall ever hold a bitter day,
> Yet ever honour'd (so my God t'obey).

I do but languish, I do but sorrow. And even those pleasures all things present me with, instead of yielding me comfort, do but re-double the grief of his loss. We were co-partners in all things. All things were with us at half; methinks I have stolen his part from him.

———*Nec fas esse ulla me voluptate hic frui*
Decrevi, tantisper dumille abest meus particeps.
I have set down, no joy enjoy I may.
As long as he my partner is away.[56]

I was so accustomed to be ever two, and so inured to be never single, that methinks I am but half my self.

Illam mea si partem animæ tulit,
Maturior vis, quid moror altera,
Nec charus æque nec superestes,
Integer? Ille dies utramque
Duxit ruinam.
Since that part of my soul riper fate reft me,
Why stay I here the other part he left me?
Not so dear, nor entire, while here I rest:
That day hath in one ruin both opprest.[57]

There is no action can betide me or imagination possess me but I hear him saying,[58] as indeed he would have done to me. For even as he did excel me by an infinite distance in all other sufficiencies and virtues, so did he in all offices and duties of friendship.

Quis desiderio sit pudor aut modus,
Tam chari capitis?
What modesty or measure may I bear,
In want and wish of him that was so dear?[59]

O misero frater adempte mihi!
Omnia tecum una perierunt gaudia nostra.
Quæ tuus in vita dulcis alebat amor.
Tu mea, tu moriens fregisti commoda frater.
Tecum una tota est nostra sepulta anima,
Cuius ego interitu tota demente fugavi
Hæc studia, atque omnes delicias animi.

Alloquar? audiero nunquam tua verba loquentem
Numquam eqo te vita frater amabilior,
Aspiciam posthac? at certe semper amabo.
O brother rest from miserable me,
All our delights are perished with thee,
Which thy sweet love did nourish in my breath;
With thee my soul is all and whole enshrined,
At whose death I have cast out of my mind
All my mind's sweet-meats, studies of this kind.
Never shall I hear thee speak, speak with thee?
Thee brother, than life dearer, never see?
Yet shalt thou ever be belov'd of me.[60]

But let us a little hear this young man speak, being but sixteen years of age.

Because I have found this work to have since been published (and to an ill end) by such as seek to trouble and subvert the state of our commonwealth, nor caring whether they shall reform it or no, which they have fondly inserted among other writings of their invention, I have revoked my intent, which was to place it here.[61] And lest the author's memory should any way be interessed[62] with those that could not thoroughly know his opinions and actions, they shall understand that this subject was by him treated of in his infancy, only by way of exercise, as a subject, common, bare-worn, and wire-drawn[63] in a thousand books. I will never doubt but he believed what he writ and writ as be thought, for he was so conscientious that no lie did ever pass his lips, yea, were it but in matters of sport or play. And I know that had it been in his choice, he would rather have been born at *Venice* than at *Sarlac*,[64] and good reason why. But he had another maxim deeply imprinted in his mind, which was carefully to obey and religiously to submit himself to the laws under which he was born. There was never a better citizen, nor more affected to the welfare and quietness of his country, nor a sharper enemy of the changes, innovations, new-fangles, and hurly-burlies of his time. He would more willingly have employed the utmost of his endeavours to extinguish and suppress than to favour or further them. His mind was modeled to the pattern of other best ages.

But yet in exchange of his serious treatise, I will here set you down another, more pithy material, and of more consequence, by him likewise produced at that tender age.[65]

Of the Cannibals

AT WHAT time King *Pyrrhus* came into *Italy*, after he had sur-
veyed the marshalling of the Army, which the Romans sent against
him: *I wot not*, said he, *what barbarous men these are* (for so were the
Græcians wont to call all strange nations) *but the disposition of this
Army, which I see, is nothing barbarous*. So said the Græcians of that
which *Flaminius* sent into their country. And *Philip* viewing from a
tower the order and distribution of the Roman camp, in his kingdom under *Publius Sulpitius Galba*. Lo, how a man ought to take
heed, lest he over-weeningly follow vulgar opinions, which should
be measured by the rule of reason and not by the common report.

I have had long time dwelling with me a man, who for the space
of ten or twelve years had dwelt in that other world which in our age
was lately discovered in those parts where *Villegaignon* first landed
and surnamed *Antartike France*.[1] This discovery of so infinite and
vast a country seemeth worthy great consideration. I wot not
whether I can warrant myself that some other be not discovered
hereafter, sithence[2] so many worthy men, and better learned than we
are, have so many ages been deceived in this. I fear me our eyes be
greater than our bellies, and that we have more curiosity than capacity. We embrace all, but we fasten nothing but wind.

Plato maketh *Solon* to report that he had learn't of the priests of
the city of *Says* in *Egypt*, that whilom, and before the general deluge,
there was a great island called *Atlantis*, situated at the mouth of the
strait of *Gibraltar*, which contained more firm land than *Africa* and
Asia together. And that the kings of that country—who did not

only possess that island but had so far entered into the mainland that of the breadth of *Africa* they held as far as *Egypt*; and of *Europe's* length, as far as *Tuscany*—and that they undertook to invade *Asia* and to subdue all the nations that compass the Mediterranean Sea, to the gulf of *Mare-Maggiore*[3] and to that end they traversed all *Spain, France,* and *Italy*, so far as *Greece*, where the Athenians made head against them. But that awhile after both the Athenians themselves and that great island were swallowed up by the Deluge.[4]

It is very likely this extreme ruin of waters wrought strange alterations in the habitations of the earth, as some hold that the sea hath divided *Sicily* from *Italy*,

> *Hæc loca vi quandam, et vasta convulsa ruina*
> *Dissiluisse ferunt, cum protinus utraque tellus*
> *Una foret.*
> Men say, sometimes this land by that forsaken,
> And that by this, were split and ruin-shaken,
> Whereas till then both lands as one were taken.[5]

Cyprus from *Soria*, the island of *Negroponte* from the mainland of *Beotia*, and in other places joined lands that were sundered by the sea, filling with mud and sand the channels between them.[6]

> ——*sterilisque diu palus aptaque remis*
> *Vicinas urbes alit, et grave sentit aratrum.*
> The fen long barren, to be row'd in, now
> Both feeds the neighbour towns, and feels the plow.[7]

But there is no great appearance the said island should be the new world we have lately discovered. For it well-nigh touched *Spain*, and it were an incredible effect of inundation, to have removed the same more than twelve hundred leagues, as we see it is. Besides, our modern navigations have now almost discovered that it is not an island, but rather firm land, and a continent, with the East *Indies* on one side, and the countries lying under the two poles on the other; from which if it be divided, it is with so narrow a strait and interval that it no way deserveth to be named an island.

For it seemeth there are certain motions in these vast bodies, some natural and other-some febricitant,[8] as well as in ours. When I consider the impression my river of *Dordogne* worketh in my time toward the right shore of her descent, and how much it hath gained in twenty years, and how many foundations of diverse houses it hath overwhelmed and violently carried away, I confess it to be an extraordinary agitation. For should it always keep one course, or had it ever kept the same, the figure of the world had ere this been overthrown. But they are subject to changes and alterations. Sometimes they overflow and spread themselves on one side, sometimes on another; and other times they contain themselves in their natural beds or channels. I speak not of sudden inundations, whereof we now treat the causes. In *Medoc* along the seacoast, my brother the Lord of *Arsac* may see a town of his buried under the sands, which the sea casteth up before it. The tops of some buildings are yet to be discerned. His rents and domains[9] have been changed into barren pastures. The inhabitants thereabouts affirm that some years since the sea encroacheth so much upon them that they have lost four leagues of firm land. These sands are her forerunners. And we see great hillocks of gravel moving, which march half a league before it and usurp on the firm land.

The other testimony of antiquity to which some will refer this discovery is in *Aristotle* (if at least that little book of unheard of wonders be his)[10] where he reporteth that certain *Carthaginians*, having sailed athwart the *Atlantic* Sea without the strait of *Gibraltar*, after long time they at last discovered a great fertile island—all replenished with goodly woods and watered with great and deep rivers, far-distant from all land; and that both they and others, allured by the goodness and fertility of the soil, went thither with their wives, children, and household, and there began to habituate and settle themselves. The lords of *Carthage* seeing their country by little and little to be dispeopled, made a law and express inhibition that upon pain of death no more men should go thither and banished all that were gone thither to dwell, fearing (as they said) that in success of time, they would so multiply as they might one day supplant them and overthrow their own estate. This narration of *Aristotle* hath no reference unto our new-found countries.

This servant I had was a simple and rough-hewn fellow:[11] a condition fit to yield a true testimony. For subtle people may indeed mark more curiously and observe things more exactly, but they amplify and gloss them. And the better to persuade and make their interpretations of more validity, they cannot choose but somewhat alter the story. They never represent things truly but fashion and mask them according to the visage they saw them in. And to purchase credit to their judgement and draw you on to believe them, they commonly adorn, enlarge, yea, and hyperbolise the matter. Wherein is required either a most sincere reporter or a man so simple that he may have no invention to build upon and to give a true likelihood unto false devices and be not wedded to his own will. Such a one was my man who, besides his own report, hath many times showed me diverse mariners and merchants whom he had known in that voyage. So am I pleased with his information that I never inquire what cosmographers say of it.

We had need of topographers to make us particular narrations of the places they have been in. For some of them, if they have the advantage of us, that they have seen *Palestine*, will challenge a privilege to tell us news of all the world besides. I would have every man write what he knows and no more: not only in that but in all other subjects. For one may have particular knowledge of the nature of one river and experience of the quality of one fountain that in other things knows no more than another man: who, nevertheless, to publish this little scantling[12] will undertake to write of all the physics. From which vice proceed diverse great inconveniences.

Now (to return to my purpose) I find (as far as I have been informed) there is nothing in that nation that is either barbarous or savage, unless men call that barbarism which is not common to them. As indeed, we have no other aim of truth and reason than the example and *Idea* of the opinions and customs of the country we live in. Where[13] is ever perfect religion, perfect policy, perfect and complete use of all things. They are even savage, as we call those fruits wild, which nature of herself and of her ordinary progress hath produced. Whereas indeed they are those[14] which ourselves have altered by our artificial devices and diverted from their common order we should rather term savage. In those are the true and most profitable virtues and natural proprieties most lively and vigorous, which in these we have bastardized, applying them to the pleasure of our corrupted taste.[15] And if notwithstanding, in diverse fruits of those countries that were never tilled, we shall find that in respect of ours they are most excellent and as delicate unto our taste, there is no reason art should gain the point of honour of our great and puissant mother Nature. We have so much, by our inventions, surcharged the beauties and riches of her works that we have altogether over-choked her. Yet wherever her purity shineth, she makes our vain and frivolous enterprises wonderfully ashamed.[16]

> *Et veniunt haderæ sponte sua melius,*
> *Surgit et in solis formosior arbutus antris,*
> *Et volucres nulla dulcius arte canunt.*
> Ivies spring better of their own accord,
> Un-hanted[17] plots much fairer trees afford.
> Birds by no art much sweeter notes record.[18]

All our endeavours or wit cannot so much as reach to represent the nest of the least birdlet,[19] its contexture, beauty, profit, and use, no nor the web of a seely[20] spider. *All things* (sayeth *Plato*) *are produced either by nature, by fortune, or by art. The greatest and fairest by one or other of the two first, the least and imperfect by the last.*[21]

Those nations seem therefore so barbarous unto me because they have received very little fashion from human wit, and are yet near their original naturality. The laws of nature do yet command them, which are but little bastardized by ours. And that with such purity, as I am sometimes grieved the knowledge of it came no sooner to light, at what time there were men that better than we could have judged of it. I am sorry *Lycurgus* and *Plato* had it not. For me seemeth that what in those nations we see by experience doth not only exceed all the pictures wherewith licentious Poesy hath proudly embellished the golden age and all her quaint inventions to feign a happy condition of man but also the conception and desire of philosophy. They could not imagine a genuitie[22] so pure and simple as we see it by experience; nor ever believe our society might be maintained with so little art and human combination. It is a nation, would I answer *Plato*, that hath no kind of traffic, no knowledge of letters, no intelligence of numbers, no name of magistrate, nor of politic superiority; no use of service, of riches, or of poverty; no contracts, no successions, no dividences,[23] no occupation but idle; no respect of kindred, but common; no apparel, but natural; no manuring[24] of lands, no use of wine, corn, or metal. The very words that import lying, falsehood, treason, dissimulation, covetousness, envy, detraction, and pardon were never heard of amongst them.[25] How dissonant would he find his imaginary common-wealth from this perfection?

Hos natura modos primum dedit.
Nature at first uprise,
These manners did devise.[26]

Furthermore, they live in a country of so exceeding pleasant and temperate situation that, as my testimonies have told me, it is very rare to see a sick body amongst them. And they have further assured me they never saw any man there either shaking with the palsy, toothless, with eyes dropping, or crooked and stooping through age. They are seated alongst the sea coast, encompassed toward the land with huge and steepie[27] mountains, having between both, a hundred leagues or thereabouts of open and champaine[28] ground. They have great abundance of fish and flesh that have no resemblance at all with ours, and eat them without any sauces or skill of cookery, but plain boiled or broiled. The first man that brought a horse thither, although he had in many other voyages conversed with them, bred so great a horror in the land that, before they could take notice of him, they slew him with arrows.

Their buildings are very long and able to contain two or three hundred souls: covered with barks of great trees, fastened in the ground at one end, interlaced and joined close together by the tops, after the manner of some of our granges; the covering whereof hangs down to the ground and steadeth them as a flank.[29] They have a kind of wood so hard that riving[30] and cleaving the same, they make blades, swords, and gridirons to broil their meat with. Their beds are of a kind of cotton cloth, fastened to the house roof, as our ship cabins: every one hath his several[31] couch, for the women lie from[32] their husbands.

They rise with the sun and feed for all day, as soon as they are up, and make no more meals after that. They drink not at meat, as *Suidas* reporteth of some other people of the East, which drank after meals, but drink many times a day and are much given to pledge carouses.[33] Their drink is made of a certain root and of the colour of our claret wines which lasteth but two or three days. They drink it warm. It hath somewhat a sharp taste, wholesome for the stomach, nothing heady but laxative for such as are not used unto it, yet very pleasing to such as are accustomed unto it. Instead of bread, they use a certain white composition, like unto corianders confected.[34] I have eaten some, the taste whereof is somewhat sweet and wallowish.[35]

They spend the whole day in dancing. Their young men go a-hunting after wild beasts with bows and arrows. Their women busy themselves therwhil'st with warming of their drink, which is their chiefest office. Some of their old men, in the morning before they go to eating, preach in common to all the household, walking from one end of the house to the other, repeating one self-same sentence many times, till he have ended his turn (for their buildings are a hundred paces in length) he commends but two things unto his auditory[36]: *First, valor against their enemies, then lovingness unto their wives.* They never miss (for their restraint[37]) to put men in mind of this duty that it is their wives which keep their drink lukewarm and well-seasoned. The form of their beds, cords, swords, blades, and wooden bracelets, wherewith they cover their hand-wrists when they fight, and great canes open at one end, by the sound of which they keep time and cadence in their dancing, are in many places to be seen and, namely, in mine own house. They are shaven all over, much more close and cleaner than we are, with no other razors than of wood or stone. They believe their souls to be eternal, and those that have deserved well of their gods to be placed in that part of heaven where the sun riseth, and the cursed toward the west in opposition.

They have certain prophets and priests, which commonly abide in the mountains and very seldom show themselves unto the people. But when they come down, there is a great feast prepared and a solemn assembly of many townships together. (Each grange as I have described maketh a village, and they are about a French league[38] one from an other.) The prophet speaks to the people in public, exhorting them to embrace virtue and follow their duty. All their moral discipline containeth but these two articles: first, an undismayed resolution to war; then, an inviolable affection to their wives. He doth also prognosticate of things to come and what success they shall hope for in their enterprises: he either persuadeth or dissuadeth them from war. But if he chance to miss of his divination and that it succeed otherwise than he foretold them, if he be taken, he is hewn in a thousand pieces and condemned for a false prophet. And therefore he that hath once mis-reckoned himself is never seen again.

Divination is the gift of God; the abusing whereof should be a punishable imposture. When the divines amongst the Scythians had foretold an untruth, they were couched along upon hurdles full of heath or brushwood, drawn by oxen, and so manacled hand and foot, burned to death. Those which manage matters subject to the conduct of man's sufficiency[39] are excusable, although they show the utmost of their skill. But those that gull and cony-catch[40] us with the assurance of an extraordinary faculty and which is beyond our knowledge ought to be double punished: first, because they perform not the effect of their promise; then, for the rashness of their imposture and unadvisedness of their fraud.

They war against the nations that lie beyond their mountains, to which they go naked, having no other weapons than bows or wooden swords, sharp at one end, as our broaches[41] are. It is an admirable thing to see the constant resolution of their combats, which never end but by effusion of blood and murder: for they know not what fear or rowts[42] are.

Every victor brings home the head of the enemy he hath slain as a trophy of his victory and fasteneth the same at the entrance of his dwelling place. After they have long time used and entreated their prisoners well, and with all commodities they can devise, he that is the master of them, summoning a great assembly of his acquaintance, tieth a cord to one of the prisoners arms, by the end whereof he holds him fast, with some distance from him for fear he might offend him, and giveth the other arm, bound in like manner, to the dearest friend he hath. And both in the presence of all the assembly kill him with swords. Which done, they roast and then eat him in common and send some slices of him to such of their friends as are absent. It is not, as some imagine, to nourish themselves with it (as anciently the Scythians wont to do,) but to represent an extreme and inexpiable revenge. Which we prove thus. Some of them perceiving the Portugales,[43] who had confederated themselves with their adversaries, to use another kind of death when they took them prisoners, which was to bury them up to the middle, and against the upper part of the body to shoot arrows, and then being almost dead, to hang them up. They supposed that these people of the other world (as they who had sowed the knowledge of many vices amongst their neighbours and were much more cunning in all kinds of evils and mischief than they) undertook not this manner of revenge without cause and that consequently it was more smartful[44] and cruel than theirs, and thereupon began to leave their old fashion to follow this.

I am not sorry we note the barbarous horror of such an action but grieved that, prying so narrowly into their faults, we are so blinded in ours. I think there is more barbarism in eating men alive than to feed upon them being dead; to mangle by tortures and torments a body full of lively sense, to roast him in pieces, and to make dogs and swine to gnaw and tear him in mammockes[45] (as we have not only read, but seen very lately, yea and in our own memory, not amongst ancient enemies, but our neighbours and fellow citizens, and which is worse, under pretense of piety and religion) than to roast and tear him after he is dead.

Chrysippus and *Zeno*, arch-pillars of the Stoic sect, have supposed that it was no hurt at all, in time of need, and to what end soever, to make use of our carrion bodies and to feed upon them, as did our forefathers who, being besieged by *Cæsar* in the city of *Alesia*, resolved to sustain the famine of the siege with the bodies of old men, women, and other persons unserviceable and unfit to fight.

> *Vascones (fama est) alimentis talibus usi*
> *Produxere animas.*
> *Gascoynes* (as fame reports)
> Liv'd with meats of such sorts. [46]

And physicians fear not, in all kinds of compositions availful to[47] our health, to make use of it, be it for outward or inward applications.[48]

But there was never any opinion found so unnatural and immodest that would excuse treason, treachery, disloyalty, tyranny, cruelty, and such like, which are our ordinary faults.[49] We may then well call them barbarous, in regard of reason's rules, but not in respect of us that exceed them in all kind of barbarism. Their wars are noble and generous and have as much excuse and beauty as this human infirmity may admit: they aim at nought so much and have no other foundation amongst them but the mere jealousy of virtue. They contend not for the gaining of new lands, for to this day they yet enjoy that natural ubertie[50] and fruitfulness which without labouring-toil doth in such plenteous abundance furnish them with all necessary things that they need not enlarge their limits.[51] They are yet in that happy estate as they desire no more than what their natural necessities direct them: whatsoever is beyond it is to them superfluous.

Those that are much about one age do generally enter-call[52] one another brethren, and such as are younger, they call children, and the aged are esteemed as fathers to all the rest. These leave this full possession of goods in common and without division to their heirs, without other claim or title but that which Nature doth plainly impart unto all creatures, even as she brings them into the world.

If their neighbours chance to come over the mountains to assail or invade them, and that they get the victory over them, the victors conquest is glory, and the advantage to be and remain superior in valour and virtue; else have they nothing to do with the goods and spoils of the vanquished and so return into their country, where they neither want any necessary thing, nor lack this great portion, to know how to enjoy their condition happily, and are contented with what nature affordeth them. So do these when their turn commeth. They require no other ransom of their prisoners but an acknowledgement and confession that they are vanquished. And in a whole age, a man shall not find one that doth not rather embrace death than either by word or countenance remissely[53] to yield one jot of an invincible courage. There is none seen that would not rather be slain and devoured than sue for life or show any fear. They use their prisoners with all liberty that they may so much the more hold their lives dear and precious and commonly entertain them with threats of future death, with the torments they shall endure, with the preparations intended for that purpose, with mangling and slicing of their members, and with the feast that shall be kept at their charge. All which is done to wrest some remisse and exact some faint-yielding speech of submission from them, or to possess them with a desire to escape or run away. That so they may have the advantage to have danted[54] and made them afraid and to have forced their constancy. For certainly true victory consisteth in that only point.

——*Victoria nulla est*
Quam quæ confessos animo quoque subjugat hostes.
No conquest such, as to suppress
Foes' hearts, the conquest to confess.[55]

The Hungarians, a most war-like nation, were whilom wont to pursue their prey no longer than they had forced their enemy to yield unto their mercy. For, having wrested this confession from him, they set him at liberty without offense or ransom, except it were to make him swear never after to bear arms against them.

We get many advantages of our enemies that are but borrowed and not ours. It is the quality of porterly-rascal[56] and not of virtue, to have stronger arms and sturdier legs. Disposition[57] is a dead and corporal quality. It is a trick of fortune to make our enemy stoop and to blear his eyes with the sun's light. It is a prank of skill and knowledge to be cunning in the art of fencing, and which may happen unto a base and worthless man. The reputation and worth of a man consisteth in his heart and will; therein consists true honour. Constancy is valour, not of arms and legs, but of mind and courage; it consisteth not in the spirit and courage of our horse, nor of our arms, but in ours. He that obstinately faileth in his courage, *Si succiderit, de genu pugnat. If he slip or fall, he fights upon his knee.*[58] He that in danger of imminent death is no whit daunted in his assuredness; he that in yielding up his ghost beholdeth his enemy with a scornful and fierce look, he is vanquished not by us but by fortune; he is slain, but not conquered.

The most valiant are often the most unfortunate. So are there triumphant losses in envy of victories. Not those four sister-victories, the fairest that ever the sun beheld with his all-seeing eye, of *Salamine*,[59] of *Platea*, of *Mycale*, and of *Sicily*, durst ever dare to oppose all their glory together to the glory of the King *Leonidas* his discomfiture and of his men at the passage of *Thermopyles*.

What man did ever run with so glorious an envy or more ambitious desire to the goal of a combat than Captain *Ischolas* to an evident loss and overthrow? Who so ingeniously or more politikely[60] did ever assure himself of his welfare than he of his ruin? He was appointed to defend a certain passage of *Peloponnesus* against the *Arcadians*, which finding himself altogether unable to perform, seeing the nature of the place and inequality of the forces and resolving that whatsoever should present itself unto his enemy must necessarily be utterly defeated. On the other side, deeming it unworthy both his virtue and magnanimity, and the Lacedemonian name, to fail or faint in his charge, between these two extremities he resolved upon a mean and indifferent course,[61] which was this. The youngest and best-disposed of his troupe he reserved for the service and defence of their country, to which he sent them back. And with those whose loss was least and who might best be spared, he determined to maintain that passage, and by their death to force the enemy to purchase the entrance of it as dear as possibly he could. As indeed it followed. For being suddenly environed round by the Arcadians, [and] after a great slaughter made of them, both himself and all his were put to the sword. Is any trophy assigned for conquerours that is not more duly due unto these conquered? A true conquest respecteth rather an undaunted resolution and honourable end than a fair escape, and the honour of virtue doth more consist in combating than in beating.

But to return to our history, these prisoners, howsoever they are dealt withal, are so far from yielding that, contrariwise, during two or three months that they are kept, they ever carry a cheerful countenance and urge their keepers to hasten their trial; they outrageously defy and injure them. They upbraid them with their cowardliness and with the number of battles they have lost against theirs.

I have a song made by a prisoner, wherein is this clause: Let them boldly come altogether and flock in multitudes to feed on him. For, with him they shall feed upon their fathers and grandfathers, that heretofore have served his body for food and nourishment. These muscles (saith he), this flesh, and these veins are your own. Fond men as you are, know you not that the substance of your forefathers limbs is yet tied unto ours? Taste them well, for in them shall you find the relish of your own flesh: An invention[62] that hath no show of barbarism. Those that paint them dying, and that represent this action, when they are put to execution, delineate the prisoners spitting in their executioners' faces and making mowes[63] at them. Verily, so long as breath is in their body, they never cease to brave and defy them, both in speech and countenance. Surely, in respect of us, these are very savage men: for either they must be so in good sooth, or we must be so indeed; there is a wondrous difference between their form and ours.

Their men have many wives, and by how much more they are reputed valiant, so much the greater is their number. The manner and beauty in their marriages is wondrous strange and remarkable. For, the same jealousy our wives have to keep us from the love and affection of other women, the same have theirs to procure it. Being more careful for their husbands' honour and content than of anything else, they endeavour and apply all their industry to have as many rivals as possibly they can, forasmuch as it is a testimony of their husbands' virtue.

Our women would count it a wonder, but it is not so. It is a virtue properly matrimonial, but of the highest kind. And in the Bible, *Leah, Rachel, Sarah,* and *Jacob's* wives brought their fairest maidenservants unto their husbands' beds. And *Livia* seconded the lustful appetites of *Augustus* to her great prejudice. And *Stratonica*, the wife of King *Deiotarus*, did not only bring a most beauteous chambermaid, that served her to her husband's bed, but very carefully brought up the children he begot on her, and by all possible means aided and furthered them to succeed in their father's royalty.

And lest a man should think that all this is done by a simple and servile or awful[64] duty unto their custom and by the impression of their ancient custom's authority, without discourse or judgement, and because they are so blockish and dull-spirited that they can take no other resolution, it is not amiss we allege some evidence of their sufficiency. Besides what I have said of one of their warlike songs, I have another amorous canzonet,[65] which beginneth in this sense: *Adder stay, stay good adder, that my sister may, by the pattern of thy parti-coloured coat, draw the fashion and work of a rich lace, for me to give unto my love; so may thy beauty, thy nimbleness, or disposition be ever preferred before all other serpents.* The first couplet is the burden of the song. I am so conversant with poesy that I may judge this invention hath no barbarism at all in it but is altogether Anacreontike.[66] Their language is a kind of pleasant speech and hath a pleasing sound, and some affinity with the Greek terminations.[67]

Three of that nation, ignoring how dear the knowledge of our corruptions will one day cost their repose, security, and happiness, and how their ruin shall proceed from this commerce, which I imagine is already well advanced (miserable as they are to have suffered themselves to be so cozened by a desire of new-fangled novelties[68] and to have quit the calmness of their climate to come and see ours), were at *Roane*[69] in the time of our late King *Charles* the Ninth, who talked with them a great while. They were showed our fashions, our pomp, and the form of a fair city. Afterward, some demanded their advice and would needs know of them what things of note and admirable they had observed amongst us. They answered three things, the last of which I have forgotten, and am very sorry for it; the other two I yet remember. They said, *First, they found it very strange that so many tall men with long beards, strong and well armed, as it were about the King's person (it is very likely they meant the Swizzers[70] of his guard) would submit themselves to obey a beardless child and that we did not rather choose one amongst them to command the rest.* Secondly (they have a manner of phrase whereby they call men but a moiety of men from others[71]), *they had perceived there were men amongst us full gorged with all sorts of commodities and others which, hunger-starven and bare with need and poverty, begged at their gates. And found it strange these moieties so needy could endure such an injustice and that they took not the others by the throat or set fire on their houses.*

I talked a good while with one of them, but I had so bad an interpreter, who did so ill apprehend my meaning and who through his foolishness was so troubled to conceive my imaginations, that I could draw no great matter from him. Touching that point, wherein I demanded of him what good he received by the superiority he had amongst his countrymen (for he was a captain, and our mariners called him king), he told me, it was to march foremost in any charge of war. Further, I asked him how many men did follow him. He showed me a distance of place to signify they were as many as might be contained in so much ground, which I guessed to be about 4 or 5 thousand men. Moreover, I demanded, if when wars were ended, all his authority expired? He answered that he had only this left him, which was that when he went on progress and visited the villages depending on him, the inhabitants prepared paths and highways athwart the hedges of their woods for him to pass through at ease.

All that is not very ill; but what of that? They wear no kind of breeches or hose.

Of the Inequality That Is Between Us

PLUTARCH sayeth in some place, *That he finds no such great differ-ence between beast and beast, as he findeth diversity between man and man.* He speaketh of the sufficiency of the mind and of internal qualities.[1] Verily, I find *Epaminondas* so far (taking him as I suppose him) from some that I know (I mean capable of common sense) as I could find in my heart to endear upon *Plutarch* and say there is more difference between such and such a man than there is diversity be-tween such a man and such a beast.

> *Hem vir viro quid præstat!*
> O Sir, how much hath one,
> Another man out-gone?[2]

And that there be so many degrees of spirits as there are steps be-tween heaven and earth, and as innumerable.

But concerning the estimation of men, it is marvel that, except ourselves, no one thing is esteemed but for its proper qualities. We commend a horse because he is strong and nimble,

> ——*volucrem*
> *Sic laudamus equum, facili cui plurima palma*
> *Fervet, et exultat rauco victoria circo.*
> We praise the horse, that bears most bells with flying,
> And triumphs most in races, hoarse with crying,[3]

and not for his furniture;[4] a greyhound for his swiftness, not for his collar; a hawk for her wing, not for her cranes[5] or bells. Why do we not likewise esteem a man for that which is his own? He hath a goodly train of men following him, a stately palace to dwell in, so great credit amongst men, and so much rent coming in. Alas, all that is about him and not in him. No man will buy a pig in a poke. If you cheapen a horse,[6] you will take his saddle and clothes from him, you will see him bare and abroad.[7] Or if he be covered, as in old times they wont to present them unto princes to be sold, it is only his least necessary parts, lest you should amuse yourself to consider his colour or breadth of his crupper.[8] But chiefly to view his legs, his head, his eyes, and his foot, which are the most remarkable parts, and above all to be considered and required in him:

> *Regibus hic mos est, ubi equos mercantur, opertos*
> *Inspiciunt, ne si facies, ut sæpe, decora*
> *Molli fulta pede est, emptorem inducat hiantem,*
> *Quod pulchra clunes, breve quod caput, ardua cervix.*
> This is King's manner, when they horses buy,
> They see them bare, lest if, as oft we try,
> Fair face have soft hoofs, gull'd the buyer be,
> They buttocks round, short head, high crest may see.[9]

When you will esteem a man, why should you survey him all wrapped and enveloped? He then but showeth us those parts that are no whit his own and hideth those from us, by which alone his worth is to be judged. It is the goodness of the sword you seek after and not the worth of the scabbard; for which peradventure you would not give a farthing, if it want his lining. A man should be judged by himself, and not by his complements. And as an ancient sayeth very pleasantly: Do you know wherefore you esteem him tall? You account the height of his pattins.[10] The base is no part of his stature[11]: measure him without his stilts. Let him lay aside his riches and external honors and show himself in his shirt.[12] Hath he a body proper to his functions, sound and cheerful? What mind hath he? Is it fair, capable, and unpolluted, and happily provided with all her necessary parts? Is she rich of her own, or of others' goods? Hath fortune nothing of hers to survey therein? If broad-waking, she will look upon a naked sword. If she care not which way her life goeth from her, whether by the mouth or by the throat; whether it be settled, equable, and contented? It is that a man must see and consider and thereby judge the extreme differences that are between us. Is he

> ——*sapiens, sibique imperiosus,*
> *Quem neque pauperies, neque mors neque vincula terrent,*
> *Responsare cupidinibus, contemnere honores*
> *Fortis, et in seipso totus teres atque rotundus,*
> *Externi ne quid valeat per læve morari,*
> *In quem manca ruit semper fortuna?*
> A wise man, of himself commander high,
> Whom want, nor death, nor bands can terrify,
> Resolv'd t'affront desires, honors to scorn,
> All in himself, close, round, and neatly-borne,
> As nothing outward on his smooth can stay,
> Gainst whom still fortune makes a lame assay?[13]

Such a man is five hundred degrees beyond kingdoms and principalities; himself is a kingdom unto himself.

> *Sapiens pol ipse fingit fortunam sibi.*
> Trust me, who bears a wiseman's name,
> His fortune to himself may frame.[14]

What is there else for him to wish for?

> ——*nonne videmus*
> *Nil aliud sibi naturam latrare, nisi ut quoi*
> *Corpore seiunctus dolor absit, mente fruatur,*
> *Incundo sensu, cura semiotus metuque?*
> See we not nature nothing else doth bark
> Unto herself, but he, whose body's bark[15]

Is free from pain's touch, should his mind enjoy,
Remov'd from care and fear, with sense of joy?[16]

Compare the vulgar troupes of our men unto him—stupid, base, servile, wavering, and continually floating on the tempestuous ocean of diverse passions which toss and retoss the same, wholly depending on others. There is more difference than is between heaven and earth, and yet such is the blindness of our custom that we make little or no account of it. Whereas if we consider a cottager and a king, a noble and a handy-craftsman, a magistrate and a private man, a rich man and a poor, an extreme disparity doth immediately present it self unto our eyes which, as a man may say, differ in nothing but in their clothes.

In *Thrace* the king was after a pleasant manner distinguished from his people, and which was much endeared. He had a religion apart: a god several[17] unto himself whom his subjects might no ways adore. It was *Mercury*. And he disdained their gods, which were *Mars*, *Bacchus*, and *Diana*.

Yet are they but pictures which make no essential dissemblance.[18] For, as interlude-players,[19] you shall now see them on the stage play a King, an Emperor, or a Duke, but they are no sooner off the stage, but they are base rascals, vagabond abjects, and porterly-hirelings,[20] which is their natural and original condition. Even so the emperor, whose glorious pomp doth so dazzle you in public—

> *Scilicet et grandes viridi cum luce smaragdi*
> *Auro includuntur, teriturque Thalassina vestis*
> *Assidué, et Veneris sudorem exercita potat.*
> Great emeralds with their grass-green light in gold
> Are clos'd, nor long can marriage-linen hold,
> But worn with use and heat
> Of venery drink's the sweat.[21]

—view him behind the curtain, and you see but an ordinary man, and peradventure more vile and more seely[22] than the least of his subjects. *Ille beatus introrsum est; istius bracteata felicitas est. One is inwardly happy: another's felicity is plated and guilt-over.*[23] Cowardice, irresolution, ambition, spite, anger, and envy move and work in him as in another:

> *Non enim gazæ, neque consularis*
> *Summovet lictor miseres tumultus*
> *Mentis et curas, laqueata circum*
> *——Tecta volantes:*
> Nor treasures, nor Maires officers[24] remove
> The miserable tumults of the mind,
> Or cares that lie about, or fly above
> Their high-roof't houses with huge beams combined.[25]

And fear, and care, and suspect haunt and follow him, even in the midst of his armed troupes.

> *Reveraque metus hominum, curæque sequaces,*
> *Nec metuunt sonitus armorum, nec fera tela,*
> *Audacterque inter reges, rerumque potentes*
> *Versantur, neque fulgorem reverentur ab auro.*
> Indeed men's still-attending cares and fear,
> Nor armors clashing, nor fierce weapons fear,
> With kings converse they boldly, and kings' peers,
> Fearing no lightning that from gold appears.[26]

Doth the ague, the megrim, or the gout spare him more than us?[27] When age shall once seize on his shoulders, can then the tall yeomen of his guard discharge him of it? When the terror of ruthless baleful death shall assail him, can he be comforted by the assistance of the gentlemen of his chamber? If he chance to be jealous or capricious, will our lowting-curtzies or putting-off of hats[28] bring him in tune again? His bedstead enchased[29] all with gold and pearls hath no virtue to allay the pinching pangs of the colic.[30]

Nec calidæ citius decedent corpore febres,
Textilibus si in picturis ostroque rubenti
Iacteris, quam si plebeia in veste cubandum est.
Fevers no sooner from thy body fly
If thou on arras or red scarlet lie
Tossing, then if thou rest
On coverlets home-dressed.[31]

The flatterers of *Alexander*[32] the great made him believe that he was the son of *Jupiter*. But being one day sore-hurt and seeing the blood gush out of his wounds: *"And what think you of this?"* (said he unto them) *"Is not this blood of a lively-red hue and merely human?* Methinks it is not of that temper which *Homer* faineth to trill from the gods' wounds." *Hermodorus* the poet made certain verses in honour of *Antigonus*, in which he called him the son of *Phoebus*. To whom he replied, *My friend, He that emptieth my close-stool*[33] *knoweth well there is no such matter.*

He is but a man, at all assays.[34] And if of himself he be a man ill born, the empire of the whole world cannot restore him.

——*puellæ*
Hunc rapiant, quidquid calcaverit, hic rosa fiat.
Wenches must ravish him, what ever he
Shall tread upon, eftsoones[35] a rose must be.[36]

What of that, if he be of a gross, stupid, and senseless mind? Voluptuousness and good fortune itself are not perceived without vigor, wit, and liveliness.

Hæc perinde sunt, ut illius animus qui ea possidet,
Qui uti scit, ei bona, illi qui non utitur recte, mala.
These things are such, as the possessor's mind,
Good, if well us'd; if ill, them ill we find.[37]

Whatsoever the goods of fortune are, a man must have a proper sense to savour them. It is the enjoying, and not the possessing of them, that makes us happy.

> *Non domus et fundus, non æris aceruus et auri,*
> *Ægroto domini deduxit corpore febres,*
> *Non animo curas, valeat possessor oportet,*
> *Qui comportatis rebus bene cogitat uti.*
> *Qui cupit, aut metuit, iuvat illum sic domus aut res,*
> *Ut lippum pictæ tabulæ, fomenta podagram.*
> Not house and land, and heaps of coin and gold
> Rid agues, which their sick lord's body hold,
> Or cares from mind: th'owner must be in health,
> That well doth think to use his hoarded wealth.
> Him that desires or fears, house, goods, delight,
> As foments do the gout, pictures sore-sight.[38]
> Be not cask clean, all that you power
> Into the cask, will straight be sour.[39]

He is a fool, his taste is wallowish and distracted. He enjoyeth it no more than one that hath a great cold doth the sweetness of Greek wine, or a horse the riches of a costly-fair furniture wherewith he is trapped. Even as *Plato* sayeth, *That health, beauty, strength, riches, and all things else he calleth good, are equally as ill to the unjust, as good to the just; and the evil contrariwise.*[40]

And then, where the body and the soul are in ill plight, what need these external commodities, seeing the least prick of a needle and passion of the mind is able to deprive us of the pleasure of the world's monarchy? The first fit of an ague or the first guird[41] that the gout gives him, what avail his goodly titles of majesty?[42]

> *Totus et argento conflatus, totus et auro.*
> All made of silver fine,
> All gold pure from the mine.[43]

Doth he not forthwith lose the remembrance of his palaces and states? If he be angry or vexed, can his principality keep him from blushing, from growing pale, from fretting, or from gnashing his teeth? Now if he be a man of worth and well-born, his royalty and his glorious titles will add but little unto his good fortune.

> *Si ventri bene, si lateri est, pedibusque tuis, nil*
> *Divitiæ poterunt regales addere maius.*
> If it be well with belly, feet, and sides,
> A king's estate, no greater good provides.[44]

He seeth they are but illusions and vain deceits. He may happily be of King *Seleucus* his advice: *That he who fore-knew the weight of a scepter, should he find it lying on the ground, he would not deign to take it up.* This he said, by reason of the weighty, irksome, and painful charges that are incident unto a good king.

Truly, it is no small in matter to govern others, since so many crosses and difficulties offer themselves, if we will govern ourselves well. Touching commanding of others, which in show seemeth to be so sweet: considering the imbecility of man's judgment and the difficulty of choice in new and doubtful things, I am confidently of this opinion, that it is much more easy and plausible to follow than to guide, and that it is a great settling of the mind to be tied but to one beaten-path and to answer but for himself.

> *Ut satius multo iam sit, parere quietum,*
> *Quam regere imperio res velle.*
> Much better t'is, in quiet to obey,
> Then to desire with king's-power all to sway.[45]

Seeing *Cyrus* said, *That it belongs not to a man to command that is not of more worth than those whom he commandeth.* But King *Hieron*[46] in *Xenophon* addeth, moreover, *That in truly enjoying of carnal sensualities, they*[47] *are of much worse condition than private men. Forasmuch as ease and facility depriveth them of that sour-sweet tickling which we find in them.*

Pinguis amor nimiumque potens, in tædia nobis,
Vertitur, et stomacho dulcis ut esca nocet.
Fat over powerful love doth loathsome grow,
As fulsome sweet-meats stomachs overthrow.[48]

Think we that high-minded men[49] take great pleasure in music?
The satiety thereof makes it rather tedious unto them. Feasts, banquets, revels, dancings, masques, and tourneys rejoice them that but
seldom see them and that have much desired to see them; the taste of
which becometh cloysome and unpleasing to those that daily see
and ordinarily have them. Nor do ladies tickle those that at pleasure
and without suspect may be glutted with them. He that cannot stay
till he be thirsty can take no pleasure in drinking. Interludes and
comedies rejoice and make us merry, but to players they are tedious
and tasteless.[50] Which to prove, we see, it is a delight for princes, and
a recreation for them, sometimes to disguise themselves and to take
upon them a base and popular kind of life.[51]

Plerumque gratæ principibus vices,
Mundæque parvo sub lare pauperum
Cænæ sine aulæis et ostro,
Sollicitam explicuere frontem.
Princes do commonly like interchange,
And cleanly meals where poor-men poorly house,
Without all tapestry or carpets strange,
Unwrinkled have their care-knit, thought-bent brows.[52]

Nothing doth sooner breed a distaste or satiety than plenty.
What longing-lust would not be allayed to see three hundred women
at his dispose and pleasure, as hath the Grand *Turk* in his seraille?[53]
And what a desire and show of hawking had he reserved to himself
from his ancestors that never went abroad without seven thousand
falkners[54] at least? Besides which, I think, the luster of greatness
brings no small incommodities to the enjoying of sweeter pleasures:
They lie too open, and are too much in sight.

And I wot not why a man should longer desire them to conceal or hide their fault. For what in us is indiscretion, the people judgeth to be tyranny, contempt, and disdain of the laws in them. And besides the ready inclination unto vice, it seemeth they also add unto it the pleasure of gourmandizing and to prostrate public observances under their feet. Verily, *Plato* in his Gorgias *defineth him to be a tyrant that in a city hath leave and power to do whatever he list.*[55] And therefore often the show and publication of their vice hurteth more than the sin itself. Every man feareth to be spied and controlled, which they are even in their countenances and thoughts, all the people esteeming to have right and interest to judge of them. And we see that blemishes grow either lesser or bigger, according to the eminence and light of the place where they are set, and that a mole or a wart in one's forehead is more apparently perceived than a scar in another place.

And that is the reason why poets feign *Jupiter's* loves to have been affected under other countenances than his own. And of so many amorous-shifts and love-practices they impute to him, there is but one (as far as I remember) where he is to be seen in his greatness and majesty.

But return we to *Hieron*. He also relateth how many incommodities he findeth in his royalty, being so barred that he cannot at his liberty travel or go whither he pleaseth, being as it were a prisoner within the limits of his country. And that in all his actions he is encircled and hemmed-in with an importunate and tedious multitude. Truly, to see our princes all alone, sitting at their meat, beleaguered-round with so many talkers, whisperers, and gazing-beholders, unknown what they are or whence they come, I have often rather pitied than envied them. King *Alphonsus* was wont to say *that burden-bearing asses were in that in far better condition than kings. For their masters suffer them to feed at their ease, whereas kings can not obtain that privilege of their servants.* And it could never fall into my mind that it might be any special commodity to the life of a man of understanding to have a score of find-faults, pick-thanks, and controllers about his close-stool.[56] Nor that the service of a man that hath a thousand pound rent a year or that hath taken *Cales* or defended

Sienna[57] is more commodious or acceptable to him than that of a sufficient and well-experienced groom.

Prince-like advantages are in a manner but imaginary pre-eminences. Every degree of fortune hath some image of principality. *Cæsar* termeth all the lords, which in his time had justice in *France*, to be kinglets, or petit-kings. And truly, except the name of *Sire*, we go very far with our kings. Look but in the provinces remote and far from the court. As for example, in *Brittany*, the attending train, the flocking subjects, the number of officers, the many affairs, the diligent service, the obsequious ceremonies of a lord that liveth retired and in his own house, brought up amongst his own servants, tenants, and followers. And note also the high pitch of his imaginations and humours; there is no greater royalty can be seen. He heareth no more talk of his master than of the *Persian* king and happily but once a year, and knows but some far-fetched and old kindred or pedigree, which his secretary finds or keeps upon some ancient record or evidence. Verily, our laws are very free, and the burden of sovereignty doth scarcely concern a gentleman of *France* twice in his whole life. Essential and effectual subjection amongst us doth not respect any but such as allure themselves unto it and that affect to honour and love to enrich themselves by such service. For he that can shroud and retire himself in his own home and can manage and direct his house without suits in law or quarrel with his neighbours or domestic encumbrances is as free as the Duke of *Venice*.[58] *Paucos servitus, plures servitutem tenent. Service holds few, but many hold service.*[59]

But above all things *Hieron* seemeth to complain that he perceiveth himself deprived of all mutual friendship, reciprocal society, and familiar conversation, wherein consisteth the most perfect and sweetest fruit of human life.[60] For what undoubted testimony of affection and good will can I expect or exact from him, that will-he or nill-he[61] oweth me all he hath, all he can? Can I make account of his humble speech, of his low-lowting curtzie[62] or of his courteous offers, since it lieth not in his power to refuse them me? The honour we receive of those which fear and stand in awe of us is no true honour. Such respects are rather due to royalty, to majesty, than to me.

——*maximum hoc regni bonum est,*
Quod facta domini cogitur populus sui
Quam ferre, tam laudare.
This is chief good of prince's dominations,
Subjects are forc't their sov'reign's acts and fashions
To bear with patience, pass with commendations.[63]

Do I not see that both the bad and the good king are served alike? That he who is hated and he that is beloved are both courted alike? And the one as much fawned upon as the other? My predecessor was served with the same appearances and waited upon with the like ceremonies, and so shall my successor be. If my subjects offend me not, it is no testimony of any good affection. Wherefore shall I take it in that sense, sithence[64] they cannot if they would? No man followeth me for any friendship that is between him and me; inasmuch as no firm friendship can be contracted where is so small relation, so slender correspondence, and such disparity. My high degree hath excluded me from the commerce of men. There is too great an inequality and distant disproportion. They follow for countenance and of custom, or rather my fortune than myself, hoping thereby to increase theirs. Whatsoever they say, all they do unto me is but a gloss and but dissimulation, their liberty being every where bridled and checked by the great power I have over them. I see nothing about me but inscrutable hearts, hollow minds, feigned looks, dissembled speeches, and counterfeit actions.[65]

His courtiers one day commended *Julian* the Emperor for ministering of right and doing of justice. *I should easily grow proud* (said he) *for these praises, if they came from such as durst either accuse or discommend my contrary actions, should I commit any.*

All the true commodities that princes have are common unto them with men of mean fortune. It is for gods to mount winged horses and to feed on ambrosia. They have no other sleep, nor no other appetite than ours. Their steel is of no better temper than that wherewith we arm ourselves. Their crown, their diadem can neither hide them from the sun nor shelter them from the rain. *Dioclesian* that wore one, so much reverenced and so fortunate, did voluntarily resign the same to withdraw himself unto the pleasure of a private life. But a while after, the urgent necessity of public affairs requiring his presence and that he should return to re-assume his charge again, he answered those that solicited him unto it, "You would never undertake to persuade me to that had you but seen the goodly ranks of trees, which my self have planted in mine orchard or the fair muskmelons I have set in my garden."

According to *Anacharsis* his opinion, *The happiest estate of a well-ordered commonwealth should be where, all other things being equally common, precedence should be measured and preferments suited according to virtue and desert, and the contrary according to vice.*[66]

At what time King *Pyrrhus* undertook to pass into *Italy*, *Cyneas* his wise and trusty counselor, going about to make him perceive the vanity of his ambition, one day bespake him thus: *"My good Sir,"* (said he) *"To what end do you prepare for so great an enterprise?"* He answered suddenly, *"To make myself lord of* Italy." *"That done, what will you do then?"* (replied *Cyneas*). *"I will then pass"* (said *Pyrrhus*) *"into* Gaul *and then into* Spain." *"And what afterwards?"* *"I will then invade Africa and subdue the same and, at last, when I shall have brought all the world under my subjection, I will then take my rest and live contented at mine ease."* *"Now, for God's sake, Sir"* (replied *Cyneas*), *"Tell me what hinders you that you be not now, if so you please, in that estate? Wherefore do you not now place yourself where you mean to aspire and save so much danger, so many hazards, and so great troubles as you interpose between both?"*[67]

> *Nimirum quia non bene norat quæ esset habendi*
> *Finis, et omnino quoad crescat vera voluptas.*
> The cause forsooth, he knew not what should be the end
> Of having, nor how far true pleasure should extend.[68]

I will exclude[69] and shut up this treatise with an ancient verse, which I singularly applaud and deem fit to this purpose:

Mores cuique sui fingunt fortunam.
Ev'ry man's manners and his mind,
His fortune to him frame and find.[70]

Of Age

I CANNOT receive[1] that manner whereby we establish the continuance[2] of our life.[3] I see that some of the wiser sort do greatly shorten the same, in respect of the common opinion. "What," said *Cato Junior*, to those who sought to hinder him from killing himself, *"Do I now live the age wherein I may justly be reproved to leave my life too soon?"* Yet was he but eight and forty years old. He thought that age very ripe, yea and well advanced, considering how few men come unto it. And such as entertain themselves with I wot not what kind of course—which they call natural—promiseth some few years beyond, might do it[4] had they a privilege that could exempt them from so great a number of accidents unto which each one of us stands subject by a natural subjection, and which may interrupt the said course they propose unto themselves.

What fondness is it for a man to think he shall die for, and through, a failing and defect of strength which extreme age draweth with it, and to propose that term unto our life, seeing it is the rarest kind of all deaths and least in use! We only call it natural, as if it were against nature to see a man break his neck with a fall; to be drowned by shipwreck; to be surprised with a pestilence or pleurisy; and as if our ordinary condition did not present these inconveniences unto us all. Let us not flatter ourselves with these fond-goodly[5] words. A man may peradventure rather call that natural which is general, common, and universal.

To die of age is a rare, singular, and extraordinary death, and so much less natural than others. It is the last and extremest kind of dying. The further it is from us, so much the less is it to be hoped for.

Indeed, it is the limit, beyond which we shall not pass and which the law of nature hath prescribed unto us, as that which should not be outgone by any.[6] But it is a rare privilege peculiar unto herself to make us continue unto it. It is an exemption which through some particular favor she bestoweth on some one man in the space of two or three ages,[7] discharging him from the crosses, troubles, and difficulties she hath interposed between both in this long cariere[8] and pilgrimage.

Therefore my opinion is to consider that the age unto which we are come is an age whereto few arrive. Since men come not unto it by any ordinary course, it is a sign we are very forward.[9] And since we have passed the accustomed bounds which is the true measure of our life, we must not hope that we shall go much further. Having escaped so many occasions of death, wherein we see the world to fall, we must acknowledge that such an extraordinary fortune as that is, which maintaineth us and is beyond the common use, is not likely to continue long.

It is a fault of the very laws to have this false imagination. They allow not a man to be capable and of discretion, to manage and dispose of his own goods, until he be five and twenty years old, yet shall he hardly preserve the state of his life so long. *Augustus* abridged five years of the ancient Roman laws and declared that for any man that should take upon him the charge of judgement,[10] it sufficed to be thirty years old. *Servius Tullius* dispensed[11] the knights who were seven and forty years of age from all voluntary services of war. *Augustus* brought them to forty and five. To send men to their place of sejourning[12] before they be five and fifty or three score[13] years of age, me seemeth, carrieth no great appearance[14] with it. My advice would be that our vocation and employment should be extended as far as might be for the public commodity. But I blame some, and condemn most, that we begin not soon enough to employ ourselves. The same *Augustus* had been universal and supreme judge of the world, when he was but nineteen years old, and would have another to be thirty before he shall be made a competent judge of a cottage or farm.[15]

As for my part, I think our minds are as full grown and perfectly jointed at twenty years as they should be, and promise as much as they can. A mind which at that age hath not given some evident token or earnest of her sufficiency shall hardly give it afterward; put her to what trial you list. Natural qualities and virtues, if they have any vigorous or beauteous thing in them, will produce and show the same within that time or never. They say in *Delphinate*,[16]

Si l'espine nou picque quand nai,
A peine que picque jamai.
A thorn, unless at first it prick,
Will hardly ever pierce to th'quick.

Of all human honourable and glorious actions that ever came unto my knowledge, of what nature soever they be, I am persuaded I should have a harder task to number those which, both in ancient times and in ours, have been produced and achieved before the age of thirty years than such as were performed after. Yea, often in the life of the same men.

May not I boldly speak it of those of *Hannibal* and *Scipio* his great adversary? They lived the better part of their life with the glory which they had gotten in their youth. And though afterward they were great men in respect of all others, yet were they but mean in regard of themselves.

As for my particular, I am verily persuaded that since that age both my spirit and my body have more decreased than increased, more recoiled than advanced. It may be that knowledge and experience shall increase in them, together with life, that bestow their time well. But vivacity, promptitude, constancy, and other parts much more our own, more important and more essential, they droop, they languish, and they faint.

——*ubi iam validis quassatum est viribus ævi*
Corpus, et obtusis ceciderunt viribus artus,
Claudicat ingenium, delirat linguaque mensque.
When once the body by shrewd strength of years

Is shak't, and limbs drawn-down from strength that wears,
Wit halts, both tongue and mind
Do daily dote, we find.[17]

It is the body which sometimes yieldeth first unto age and other times the mind. And I have seen many that have had their brains weakened before their stomach or legs. And forasmuch as it is a disease, little or nothing sensible[18] unto him that endureth it and maketh no great show, it is so much the more dangerous. Here I exclaim against our laws, not because they leave us so long and late in working and employment, but that they set us a-work no sooner, and it is so late before we be employed. Methinks that considering the weakness of our life, and seeing the infinite number of ordinary rocks and natural dangers it is subject unto,[19] we should not so soon as we come into the world allot so great a share thereof unto unprofitable wantonness in youth, ill-breeding idleness, and slow-learning prentissage.[20]

Of the Inconstancy of Our Actions

THOSE which exercise themselves in controlling human actions find no such let[1] in any one part as to piece them together and bring them to one same lustre. For they commonly contradict one another so strangely as it seemeth impossible they should be parcels of one warehouse. Young *Marius* is sometimes found to be the son of *Mars* and other times the child of *Venus*. Pope *Boniface* the Eighth is reported to have entered into his charge[2] as a fox, to have carried himself therein as a lion, and to have died like a dog. And who would think it was *Nero*, that lively image of cruelty who, being required to sign (as the custom was) the sentence of a criminal offender that had been condemned to die, that ever he should answer, "Oh, would to God I could never have written!" So near was his heart grieved to doom a man to death.

The world is so full of such examples, that every man may store himself. And I wonder to see men of understanding trouble themselves with sorting these parcels, sithence[3] (me seemeth) irresolution is the most apparent and common vice of our nature, as witnesseth that famous verse of *Publius* the Comedian:

> *Malum consilium est, quod mutari non potest.*
> The counsel is but bad,
> Whose change may not be had.[4]

There is some appearance to judge a man by the most common conditions of his life. But seeing the natural instability of our customs and opinions, I have often thought that even good authors do ill and take a wrong course, willfully to opinionate themselves about framing a constant and solid contexture[5] of us. They choose an universal air and, following that image, range and interpret all a man's actions. Which, if they cannot wrest sufficiently, they remit them unto dissimulation. *Augustus* hath escaped their hands, for there is so apparent, so sudden and continual a variety of actions found in him through the course of his life that even the boldest judges and strictest censurers have been fain to give him over and leave him undecided. *There is nothing I so hardly believe to be in man as constancy, and nothing so easy to be found in him as inconstancy.* He that should distinctly and part by part judge of him should often jump to speak truth.[6]

View all antiquity over, and you shall find it a hard matter to choose out of a dozen of men that have directed their life unto one certain, settled, and assured course, which is the surest drift of wisdom. For, to comprehend all in one word, sayeth an ancient writer, and to embrace all the rules of our life into one, it is at all times to will and not to will one same thing. I would not vouchsafe (sayeth he) to add anything, always provided the will be just. For, if it be unjust, it is impossible it should ever continue one. Verily, I have heretofore learned that vice is nothing but a disorder and want of measure and, by consequence, it is impossible to fasten constancy unto it. It is a saying of *Demosthenes* (as some report), *That consultation and deliberation is the beginning of all virtue, and constancy the end and perfection.* If by reason or discourse we should take a certain way, we should then take the fairest: but no man hath thought on it.

> *Quod petiit, spernit, repetit quod nuper omisit,*
> *Æstuat, et vitæ disconvenit ordine toto.*
> He scorns that which he sought, seeks that he scorn'd of late,
> He flows, ebbs, disagrees in his life's whole estate.[7]

Our ordinary manner is to follow the inclination of our appetite, this way and that way, on the left and on the right hand, upward and downward, according as the wind of occasions doth transport us.

We never think on what we would have but at the instant we would have it, and change as that beast that takes the colour of the place wherein it is laid.[8] What we even now purposed, we alter by and by, and presently return to our former bias; all is but changing, motion, and inconstancy:

> *Ducimur ut nervis alienis mobile lignum.*
> So are we drawn, as wood is shoved,
> By others sinews each way moved.[9]

We go not, but we are carried: as things that float, now gliding gently, now hulling[10] violently, according as the water is, either stormy or calm.

> ——*nonne videmus*
> *Quid sibi quisque velit nescire et quærere semper,*
> *Commutare locum quasi onus deponere possit?*
> See we not, every man in his thought's height
> Knows not what he would have, yet seeks he straight
> To change place, as he could lay down his weight?[11]

Every day new toys, each hour new fantasies, and our humours move and fleet with the fleetings and movings of time.

> *Tales sunt hominum mentes, quali Pater ipse*
> *Iuppiter auctifero lustravit lumine terras.*
> Such are men's minds, as that great God of might
> Surveys the earth with increase-bearing light.[12]

We float and waver between diverse opinions: we will nothing freely, nothing absolutely, nothing constantly. Had any man prescribed certain laws or established assured policies in his own head, in his life should we daily see to shine an equality of customs, an assured order, and an infallible relation from one thing to another. *Empedocles* noted this deformity[13] to be amongst the Agrigentines, that they gave themselves so over unto delights as if they should die tomorrow next, and built as if they should never die, the discourse thereof were easy to be made.[14]

As is seen in young *Cato*. He that touched but one step of it hath touched all. It is an harmony of well-according tunes and which cannot contradict itself. With us it is clean contrary: so many actions, so many particular judgments are there required. The surest way (in mine opinion) were to refer them unto the next circumstances without entering into further search and without concluding any other consequence of them.

During the late tumultuous broils of our mangled estate, it was told me that a young woman not far from me had headlong cast herself out of a high window with intent to kill herself, only to avoid the ravishment of a rascally base soldier that lay in her house who offered to force[15] her And perceiving that with the fall she had not killed herself, to make an end of her enterprise, she would have cut her own throat with a knife but that she was hindered by some that came in to her. Nevertheless, having sore wounded herself, she voluntarily confessed that the soldier had yet but urged her with importunate requests, suing-solicitations, and golden bribes. But she feared he would in the end have obtained his purpose by compulsion. By whose earnest speeches, resolute countenance, and gored blood (a true testimony of her chaste virtue) she might appear to be the lively pattern of another *Lucrece*. Yet know I certainly that, both before that time and afterward, she had been enjoyed of others upon easier composition.[16] And as the common saying is, fair and soft, as squeamish-honest as she seems, although you miss of your intent, conclude not rashly an inviolable chastity to be in your mistress. For a groom or a horse-keeper may find an hour to thrive in, and a dog hath a day.

Antigonus, having taken upon him to favor a soldier of his by reason of his virtue and valour, commanded his physicians to have great care of him and see whether they could recover him of a lingering and inward disease which had long tormented him. Who being perfectly cured, he afterward perceived him to be nothing so earnest and diligent in his affairs, demanded of him how he was so changed from himself and become so cowardish. "Yourself, good sir" (answered he), have made me so, by ridding me of those infirmities which so did grieve me that I made no account of my life." A soldier of *Lucullus*, having by his enemies been robbed of all he had, to revenge himself undertook a notable and desperate attempt upon them. And having recovered his losses, *Lucullus* conceived a very good opinion of him and, with the greatest shows of assured trust and loving kindness he could bethink himself, made especial account of him and in any dangerous enterprise seemed to trust and employ him only:

> *Verbis quæ timido quoque possent addere mentem.*
> With words, which to a coward might
> Add courage, had he any spright.[17]

"Employ" (said he unto him[18]) "some wretch-stripped and robbed soldier,"

> ——(*quantumvis rusticus ibit,*
> *Ibit eo quo vis, qui zonam perdidit, inquit.*)
> (None is, saith he, so clownish, but will on,
> Where you will have him, if his purse be gone)[19]

and absolutely refused to obey him.

When we read that *Mahomet*,[20] having outrageously rated[21] *Chasan*, chief leader of his Ianizers,[22] because he saw his troupe well-nigh defeated by the Hungarians, and he to behave himself but faintly in the fight. *Chasan*, without making other reply, alone as he was and without more ado, with his weapon in his hand rushed furiously in the thickest throng of his enemies that he first met withal, of whom he was instantly slain. This may haply be deemed rather a rash conceit than a justification,[23] and a new spite than a natural prowess.

He whom you saw yesterday so boldly venturous, wonder not if you see him a dastardly meacocke[24] tomorrow next. For either anger or necessity, company or wine, a sudden fury or the clang of a trumpet, might rouse up his heart and stir up his courage. It is no heart nor courage so framed by discourse or deliberation. These circumstances have settled the same in him. Therefore is it no marvel if by other contrary circumstances he become a craven and change copy.[25]

This supple variation and easy-yielding contradiction which is seen in us hath made some to imagine that we had two souls, and others, two faculties, whereof everyone as best she pleaseth accompanieth and doth agitate us—the one towards good, the other towards evil. Forsomuch as such a rough diversity cannot well sort and agree in one simple subject.

The blast of accidents doth not only remove me according to his inclination. For besides, I remove and trouble myself by the instability of my posture, and whosoever looketh narrowly about himself shall hardly see himself twice in one same state. Sometimes I give my soul one visage, and sometimes another, according unto the posture or side I lay her in. If I speak diversely of myself, it is because I look diversely upon myself. All contrarieties are found in her, according to some turn or removing, and in some fashion or other. Shamefaced, bashful, insolent, chaste, luxurious, peevish, prattling, silent, fond, doting, labourious, nice, delicate, ingenious, slow, dull, froward,[26] humorous, debonair, wise, ignorant, false in words, true-speaking, both liberal,[27] covetous, and prodigal. All these I perceive in some measure or other to be in mine, according as I stir or turn myself. And whosoever shall heedfully survey and consider himself shall find this volubility and discordance to be in himself, yea, and in his very judgement. I have nothing to say entirely, simply, and with solidity of myself, without confusion, disorder, blending, mingling; and in one word, *Distinguo*[28] is the most universal part of my logic.

Although I ever purpose to speak good of good and rather to interpret those things that will bear it unto a good sense, yet is it that the strangeness of our condition admitteth that we are often urged to do well by vice itself, if well doing were not judged by the intention only.

Therefore may not a courageous act conclude a man to be valiant.[29] He that is so, when just occasion serveth, shall ever be so and upon all occasions. If it were an habitude of virtue and not a sudden humour, it would make a man equally resolute at all assays, in all accidents. Such alone, as in company; such in a single combat, as in a set battle. For, whatsoever some say, valour is all alike, and not one in the street or town and another in the camp or field. As courageously should a man bear a sickness in his bed as a hurt in the field, and fear death no more at home in his house than abroad in an assault. We should not then see one same man enter the breach, or charge his enemy with an assured and undaunted fierceness, and afterward having escaped that, to vex, to grieve, and torment himself like unto a seely[30] woman or faint-hearted milk-sop[31] for the loss of a suit[32] or death of a child. If one chance to be carelessly base-minded in his infancy,[33] and constantly-resolute in poverty; if he be timorously-fearful at sight of a barber's razor,[34] and afterward stoutly-undismayed against his enemies' swords, the action is commendable, but not the man.

Diverse Grecians (sayeth *Cicero*) cannot endure to look their enemy in the face, yet are they most constant[35] in their sicknesses. Whereas the *Cimbrians* and *Celtiberians*[36] are mere contrary. *Nihil enim potest esse æquabile, quod non a certa ratione proficiscatur: For nothing can bear itself even, which proceedeth not from resolved reason.*[37]

There is no valor more extreme in his kind than that of *Alexander*; yet it is but in *species*,[38] nor everywhere sufficiently full and universal. As incomparable as it is, it hath his blemishes, which is the reason that in the idlest suspicions he apprehendeth at the conspiracies of his followers against his life, we see him so earnestly to vex and so desperately to trouble himself. In search and pursuit whereof, he demeaneth himself with so vehement and indiscreet an injustice and with such a demisse[39] fear that even his natural reason is thereby subverted. Also the superstition, wherewith he is so thoroughly tainted, beareth some show of pusillanimity.[40] And the unlimited excess of the repentance he showed for the murder of *Clitus* is also a witness of the inequality of his courage.[41]

Our matters are but parcels huddled up and pieces patched together, and we endeavour to acquire honour by false means and untrue tokens. *Virtue will not be followed but by herself.* And if at any time we borrow her mask upon some other occasion, she will as soon pull it from our face. It is a lively hue and strong dye, if the soul be once dyed with the same perfectly, and which will never fade or be gone, except it carry the skin away with it. Therefore to judge a man, we must a long time follow and very curiously mark his steps. Whether constancy do wholly subsist and continue upon her own foundation in him, *Cui vivendi via considerata atque provisa est, who hath forecast and considered the way of life;*[42] whether the variety of occurrences make him change his pace (I mean his way,[43] for his pace may either be hastened or slowed), let him run on: such a one (as sayeth the imprease of our good *Talbot*[44]) goeth before the wind.

It is no marvel (sayeth an old writer) that hazard hath such power over us, since we live by hazard. It is impossible for him to dispose of his particular actions that hath not in gross directed his life unto one certain end. It is impossible for him to range all pieces in order that hath not a plot or form of the total frame in his head.[45] What availeth the provision of all sorts of colours unto one that knows not what he is to draw? No man makes any certain design of his life, and we deliberate of it but by parcels. A skilful archer ought first to know the mark he aimeth at and then apply his hand, his bow, his string, his arrow, and his motion accordingly. Our counsels go astray because they are not rightly addressed and have no fixed end. *No wind makes for him that hath no intended port to sail unto.*

As for me, I allow not greatly of that judgment which some made of *Sophocles,* and to have concluded him sufficient in the managing of domestic matters against the accusation of his own son, only by the sight of one of his tragedies.[46] Nor do I commend the conjecture of the *Parians* sent to reform the *Milesians* as sufficient to the consequence they drew thence. In visiting and surveying the isle, they

marked the lands that were best husbanded and observed the country houses that were best governed. And having registered the names
of their owners and afterward made an assembly of the townsmen of
the city, they named and instituted those owners as new governours
and magistrates, judging and concluding that being good husbands
and careful of their household affairs, they must consequently be so
of public matters.

We are all framed of flaps and patches, and of so shapeless and
diverse a contexture, that every piece and every moment playeth his
part. And there is as much difference found between us and ourselves as there is between ourselves and others. *Magnam rem puta,
unum hominem agere. Esteem it a great matter, to play but one man.*[47]
Since ambition may teach men both valour, temperance, liberality,
yea, and justice. Sith[48] covetousness may settle in the mind of a shop-
apprentice boy, brought up in ease and idleness, a dreadless assurance to leave his home-bred ease and forgo his place of education,
and in a small bark to yield himself unto the mercy of blustering
waves, merciless winds, and wrathful *Neptune*. And that it also
teacheth discretion and wisdom. And that *Venus* herself ministereth
resolution and hardiness unto tender youth as yet subject to the discipline of the rod, and teacheth the ruthless soldier the soft and
tenderly-effeminate heart of women in their mothers' laps:[49]

> *Hac duce custodes furtim transgressa iacentes,*
> *Ad iuvenem tenebris sola puella venit.*
> The wench by stealth her lodg'd guards having stript,
> By this guide, sole, i'th dark, to' the yonker skipt.[50]

*It is no part of a well-grounded judgement simply to judge ourselves by
our exterior actions.* A man must thoroughly sound himself and dive
into his heart, and there see by what wards or springs the motions
stir. But forsasmuch as it is a hazardous and high enterprise, I would
not have so many to meddle with it as do.

A Custom of the Isle of Cea[1]

IF, AS some say, to philosophate[2] be to doubt, with much more reason to rave and fantastiquize[3] as I do must necessarily be to doubt. For, to inquire and debate belongeth to a scholar, and to resolve appertains to a cathedral master.[4] But know, my cathedral,[5] it is the authority of God's divine will, that without any contradiction doth sway us and hath her rank beyond these human and vain contestations.

Philip being with an armed hand[6] entered the country of *Peloponnesus*, someone told *Damidas* the Lacedemonians[7] were like to endure much, if they sought not to reobtain his lost favour. "Oh varlet[8] as thou art" (answered he). "And what can they suffer who have no fear at all of death?" *Agis* being demanded how a man might do to live free, answered, *"Despising and contemning to die."*

These and a thousand like propositions which concur in this purpose do evidently infer something beyond the patient expecting of death itself to be suffered in this life. Witness the Lacedemonian child, taken by *Antigonus* and sold for a slave, who urged by his master to perform some abject service. "Thou shalt see," (said he), "whom thou hast bought; for, it were a shame for me to serve, having liberty so near at hand." And therewithal threw himself headlong down from the top of the house. *Antipater*, sharply threatening the Lacedemonians to make them yield to a certain request of his, they answered, "Shouldest thou menace us worse than death, we will rather die." And to *Philip*, who having written unto them that he would hinder all their enterprises, "What? (say they), "wilt thou also hinder us from dying?"

That is the reason why some say that the wiseman liveth as long as he ought, and not so long as he can. And that the favourablest gift nature hath bequeathed us and which removeth all means from us to complain of our condition is that she hath left us the key of the fields. She hath appointed but one entrance unto life but many a thousand ways out of it: *Well may we want ground dot*[9] *to live upon but never ground to die in*, as *Boiocatus*[10] answered the *Romans*. Why dost thou complain against this world? It doth not contain thee. If thou livest in pain and sorrow, thy base courage is the cause of it. To die there wanteth but will.

> *Ubique mors est: optime hoc cavit Deus,*
> *Eripere vitam nemo non homini potest:*
> *At nemo mortem: mille ad hanc aditus patent.*
> Each where death is: God did this well purvey,
> No man but can from man life take away,
> But none bars death, to it lies many'a way.[11]

And it is not a receipt[12] to one malady alone. *Death is a remedy against all evils.* It is a most assured haven, never to be feared and often to be sought. All comes to one period, whether man make an end of himself or whether he endure it; whether he run before his day, or whether he expect it. Whence soever it come, it is ever his own, wherever the thread be broken, it is all there; it's the end of the web. The voluntariest death is the fairest. *Life dependeth on the will of others, death on ours.* In nothing should we so much accommodate ourselves to our humors as in that. Reputation doth nothing concern such an enterprise; it is folly to have any respect unto it. *To live is to serve, if the liberty to die be wanting.* The common course of curing any infirmity is ever directed at the charge[13] of life: we have incisions made into us, we are cauterized, we have limbs cut and mangled, we are let blood, we are dieted. Go we but one step further, we need no more physic[14]; we are perfectly whole. Why is not our jugular or throat-vein as much at our command as the mediane?[15] To extreme sicknesses, extreme remedies. *Servius* the Grammarian, being troubled with the gout, found no better means to be rid of it than to apply poison to mortify[16] his legs. He cared not whether they were *Podagrees*[17] or no, so they were insensible. God giveth us sufficient privilege, when he placeth us in such an estate, as life is worse than death unto us. *It is weakness to yield to evils but folly to foster them.*

The Stoics say it is a convenient natural life for a wise man to forgo life, although he abound in all happiness, if he do it opportunely. And for a fool to prolong his life, albeit he be most miserable, provided he be in most part of things which they say to be according unto nature.[18] As I offend not the laws made against thieves when I cut mine own purse and carry away mine own goods, nor of destroyers when I burn mine own wood, so am I nothing tied unto laws made against murderers, if I deprive myself of mine own life.

Hegesias was wont to say that even as the condition of life so should the quality of death depend on our election. And *Diogenes* meeting with the philosopher *Speusippus*, long time afflicted with the dropsy and therefore carried in a litter, cried out unto him, "All hail, *Diogenes*."[19] "And to thee no health at all" (replied *Diogenes*), "that endurest to live in so wretched an estate." True it is that a while after *Speusippus*, as overtired with so languishing a condition of life, compassed his own death.

But this goeth not without some contradiction. For many are of opinion that, without the express commandment of him that hath placed us in this world, we may by no means forsake the garrison of it and that it is in the hands of God only, who therein hath placed us, not for ourselves alone but for his glory and others' service, whenever it shall please him to discharge us hence and not for us to take leave. *That we are not born for ourselves but for our country.* The laws for their own interest require an account at our hands for ourselves and have a just action of murder against us. Else as destroyers of our own charge, we are punished in the other world.

Proxima deinde tenent mæsti loca, qui sibi lethum
Insontes peperere manu, lucemque perosi

Proiecere animas.
Next place they lamentable hold in hell,
Whose hand their death caus'd causeless, (but not well)
And hating life did thence their souls expel.[20]

There is more constancy in using the chain that holds us than in breaking the same and more trial of steadfastness in *Regulus* than in *Cato*.[21] It is indiscretion and impatience that hasteneth our way. *No accidents can force a man to turn his back from lively virtue.* She seeketh out evils and sorrows as her nourishment. The threats of fell tyrants, tortures and torments, executioners and torturers do animate and quicken her.

Duris ut ilex tonsa bipennibus
Nigræ feraci frondis in Algido
Per damna, per cædes, ab ipso
Ducit opes animumque ferro.
As holme-trees[22] do with hard ax lopt
On hills with many holme-trees topt,
From loss, from cuttings it doth feel,
Courage and store rise ev'n from steel.[23]

And as the other sayeth,

Non est ut putas virtus, pater,
Timere vitam, sed malis ingentibus
Obstare, nec se vertere ac retro dare.
Sir, 'tis not virtue, as you understand,
To fear life, but gross mischief to withstand,
Not to retire, turn back, at any hand.[24]
Rebus in adversis facile est contemnere mortem.
Fortius ille facit, qui miser esse potest.
T'is easy in cross chance death to despise
He that can wretched be, doth stronger rise.[25]

It is the part of cowardliness and not of virtue to seek to squat itself in some hollow-lurking hole, or to hide herself under some massy tomb, thereby to shun the strokes of fortune. She never forsakes her course, nor leaves her way, what stormy weather soever cross her.

> *Si fractus illabatur orbis,*
> *Impavidam ferient ruinæ.*
> If the world broken should upon him fall,
> The ruins may him strike but not appall.[26]

The avoiding of other inconveniences doth most commonly drive us into this; yea, sometimes the shunning of death makes us to run into it.

> *Hic, rogo, non furor est, ne moriare, mori?*
> Madness is't not, say I,
> To die, lest you should die?[27]

As those who for fear of a downright precipice do headlong cast themselves into it.

> ——*multos in summa pericula misit*
> *Venturi timor ipse mali: fortissimus ille est,*
> *Qui promptus metuenda pati, si cominus instent,*
> *Et differre potest.*
> The very fear of ills to come hath sent
> Many to mighty dangers: strongest they,
> Who fearful things t'endure are ready bent,
> If they confront them, yet can them delay.[28]
> ——*usque adeo mortis formidine, vitæ*
> *Percipit humanos odium, lucisque videndæ,*
> *Ut sibi consciscant mærenti pectore lethum,*
> *Obliti fontem curarum hunc esse timorem.*

> So far the fear of death, the hate of life
> And seeing-light doth men as men possess,[29]
> They grieving kill themselves to end the strife,
> Forgetting fear is spring of their distress.[30]

Plato, in his *Laws*, allots him that hath deprived his nearest and dearest friend of life (that is to say himself) and abridged him of the destiny's course, not constrained by any public judgment, nor by any lewd and inevitable accident of fortune, nor by any intolerable shame or infamy, but through baseness of mind and weakness of a faint-fearful courage, to have a most ignominious and ever-reproachful burial.

And the opinion which disdaineth our life is ridiculous. For, in fine,[31] it is our being; it is our all in all. Things that have a nobler and richer being may accuse ours. But it is against nature we should despise and carelessly set ourselves at naught. It is a particular infirmity, and which is not seen in any other creature, to hate and disdain himself. It is of like vanity that we desire to be other than we are. The fruit of such a desire doth not concern us, forasmuch as it contradicteth and hindereth itself in itself. He that desireth to be made of a man an angel[32] doth nothing for himself. He should be nothing the better by it. And being no more, who shall rejoice or conceive any gladness of this change or amendment for him?

> *Debet enim misere cui forte ægreque futuram est,*
> *Ipse quoque esse in eo tum tempore, cum male possit*
> *Accidere.*
> For he, who shall perchance prove miserable,
> And speed but ill, should then himself be able
> To be himself, when ills may chance unstable.[33]

The security, indolence, impassibility, and privation of this life's evils, which we purchase at the price of death, bring us no commodity at all. *In vain doth he avoid war that cannot enjoy peace, and bootless doth he shun pain that hath no means to feel rest.*

Amongst those of the first opinion, great questioning hath been to know what occasions are sufficiently just and lawful to make a man undertake the killing of himself. They call that ... *a reasonable orderly outlet*.[34] For, although they say a man must often die for slight causes, since these that keep us alive are not very strong, yet is some measure required in them. There are certain fantastical and brain-sick humors which have not only provoked particular men but whole nations to defeat themselves. I have heretofore alleged some examples of them. And moreover we read of certain Milesian virgins, who upon a furious conspiracy hanged themselves one after another, until such time as the magistrate provided for it,[35] appointing that such as should be found so hanged should with their own halters[36] be dragged naked through the streets of the city.

When *Threicion* persuadeth *Cleomenes* to kill himself by reason of the bad and desperate estate his affairs stood in, and having escaped a more honourable death in the battle which he had lately lost, moveth him to accept of this other, which is second to him in honour, and give the conqueror no leisure to make him endure either another death or else a shameful life. *Cleomenes* with a Lacedemonian and Stoic courage refuseth this counsel as base and effeminate. "It is a receipt"[37] (saith he), "which can never fail me and whereof a man should make no use, so long as there remaineth but one inch of hope." That to live is sometimes constancy and valour; that he will have his very death serve his country and by it show an act of honour and of virtue. *Threicion* then believed and killed himself. *Cleomenes* did afterwards as much, but not before he had tried and assayed the utmost power of fortune. All inconveniences are not so much worth that a man should die to eschew them.

Moreover, there being so many sudden changes and violent alterations in human things, it is hard to judge in what state or point we are justly at the end of our hope:

Sperat et in sæva victus gladiator arena,
——Sit licet infesto pollice turba minax.

The fencer[38] hopes, though down in lists he lie,
And people with turn'd hand threats he must die.[39]

All things, sayeth an ancient proverb, may a man hope for so long as he liveth. "Yea but," answereth *Seneca*, "wherefore shall I rather have that in mind, that fortune can do all things for him that is living than this—that fortune hath no power at all over him who knoweth how to die?"[40] *Joseph*[41] is seen engaged in so apparent-approaching danger, with a whole nation against him that, according to human reason, there was no way for him to escape. Notwithstanding being (as he saith) counseled by a friend of his at that instant to kill himself, it fell out well for him to opiniate[42] himself yet in hope. For fortune, beyond all man's discourse, did so turn and change that accident that, without any inconvenience at all, he saw himself delivered.

Whereas on the contrary *Brutus* and *Cassius*, by reason of the downfall and rashness wherewith before due-time and occasion they killed themselves, did utterly lose the relics of the Roman liberty whereof they were protectors. The Lord of *Anguien* in the battle of *Serisolles*,[43] as one desperate of the combat's success, which on his side went to wrack, attempted twice to run himself through the throat with his rapier and thought by precipitation to bereave himself of the enjoying of so notable a victory. I have seen a hundred hares save themselves even in the greyhounds' jaws: *Aliquis carnifici suo superstes fuit. Some man hath outlived his hangman.*[44]

Multa dies variusque labor mutabilis ævi
Rettulit in melius, multos alterna revisens
Lusit, et in solido rursus fortuna locavit.
Time, and of turning age the diverse strain,
Hath much to better brought, fortunes turn'd train,
Hath many mock't, and set them fast again.[45]

Pliny sayeth there are but three sorts of sicknesses, which to avoid a man may have some colour of reason to kill himself. The sharpest of all is the stone in the bladder when the urine is there stopped. *Seneca*, those only which for long time disturb and distract the offices of the mind.[46]

To avoid a worse death, some are of opinion a man should take it at his own pleasure. *Democritus,* chief of the *Ætolians*, being led captive to *Rome*, found means to escape by night. But being pursued by his keepers, rather than he would be taken again, ran himself through with his sword.

Antinoüs and *Theodotus*, their city of *Epirus* being by the Romans reduced unto great extremity, concluded and persuaded all the people to kill themselves. But the counsel rather to yield having prevailed, they went to seek their own death and rushed amidst the thickest of their enemies, with an intention rather to strike than to ward[47] themselves. The island of *Gosa*,[48] being some years since surprised and overrun by the Turks, a certain Sicilian therein dwelling, having two fair daughters ready to be married, killed them both with his own hands, together with their mother, that came in to help them. That done, running out into the streets with a crossbow in one hand and a caliver[49] in the other, at two shoots slew the two first Turks that came next to his gates, then resolutely drawing his sword, ran furiously among them, by whom he was suddenly hewn in pieces. Thus did he save himself from slavish bondage, having first delivered his own from it.

The Jewish women, after they had caused their children to be circumcised, to avoid the cruelty of *Antiochus*, did headlong precipitate themselves and them unto death.

I have heard it credibly reported that a gentleman of good quality, being prisoner in one of our gaols[50] and his parents advertised that he should assuredly be condemned, to avoid the infamy of so reproachful a death, appointed a priest to tell him that the best remedy for his delivery was to recommend himself to such a saint, with such and such a vow, and to continue eight days without taking any sustenance, what faintness or weakness soever he should feel in himself. He believed them, and so without thinking on it, was delivered both of life and danger.

Scribonia, persuading *Libo* her nephew to kill himself rather than to expect the stroke of justice, told him that for a man to preserve his own life, to put it into the hands of such as three or four days after should come and seek it, was even to dispatch another man's business and that it was no other than for one to serve his enemies to preserve his blood, therewith to make them food.

We read in the holy Bible that *Nicanor* the persecutor of God's law, having sent his satellites to apprehend the good old man *Rasias*, for the honor of his virtue surnamed the father of the *Jews*. When that good man saw no other means left him, his gate being burned and his enemies ready to lay hold on him, chose—rather than to fall into the hands of such villains and be so basely abused against the honour of his place—to die nobly and so smote himself with his own sword. But by reason of his haste, having not thoroughly slain himself, he ran to throw himself down from an high wall amongst the throng of people, which making him room, he fell right upon his head. All which notwithstanding, perceiving life to remain in him, he took heart of grace again and getting up on his feet, all gored with blood and laden with strokes, making way through the prease,[51] came to a craggy and down-steepy rock where, unable to go any further, by[52] one of his wounds with both his hands he pulled out his guts, and tearing and breaking them, cast them amongst such as pursued him, calling and attesting the vengeance of God to light upon them.

Of all violences committed against conscience, the most in mine opinion to be avoided is that which is offered against the chastity of women, forsomuch as there is naturally some corporal pleasure commixed with it. And therefore the dissent cannot fully enough be joined thereunto, and it seemeth that force is in some sort intermixed with some will.[53] The ecclesiastical story hath in especial reverence sundry such examples of devout persons, who called for death to warrant them from the outrages which some tyrants prepared against their religion and consciences. *Pelagia* and *Sophronia*, both canonized; the first, together with her mother and sisters, to escape the outrageous rapes of some soldiers, threw herself into a river; the other, to shun the force of *Maxentius* the Emperor, slew herself.

It shall peradventure redound to our honour in future ages that a wise author of these days and namely a Parisian[54] doth labour to persuade the ladies of our times rather to hazard upon any resolution than to embrace so horrible a counsel of such desperation. I am sorry that to put amongst his discourses he knew not the good saying I learnt of a woman at *Toulouse*, who had passed through the hands of some soldiers: "God be praised" (said she), "that once in my life I have had my belly-full without sin." Verily, these cruelties[55] are not worthy of the French courtesy. And God be thanked, since this good advertisement,[56] our air is infinitely purged of them. Let it suffice, that in doing it, they say, *No*, and take it, following the rule of *Marot*.[57]

The history is very full of such who a thousand ways have changed lingering-toilsome life with death.

Lucius Aruntius killed himself (as he said) to avoid what was past and eschew what was to come.

Granius Sylvanus and *Statius Proximus*, after they had been pardoned by *Nero*, killed themselves, either because they scorned to live by the favor of so wicked a man or because they would not another time be in danger of a second pardon, seeing his so easy-yielding unto suspicions and accusations against honest men.

Spargapizes, son unto Queen *Tomiris*, prisoner by the law of war unto *Cyrus*, employed the first favor that *Cyrus* did him by setting him free, to kill himself; as he who never pretended to reap other fruit by his liberty than to revenge the infamy of his taking[58] upon himself.

Boges, a governour for King *Xerxes* in the country of *Ionia*, being besieged by the *Athenians* army under the conduct of *Cymon*, refused the composition to return safely, together with his goods and treasure into *Asia*, as one impatient to survive the loss of what his master had given him in charge. And after he had stoutly, and even to the last extremity, defended the town, having no manner of victuals left him, first he cast all the gold and treasure, with whatsoever he imagined the enemy might reap any commodity by, into the river *Strimon*. Then, having caused a great pile of wood to be set on fire and made all women, children, concubines, and servants to be stripped and thrown into the flames, afterward ran in himself, where all were burned.

Minachetuen,[59] a lord in the East *Indies*, having had an inkling of the king of *Portugal's* viceroy's deliberation to dispossess him without any apparent cause of the charge he had in *Malaca*, for to give it unto the King of *Campar*, of himself resolved upon this resolution. First, he caused an high scaffold to be set up, somewhat longer than broad, under-propped with pillars, all gorgeously hanged with rich tapestry, strewed with flowers, and adorned with precious perfumes. Then, having put on a sumptuous long robe of cloth of gold, richly beset with store of precious stones of inestimable worth, he came out of the palace into the street and by certain steps ascended the scaffold, in one of the corners whereof was a pile of aromatic wood set afire. All the people of the city were flocked together to see what the meaning of such unaccustomed preparation might tend unto. *Minachetuen*, with an undaunted-bold, yet seeming-discontented countenance, declared the manifold obligations which the *Portugal* nation was indebted unto him for; expostulated how faithfully and truly he had dealt in his charge; that having so often witnessed, armed at all assays for others; that his honour was much dearer unto him than life, he was not to forsake the care of it for himself; that fortune refusing him all means to oppose himself against the injury intended against him, his courage at the least willed him to remove the feeling thereof and not become a laughing stock unto the people and a triumph to men of less worth than himself. Which words as he was speaking, he cast himself into the fire.

Sextilia, the wife of *Scaurus,* and *Paxea,* wife unto *Labeo*, to encourage their husbands to avoid the dangers which pressed them, wherein they had no share (but in regard of the interest of their conjugal affection) voluntarily engaged their life[60] in this extreme necessity to serve them as an example to imitate and company to regard. What they performed for their husbands, *Cocceius Nerva* acted for his country, and though less profitable yet equal in true-love. That famous interpreter of the laws, abounding in riches, in reputation, in credit, and flourishing in health about the emperor, had no other cause to rid himself of life but the compassion of the miserable estate wherein he saw the Roman commonwealth.

There is nothing can be added unto the daintiness of *Fulvius's* wife's death, who was so inward with *Augustus*.[61] *Augustus*, perceiving he[62] had blabbed a certain secret of importance which he on trust had revealed unto him, one morning coming to visit him, he seemed to frown upon him for it. Whereupon as guilty he returneth home, as one full of despair and in piteous sort, told his wife that sithence[63] he was fallen into such a mischief, he was resolved to kill himself. She, as one no whit dismayed, replied unto him, "Thou shalt do but right, since having so often experienced the inconvenience[64] of my tongue, thou hast not learnt to beware of it. Yet give me leave to kill myself first." And without more ado, ran herself through with a sword.

Vibius Virius, despairing of his city's safety, besieged by the Romans, and mistrusting their mercy, in their senate's last consultation, after many remonstrances employed to that end, concluded that the best and fairest way was to escape fortune by their own hands. The very enemies should have them in more honour, and *Hannibal* might perceive what faithful friends he had forsaken. Inviting those that should allow of his advice to come and take a good supper which was prepared in his house where, after great cheer, they should drink together whatsoever should be presented unto him—"a drink that shall deliver our bodies from torments, free our minds from injuries, and release our eyes and ears from seeing and hearing so horrible mischiefs, which the conquered must endure at the hands of most cruel and offended conquerors. I have," (quoth he), "taken order that men fit for that purpose shall be ready, when we shall be expired, to cast us into a great burning pile of wood."

Diverse[65] approved of his high resolution, but few did imitate the same. Seven and twenty senators followed him, who after they had attempted to stifle so irksome, and suppress so terror-moving, a thought, with quaffing and swilling of wine they ended their repast by this deadly mess. And entre-embracing one another, after they had in common deplored and bewailed their country's misfortune, some went home to their own houses, othersome stayed there, to be entombed with *Vibius* in his own fire, whose death was so long and lingering. Forsomuch as the vapor of the wine having possessed their veins and slowed the effect and operation of the poison that some lived an hour after they had seen their enemies enter *Capoa*, which they carried the next day after, and incurred the miseries and saw the calamities which at so high a rate they had sought to eschew.[66]

Taurea Jubellius, another citizen there,[67] the consul *Fulvius* returning from that shameful slaughter which he had committed of 225 senators, called him churlishly by his name and, having arrested[68] him, "Command" (quoth he) "unto him that I also be massacred after so many others that so thou mayest brag to have murdered a much more valiant man than ever thou wast." *Fulvius*, as one enraged, disdaining him forsomuch as he had newly received letters from *Rome* contrary to the inhumanity of his execution, which inhibited him to proceed any further. *Jubellius* continuing his speech, said, "Sithence my country is taken, my friends butchered, and having with mine own hands slain my wife and children, as the only mean to free them from the desolation of this ruin, I may not die the death of my fellow-citizens, let us borrow the vengeance of this hateful life from virtue." And drawing a blade he had hidden under his garments, therewith ran himself through and, falling on his face, died at the consul's feet.

Alexander besieged a city in *India*, the inhabitants whereof, perceiving themselves brought to a very narrow pinch,[69] resolved obstinately to deprive him of the pleasure he might get of his victory, and together with their city, in despite of his humanity, set both the town and themselves on a light fire and so were all consumed. A new kind of warring, where the enemies did all they could and sought to save them, they to lose themselves; and to be assured of their death, did all a man can possibly effect to warrant[70] his life.

Astapa, a city in *Spain*, being very weak of walls and other defences, to withstand the Romans that besieged the same, the inhabitants drew all their riches and wealth into the marketplace, whereof having made a heap and on the top of it placed their wives and children, and encompassed and covered the same with dry brush wood that it might burn the easier. And, having appointed fifty lusty young men of theirs for the performance of their resolution, made a sally where, following their determined vow, seeing they could not vanquish, suffered themselves to be slain, every mother's child. The fifty, after they had massacred every living soul remaining in the city and set fire to the heap, joyfully leaped thereinto, ending their generous liberty in a state rather insensible than dolorous and reproachful; showing their enemies that, if fortune had been so pleased, they should as well have had the courage to bereave them of the victory, as they had to yield it them both vain and hideous. Yea, and mortal to those who, allured by the glittering of the gold that molten ran from out the flame, thick and three-fold approaching greedily unto it, were therein smothered and burned, the foremost being unable to give back,[71] by reason of the throng that followed them.

The *Abideans*, pressed by *Philip*, resolved upon the very same but, being prevented, the King whose heart yearned and abhorred to see the fond-rash precipitation of such an execution (having first seized upon and saved the treasure and movables, which they had diversely condemned to the flames and utter spoil), retiring all the soldiers, granted them the full space of 3 days to make themselves away, that so they might do it with more order and leisure; which three days they replenished with blood and murder beyond all hostile cruelty. And which is strange, there was no one person saved that had power upon himself.

There are infinite examples of such-like popular conclusions, which seem more violent by how much more the effect of them is more universal. They are less than several; what discourse would not do in every one, it doth in all, the vehemence of society ravishing particular judgments.[72]

Such as were condemned to die in the time of *Tiberius* and delayed their execution any while lost their goods and could not be buried, but such as prevented the same in killing themselves were solemnly enterred[73] and might, at their pleasure, bequeath such goods as they had to whom they list.

But a man doth also sometimes desire death, in hope of a greater good. "I desire" (sayeth Saint *Paul*), "to be out of this world, that I may be with *Jesus Christ*." And "who shall release me out of these bonds?" *Cleombrotus Ambraciota*, having read *Plato's Phædon*, was so possessed with a desire and longing for an after-life that, without other occasion or more ado, he went and headlong cast himself into the sea. Whereby it appeareth how improperly we call this voluntary dissolution "despair," unto which the violence of hope doth often transport us, and as often a peaceful and settled inclination of judgment.

Jaques du Castell, Bishop of *Soissons*, in the voyage which Saint *Louis* undertook beyond the seas, seeing the king and all his army ready to return into *France* and leave the affairs of religion imperfect, resolved with himself rather to go to heaven. And having bidden his friends farewell, in the open view of all men, rushed alone into the enemy's troops, of whom he was forthwith hewn in pieces.

In a certain kingdom of these late-discovered *Indies*,[74] upon a day of a solemn procession, in which the idols they adore are publicly carried up and down upon a chariot of exceeding greatness; besides that, there are many seen to cut and slice great mammocks[75] of their quick flesh, to offer the said idols. There are numbers of others seen who, prostrating themselves alongst upon the ground, endure very patiently to be moldered[76] and crushed to death under the chariot's wheels, thinking thereby to purchase after their death a veneration of holiness, of which they are not defrauded. The death of this Bishop,[77] armed as we have said, argueth more generosity and less sense, the heat of the combat amusing one part of it.[78]

Some commonwealths there are that have gone about to sway the justice and direct the opportunity of voluntary deaths. In our city of *Marseille* they were wont in former ages ever to keep some poison in store, prepared and compounded with hemlock at the city's charge, for such as would upon any occasion shorten their days, having first approved the reasons of their enterprise unto the six hundred elders of the town, which was their senate. For otherwise it was unlawful for any body, except by the magistrate's permission and for very lawfully-urgent occasions, to lay violent hands upon himself. The very same law was likewise used in other places.

Sextus Pompeius going into *Asia* passed through the island of *Cea*, belonging to *Negroponto*; it fortuned whilst he abode there (as one reporteth that was in his company) that a woman of great authority, having first yielded an account unto her citizens and showed good reasons why she was resolved to end her life, earnestly entreated *Pompey* to be an assistant at her death that so it might be esteemed more honourable, which he assented unto. And having long time in vain sought, by virtue of his eloquence (wherein he was exceedingly ready) and force of persuasion, to alter her intent and remove her from her purpose, in the end yielded to her request. She had lived four score and ten years in a most happy estate of mind and body, but then lying on her bed, better adorned than before she was accustomed to have it and leaning on her elbow, thus she bespake: "The gods, O *Sextus Pompeius*, and rather those I forgo than those I go unto, reward and appay[79] thee, for that thou hast vouchsafed to be both a counselor of my life and a witness of my death. As for my part, having hitherto ever tasted the favourable visage of fortune, for fear the desire of living overlong should make me taste of her frowns, with an happy and successful end, I will now depart and licence the remainder of my soul, leaving behind me two daughters of mine, with a legion of grandchildren and nephews." That done, having preached unto and exhorted all her people and kinfolks to an unity and peace and divided her goods amongst them and recommended her household gods unto her eldest daughters, with an assuredly-staid hand she took the cup wherein the poison was, and having made her vows unto *Mercury* and prayers to conduct her unto some happy place in the other world, roundly swallowed that mortal potion. Which done, she entertained the company with the progress of her behaviour, and as the parts of her body were one after another possessed with the cold operation of that venom, until such time as she said she felt it work at the heart and in her entrails, she called her daughter to do her the last office and close her eyes.

Pliny reporteth of a certain *Hiperborean*[80] nation wherein, by reason of the mild temperature of the air, the inhabitants thereof commonly never die but when they please to make themselves away. And that being weary and tired with living, they are accustomed at the end of a long-long age, having first made merry and good cheer with their friends, from the top of an high-steepy rock appointed for that purpose, to cast themselves headlong into the sea.

Grieving-smart[81] and a worse death seem to me the most excusable incitations.[82]

Of the Affection of Fathers to Their Children

2.8

MADAME, if strangeness do not save or novelty shield me, which are wont to give things reputation, I shall never with honesty quit myself of this enterprise[2]; yet is it so fantastical and bears a show so different from common custom that that may haply purchase it free passage. It is a melancholy humour, and consequently a hateful enemy to my natural complexion, bred by the anxiety and produced by the anguish of carking[3] care whereinto some years since I cast myself, that first put this humorous conceit of writing into my head. And finding myself afterward wholly unprovided of subject and void of other matter, I have presented myself unto myself for a subject to write and argument to descant[4] upon. It is the only book in the world of this kind and of a wild extravagant design. Moreover, there is nothing in it worthy the marking but this fantasticalness. For to so vain a ground and base a subject, the world's best workman could never have given a fashion deserving to be accounted of.

Now (worthy Lady), sithence I must portray myself to the life, I should have forgotten a part of importance, if therewithal I had not represented the honour I have ever yielded to your deserts which I have especially been willing to declare in the forefront of this chapter. Forasmuch as amongst your other good parts and commendable qualities that of loving amity which you have shown to your children holdeth one of the first ranks. Whosoever shall understand and know the age wherein your late husband the Lord of *Estissac* left you a widow; the great and honorable matches have been offered you (as worthy and as many as to any other Lady in *France* of your condition); the constant resolution and resolute constancy wherewith so many years you have sustained and even in spite or athwart so manifold thorny difficulties, the charge and conduct of their affairs, which have tossed, turmoiled, and removed you in all corners of *France* and still hold you besieged; the happy and successful forwardness[5] you, which only through your wisdom or good fortune have given them—he will easily say with me that in our age we have no pattern of motherly affection more exemplary than yours.

I praise God (Madame) it hath been so well employed. For the good hopes which the young Lord of *Estissac*, your son, giveth of himself fore-show he shall come to an undoubted assurance that, when he shall come to years of discretion, you shall reap the obedience of a noble, and find the acknowledgement of a good, child. But because, by reason of his childhood, he could not take notice of the exceeding kindness and manifold offices he hath received from you, my meaning is that if ever these my compositions shall haply one day come into his hands (when peradventure I shall neither have mouth nor speech to declare it unto him), he receive this testimony in all verity from me; which shall also more lively be testified unto him by the good effects (whereof, if so it please God, he shall have a sensible feeling) that there is no gentleman in *France* more endebted to his mother than he; and that hereafter he cannot yield a more certain proof of his goodness and testimony of his virtue than in acknowledging and confessing you for such.

If there be any truly natural law, that is to say, any instinct universally and perpetually imprinted both in beasts and us (which is not without controversy), I may, according to mine opinion, say that next to the care which each living creature hath to his preservation and to fly what doth hurt him, the affection which the engenderer beareth his offspring holds the second place in this rank. And forasmuch as Nature seemeth to have recommended the same unto us, aiming to extend, increase, and advance the successive parts or parcels of this her frame, it is no wonder if back again it[6] is not so great from children unto fathers.

This other Aristotelian consideration remembered: that *he who doth benefit another loveth him better than he is beloved of him again*;

and he to whom a debt is owing loveth better than he that oweth. And every workman loveth his work better than he should be beloved of it again, if it had sense or feeling. Forasmuch as we love to be, and being consisteth in moving and action. Therefore is every man, in some sort or other, in his own workmanship. *Whosoever doth a good deed exerciseth a fair and honest action; whosoever receiveth exerciseth only a profitable[7] action.* And profit is nothing so much to be esteemed or loved as honesty. Honesty is firm and permanent, affording him that did it a constant gratification. Profit is very slippery and easily lost, nor is the memory of it so sweet or so fresh. Such things are dearest unto us that have cost us most; and to give is of more cost than to take.

Since it hath pleased God to endow us with some capacity of discourse, that as beasts we should not servilely be subjected to common laws[8] but rather with judgement and voluntary liberty apply ourselves unto them, we ought somewhat to yield unto the simple authority of Nature, but not suffer her tyranny to carry us away: only reason ought to have the conduct of our inclinations.

As for me, my taste is strangely distasted[9] to its propensions,[10] which in us are produced without the ordinance and direction of our judgement. As upon this subject I speak of, I cannot receive this passion wherewith some embrace children scarcely born, having neither motion in the soul nor form well to be distinguished in the body whereby they might make themselves lovely or amiable. And I could never well endure to have them brought up or nursed near about me.

A true and well-ordered affection ought to be born and augmented with the knowledge they owe us of themselves; and then, if they deserve it (natural inclination marching hand in hand with reason), to cherish and make much of them with a perfect fatherly love and loving friendship; and conformably to judge of them if they be otherwise, always yielding ourselves unto reason, notwithstanding natural power. For the most part, it goeth clean contrary, and commonly we feel ourselves more moved with the sports, idlenesses, wantonness, and infant-trifles of our children than afterward we do with all their actions when they be men, as if we had loved them for our pastimes, as we do apes, monkeys, or perokitoes,[11] and not as men. And some that liberally furnish them with sporting babbles[12] while they be children will miserably pinch it in the least expense for necessaries when they grow men. Nay, it seemeth that the jealousy we have to see them appear into and enjoy the world, when we are ready to leave them, makes us more sparing and close-handed toward them. It vexeth and grieveth us when we see them following us at our heels, supposing they solicit us to be gone hence. And if we were to fear that, since the order of things beareth that they cannot indeed neither be nor live but by our being and life, we should not meddle to be fathers.

As for me, I deem it a kind of cruelty and injustice not to receive them into the share and society of our goods and to admit them as partners in the understanding of our domestical affairs (if they be once capable of it) and not to cut off and shut up our commodities to provide for theirs, since we have engendered them to that purpose. It is mere injustice to see an old, crazed, sinew-shrunken, and nigh-dead father sitting alone in a chimney-corner to enjoy so many goods as would suffice for the preferment and entertainment of many children, and in the meanwhile, for want of means, to suffer them to lose their best days and years without thrusting them into public service and knowledge of men; whereby they are often cast into despair, to seek by some way how unlawful soever to provide for their necessaries.[13] And in my days, I have seen diverse young men of good houses so given to stealing and filching that no correction could divert them from it. I know one, very well allied, to whom, at the instance of a brother of his (a most honest, gallant, and virtuous gentleman) I spoke to that purpose, who boldly answered and confessed unto me that only by the rigor and covetism[14] of his father he had been forced and driven to fall into such lewdness and wickedness. And even at that time he came from stealing certain jewels from a lady in whose bed-chamber he fortuned to come with certain gentlemen when she was rising and had almost been taken. He made me remember a tale I had heard of another gentleman, from his youth so fashioned and inclined to this goodly trade of pilfering that, coming afterward to be heir and lord of his own goods [and] resolved to give over that manner of life, could notwithstanding (if he chanced to come near a shop where he saw anything he stood in need of) not choose but steal the same, though afterward he would ever send money and pay for it. And I have seen diverse so inured to that vice that amongst their companions they would ordinarily steal such things as they would restore again.

I am a Gascon, and there is no vice wherein I have less skill. I hate it somewhat more by complexion than I accuse it by discourse.[15] I do not so much as desire another man's goods. And although my countrymen be indeed somewhat more taxed with this fault than other provinces of *France*, yet have we seen of late days and that sundry times men well born and of good parentage in other parts of *France* in the hands of justice, and lawfully convicted of many most horrible robberies. I am of opinion that in regard of these debauches and lewd actions fathers may, in some sort, be blamed, and that it is only long of[16] them.

And if any shall answer me, as did once a gentleman of good worth and understanding, that he thriftily endeavoured to hoard up riches to no other purpose nor to have any use and commodity of them than to be honoured, respected, and suingly sought[17] unto by his friends and kinsfolk and that, age having bereaved him of all other forces, it was the only remedy he had left to maintain himself in authority with his household and keep him from falling into contempt and disdain of all the world. And truly according to *Aristotle*, not only old age but each imbecility is the promoter and motive of covetousness. That is something, but it is a remedy for an evil whereof the birth should have been hindered and breeding avoided.

That father may truly be said miserable that holdeth the affection of his children tied unto him by no other means than by the need they have of his help or want of his assistance, if that may be termed affection. *A man should yield himself respectable by virtue and sufficiency, and amiable by his goodness and gentleness of manners.* The very cinders of so rich a matter have their value; so have the bones and relics of honourable men whom we hold in respect and reverence.

No age can be so crazed and drooping in a man that hath lived honourably but must needs prove venerable, and especially unto his children, whose minds ought so to be directed by the parents that reason and wisdom, not necessity and need nor rudeness and compulsion, may make them know and perform their duty.

> ——*et errat longe, mea quidem sententia,*
> *Qui imperium credat esse gravius aut stabilius,*
> *Vi quod fit, quam illud quod amicitia adjungitur.*
> In mine opinion he doth much mistake,
> Who, that command more grave, more firm doth take,
> Which force doth get, than that which friendships make.[18]

I utterly condemn all manner of violence in the education of a young spirit, brought up to honour and liberty. There is a kind of slavishness in churlish rigour and servility in compulsion; and I hold that *that which cannot be compassed by reason, wisdom, and discretion, can never be attained by force and constraint.* So was I brought up: they tell me that in all my youth I never felt rod but twice, and that very lightly. And what education I have had myself, the same have I given my children. But such is my ill hap that they die all very young; yet hath Leonora, my only daughter, escaped this misfortune and attained to the age of six years and somewhat more; for the conduct of whose youth and punishment of her childish faults (the indulgence of her mother applying itself very mildly unto it) was never other means used but gentle words. And were my desire frustrate,[19] there are diverse other causes to take hold of without reproving my discipline,[20] which I know to be just and natural. I would also have been much more religious in that towards male children, not born to serve as women and of a freer condition. I should have loved to have stored their mind with ingenuity and liberty. I have seen no other effects in rods but to make children's minds more remiss or more maliciously headstrong.

Desire we to be loved of our children? Will we remove all occasions from them to wish our death? (although no occasion of so horrible and unnatural wishes can either be just or excusable) *nullum scelus rationem habet*, no ill deed hath a good reason.[21]

Let us reasonably accommodate their life with such things as are in our power. And therefore should not we marry so young that our age do in a manner confound itself with theirs. For this inconvenience doth unavoidably cast us into many difficulties and encumbrances. This I speak chiefly unto nobility, which is of an idle disposition or loitering condition and which (as we say) liveth only by her lands or rents. For else, where life standeth upon gain, plurality, and company of children is an easeful furtherance of husbandry. They are as many new implements to thrive and instruments to grow rich.

I was married at thirty years of age and commend the opinion of thirty-five, which is said to be *Aristotle's*. *Plato* would have no man married before thirty and hath good reason to scoff at them that will defer it till after fifty-five and then marry; and condemneth their breed[22] as unworthy of life and sustenance. *Thales* appointed the best limits, who by his mother being instantly urged to marry whilst he was young, answered that it was not yet time; and when he came to be old, he said it was no more time. A man must refuse opportunity to every importunate action.

The ancient *Gauls* deemed it a shameful reproach to have the acquaintance of a woman before the age of twenty years, and did especially recommend unto men that sought to be trained up in wars the careful preservation of their maidenhead until they were of good years, forsomuch as by losing it in youth, courages are thereby much weakened and greatly impaired, and by coupling with women diverted from all virtuous action.

> *Ma hor congiunto a giovinetta sposa,*
> *Lieto homai de' figli, era invilito*
> *Ne gli afetti di padre et di marito.*
> But now conjoyn'd to a fresh-springing spouse,
> Joy'd in his children, he was thought-abased,
> In passions twixt a sire and husband placed.[23]

Muleasses, King of *Thunes*,[24] he whom the Emperor *Charles* the Fifth restored unto his own state again, was wont to upbraid his father's memory for so dissolutely-frequenting of women, terming him a sloven, effeminate, and a lustful engenderer of children. The Greek story doth note *Iccus* the *Tarentine, Crisso, Astyllus, Diopompus*, and others, who to keep their bodies tough and strong for the service of the Olympic courses, wrestlings, and such bodily exercises they did, as long as they were possessed with that care, heedfully abstain from all venerian[25] acts and touching of women. In a certain country of the Spanish *Indies*, no man was suffered to take a wife before he were thirty years old, and women might marry at ten years of age.

There is no reason, neither is it convenient, that a gentleman of five and thirty years should give place to his son that is but twenty. For then is the father as seemly and may as well appear and set himself forward, in all manner of voyages of wars as well by land as sea, and do his prince as good service, in court or elsewhere, as his son. He hath need of all his parts and ought truly to impart them, but so that be forget not himself for others. And to such may justly that answer serve which fathers have commonly in their mouths: *I will not put off my clothes before I be ready to go to bed.*

But a father over-burdened with years and crazed through sickness and, by reason of weakness and want of health barred from the common society of men, doth both wrong himself and injure his[26] idly and to no use to hoard up and keep close a great heap of riches and deal of pelf. He is in state good enough if he be wise to have a desire to put off his clothes to go to bed—I will not say to his shirt, but to a good warm night gown. As for other pomp and trash whereof he hath no longer use or need, he ought willingly to distribute and bestow them amongst those to whom by natural degree they ought to belong. It is reason he should have the use and bequeath the fruition of them, since nature doth also deprive him of them; otherwise without doubt there is both envy and malice stirring.

The worthiest action that ever the Emperour *Charles* the Fifth performed was this: in imitation of some ancients of his quality, that he had the discretion to know that reason commanded us to strip or shift ourselves when our clothes trouble and are too heavy for us, and that it is high time to go to bed when our legs fail us. He resigned his means, his greatness, and kingdom to his son at what time he found his former undaunted resolution to decay and force to conduct his affairs to droop in himself, together with the glory he had thereby acquired.

> *Solve senescentem mature sanus equum, ne*
> *Peccet ad extremum ridentus, et ilia ducat.*
> If you be wise, the horse grown-old betimes cast-off,
> Lest he at last fall lame, falter, and breed a skoffe.[27]

This fault for a man not to be able to know himself betimes[28] and not to feel the impuissance and extreme alteration that age doth naturally bring both to the body and the mind (which in my opinion is equal if the mind hath but one half), hath lost the reputation of the most part of the great men in the world. I have in my days both seen and familiarly known some men of great authority, whom a man might easily discern to be strangely fallen from that ancient sufficiency, which I know by the reputation they had thereby attained unto in their best years. I could willingly for their honor's sake have wished them at home about their own business, discharged from all negotiations of the commonwealth and employments of war that were no longer fit for them.

I have sometimes been familiar in a gentleman's house, who was both an old man and a widower yet lusty of his age. This man had many daughters marriageable and a son grown to man's state and ready to appear in the world; a thing that drew on and was the cause of great charges and many visitations, wherein he took but little pleasure, not only for the continual care he had to save, but more by reason of his age he had betaken himself to a manner of life far different from ours. I chanced one day to tell him somewhat boldly (as my custom is) that it would better beseem him to give us[29] place and resign his chief house to his son (for he had no other manor-house conveniently well furnished), and quietly retire himself to some farm of his where no man might trouble him or disturb his rest, since he could not otherwise avoid our importunity, seeing the condition of his children; who afterward followed my counsel and found great ease by it.

It is not to be said that they have anything given them[30] by such a way of obligation which a man may not recall again. I, that am ready to play such a part, would give over unto them the full possession of my house and enjoying of my goods, but with liberty and limited condition, as if they should give me occasion, I might repent myself of my gift and revoke my deed. I would leave the use and fruition of all unto them, the rather because it were no longer fit for me to wield the same. And touching the disposing of all matters in gross, I would reserve what I pleased unto myself. Having ever judged that it must be a great contentment to an aged father, himself to direct his children in the government of his household affairs and to be able, whilst himself liveth, to check and control their demeanors, storing them with instruction and advised counsel according to the experience he hath had of them, and himself to address the ancient honour and order of his house in the hands of his successours, and that way warrant himself of the hope he may conceive of their future conduct and or success.

And to this effect I would not shun their company. I would not be far from them, but as much as the condition of my age would permit, enjoy and be a partner of their sports, mirths, and feasts. If I did not continually live amongst them (as I could not well without offending their meetings and hindering their recreation, by reason of the peevish forwardness of my age and the trouble of my infirmities, and also without forcing their rules and resisting the form of life I should then follow), I would at least live near them in some corner of my house, not the best and fairest in show but the most easeful and commodious. And not as some years since I saw a dean of S. *Hillarie* of *Poitiers*, reduced by reason and the incommodity of his melancholy to such a continual solitariness that when I entered into his chamber he had never removed one step out of it in two and twenty years before; yet had all his faculties free and easy, only a rheume[31] excepted that fell into his stomach. Scarce once a week would he suffer anybody to come and see him. He would ever be shut up in his chamber all alone, where no man should come, except a boy, who once a day brought him meat and who might not tarry there, but as soon as he was in must go out again. All his exercise was sometimes to walk up and down his chamber, and now and then read on some book (for he had some understanding of letters); but obstinately resolved to live and die in that course, as he did shortly after.

I would endeavour by a kind of civil demeanour and mild conversation to breed and settle in my children a true-hearty loving friendship and unfained good will towards me, a thing easily obtained amongst well-born minds. For if they prove or be such surly-furious beasts or given to churlish disobedience, as our age bringeth forth thousands, they must as beasts be hated, as churls neglected, and as degenerate[32] avoided.

I hate this custom to forbid children to call their fathers "father" and to teach them another strange name, as of more reverence; as if nature had not sufficiently provided for our authority. We call God Almighty by the name of father and disdain our children should call us so. I have reformed this fault in mine own household. It is also folly and injustice to deprive children, especially being of competent age, of their fathers' familiarity and ever to show them a surly, austere, grim, and disdainful countenance, hoping thereby to keep them in awful fear and duteous obedience. For it is a very unprofitable proceeding and which maketh fathers irksome unto children, and which is worse, ridiculous. They have youth and strength in their hands, and consequently the breath and favour of the world, and do with mockery and contempt receive these churlish, fierce, and tyrannical countenances from a man that hath no lusty blood left him, neither in his heart nor in his veins—mere bugbears and scarecrows, to scare birds withal. If it lay in my power to make myself feared, I had rather make myself beloved.[33]

There are so many sorts of defects in age and so much impuissance,[34] it is so subject to contempt, that the best purchase it can make is the good will, love, and affection of others. Commandment and fear are no longer her weapons. I have known one whose youth had been very imperious and rough, but when he came to man's age, although he live in as good plight and health as may be, yet he chaseth, he scoldeth, he brawleth, he fighteth, he sweareth and biteth, as the most boisterous and tempestuous master of *France*. He frets and consumes himself with carke[35] and care and vigilancy (all which is but a juggling and ground for his familiar to play upon and cozen him the more) as for his goods, his garners, his cellars, his coffers, yea, his purse. Whilst himself keeps the keys of them close in his bosom and under his boulster[36] as charily as he doth his eyes, other enjoy and command the better part of them. Whilst he pleaseth and flattereth himself with the niggardly sparing of his table, all goeth to wrack and is lavishly wasted in diverse corners of his house—in play, in riotous spending, and in soothingly entertaining the accounts or tales of his vain chasing, foresight, and providing. Every man watcheth and keepeth sentinel against him. If any silly or heedless servant do by fortune apply himself unto it, he is presently made to suspect him,[37] a quality on which age doth immediately bite of itself. How many times hath he vaunted and, applauding himself, told me of the strict orders of his house, of his good husbandry, of the awe he kept his household in, and of the exact obedience and regardful reverence he received of all his family, and how clear-sighted he was in his own business:

Ille solus nescit omnia.
Of all things none but he,
Most ignorant must be.[38]

I know no man that could produce more parts, both natural and artificial, fit to preserve his mastery and to maintain his absoluteness than he doth; yet is he clean fallen from them like a child. Therefore have I made choice of him amongst many such conditions that I know, as most exemplary.

It were a matter beseeming a scholastical[39] question whether it be better so or otherwise. In his presence all things give place unto him.[40] This vain course is ever left unto his authority that he is never gainsaid. He is had in awe, he is feared, he is believed, he is respected his belly-full. Doth he discharge any boy or servant? He presently trusseth up his pack, then he is gone. But whither? Only out of his sight, not out of his house. The steps of age are so slow, the senses so troubled, the mind so distracted, that he shall live and do his office a whole year in one same house and never be perceived. And when fit time or occasion serveth, letters are produced from far places, humbly suing and pitifully complaining, with promises to do better and to amend, by which he is brought into favour and office again. Doth the master make any bargain or dispatch that pleaseth not, it is immediately smothered and suppressed soon after forging causes and devising colourable excuses, to excuse the want of execution or answer. No foreign letters being first presented unto him, he seeth but such as are fit for his knowledge. If peradventure they come into his hands, as he that trusteth some one of his men to read them unto him, he will presently devise what he thinketh good, whereby they often invent that such a one seemeth to ask him forgiveness that wrongeth him by his letter. To conclude, he never looks into his own business but by a disposed, designed, and as much as may be pleasing image, so contrived by such as are about him, because they will not stir up his choler, move his impatience, and exasperate his frowardness.[41] I have seen under different forms many long and constant, and of like effect, economies.

It is ever proper unto women to be readily bent to contradict and cross their husbands. They will with might and main,[42] hand over head, take hold of any colour to thwart and withstand them; the first excuse they meet with serves them as a plenary justification. I have seen some that would in gross steal from their husbands to the end (as they told their confessor) they might give the greater alms. Trust you to such religious dispensations! They think no liberty to have or managing to possess sufficient authority if it come from their husbands' consent.[43] They must necessarily usurp it, either by wily craft or main force, and ever injuriously, thereby to give it more grace and authority. As in my discourse, when it is against a poor old man and for children, then take they hold of this title and therewith gloriously serve their turn and passion, and, as in a common servitude, easily usurp and monopolize against his government and domination. If they be men-children, tall, of good spirit, and forward, then they presently suborn—either by threats, force, or favour—both steward, bailiff, clerk, receiver, and all the father's officers and servants.

Such as have neither wife nor children do more hardly[44] fall into his mischief, but yet more cruelly and unworthily. Old *Cato* was wont to say, *So many servants, so many enemies.* Note whether according to the distance that was between the purity of his age and the corruption of our times, he did not forewarn us that *wives, children, and servants are to us so many enemies.* Well fits it decrepitude to store us with the sweet benefit of ignorance and unperceiving facility wherewith we are deceived. If we did yield unto it, what would become of us? Do we not see that even then if we have any suits in law or matters to be decided before judges, both lawyers and judges will commonly take part with and favour our children's causes against us, as men interested in the same?

And if I chance not to spy or plainly perceive how I am cheated, cozened, and beguiled, I must of necessity discover in the end how I am subject, and may be cheated, beguiled, and cozened. And shall the tongue of man ever be able to express the invaluable worth of a friend, in comparison of these civil bonds? The lively image and idea whereof which so unspotted I perceive to be among beasts—oh, with what religion do I respect and observe the same!

If others deceive me, yet do I not deceive myself, to esteem myself capable and of power to look unto myself, nor to trouble my brains to yield myself unto it. I do beware and keep myself from such treasons and cunny-catching[45] in mine own bosom, not by an unquiet and tumultuary[46] curiosity, but rather by a diversion and resolution.

When I hear the state of any one reported or discoursed of, I amuse not myself on him but presently cast mine eyes on myself and all my wits together, to see in what state I am and how it goeth with me. Whatsoever concerneth him, the same hath relation to me. His fortunes forewarn me and summon up my spirits that way. *There is no day nor hour but we speak that of others we might properly speak of ourselves, could we as well enfold as we can unfold our consideration.*

And many authors do in this manner wound the protection of their cause by over-rashly running against that which they take hold of, thirling[47] such darts at their enemies that might with much more advantage be cast at them.

The Lord of *Montluc*, late one of the Lord Marshals of *France*, having lost his son, who died in the island of *Madeira*—a worthy, forward, and gallant young gentleman, and truly of good hope—amongst other his griefs and regrets did greatly move me to condole the infinite displeasure and heart's-sorrow that he felt, inasmuch as he had never communicated and opened himself unto him. For with his austere humour and continual endeavouring to hold a grim-stern-fatherly gravity over him, he had lost the means perfectly to find and thoroughly to know his son and so to manifest unto him the extreme affection he bore him and the worthy judgement he made of his virtue. "Alas," was he wont to say, "the poor lad saw never anything in me but a severe-surly countenance, full of disdain, and haply[48] was possessed with this conceit that I could neither love nor esteem him according to his merits. Ay-me, to whom did I reserve to discover that singular and loving affection which in my soul I bare unto him? Was it not he that should have had all the pleasure and acknowledgement thereof? I have forced and tormented myself to maintain this vain mask and have utterly lost the pleasure of his conversation and therewithal his good will, which surely was but faintly cold towards me, forsomuch as he never received but rude entertainment of me and never felt but a tyrannical proceeding in me towards him." I am of opinion his complaint was reasonable and well grounded. For, as I know by certain experience, there is no comfort so sweet in the loss of friends as that our own knowledge or conscience tells us we never omitted to tell them everything and expostulate all matters unto them and to have had a perfect and free communication with them. Tell me, my good friend, am I the better or the worse by having a taste of it?[49] Surely I am much the better. His grief doth both comfort and honour me. Is it not a religious and pleasing office of my life for ever to make the obsequies thereof? Can there be any pleasure worth this privation?

I do unfold and open myself as much as I can to mine own people,[50] and willingly declare the state of my will and judgment towards them, as commonly I do towards all men. I make haste to produce and present myself, for I would have no man mistake me, in what part soever.

Amongst other particular customs which our ancient Gauls had (as *Cæsar* affirmeth), this was one, that children never came before their fathers nor were in any public assembly seen in their company but when they began to bear arms; as if they would infer that then was the time fathers should admit them to their acquaintance and familiarity.

I have also observed another kind of indiscretion in some fathers of our times, who during their own life would never be induced to acquaint or impart unto their children that share or portion which, by the Law of Nature, they were to have in their fortunes: nay, some there are who, after their death, bequeath and commit the same authority over them and their goods unto their wives, with full power and law to dispose of them at their pleasure. And myself have known a gentleman, a chief officer of our crown that by right and hope of succession (had he lived unto it) was to inherit above fifty thousand crowns a year good land, who at the age of more than fifty years fell into such necessity and want, and was run so far in debt that he had nothing left him and, as it is supposed, died for very need; whilst his mother, in her extreme decrepitude, enjoyed all his lands and possessed all his goods, by virtue of his father's will and testament, who had lived very near four-score years; a thing (in my conceit) no way to be commended but rather blamed.

Therefore do I think that a man but little advantaged or bettered in estate who is able to live of himself and is out of debt, especially if he have children and goeth about to marry a wife that must have a great jointer[51] out of his lands, assuredly there is no other debt that brings more ruin unto houses than that. My predecessors have commonly followed this counsel and so have I, and all have found good by it. But those that dissuade us from marrying of rich wives lest they might prove over disdainful and peevish, or less tractable and loving, are also deceived to make us neglect and forego a real commodity for so frivolous a conjecture. To an unreasonable woman, it is all one cost to her whether they pass under one reason or under another. *They love to be where they are most wronged.* Injustice doth allure them, as the honour of their virtuous actions enticeth the good. And by how much richer they are, so much more mild and gentle are they, as more willingly and gloriously chaste by how much fairer they are.

Some colour of reason there is men should leave the administration of their goods and affairs unto mothers whilst their children are not of competent age or fit according to the laws to manage the charge of them. And ill hath their father brought them up if he cannot hope these, coming to years of discretion, they shall have no more wit, reason, and sufficiency than his wife, considering the weakness of their sex. Yet truly were it as much against nature so to order things that mothers must wholly depend on their children's discretion. They ought largely and competently to be provided wherewith to maintain their estate according to the quality of their house and age because *need and want is much more unseemly and hard to be endured in women than in men*. And children rather than mothers ought to be charged therewith.

In general, my opinion is that the best distribution of goods is, when we die, to distribute them according to the custom of the country. The laws have better thought upon them than we. And better is it to let them err in their election than for us rashly to hazard to fail in ours. They are not properly our own since, without us and by a civil prescription, they are appointed to certain successors. And albeit we have some further liberty, I think it should be a great and most apparent cause to induce us to take from one and bar him from that which Fortune hath allotted him and the common laws and justice hath called him unto. And that against reason we abuse this liberty, by suiting the same unto our private humours and frivolous fantasies. My fortune hath been good, inasmuch as yet it never presented me with any occasions that might tempt or divert my affections from the common and lawful ordinance.

I see some towards whom it is but labour lost carefully to endeavour to do any good offices. *A word ill taken defaceth the merit of ten years.* Happy he that, at this last passage, is ready to soothe and applaud their will. The next action transporteth him; not the best and most frequent offices, but the freshest and present, work the deed.[52] They are the people that play with their wills and testaments as with apples and rods, to gratify or chastise every action of those who pretend any interest thereunto. It is a matter of over-long pursuit and of exceeding consequence at every instance to be thus dilated,[53] and wherein the wiser sort establish themselves once for all, chiefly respecting reason and public observance.

We somewhat over-much take these masculine substitutions[54] to heart and propose a ridiculous eternity unto our names. We also over-weight such vain future conjectures which infant-spirits[55] give us. It might peradventure have been from out my rank because I was the dullest, the slowest, the unwillingest, the most leaden-pated to learn my lesson or any good that ever was not only of all my brethren but of all the children in my country, were the lesson concerning my exercise of the mind or body. It is folly to try any extraordinary conclusions upon the trust of their divinations, wherein we are so often deceived. If this rule may be contradicted and the destinies corrected in the choice they have made of our heirs, with so much more appearance may it be done in consideration of some remarkable and enormous corporal deformity, a constant and incorrigible vice, and, according to us great esteemers of beauty, a matter of important prejudice.

The pleasant dialogue of *Plato's* the law-giver with his citizens will much honour this passage: "Why then," say they, perceiving their end to approach, "shall we not dispose of that which is our own to whom and according as we please? O Gods, what cruelty is this, that it shall not be lawful for us to give or bequeath more or less according to our fantasies[56] to such as have served us and taken pains with us in our sicknesses, in our age, and in our business?" To whom the law-giver answereth in this manner: "My friends," sayeth he, "who doubtless shall shortly die, it is a hard matter for you both to know yourselves and what is yours according to the *Delphic* inscription. As for me, who am the maker of your laws, I am of opinion that neither yourselves are your own nor that which you enjoy. And both you and your goods, past and to come, belong to your family. And, moreover, both your families and your goods are the commonwealth's. Wherefore, lest any flatterer, either in your age or in time of sickness, or any other passion, should unadvisedly induce you to make any unlawful conveyance or unjust will and testament, I will look to you and keep you from it. But having an especial respect both to the universal interest of your city and particular state of your houses, I will establish laws and by reason make you perceive and confess that *a particular commodity ought to yield to a public benefit.* Follow that course merely whereto human necessity doth call you. To me it belongeth, who have no more regard to one thing than to another, and who, as much as I can, take care for the general, to have a regardful respect of that which you leave behind you."

But to return to my former discourse, methinks we seldom see that woman born to whom the superiority or majesty over men is due, except the motherly and natural, unless it be for the chastisement of such as by some fond-febricitant[57] humour have voluntarily submitted themselves unto them. But that doth nothing concern old women, of whom we speak here. It is the appearance of this consideration hath made us to frame and willingly to establish this law (never seen elsewhere) that barreth women from the succession of this crown; and there are few principalities in the world where it is not alleged, as well as here, by a likely and apparent reason which authoriseth the same. But fortune hath given more credit unto it in some places than in other some.[58]

It is dangerous to leave the dispensation of our succession unto their[59] judgement, according to the choice they shall make of their children, which is most commonly unjust and fantastical. For the same unruly appetite and distasted relish, or strange longings, which they have when they are great with child, the same have they at all times in their minds. They are commonly seen to affect the weakest, the simplest, and most abject, or such, if they have any, that had more need to suck. For, wanting reasonable discourse to choose and embrace what they ought, they rather suffer themselves to be directed where nature's impressions are most single, as other creatures, which take no longer knowledge of their young ones than they are sucking.

Moreover, experience doth manifestly show unto us that the same natural affection to which we ascribe so much authority hath but a weak foundation. For a very small gain we daily take mothers' own children from them and induce them to take charge of ours. Do we not often procure them to bequeath their children to some fond, filthy, sluttish, and unhealthy nurse, to whom we would be very loath to commit ours, or to some brutish goat; not only forbidding them to nurse and feed their own children, what danger soever may betide them, but also to have any care of them, to the end they may the more diligently follow and carefully attend the service of ours? Whereby we soon see through custom a certain kind of bastard affection to be engendered in them, more vehement than the natural, and to be much more tender and careful for the welfare and preservation of other men's children than for their own.

And the reason why I have made mention of goats is because it is an ordinary thing round about me where I dwell to see the country women, when they have not milk enough to feed their infants with their own breasts, to call for goats to help them. And myself have now two lackeys waiting on me who, except it were eight days, never sucked other milk than goats'. They are presently to come at call and give young infants suck, and become so well acquainted with their voice that, when they hear them cry, they run forthwith unto them. And if by chance they have any other child put to their teats than their nurseling, they refuse and reject him; and so doth the child a strange goat. Myself saw that one not long since, from whom the father took a goat which he had sucked two or three days because he had but borrowed it of one of his neighbours, who could never be induced to suck any other; whereby he shortly died, and, as I verily think, of mere hunger. *Beasts, as well as we, do soon alter and easily bastardize their natural affection.*

I believe that, in that which *Herodotus* reporteth of a certain province of *Libya*, there often followeth great error and mistaking. He sayeth that men do indifferently use and, as it were, in common frequent women and that the child, as soon as he is able to go,[60] coming to any solemn meetings and great assemblies, led by a natural instinct, findeth out his own father; where being turned loose in the midst of the multitude, look what man the child doth first address his steps unto and then go to him, the same is ever afterward reputed to be his right father.

Now if we shall duly consider this simple occasion of loving our children—because we have begotten them, for which we call them our other selves—it seems there is another production coming from us and which is of no less recommendation and consequence. For what we engender by the mind, the fruits of our courage, sufficiency, or spirit, are brought forth by a far more noble part than the corporal and more our own. We are both father and mother together in this generation. Such fruits cost us much dearer and bring us more honour, and chiefly if they have any good or rare thing in them. For the value of our other children is much more theirs than ours. The share we have in them is but little, but of these all the beauty, all the grace, and all the worth is ours. And therefore do they represent and resemble us much more lively than others. Plato addeth, moreover, that these are immortal issues, and immortalize their fathers, yea, and deify them, as *Licurgus*, *Solon*, and *Minos*.

All histories being full of examples of this mutual friendship of fathers toward their children, I have not thought it amiss to set down some choice ones of this kind.[61]

Heliodorus, that good Bishop of *Tricea*, loved rather to lose the dignity, profit, and devotion of so venerable a prelateship than to forgo his daughter, a young woman to this day commended for her beauty but haply somewhat more curiously and wantonly pranked up than beseemed the daughter of a churchman and a bishop, and of over-amorous behaviour.[62]

There was one *Labienus* in *Rome* a man of great worth and authority, and amongst other commendable qualities, most excellent in all manner of learning; who, as I think, was the son of that great *Labienus*, chief of all the captains that followed and were under *Cæsar* in the wars against the Gauls, and who afterward, taking great *Pompey*'s part, behaved himself so valiantly and so constantly that he never forsook him until *Cæsar* defeated him in *Spain*. This *Labienus* of whom I speak had many that envied his virtues, but above all, as it is likely, courtiers and such as in his time were favored of the emperors who hated his frankness, his fatherly humors, and distaste he bore still against tyranny, wherewith it may be supposed he had stuffed his books and compositions. His adversaries vehemently pursued him before the magistrate of *Rome* and prevailed so far that many of his works which he had published were condemned to be burned. He was the first on whom this new example of punishment was put in practice, which after continued long in Rome and executed on diverse others, to punish learning, studies, and writings with death and consuming fire. There were neither means enough or matter sufficient of cruelty, unless we had intermingled among them things which nature hath exempted from all sense and sufferance, as reputation and the inventions of our mind, and except we communicated corporal mischiefs unto disciplines and monuments of the muses.

Which loss *Labienus* could not endure nor brook to survive those his dear and highly-esteemed issues;[63] and therefore caused himself to be carried and shut up alive within his ancestors' monument where, with a dreadless resolution, he at once provided both to kill himself and be buried together.[64] It is hard to show any more vehement fatherly affection than that. *Cassius Severus,* a most eloquent man and his familiar friend, seeing his books burnt, exclaimed that by the same sentence he should therewithal be condemned to be burned alive, for he still bare[65] and kept in mind what they contained in them.

A like accident happened to *Geruntius Cordus*, who was accused to have commended *Brutus* and *Cassius* in his books. That base, senile, and corrupted Senate, and worthy of a far worse master than *Tiberius*, adjudged his writings to be consumed by fire; and he was pleased to accompany them in their death, for he pined away by abstaining from all manner of meat.

That notable man *Lucan*, being adjudged by that lewd varlet *Nero* to death at the latter end of his life, when all his blood was well-nigh spent from out the veins of his arm, which by his physician he had caused to be opened to hasten his death and that a chilling cold began to seize the uttermost parts of his limbs and approach his vital spirits, the last thing he had in memory was some of his own verses, written in his book of the *Pharsalian* wars, which with a distinct voice he repeated and so yielded up the ghost, having those last words in his mouth. What was that but a kind, tender, and fatherly farewell which he took of his children, representing the last adieus and parting embracements, which at our death we give unto our dearest issues? And an effect of that natural inclination, which in that last extremity puts us in mind of those things which in our life we have held dearest and most precious?

Shall we imagine that *Epicurus* who (as himself said), dying tormented with the extreme pain of the colic, had all his comfort in the beauty of the doctrine which he left behind him in the world, would have received as much contentment of a number of well-born and better-bred children (if he had had any) as he did of the production of his rich compositions? And if it had been in his choice to leave behind him either a counterfeit, deformed, or ill-born child or a foolish, trivial, and idle book, not only he but all men in the world besides of like learning and sufficiency would much rather have chosen to incur the former than the latter mischief. It might peradventure be deemed impiety in Saint *Augustine* (for example-sake) if on the one part one should propose unto him to bury all his books, whence our religion receiveth so much good, or to inter his children (if in case he had any) that he would not rather choose to bury his children or the issue of his loins than the fruits of his mind.

And I wot not well whether myself should not much rather desire to beget and produce a perfectly well-shaped and excellently-qualitied infant by the acquaintance of the muses than by the acquaintance of my wife.

Whatsoever I give to this,[66] let the world allow of it as it please, I give it as purely and irrevocably as any man can give it to his corporal children. That little good which I have done him is no longer in my disposition. He may know many things that myself know no longer and hold of me what I could not hold myself and which (if need should require) I must borrow of him as of a stranger. If I be wiser than he, he is richer than I.

There are few men given unto poesy that would not esteem it for a greater honour to be the fathers of *Virgil's Æneidos* than of the goodliest boy in *Rome* and that would not rather endure the loss of the one than the perishing of the other. For, according to *Aristotle, Of all workmen, the Poet is principally the most amorous of his productions and conceited of his labours.*

It is not easy to be believed that *Epaminondas*, who wanted to leave some daughters behind him which unto all posterity should one day highly honour their father (they were the two famous victories which he had gained of the Lacedemonians), would ever have given his free consent to change them with the best-born, most gorgeous, and goodliest damsels of all *Greece*, or that *Alexander* and *Cæsar* did ever wish to be deprived of the greatness of their glorious deeds of war for the commodity to have children and heirs of their own bodies, how absolutely-perfect and well accomplished so ever they might be.

Nay, I make a great question whether *Phidias* or any other excellent statuary[67] would as highly esteem and dearly love the preservation and successful continuance of his natural children as he would an exquisite and matchless-wrought image that with long study and diligent care he had perfected according unto art. And as concerning those vicious and furious passions which sometimes have inflamed some fathers to the love of their daughters or mothers towards their sons, the very same and more partially-earnest is also found in this other kind of child-bearing and alliance. Witness that which is reported of *Pygmalion* who, having curiously framed a goodly statue of a most singularly-beauteous woman, was so strange-fondly and passionately surprised with the lustful love of his own workmanship that the gods through his raging importunity were fain in favour of him to give it life.

> *Tentatum mollescit ebur, positoque rigore*
> *Subsidit digitis.*
> As he assayed it, th' ivory softened much,
> And (hardness left) did yield to fingers' touch.[68]

An Apology of Raymond Sebond
(selections)

Is it possible to imagine anything so ridiculous as this miserable and wretched creature, which is not so much as master of himself, exposed and subject to offences of all things, and yet dareth call
himself master and emperour of this universe?

———

Presumption is our natural and original infirmity. *Of all creatures,
man is the most miserable and frail, and therewithal the proudest and
disdainfulest.* Who perceiveth and seeth himself placed here amidst
the filth and mire of the world, fast tied and nailed to the worst,
most senseless, and drooping part of the world, in the vilest corner
of the house, and farthest from heavens'-cope,[1] with those creatures
that are the worst of the three conditions.[2] And yet dareth imagi-
narily place himself above the circle of the moon and reduce heaven
under his feet. It is through the vanity of the same imagination that
he dare equal himself to God, that he ascribeth divine conditions
unto himself, that he selecteth and separateth himself from out the
rank of other creatures. To which his fellow-brethren and compeers,
he cuts out and shareth their parts and allotteth them what portions
of means or forces he thinks good. How knoweth he by the virtue of
his understanding the inward and secret motions of beasts? By what
comparison from them to us doth he conclude the brutishness he
ascribeth unto them?

When I am playing with my cat, who knows whether she have
more sport in dallying with me than I have in gaming with her? We

entertain one another with mutual apish tricks. If I have my hour to begin or to refuse, so hath she hers. *Plato* in setting forth the golden age under *Saturn*, amongst the chief advantages that man had then, reporteth the communication he had with beasts, of whom inquiring and taking instruction, he knew the true qualities and differences of every one of them; by and from whom, he got an absolute understanding and perfect wisdom, whereby he led a happier life than we can do. Can we have a better proof to judge of man's impudence touching beasts? This notable author[3] was of opinion that in the greatest part of the corporal form which nature hath bestowed on them she hath only respected the use of the prognostications which in his days were thereby gathered.

The defect which hindreth the communication between them and us, why may it not as well be in us as in them? It is a matter of divination to guess in whom the fault is that we understand not one another. For we understand them no more than they us. By the same reason, may they as well esteem us beasts as we them. It is no great marvel if we understand them not: no more do we the Cornish, the Welsh, or Irish.[4] Yet have some boasted that they understood them, as *Apollonius Thyaneus, Melampus, Tiresias, Thales,* and others. And if it be (as cosmographers report) that there are nations who receive and admit a dog to be their king, it must necessarily follow that they give a certain interpretation to his voice and moving. We must note the parity that is between us. We have some mean understanding of their senses; so have beasts of ours, about the same measure. They flatter and fawn upon us, they threat and entreat us, so do we them.

Touching other matters, we manifestly perceive that there is a full and perfect communication amongst them and that not only those of one same kind understand one another, but even such as are of different kinds.

> *Et mutæ pecudes, et denique secla ferarum*
> *Dissimiles fuerunt voces variasque cluere,*
> *Cum metus aut dolor est, aut cum iam gaudia gliscunt.*
> Whole herds (though dumb) of beasts, both wild and tame,

Use diverse voices, different sounds to frame,
As joy, or grief, or fear,
Upspringing passions bear.[5]

By one kind of barking of a dog, the horse knoweth he is angry; by
another voice of his, he is nothing dismayed. Even in beasts that
have no voice at all, by the reciprocal kindness which we see in them,
we easily infer there is some other mean of intercommunication:
their gestures treat,[6] and their motions discourse.

Non alia longe ratione atque ipsa videtur
Protrahere ad gestum, pueros infantia linguæ.
No otherwise, then, for they cannot speak,
Children are drawn by signs their minds to break.[7]

And why not, as well as our dumb-men dispute, argue, and tell histories by signs? I have seen some so readie, and so excellent in it, that
(in good sooth) they wanted nothing to have their meaning perfectly understood. Do we not daily see lovers with the looks and rolling of their eyes plainly show when they are angry or pleased, and
how they entreat and thank one another, assign meetings, and express any passion?

E'l silentio ancor suole
Haver prieghi e parole.
Silence also hath a way,
Words and prayers to convey.[8]

What do we with our hands? Do we not sue and entreat, promise
and perform, call men unto us and discharge them, bid them farewell and be gone, threaten, pray, beseech, deny, refuse, demand, admire, number, confess, repent, fear, be ashamed, doubt, instruct,
command, incite, encourage, swear, witness, accuse, condemn, ab-
solve, injure, despise, defy, despite,[9] flatter, applaud, bless, humble,
mock, reconcile, recommend, exalt, show-gladness, rejoice, com-

plain, wail, sorrow, discomfort, despair, cry-out, forbid, declare silence and astonishment, and what not? With so great variation and amplifying, as if they would contend with the tongue. And with our head, do we not invite and call to us, discharge and send away, avow, disavow, belie, welcome, honour, worship, disdain, demand, direct, rejoice, affirm, deny, complain, cherish, blandish, chide, yield, submit, brag, boast, threaten, exhort, warrant, assure, and inquire? What do we with our eyelids? And with our shoulders? To conclude, there is no motion nor jesture that doth not speak, and speaks in a language very easy and without any teaching to be understood. Nay, which is more, it is a language common and public to all; whereby it followeth (seeing the variety and several use it hath from others) that this must rather be deemed the proper and peculiar speech of human nature. I omit that which necessity, in time of need, doth particularly instruct and suddenly teach such as need it; and the alphabets upon fingers and grammars by gestures; and the sciences, which are only exercised and expressed by them; and the nations *Pliny* reporteth to have no other speech.

An ambassador of the city of *Abdera*, after he had talked a long time unto *Agis*, King of *Sparta*, said thus unto him: "O King, what answer wilt thou that I bear back unto our citizens?" "Thus" (answered he) "that I have suffered thee to speak all thou wouldest and as long as thou pleasedst, without ever speaking one word." Is not this a kind of speaking silence and easy to be understood?

And as for other matters, what sufficiency is there in us that we must not acknowledge from the industry and labours of beasts? Can there be a more formal and better ordered policy, divided into so several charges and offices, more constantly entertained, and better maintained, than that of bees? Shall we imagine their so orderly disposing of their actions and managing of their vacations[10] have so proportioned and formal a conduct without discourse, reason, and forecast?

His quidam signis at que hæc exempla sequuti,
Esse apibus partem divinæ mentis, and haustus

Æthereos dixere.
Some by these signs, by these examples moved,
Said that in bees there is and may be proved
Some taste of heav'nly kind,
Part of celestial mind.[11]

The swallows which at the approach of spring-time we see to pry, to search, and ferret all the corners of our houses—is it without judgement they seek or without discretion they choose from out a thousand places that which is fittest for them to build their nests and lodge in? And in that pretty-cunning contexture and admirable framing of their houses would birds rather fit themselves with a round than a square figure, with an obtuse than a right angle, except they knew both the commodities and effects of them? Would they (suppose you) first take water and then clay, unless they guessed that the hardness of the one is softened by the moistness of the other? Would they floor their palace with moss or down, except they foresaw that the tender parts of their young ones shall thereby be more soft and easy? Would they shroud and shelter themselves from stormy weather and build their cabins toward the East, unless they knew the different conditions of winds and considered that some are more healthful and safe for them than some others? Why doth the spider spin her artificial web thick in one place and thin in another? And now useth one, and then another knot, except she had an imaginary kind of deliberation, forethought, and conclusion?

We perceive by the greater part of their works what excellency beasts have over us and how weak our art and short our cunning is, if we go about to imitate them. We see notwithstanding, even in our grossest works, what faculties we employ in them and how our mind employeth the uttermost of her skill and forces in them. Why should we not think as much of them? Wherefore do we attribute the works which excel whatever we can perform, either by nature or by art, into a kind of unknown, natural, and servile inclination? Wherein unawares, we give them a great advantage over us to infer that nature, led by a certain loving kindness, leadeth and accompanieth them (as it were by the hand) unto all the actions and commodities of their life. And that she forsaketh and leaveth us to the hazard of fortune, and by art to quest and find out those things that are behooveful and necessary for our preservation. And therewithal denieth us the means to attain by any institution and contention of spirit to the natural sufficiency of brute beasts. So that their brutish stupidity doth in all commodities exceed whatsoever our divine intelligence can effect.

Truly, when I consider man all naked (yea, be it in that sex which seemeth to have and challenge the greatest share of eye-pleasing beauty[12]) and view his defects, his natural subjection, and manifold imperfections, I find we have had much more reason to hide and cover our nakedness than any creature else. We may be excused for borrowing those which nature had therein favored more than us with their beauties, to adorn us and under their spoils of wool, of hair, of feathers, and of silk to shroud us.

That which is told of those that inhabit *Brazil*, who die only through age, which some impute to the clearness and calmness of their air, I rather ascribe to the calmness and clearness of their minds, void and free from all passions, cares, toiling, and unpleasant labours, as a people that pass their life in a wonderful kind of simplicity and ignorance, without letters, or laws, and without kings or any religion.

The participation which we have of the knowledge of truth, whatsoever she is, it is not by our own strength we have gotten it. God hath sufficiently taught it us, in that he hath made choice of the simple, common, and ignorant to teach us his wonderful secrets. Our faith hath not been purchased by us: it is a gift proceeding from the liberality of others. It is not by our discourse or understanding that we have received our religion; it is by a foreign authority and commandment. The weakness of our judgment helps us more than our strength to compass the same, and our blindness more than our clear-sighted eyes. It is more by the means of our ignorance than of our skill that we are wise in heavenly knowledge. It is no marvel if our natural and terrestrial means cannot conceive the supernatural or apprehend the celestial knowledge. Let us add nothing of our own unto it but obedience and subjection. For, (as it is written), *I will confound the wisdom of the wise and destroy the understanding of the prudent. Where is the wise? Where is the scribe? Where is the disputer of this world?*[13] Hath not God made the wisdom of this world foolishness? For seeing the world by wisdom knew not God in the wisdom of God, it hath pleased him by the vanity of preaching to save them that believe.

Yet must I see at last whether it be in man's power to find what he seeks for and if this long search, wherein he hath continued so many ages, hath enriched him with any new strength or solid truth.

I am persuaded, if he speak in conscience, he will confess that all the benefit he hath gotten by so tedious a pursuit hath been that he hath learned to know his own weakness. That ignorance which in us was natural we have with long study confirmed and averred. It hath happened unto those that are truly learned as it happeneth unto ears of corn which, as long as they are empty, grow and raise their head aloft, upright, and stout. But if they once become full and big with ripe corn, they begin to humble and droop downward. So men having tried and sounded all—and in all this chaos and huge heap of learning and provision of so infinite different things—and found nothing that is substantial, firm, and steady, but all vanity, have renounced their presumption and too late known their natural condition. It is that which *Velleius* upbraids *Cotta* and *Cicero* withal, that they have learned of *Philo* to have learned nothing.[14]

Pherecydes, one of the seven wise,[15] writing to *Thales* even as he was yielding up the Ghost, "I have" (saith he) "appointed my friends, as soon as I shall be laid in my grave, to bring thee all my writings. If they please thee and the other Sages, publish them; if not, conceal them. They contain no certainty nor do they any whit satisfy me. My profession is not to know the truth, nor to attain it. I rather open than discover things."

The wisest that ever was, being demanded what he knew, answered he knew that he knew nothing.[16] He verified what some say, that the greatest part of what we know is the least part of what we know not; that is, that that which we think to know is but a parcel, yea and a small particle of our ignorance. We know things in a dream (sayeth *Plato*), and we are ignorant of them in truth. *Omnes pene veteres nihil cognosci, nihil percipi, nihil sciri posse dixerunt: angustos sensus, imbecilles animos, brevia curricula vitæ: Almost all the ancients affirmed nothing may be known, nothing perceived, nothing understood; that our senses are narrow, our minds are weak, and the race of our life is short.*[17]

Cicero himself, who ought[18] all he had unto learning, *Valerius* sayeth that in his age he began to disesteem letters. And whilst he practised them, it was without bond to any special body, following what seemed probable unto him, now in the one, and now in the other sect, ever holding himself under the Academy's doubtfulness. *Dicendum est, sed ita ut nihil affirmem: quæram omnia, dubitans plurumque, et mihi diffidens. Speak I must, but so as I avouch nothing; question all things, for the most part in doubt and distrust of myself.*[19]

I should have too much ado[20] if I would consider man after his own fashion and in gross; which I might do by his own rule, who is wont to judge of truth not by the weight or value of voices but by the number. But leave we the common people,

> *Qui vigilans stertit,*
> Who snore while they are awake.
> *Mortua cui vita est, prope iam vivo atque videnti:*
> Whose life is dead while yet they see,
> And in a manner living be,[21]

who feeleth not himself, who judgeth not himself, who leaves the greatest part of his natural parts idle.

I will take man even in his highest estate. Let us consider him in this small number of excellent and choice men who, having naturally been endowed with a peculiar and exquisite wit, have also fostered and sharpened the same with care, with study, and with art, and have brought and strained unto the highest pitch of wisdom it may possibly reach unto. They have fitted their soul unto all senses and squared the same to all biases[22]; they have strengthened and under-propped it with all foreign helps that might any way fit or stead[23] her and have enriched and adorned her with whatsoever they have been able to borrow, either within or without the world for her avail. It is in them that the extreme height of human nature doth lodge. They have reformed the world with policies and laws. They have instructed the same with arts and sciences, as also by example of their wonderful manners and life. I will but make account of such people, of their witness, and of their experience. Let us see how far they have gone and what holdfast[24] they have held by. The maladies and defects which we shall find in that college[25] the world may boldly allow them to be his.[26]

Whosoever seeks for any thing, cometh at last to this conclusion and sayeth that either he hath found it, or that it cannot be found, or that he is still in pursuit after it. All philosophy is divided into these three kinds. Her purpose is to seek out the truth, the knowledge, and the certainty.

The Peripatetics, the Epicurians, the Stoics, and others have thought they had found it. These have established the sciences[27] that we have, and as of certain notions have treated of them.

Clitomachus, Carneades, and the *Academics* have despaired the finding of it and judged that truth could not be conceived by our means. The end of these is weakness and ignorance. The former had more followers and the worthiest sectaries.

Pyrrho[28]and other *Sceptics,* or *Epechists,*[29] whose doctrine or manner of teaching many ancient learned men have thought to have been drawn from *Homer,* from the Seven Wise Men, from *Archilo-*

chus and *Euripides*—to whom they join *Zeno*, *Democritus* and *Xenophanes*—say that they are still seeking after truth. These judge that those are infinitely deceived who imagine they have found it and that the second degree is over-boldly vain in affirming that man's power is altogether unable to attain unto it. For, to establish the measure of our strength, to know and distinguish of the difficulty of things, is a great, a notable, and extreme science, which they doubt whether man be capable thereof or no.

> *Nil sciri quisquis putat, id quoque nescit,*
> *An sciri possit, quo se nil scire fatetur.*
> Who thinks nothing is known, knows not that, whereby he,
> Grants he knows nothing if it known may be.[30]

That ignorance which is known, judged, and condemned is not an absolute ignorance. For, to be so, she must altogether be ignorant of herself. So that the profession of the Pyrrhonians is ever to waver, to doubt, and to inquire, never to be assured of anything, nor to take any warrant of himself. Of the three actions or faculties of the soul, that is to say, the imaginative, the concupiscible,[31] and the consenting, they allow and conceive the two former; the last they hold and defend to be ambiguous, without inclination or approbation either of one or other side, be it never so light.

Zeno in gesture painted forth his imagination upon this division of the soul's faculties: the open and out-stretched hand was appearance; the hand half-shut and fingers somewhat bending, consent; the fist closed, comprehension; if the fist of the left hand were closely clinched together, it signified science.

Now this situation of their judgement, straight and inflexible, receiving all objects with application or consent, leads them unto their Ataraxie [*ataraxia*], which is the condition of a quiet and settled life, exempted from the agitations which we receive by the impression of the opinion and knowledge we imagine to have of things. Whence proceed fear, avarice, envy, immoderate desires, ambition, pride, superstition, love of novelties, rebellion, disobedience, obstinacy, and the greatest number of corporal evils. Yea, by that means they are exempted from the jealousy of their own discipline,[32] for they contend but faintly. They fear not revenge nor contradiction in their disputations. When they say that heavy things descend downward, they would be loath to be believed but desire to be contradicted, thereby to engender doubt and suspense of judgement, which is their end and drift. They put forth their propositions but to[33] contend with those they imagine we hold in our conceipt.[34]

If you take theirs, then will they undertake to maintain the contrary: all is one to them, nor will they give a penny to choose. If you propose that snow is black, they will argue on the other side that it is white. If you say it is neither one nor other, they will maintain it to be both. If by a certain judgement you say that you cannot tell, they will maintain that you can tell. Nay, if by an affirmative axiom, you swear that you stand in some doubt, they will dispute that you doubt not of it or that you cannot judge or maintain that you are in doubt. And by this extremity of doubt which staggereth itself they separate and divide themselves from many opinions, yea from those which diverse ways have maintained both the doubt and the ignorance.

Why shall it not be granted then (say they) as to Dogmatists, or doctrine-teachers, for one to say green and another yellow, so for them to doubt? *Is there anything can be proposed unto you, either to allow or refuse, which may not lawfully be considered as ambiguous and doubtful?* And whereas others be carried either by the custom of their country or by the institution of their parents or by chance—as by a tempest, without choice or judgement, yea sometimes before the age of discretion, to such and such another opinion, to the Stoic or Epicurean sect, to which they find themselves more engaged, subjected or fast-tied, as to a prize they cannot let go: *Ad quamcumque disciplinam, velut tempestate, delati, ad eam tanquam ad saxum, adhærescunt. Being carried as it were by a tempest, to any kind of doctrine, they stick close to it, as it were to a rock.*[35]

Why shall not these likewise be permitted to maintain their liberty and consider of things without duty or compulsion? *Hoc liberiores, et solutiores, quod integra illis est iudicandi potestas: They are so much the freer and at liberty, for that their power of judgement is kept entire.*[36] Is it not some advantage for one to find himself disengaged from necessity which brideleth others? Is it not better to remain in suspense than to entangle himself in so many errors that human fantasy hath brought forth? Is it not better for a man to suspend his own persuasion than to meddle with these seditious and quarrelous[37] divisions?

What shall I choose? Marry, what you list, so you choose. A very foolish answer, to which it seemeth nevertheless that all dogmatism arriveth, by which it is not lawful for you to be ignorant of that we know not.

Take the best and strongest side, it shall never be so sure, but you shall have occasion to defend the same, to close and combat a hundred and a hundred[38] sides? Is it not better to keep out of this confusion? You are suffered to embrace, as your honour and life, *Aristotle's* opinion upon the eternity of the soul, and to belie and contradict whatsoever *Plato* saith concerning that; and shall they be interdicted[39] to doubt of it?

If it be lawful for *Panæcius* to maintain his judgement about auspices, dreams, oracles, and prophecies, whereof the Stoics make no doubt at all, wherefore shall not a wise man dare that in all things which this man dareth in such as he hath learned of his masters? Confirmed and established by the general consent of the school whereof he is a sectary and a professor? If it be a child that judgeth, he wots[40] not what it is; if a learned man, he is forestalled.

They [the Pyrrhonists] have reserved a great advantage for themselves in the combat, having discharged themselves of the care how to shroud themselves. They care not to be beaten, so they may strike again. And all is fish that comes to net with them. If they overcome, your proposition halteth; if you, theirs is lame. If they prove that nothing is known, it is very well; if they cannot prove it, it is good alike: *Ut quum in eadem re paria contrariis in partibus momenti inveniuntur, facilius ab utraque parte assertio sustiniatur. So as when the same matter the like weight and moment is found on diverse parts, we may the more easily withhold avouching on both parts.*[41]

And they suppose to find out more easily why a thing is false than true; and that which is not than that which is; and what they believe not than what they believe.

Their manner of speech is: *I confirm nothing*; it is no more so than thus, or neither; I conceive it not; appearances are everywhere alike; the law of speaking *pro* or *contra* is all one. *Nothing seemeth true, that may not seem false.* Their sacramental word is ἐποχή which is as much to say as, I uphold and stir not. Behold the burdens[42] of their songs and other such like. Their effect is a pure, entire, and absolute surceasing and suspense of judgement. They use their reason to inquire and to debate, and not to stay and choose. Whosoever shall imagine a perpetual confession of ignorance and a judgement upright and without straggering[43] to what occasion soever may chance —that man conceives the true Pyrrhonism.

I expound this fantazie[44] as plain as I can because many deem it hard to be conceived. And the authors themselves represent it somewhat obscurely and diversely.

Touching the actions of life, in that they are after the common sort. They are lent and applied to natural inclinations, to the impulsion and constraint of passions, to the constitutions of laws and customs, and to the tradition of arts. *Non enim nos Deus ista scire, sed tantummodo uti voluit. For God would not have us know these things but only use them.*[45] By such means they suffer their common actions to be directed, without any conceit or judgement, which is the reason that I cannot well sort unto this discourse what is said of *Pyrrho.* They feign him to be stupid and unmovable, leading a kind of wild and unsociable life, not shunning to be hit with carts, presenting himself unto downfalls,[46] refusing to conform himself to the laws. It is an endearing of his discipline.[47] He would not make himself a stone or a block but a living, discoursing, and reasoning man, enjoying all pleasures and natural commodities, busying himself with, and using all, his corporal and spiritual parts, in rule and right. The fantastical and imaginary and false privileges which man hath usurped unto himself, to sway, to appoint, and to establish, he hath absolutely renounced and quit them.

Yet is there no sect but is enforced to allow her wise Secter in chief[48] to follow diverse things nor comprized[49] nor perceived nor allowed, if he will live. And if he take shipping,[50] he follows his purpose, not knowing whether it shall be profitable or no, and yields to this—that the ship is good, the pilot is skillful, and that the season is fit; circumstances only probable. After which he is bound to go and suffer himself to be removed by appearances, always provided they have no express contrariety in them. He hath a body, he hath a soul, his senses urge him forward, his mind moveth him. Although he find not this proper and singular mark of judging in himself and that he perceive he should not engage his consent, seeing some falsehood may be like unto this truth, he ceaseth not to conduct the offices of his life fully and commodiously.

How many arts are there which profess to consist more in conjecture than in the science? That distinguish not between truth and falsehood but only follow seeming? There is both true and false (say they), and there are means in us to seek it out, but not to stay it when we touch it. It is better for us to suffer the order of the world to manage us without further inquisition. A mind warranted from prejudice hath a marvellous preferment to tranquility.[51] *Men that censure and control their judges do never duly submit themselves unto them.* How much more docile and tractable are simple and uncurious minds found, both towards the laws of religion and politic decrees, than these over-vigilant and nice-wits,[52] teachers of divine and human causes?

There is nothing in man's invention wherein is so much likelihood, possibility, and profit.[53] This [Pyrrhonism] representeth man bare and naked, acknowledging his natural weakness, apt to receive from above some strange power, disfurnished of all human knowledge, and so much the more fit to harbour divine understanding, disannulling his judgement that so he may give more place unto faith. Neither misbelieving nor establishing any doctrine or opinion repugnant unto common laws and observances, humble, obedient, disciplinable,[54] and studious; a sworn enemy to heresy, and by consequence exempting himself from all vain and irreligious opinions

invented and brought up by false sects. It is a white sheet[55] prepared
to take from the finger of God, what form so ever it shall please him
to imprint therein. *The more we address and commit ourselves to God
and reject ourselves, the better it is for us.* Accept (sayeth *Ecclesiastes*)
in good part things both in show and taste, as from day to day they
are presented unto thee; the rest is beyond thy knowledge. *Dominus
novit cogitationes hominum, quoniam vanæ sunt. The Lord knows the
thoughts of men, that they are vain.*[56]

See how of three general sects of philosophy, two make express
profession of doubt and ignorance, and in the third, which is the
dogmatists, it is easy to be discerned that the greatest number have
taken the face of assurance only because they could set a better
countenance on the matter. They have not so much gone about to
establish any certainty in us as to show how far they had waded in
seeking out the truth. *Quam docti fingunt magis qam norunt: which
the learned do rather conceit[57] than know.*[58]

Thy reason hath in no one other thing more likelihood and foundation than in that which persuadeth thee a plurality of worlds.[59]

> *Terramque et solem, lunam, mare, cætera quæ sunt,*
> *Non esse unica, sed numero magis innumerali.*
> The earth, the sun, the moon, the sea and all
> In number numberless, not one they call.[60]

The famousest wits of former ages have believed it, yea, and some of
our modern, as forced thereunto by the appearance of human reason. For as much as whatsoever we see in this vast world's-frame,
there is no one thing alone, single, and one.

> ——*cum in summa res nulla sit una,*
> *unica quæ gignatur, et unica solaque crescat:*

Whereas in general sum, nothing is one,
To be bred only one, grow only one.[61]

And that all several kind are multiplied in some number. Whereby it seemeth unlikely that God hath framed this piece of work alone without a fellow and that the matter of this form hath wholly been spent in this only *Individuum*:

> *Quare etiam atqæ etiam tales fateare necesse est,*
> *Esse alios alibi congressus matiriaï,*
> *Qualis hic est avido complexu quem tenet Æther.*
> Wherefore you must confess, again again,
> Of matters such like meetings elsewhere reign.
> As this, these skies in greedy grip contain.[62]

Namely, if it[63] be a breathing creature, as its motions make it so likely that *Plato* assureth it, and diverse of ours either affirm it or dare not impugn it; no more than this old opinion that the Heaven, the stars, and other members of the world are creatures composed both of body and soul, mortal in respect of their composition but immortal by the creator's decree.

Now, if there be diverse worlds, as *Democritus, Epicurus,* and well-near all philosophy hath thought, what know we whether the principles and the rules of this one concern or touch likewise the others? Happily,[64] they have another semblance and another policy. *Epicurus* imagineth them either like or unlike. We see an infinite difference and variety in this world, only by the distance of places. There is neither corn, nor wine, no nor any of our beasts seen in that new corner of the world which our fathers have lately discovered. All things differ from ours. And in the old time, mark but in how many parts of the world they had never knowledge nor of *Bacchus* nor of *Ceres*.[65]

If any credit may be given unto *Pliny* or to *Herodotus*, there is in some places a kind of men that have very little or no resemblance at all with ours. And there be mongrel and ambiguous shapes between a human and brutish nature. Some countries there are where men are born headless, with eyes and mouths in their breasts;[66] where all are Hermaphrodites; where they creep on all four; where they have but one eye in their forehead, and heads more like unto a dog than ours; where from the navel downward they are half fish and live in the water; where women are brought a bed at five years of age[67] and live but eight; where their heads and the skin of their brows are so hard that no iron can pierce them but will rather turn edge; where men never have beards. Other nations there are that never have use of fire; others whose sperm is of a black colour.

What shall we speak of them, who naturally change themselves into wolves, into colts, and then into men again? And if it be (as *Plutarch* sayeth) that in some part of the Indies, there are men without mouths and who live only by the smell of certain sweet odors, how many of our descriptions be then false? He is no more risible, nor perhaps capable of reason and society, the direction and cause of our inward frame should for the most part be to no purpose.[68]

Moreover, how many things are there in our knowledge that oppugn these goodly rules which we have allotted and prescribed unto nature? And we undertake to join GOD himself unto her. How many things do we name miraculous and against nature? Each man and every nation doth it according to the measure of his ignorance. How many hidden proprieties and quintessences[69] do we daily discover? For us to go according to nature is but to follow according to our understanding, as far as it can follow and as much as we can perceive in it. Whatsoever is beyond it is monstrous and disordered.

By this account all shall then be monstrous to the wisest and most sufficient; for even to such, human reason hath persuaded that she had neither ground nor footing, no not so much as to warrant snow to be white: And *Anaxagoras* said it was black. Whether there be anything or nothing; whether there be knowledge or ignorance; (which *Metrodorus Chius* denied that any man might say). Or whether we live, as *Euripides* seemeth to doubt and call in question, whether the life we live be a life or no, or whether that which we call death be a life.

I have ever thought this manner of speech in a Christian is full of indiscretion and irreverence: "God cannot die, God cannot gainsay himself, God cannot do this or that." I cannot allow a man should so bound God's heavenly power under the laws of our word.[70] And that appearance, which in these propositions offers itself unto us, ought to be represented more reverently and more religiously.

Our speech hath his infirmities and defects, as all things else have. *Most of the occasions of this worlds troubles are grammatical.* Our suits and processes proceed but from the canvassing and debating the interpretation of the laws, and most of our wars from the want of knowledge in state-counsellors that could not clearly distinguish and fully express the covenants and conditions of accords between Prince and Prince. How many weighty strifes and important quarrels hath the doubt of this one syllable, *hoc*, brought forth in the world?[71]

Examine the plainest sentence that Logic itself can present unto us. If you say, "It is fair weather," and in so saying, say true, it is fair weather then. Is not this a certain forme of speech? Yet will it deceive us. That it is so, let us follow the example: If you say, "I lie," and in that you should say true, you lie then.[72] The art, the reason, the force of the conclusion of this last are like unto the other; notwithstanding we are entangled.

I see the Pyrrhonian philosophers, who can by no manner of speech express their general conceit; for they had need of a new language. Ours[73] is altogether composed of affirmative propositions which are directly against them [the Pyrrhonists]. So that, when they say "I doubt," you have them fast by the sleeve to make them avow that at least you are assured and know that they doubt. So have they been compelled to save themselves by this comparison of physic,[74] without which their conceit[75] woud be inexplicable and intricate. When they pronounce "I know not, or doubt," they say that this proposition transports itself together with the rest, even as the rhubarb doth, which scoureth ill humours away and therewith is carried away himself. This conceit is more certainly conceived by an interrogation: What can I tell [*Que sçay-je?*]? As I bear it in an impresa[76] of a pair of balances.

Note how some prevail with this kind of unreverent and unhallowed speech. In the disputations that are nowadays in our religion, if you overmuch urge the adversaries, they will roundly tell you that it lieth not in the power of GOD to make his body, at once to be in paradise and on earth and in many other places together. And how that ancient scoffer[77] made profitable use of it. At least (sayeth he) it is no small comfort unto man to see that GOD cannot do all things: for he cannot kill himself if he would, which is the greatest benefit we have in our condition; he cannot make mortal men immortal, nor raise the dead to life again, nor make him that hath lived never to have lived, and him who hath had honors not to have had them, having no other right over what is past but of forgetfulness. And, that this society between God and man may also be combined with some pleasant examples, he cannot make twice ten to be but twenty.

See what he sayeth, and which a Christian ought to abhor that ever such and so profane words should pass his mouth. Whereas, on the contrary part, it seemeth that fond men endeavour to find out this foolish-boldness of speech that so they may turn and wind God almighty according to their measure.

——*cras vel atra*
Nube polum pater occupato,
Vel sole puro, non tamen irritum
Quodcumque retro est efficiet, neque
Diffinget effectumque reddet
Quod fugiens semel hora vexit.
Tomorrow let our father fill the sky,
With dark clouds, or with clear sun, he thereby
Shall not make void what once is overpast:
Nor shall he undo, or in new mold cast,
What time hath once caught, that flies hence so fast.[78]

When we say that the infinity of ages, as well past as to come, is but one instant with God, that his wisdom, goodness, and power are one self-same thing with his essence—our tongue speaks it, but our understanding can no wit apprehend it. Yet will our self-overweening sift his divinity through our searce.[79] Whence are engendered all the vanities and errors wherewith this world is so full-fraught, reducing and weighing with his uncertain balance a thing so far from his reach and so distant from his weight. *Mirum quo procedat improbitas cordis humani, parvulo aliquo invitata successu. It is a wonder, whether the perverse wickedness of man's heart will proceed if it be but called on with any little success.*[80]

How insolently do the Stoics charge *Epicurus* because he holds that to be perfectly good and absolutely happy belongs but only unto God, and that the wise man hath but a shadow and similitude thereof? How rashly have they joined God unto destiny (which, at my request, let none that beareth the surname of a Christian do at this day), and *Thales*, *Plato*, and *Pythagoras* have subjected him unto necessity.

This over-boldness, or rather bold-fierceness, to seek to discover God by and with our eyes hath been the cause that a notable man of our times[81] hath attributed a corporal form unto divinity and is the cause of that which daily happeneth unto us, which is, by a particular assignation, to impute all important events to God. Which, because they touch us, it seemeth they also touch him, and that he regardeth them with more care and attention than those that are but slight and ordinary unto us. *Magna dii curant, parva negligunt. The Gods take some care for great things, but none for little.* Note his example; he will enlighten you with his reason: *Nec in regnis quidem reges omnia minima currant. Nor do kings in their kingdoms much care for the least matters.*[82]

As if it were all one to that king, either to remove an empire or a leaf of a tree; and if his providence were otherwise exercised, inclining or regarding no more the success of a battle than the skip of a flea. The hand of his government affords itself to all things after a like tenure, fashion, and order; our interest addeth nothing unto it;

our motions and our measures concern him nothing and move him no whit. *Deus ita artifex magnus in magnis, ut minor non sit in parvis. God is so great a workman in great things, as he is no less in small things.*[83]

Our arrogance setteth ever before us this blasphemous equality. Because our occupations charge us, *Strato* hath presented the gods with all immunity of offices, as are their priests. He maketh nature to produce and preserve all things, and by her weights and motions to compact all parts of the world, discharging human nature from the fear of divine judgements.[84] *Quod beatum æternumque sit, id nec habere, negotii quicquam, nec exhibere alteri. That which is blessed and eternal, nor is troubled itself nor troubleth others.*[85] Nature willeth that in all things alike there be also like relation.[86] Then the infinite number of mortal men concludeth a like number of immortal. The infinite things that kill and destroy presuppose as many that preserve and profit. As the souls of the Gods, sans tongues, sans eyes, and sans ears,[87] have each one in themselves a feeling of that which the other feel, and judge of our thoughts; so men's souls, when they are free and severed from the body, either by sleep or any distraction, divine, prognosticate, and see things which, being conjoined to their bodies, they could not see.

Men (sayeth Saint *Paul*), when they professed themselves to be wise, they became fools, for they turned the glory of the incorruptible God to the similitude of the image of a corruptible man.[88]

Mark, I pray you, a little the juggling[89] of ancient deifications. After the great, solemn, and proud pomp of funerals, when the fire began to burn the top of the pyramid and to take hold of the bed or hearse wherein the dead corpse lay, even at that instant they let fly an eagle, which taking her flight aloft upward, signified that the soul went directly to paradise. We have yet a thousand medals and monuments, namely, of that honest woman *Faustina*, wherein that eagle is represented, carrying a cock-horse[90] up towards heaven those deified souls. It is pity we should so deceive our selves with our own foolish devices and apish inventions—

Quod finxere timent.
Of that they stand in fear,
Which they in fancy bear.[91]

—as children will be afeard of their fellow's visage which themselves
have besmeared and blacked. *Quasi quicquam infælicius sit homine,
cui sua figmenta dominantur. As though anything were more wretched
than man over whom his own imaginations bear sway and domineere.*[92]

To honour him whom we have made is far from honouring him
that hath made us. *Augustus* had as many temples as *Jupiter* and
served with as much religion and opinion of miracles. The *Thasians*,
in requital of the benefits they had received of *Agesilaus*, came to tell
him how they had canonized him. "Hath your nation" (said he), "the
power to make those whom it pleaseth gods? Then first (for example
sake) make one of yourselves, and when I shall have seen what good
he shall have thereby, I will then thank you for your offer."

Oh senseless man, who cannot possibly make a worm and yet will
make gods by dozens.

Listen to *Trismegistus*[93] when he praiseth our sufficiency: "For
man to find out divine nature, and to make it, hath surmounted the
admiration of all admirable things."[94]

Lo, here arguments out of philosophy's schools itself:

Noscere cui Divos et cæli numina soli,
Aut soli nescire datum.
Only to whom heaven's deities to know,
Only to whom is giv'n them not to know.[95]

If God be, he is a living creature; if he be a living creature, he hath
sense;[96] and if he have sense, he is subject to corruption. If he be
without a body, he is without a soul and consequently without action; and if he have a body, he is corruptible. Is not this brave?[97]

We are incapable to have made the world, then is there some
more excellent nature that hath set her helping hand unto it. Were it

not a sottish[98] arrogance that we should think ourselves to be the perfectest thing of this universe? Then sure there is some better thing. And that is God. When you see a rich and stately mansion-house, although you know not who is owner of it, yet will you not say that it was built for rats. And this more-than-human frame and divine composition which we see of heaven's palace, must we not deem it to be the mansion of some lord greater than ourselves? Is not the highest ever the most worthy? And we are seated in the lowest place.

Nothing that is without a soul and void of reason is able to bring forth a living soul capable of reason. The world doth bring us forth, then the world hath both soul and reason. Each part of us is less than ourselves. We are part of the world, then the world is stored with wisdom and with reason, and that more plenteously than we are.

It is a goodly thing to have a great government. Then the world's government belongeth to some blessed and happy nature. The stars annoy us not, then the stars are full of goodness. We have need of nourishment, then so have the gods and feed themselves with the vapours arising here below. Worldly goods are not goods unto God, then are not they goods unto us. To offend and to be offended are equal witnesses of imbecility, then it is folly to fear God. God is good by his own nature, man by his industry. Which is more? Divine wisdom and man's wisdom have no other distinction but that the first is eternal. Now lastingness is not an accession unto wisdom. Therefore are we fellows. We have life, reason, and liberty, we esteem goodness, charity, and justice; these qualities are then in him.

In conclusion, the building and destroying the conditions of divinity are forged by man according to the relation to himself. Oh, what a pattern and what a model! Let us raise and let us amplify human qualities as much as we please. Puff-up thyself, poor man—yea, swell and swell again.

There is nothing wherein the world differeth so much as in customs and laws. Some things are here accounted abominable which in another place are esteemed commendable: as in *Lacedemonia*,[99] the slight and subtlety in stealing. Marriages in proximity of blood are amongst us forbidden as capital; elsewhere they are allowed and esteemed:

> ——*gentes esse feruntur,*
> *In quibus et nato genitrix, et nata parenti*
> *Iungitur, et pietas geminato crescit amore.*
> There are some people, where the mother weddeth
> Her son, the daughter her own father beddeth;
> And so by doubling love, their kindness spreddeth.[100]

The murdering of children and of parents; the communication with women;[101] traffic of robbing and stealing; free licence to all manner of sensuality: to conclude, there is nothing so extreme and horrible but is found to be received and allowed by the custom of some nation.

It is credible that there be natural laws, as may be seen in other creatures. But in us they are lost; this goodly human reason engrafting itself among all men, to sway and command, confounding and topsy-turvying the visage of all things, according to her inconstant vanity and vain inconstancy. *Nihil itaque amplius nostrum est, quod nostrum dico, artis est. Therefore nothing more is ours: all that I call ours belongs to art.*[102]

Subjects have diverse lustres, and several considerations, whence the diversity of opinion is chiefly engendered. One nation vieweth a subject with one visage, and thereon it stays; another with another. Nothing can be imagined so horrible as for one to eat and devour his own father. Those people, which anciently kept this custom, hold it nevertheless for a testimony of piety and good affection, seeking by that mean to give their fathers the worthiest and most honourable sepulchre, harboring their fathers' bodies and relics in themselves and in their marrow, in some sort reviving and regenerating them by the transmutation made in their quick[103] flesh by digestion and nourishment. It is easy to be considered what abomination and cruelty it had been in men accustomed and trained in this inhuman superstition to cast the carcasses of their parents into the corruption of the earth, as food for beasts and worms.

———

I have heard it reported of a judge, who when he met with any sharp conflict betweene *Bartolus* and *Baldus*[104] or with any case admitting contrariety, was wont to write in the margin of his book, *A question for a friend*—which is to say, that the truth was so entangled and disputable that in such a case he might favour which party he should think good. There was no want but of spirit and sufficiency if he set not everywhere through his books, *A question for a friend*.

The advocates and judges of our time find in all cases biases too-too-many to fit them where they think good. To so infinite a science, depending on the authority of so many opinions, and of so arbitrary a subject, it cannot be but that an exceeding confusion of judgements must arise. There are very few processes so clear but the lawyers' advises[105] upon them will be found to differ. What one company hath judged, another will adjudge the contrary, and the very same will another time change opinion. Whereof we see ordinary examples by this licence, which wonderfully blemisheth the authority and luster of our law, never to stay upon one sentence but to run from one to another judge to decide one same case.

———

This discourse hath drawn me to *the consideration of the senses, wherein consisteth the greatest foundation and trial of our ignorance.* Whatsoever is known is without peradventure[106] known by the faculty of the knower. For, since the judgement cometh from the operation of him that judgeth, reason requireth that he perform and act this operation by his means and will and not by others' compulsion. As it would follow if we knew things by the force and according to the law of their essence. Now all knowledge is addressed into us by the senses; they are our masters:

——via qua munita fidei
Proxima fert humanum in pectus, templaque mentis.
Whereby a way for credit leads well-lined
Into man's breast and temple of his mind.[107]

Science[108] begins by them and in them is resolved. After all, we should know no more than a stone, unless we know that there is sound, smell, light, savor, measure, weight, softness, hardness, sharpness, colour, smoothness, breadth, and depth. Behold here the platform of all the frame and principles of the building of all our knowledge. And according to some, science is nothing else but what is known by the senses. Whosoever can force me to contradict my senses hath me fast by the throat and cannot make me recoil one foot backward. The senses are the beginning and end of human knowledge.

Invenies primis ab sensibus esse creatam
Notitiam veri, neque sensus posse refelli.
Quid maiore fide porro, quam sensus haberi
Debet?
You shall find knowledge of the truth at first was bred
From our first senses, nor can senses be misled.
What, then our senses should
With us more credit hold?[109]

Attribute as little as may be unto them, yet must this ever be granted them, that all our instruction is addressed by their meanes and intermission. *Cicero* sayeth that *Chrysippus*, having essayed to abate the power of his senses and of their virtue, presented contrary arguments unto himself, and so vehement oppositions, that he could not satisfy himself. Whereupon *Carneades* (who defended the contrary part) boasted that he used the very same weapons and words of *Chrysippus* to combat against him and therefore cried out upon him, *Oh miserable man! Thine own strength hath failed thee.*

There is no greater absurdity in our judgement than to maintain

that fire heateth not, that light shineth not, that in iron there is neither weight nor firmness, which are notices our senses bring unto us.
Nor belief or science in man that may be compared unto that in certainty.

The first consideration I have upon the senses subject[110] is that I
make a question whether man be provided of all natural senses or
no. I see diverse creatures that live an entire and perfect life, some
without sight and some without hearing; who knoweth whether we
also want[111] either one, two, three, or many senses more? For if we
want any one, our discourse cannot discover the want or defect
thereof. It is the senses' privilege to be the extreme bounds of our
perceiving. There is nothing beyond them that may stead us to discover them. No one sense can discover another.

> *An poterunt oculos aures reprehendere, an aures*
> *Tactus, an hunc porro tactum sapor arguet oris,*
> *An confutabunt nares, oculive revincent?*
> Can ears the eyes, or can touch reprehend
> The ears, or shall mouth's taste that touch amend?
> Shall our nose it confute,
> Or eyes gainst it dispute?[112]

They all make the extremest line of our faculty.

> ——*seorsum cuique potestas*
> *Divisa est, sua vis cuique est.*
> To each distinctly, might
> Is shared, each hath its right.[113]

It is impossible to make a man naturally blind[114] to conceive that
he seeth not; impossible to make him desire to see and sorrow his
defect. Therefore ought we not to take assurance that our mind is
contented and satisfied with those we have, seeing it hath not wherewith to feel her own malady and perceive her imperfection, if it be in
any. It is impossible to tell that blind man anything, either by dis-

course, argument, or similitude, that lodgeth any apprehension of light, colour, or sight in his imagination. There is nothing more backward that may push the senses to any evidence. The blind-born, which we perceive desire to see, it is not to understand what they require; they have learned of us that something they want and something they desire that is in us with the effects and consequences thereof, which they call good. Yet wot not they what it is, nor apprehend they it near or far.

I have seen a gentleman of a good house, born blind, at least blind in such an age that he knows not what sight is. He understandeth so little what he wanteth that, as we do, he useth words fitting sight and applieth them after a manner only proper and peculiar to himself. A child being brought before him to whom he was godfather, taking him in his arms, he said, "Good Lord, what a fine child this is! It is a goodly thing to see him. What a cheerful countenance he hath, how prettily he looketh." He will say as one of us, "This hall hath a fair prospect;[115] it is very fair weather; the sun shines clear." Nay, which is more, because hunting, hawking, tennis-play, and shooting at buts[116] are our common sports and exercises (for so he hath heard), his mind will be so affected unto them, and he will so busy himself about them, that he will think to have as great an interest in them as any of us and show himself as earnestly passionate, both in liking and disliking them, as any else. Yet doth he conceive and receive them but by hearing. If he be in a fair champian ground[117] where he may ride, they will tell him yonder is a hare started or the hare is killed; he is as busily earnest of his game as he heareth others to be that have perfect sight. Give him a ball, he takes it in the left hand and with the right streekes[118] it away with his racket. In a piece[119] he shoots at random and is well pleased with what his men tell him, be it high or wide.

Who knows whether mankind commit as great a folly for want of some sense, and that by this default the greater part of the visage of things be concealed from us? Who knows whether the difficulties we find in sundry of nature's works proceed thence? And whether diverse effects of beasts, which exceed our capacity, are produced by the faculty of some sense that we want? And whether some of them have by that mean a fuller and more perfect life than ours?

We seize on an apple well nigh with all our senses: We find redness, smoothness, odor, and sweetness in it; besides which, it may have other virtues, either binding or restrictive,[120] to which we have no sense to be referred. The proprieties[121] which in many things we call secret, as in the adamant to draw iron,[122] is it not likely there should be sensitive faculties in nature able to judge and perceive them, the want whereof breedeth in us the ignorance of the true essence of such things? It is happily[123] some particular sense that unto cocks or chanticleers discovereth the morning and midnight hour and moveth them to crow; that teacheth a hen, before any use or experience, to fear a hawk and not a goose or a peacock, far greater birds; that warneth young chickens of the hostile quality which the cat hath against them and not to distrust a dog: to strut and arm themselves against the mewing of the one (in some sort a flattering and mild voice) and not against the barking of the other (a snarling and quarrelous[124] voice); that instructeth rats, wasps, and emmets[125] ever to choose the best cheese and fruit, having never tasted them before. And that addresseth the stag, the elephant, and the serpent to the knowledge of certain herbs and simples[126] which, being either wounded or sick, have the virtue to cure them.

There is no sense but hath some great domination and which by his mean affordeth not an infinite number of knowledges. If we were to report the intelligence of sounds, of harmony and of the voice, it would bring an inimaginable confusion to all the rest of our learning and science. For, besides what is tied to the proper effect of every sense, how many arguments, consequences, and conclusions draw we unto other things, by comparing one sense to another? Let a skillful wise man but imagine human nature to be originally produced without sight and discourse, how much ignorance and trouble such a defect would bring unto him and what obscurity and blindness in our mind. By that shall we perceive how much the privation of one or two or three such senses (if there be any in us) doth import us about the knowledge of truth. We have by the consultation and concurrence of our five senses formed one verity, whereas peradventure there was required the accord and consent of eight or ten senses, and their contribution to attain a perspicuous insight of her and see her in her true essence.

Those sects[127] which combat man's science do principally combat the same by the uncertainty and feebleness of our senses. For, since by their mean and intermission all knowledge comes unto us, if they chance to miss in the report they make unto us, if either they corrupt or alter that, which from abroad they bring unto us, if the light which by them is transported into our soul be obscured in the passage, we have nothing else to hold by. From this extreme difficulty are sprung all these fantasies, which every subject containeth, whatsoever we find in it. That it hath not what we suppose to find in it; and that of the *Epicurians*, which is that the sun is no greater than our sight doth judge it—

> *Quicquid id est, nihilo fertur maiore figura,*
> *Quam nostris oculis quam cernimus esse videtur.*
> What ere it be, it in no greater form doth pass,
> Than to our eyes, which it behold, it seeming was.[128]

—that the appearances which represent a great body to him that is near unto them and a much lesser to him that is further from them are both true—

> *Nec tamen hic oculis falli concedimzus hilum:*
> *Proinde animi vitium hoc oculis adfingere noli.*
> Yet grant we not, in this, our eyes deceiv'd or blind,
> Impute not then to eyes this error of the mind.[129]

—and, resolutely, that there is no deceit in the senses, that a man must stand to their mercy and elsewhere seek reasons to excuse the difference and contradiction we find in them; yea, invent all other untruths and raving conceits (so far come they) rather than accuse the senses.

Timagoras swore that howsoever he winked or turned his eyes he could never perceive the light of the candle to double. And that this seeming proceeded from the vice of opinion, and not from the instrument. Of all absurdities, the most absurd amongst the Epicurians is to disavow the force and effect of the senses.

> *Proinde quod in quoque est his visum tempore, verum est.*
> *Et si non potuit ratio dissoluere causam,*
> *Cur ea quæ fuerint iuxtim quadrata, procul sint*
> *Visa rotunda: tamen præstat rationis egentem*
> *Reddere mendos causas vtriúsque figuræ,*
> *Quam manibus manifesta suis emittere quoquam,*
> *Et violare fidem primam, et convellere tota*
> *Fundamenta, quibus nixatur vita salusque.*
> *Non modo enim ratio ruat omnis, vita quoque ipsa*
> *Concidat extemplo, nisi credere sensibus ausis,*
> *Præcipitesque locos vitare, et cætera quæ sint*
> *In genere hoc fugienda.*
> What by the eyes is seen at any time is true,
> Though the cause reason could not render of the view,
> Why what was square at hand, a far-off seemed round,
> Yet it much better were that wanting reason's ground
> The causes of both forms we harp on, but not hit,
> Then let slip from our hands things clear and them omit,
> And violate our first belief, and rashly rend
> All those groundworks, whereon both life and health depend,
> For not alone all reason falls, life likewise must
> Fail out of hand, unless your senses you dare trust,
> And break-neck places, and all other errors shun,
> From which we in this kind most carefully should run.[130]

This desperate and so little-philosophical counsel represents no other thing, but that human science cannot be maintained but by unreasonable, fond, and mad reason; yet is it better that man use it to prevail, yea, and of all other remedies else, how fantastical soever they be, rather than avow his necessary foolishness. So prejudicial and disadvantageous a verity he cannot avoid, but senses must necessarily be the sovereign masters of his knowledge. But they are uncertain and falsifiable to all circumstances. There must a man strike to the utmost of his power, and if his just forces fail him (as they are wont), to use and employ obstinacy, temerity, and impudency.

If that which the Epicurians affirm be true, that is to say, we have no science whether[131] the appearances of the senses be false, and that which the Stoics say, that it is also true that the senses' appearances are so false as they can produce us no science. We will conclude at the charges of these two great dogmatist sects that there is no science. Touching the error and uncertainty of the senses' operation, a man may store himself with as many examples as he pleaseth, so ordinary are the faults and deceits they use towards us. And the echoing or reporting of a valley, the sound of a trumpet seemeth to sound before us, which cometh a mile behind us.

> *Extantesque procul medio de gurgite montes*
> *Iidem apparent longe diversilicet.*
> *Et fugere ad puppim colles campique videntur*
> *Quos agimus propter navim.*
> *Ubi in medio nobis equus acer obhæsit*
> *Flumine, equi corpus transversum ferre videtur*
> *Vis, et in adversum flumen contrudere raptim.*
> And hills, which from the main far off to kenning[132] stand,
> Appear all one, though they far distant be, at hand.
> And hills and fields do seem unto our boat to fly,
> Which we drive by our boat as we do pass thereby,
> When in midst of a stream a stately horse doth stay,
> The stream's o'erthwarting seems his body cross to sway,
> And swiftly gainst the stream to thrust him th'other way.[133]

To roll a bullet under the forefinger, the middlemost being put over it, a man must very much enforce himself to affirm there is but one, so assuredly doth our sense present us two. That the senses do often master our discourse[134] and force it to receive impressions, which he knoweth and judgeth to be false, it is daily seen. I leave the sense of feeling which hath his functions nearer, more quick and substantial, and which by the effect of the grief or pain it brings to the body doth so often confound and re-enverse[135] all these goodly Stoical resolutions and enforceth him, who with all resolution hath established this dogma or doctrine in his mind, to cry out his belly acheth and that the colic, as every other sickness or pain, is a thing indifferent, wanting power to abate anything of sovereign good or chief felicity, wherein the wise man is placed by his own virtue.

There is no heart so demisse[136] but the rattling sound of a drum or the clang of a trumpet will rouse and inflame; nor mind so harsh and stern but the sweetness and harmony of music will move and tickle; nor any soul so skittish and stubborn that hath not a feeling of some reverence in considering the cloudy vastity[137] and gloomy canapies of our churches, the eye-pleasing diversity of ornaments and orderly order of our ceremonies, and hearing the devout and religious sound of our organs, the moderate, symphonial, and heavenly harmony of our voices. Even those that enter into them with an obstinate will and contemning mind have in their heart a feeling of remorse, of chilnesse,[138] and horror that puts them into a certain diffidence of their former opinions.

As for me, I distrust mine own strength to hear with a settled mind some of *Horace* or *Catullus* verses sung with a sufficiently well-tuned voice, uttered by and proceeding from a fair, young, and heart-alluring mouth. And *Zeno* had reason to say that the voice was the flower of beauty.

Some have gone about to make me believe that a man whom most of us French men know, in repeating of certain verses he had made, had imposed upon me that they were not such in writing as in the air and that mine eyes would judge of them otherwise than mine ears. So much credit hath pronunciation to give price and fashion to those works that pass her mercy. Whereupon *Philoxenus* was not to be blamed when, hearing one to give an ill accent to some composition of his, he took in a rage some of his pots or bricks and, breaking them, trode and trampled them under his feet, saying unto him, *I break and trample what is thine, even as thou manglest and marrest what is mine.*

Wherefore did they (who with an undaunted resolve have procured their own death because they would not see the blow or stroke coming) turn their face away? And those who for their health's sake cause themselves to be cut and cauterized cannot endure the sight of the preparations, tools, instruments, and works of the chirurgion[139] but because the sight can have no part of the pain or smart? Are not these fit examples to verify the authority which senses have over discourse? We may long enough know that such a one's locks or flaring-tresses are borrowed of a page or taken from some lacky, that this fair ruby-red[140] came from *Spain*, and this whiteness or smoothness from the ocean sea. Yet must sight force us to find and deem the subject more lovely and more pleasing, against all reason. For in that there is nothing of its[141] own:

> *Auferimur cultu: gemnis, auroque teguntur*
> *Crimina, pars minima est ipsa puelia sui.*
> *Sæpe ubi sit quod ames inter tam multa requiras:*
> *Decipit hac oculos Ægide, dives amor.*
> We are misled by ornaments: what is amiss
> Gold and gems cover, least part of herself the maiden is.
> 'Mongst things so many you may ask, where your love lies:
> Rich love by this Gorgonian shield deceives thine eyes.[142]

How much do poets ascribe unto the virtue of the senses, which makes *Narcissus* to have even fondly lost himself for the love of his shadow?

> *Cunctaque miratur, quibus est mirabilis ipse,*
> *Se cupit imprudens, et qui probat, ipse probatur,*
> *Dumque petit, petitur: pariterque accendit et ardet.*
> He all admires, whereby himself is admirable,
> Fond he, fond of himself, to himself amiable,
> He, that doth like, is lik'd, and while he doth desire;
> He is desired, at once he burns and sets on fire.[143]

And *Pygmalion's* wits so troubled by the impression of the sight of his ivory statue that he loveth and serves it as if it had life:

> *Oscula dat, reddique putat, sequiturque, tenetque,*
> *Et credit tactis digitos insidere membris,*
> *Et metuit pressos veniat ne livor in artus.*
> He kisses, and thinks kisses come again,
> He sues, pursues, and holds, believes in vain,
> His fingers sink where he doth touch the place,
> And fears lest black-and-blue touched limbs deface.[144]

Let a philosopher be put in a cage made of small and thin-set iron wire and hanged on the top of our Lady's church steeple in *Paris*.[145] He shall, by evident reason, perceive that it is impossible he should fall down out of it, yet can he not choose (except he have been brought up to the trade of tilers or thatchers[146]) but the sight of that exceeding height must needs dazzle his sight and amaze or turn his senses. For we have much ado to warrant ourselves in the walks or battlements of a high tower or steeple, if they be battlemented and wrought with pillars and somewhat wide one from another, although of stone and never so strong. Nay, some there are that can scarcely think or hear of such heights. Let a beam or plank be laid across from one of those two steeples to the other as big, as thick, as strong, and as broad as would suffice any man to walk safely upon it: there is no philosophical wisdom of so great resolution and constancy that is able to encourage and persuade us to march upon it as we would were it below on the ground.

I have sometimes made trial of it upon our mountains on this side of *Italy,* yet am I one of those that will not easily be affrighted with such things, and I could not without horror to my mind and trembling of legs and thighs endure to look on those infinite precipices and steepy down-falls, though I were not near the brim nor any danger within my length and more. And unless I had willingly gone to the peril, I could not possibly have fallen. Where I also noted that how deep soever the bottom were if but a tree, a shrub, or any out-butting crag of a rock presented itself unto our eyes upon those steepy and high alps, somewhat to uphold the sight and divide the same, it doth somewhat ease and assure us from fear, as if it were a thing which in our fall might either help or uphold us. And that we cannot without some dread and giddiness in the head so much as abide to look upon one of those even and down-right precipices: *Ut despici sine vertigine simul oculorum animique non possit. So as they cannot look down without giddiness both of eyes and minds*;[147] which is an evident deception of the sight.

Therefore was it that a worthy philosopher pulled out his eyes that so he might discharge his soul of the debauching and diverting he received by them and the better and more freely apply himself unto philosophy. But by this account he should also have stopped his ears, which (as *Theophrastus* said) are the most dangerous instruments we have to receive violent and sudden impressions to trouble and alter us and should, in the end, have deprived himself of all his other senses, that is to say both of his being and life. For they have the power to command our discourse and sway our mind: *Fit etiam sæpe specie quadam, sæpe vocum gravitate et cantibus, ut pellantur animi vehementius: sæpe etiam cura et timore. It comes to pass that many times our minds are much moved with some shadow, many times with deep-sounding or singing voices, many times with care and fear.*[148]

Physicians hold that there are certain complexions, which by some sounds and instruments, are agitated even unto fury. I have seen some who, without infringing their patience, could not well hear a bone gnawed under their table. And we see few men but are much troubled at that sharp, harsh, and teeth-edging noise that smiths make in filing of brass or scraping of iron and steel together; others will be offended if they but hear one chew his meat somewhat aloud; nay, some will be angry with, or hate, a man that either speaks in the nose or rattles in the throat. That piping prompter of *Graccus* who mollified, raised, and wound[149] his master's voice whilst he was making orations at *Rome*, what good did he, if the motion and quality of the sound had not the force to move and efficacy to alter the auditory's judgement? Verily, there is great cause to make so much ado and keep such a coyle[150] about the constancy and firmness of this goodly piece[151] which suffers itself to be handled, changed, and turned by the motion and accident of so light a wind.

The very same cheating and cozening that senses bring to our understanding themselves receive it in their turns. Our mind doth likewise take revenge of it; they lie, they cog, and deceive one another avie.[152] What we see and hear, being passionately transported by anger, we neither see nor hear it as it is.

> *Et solem geminum, et duplices se ostendere Thebas.*
> That two suns do appear,
> And double *Thebes* are there.[153]

The object which we love seemeth much more fairer unto us than it is—

> *Multimodis igitur pravas turpesque videmus*
> *Esse in delitiis, summoque in honore vigere.*
> We therefore see that those, who many ways are bad,
> And foul, are yet belov'd, and in chief honour had.[154]

—and that much fouler which we loth. To a pensive and heart-grieved man, a clear day seems gloomy and dusky. Our senses are not only altered but many times dulled by the passions of the mind. How many things see we which we perceive not if our mind be either busied or distracted elsewhere?

> ——*in rebus quoque apertis noscere possis,*
> *Si non advertas animum, proinde esse, quasi omni*
> *Tempore semotæ fuerint, longeque remotæ.*
> Ev'n in things manifest it may be seen,
> If you mark not, they are, as they had been
> At all times sever'd far, removed clean.[155]

The soul seemeth to retire herself into the inmost parts and amuseth[156] the senses' faculties, so that both the inward and outward parts of man are full of weakness and falsehood.

Those which have compared our life unto a dream have happily had more reason so to do than they were aware. When we dream, our soul liveth, worketh, and exerciseth all her faculties, even and as much as when it waketh; and if more softly, and obscurely, yet verily not so as that it may admit so great a difference as there is between a dark night and a clear day; yea, as between a night and a shadow. There it sleepeth, here it slumbereth. More or less, they are ever darknesses, yea Cimmerian[157] darknesses.

We wake sleeping, and sleep waking. In my sleep I see not so clear, yet can I never find my waking clear enough or without dimness. Sleep also in his deepest rest doth sometimes bring dreams asleep. But our waking is never so vigilant as it may clearly purge and dissipate the ravings or idle fantasies, which are the dreams of the waking, and worse than dreams.

Our reason and soul receiving the fantasies and opinions which sleeping seize on them, and authorising our dreams' actions with like approbation as it doth the day's, why make we not a doubt whether our thinking and our working be another dreaming, and our waking some kind of sleeping?

If the senses be our first judges, it is not ours that must only be called to counsel, for in this faculty beasts have as much (or more) right as we. It is most certain that some have their hearing more sharp than man; others their sight; others their smelling; others their feeling or taste. *Democritus* said that gods and beasts had the sensitive faculties much more perfect than man.

Now between the effects of their senses and ours, the difference is extreme. Our spittle[158] cleanseth and drieth our sores and killeth serpents.

> *Tantaque in his rebus distantia differitasque est,*
> *Ut quod aliis cibus est, aliis fuat acre venenum.*

Sæpe etenim serpens, hominis contacta saliva,
Disperit, ac sese mandendo conficit ipsa.
There is such distance, and such difference in these things,
As what to one is meat t'another poison brings.
For oft a serpent touched with spittle of a man
Doth die, and gnaw itself with fretting all he can.[159]

What quality shall we give unto spittle, either according to us or according to the serpent? By which two senses shall we verify its true essence, which we seek for? *Pliny* sayeth that there are certain sea-hares in *India* that to us are poison and we bane to them, so that we die if we but touch them. Now, whether is man or the hare poison? Whom shall we believe, either the fish of man, or the man of fish?

Some quality of the air infecteth man, which nothing at all hurteth the ox; some other the ox, and not man. Which of the two is either, in truth or in nature, the pestilent quality?

Such as are troubled with the yellow jandise[160] deem all things they look upon to be yellowish which seem more pale and wan to them than to us.

Lurida præterea fiunt quæcunque tuentur
Arquati.
And all that jaundis'd men behold,
They yellow straight or palish hold.[161]

Those which are sick of the disease which physicians call *Hyposphragma*, which is a suffusion of blood under the skin, imagine that all things they see are bloody and red. Those humors that so change the sight's operation, what know we whether they are predominant and ordinary in beasts? For we see some whose eyes are as yellow as theirs that have the jaundice; others that have them all bloodshot with redness. It is likely that the objects' colour they look upon seemeth otherwise to them than to us. Which of the two judgements shall be true? For it is not said that the essence of things hath reference to man alone. Hardness, whiteness, depth, and sharpness touch the service and concern the knowledge of beasts as well as ours. Nature hath given the use of them to them as well as to us.

When we wink a little with our eye, we perceive the bodies we look upon to seem longer and outstretched. Many beasts have their eye as winking as we. This length is then happily the true form of that body and not that which our eyes give it, being in their ordinary seat. If we close our eye above, things seeme double unto us.

> *Bina lucernarum florentia lumina flammis,*
> *Et duplices hominum facies, et corpora bina.*
> The lights of candles double flaming then;
> And faces twain, and bodies twain of men.[162]

If our ears chance to be hindered by anything, or that the passage of our hearing be stopped, we receive the sound otherwise than we were ordinarily wont. Such beasts as have hairy ears, or that in lieu of an ear have but a little hole, do not by consequence hear what we hear, and receive the sound other than it is.[163] We see at solemn shows or in theaters that, opposing any coloured glass between our eyes and the torch's light, whatsoever is in the room seems green or yellow or red unto us, according to the colour of the glass:

> *Et vulgo faciunt id lutea russaque vela,*
> *Et ferriginea, cum magnis intenta theatris*
> *Per malos volgata trabesque trementia pendent:*
> *Namque ibi consessum caveai subter, et omnem*
> *Scenai speciem, patrum matrumque deorumque*
> *Inficiunt, coguntque suo volitare colore.*
> And yellow, russet, rusty curtains work this feat
> In common sights abroad, wherever scaffolds great
> Stretched on masts, spread over beams, they hang still waving.
> All the seats circuit there, and all the stage's braving,
> Of fathers, mothers, gods, and all the circled show
> They double-dyed, and in their colours make to flow.[164]

It is likely that those beasts' eyes, which we see to be of diverse colours, produce the appearances of those bodies they look upon to be like their eyes.

To judge the senses' operation, it were then necessary we were first agreed with beasts and then between ourselves. Which we are not, but ever-and-anon disputing about that one seeth, heareth, or tasteth something to be other than indeed it is and contend as much as about anything else of the diversity of those images our senses reporte unto us. A young child heareth, seeth, and tasteth otherwise, by nature's ordinary rule, than a man of thirty years, and he otherwise than another of threescore.

The senses are to some more obscure and dim, and to some more open and quick. We receive things differently, according as they are and seem unto us. Things being then so uncertain and full of controversy, it is no longer a wonder if it be told us that we may avouch snow to seem white unto us but to affirm that it is in essence and in truth, we cannot warrant ourselves; which foundation being so shaken, all the science in the world must necessarily go to wrack.

What, do our senses themselves hinder one another? To the sight a picture seemeth to be raised aloft and in the handling flat. Shall we say that musk is pleasing or no, which comforteth our smelling and offendeth our taste? There are herbs and ointments which to some parts of the body are good and to othersome hurtful. Honey is pleasing to the taste but unpleasing to the sight. Those jewels wrought and fashioned like feathers or sprigs which in impreses[165] are called *feathers without ends*, no eye can discern the breadth of them, and no man warrant himself from this deception that on the one end or side it groweth not broader and broader, sharper and sharper, and on the other more and more narrow, especially being rolled about one's finger; when notwithstanding in handling it seemeth equal in breadth and everywhere alike.

Those who to increase and aid their luxury[166] were anciently wont to use perspective or looking glasses, fit to make the object they represented appear very big and great, that so the members[167] they were to use might by that ocular increase please them the more: to whether of the two senses yielded they, either to the sight presenting those members as big and great as they wished them, or to the feeling that presented them little and to be disdained?

Is it our senses that lend these diverse conditions unto subjects, when for all that, the subjects have but one? As we see in the bread we eat: it is but bread, but one using it maketh bones, blood, flesh, hair, and nails thereof:

> *Ut cibus in membra atque artus cum diditur omnet*
> *Disperit, atque aliam naturam sufficit ex se.*
> As meat distributed into the members dies,
> Another nature yet it perishing supplies.[168]

The moistness which the root of a tree sucks becomes a trunk, a leaf, and a fruit. And the air, being but one, applied unto a trumpet becometh diverse in a thousand sorts of sounds. Is it our senses (say I) who likewise fashion of diverse qualities those subjects, or whether they have them so and such? And upon this doubt, what may we conclude of their true essence?

Moreover, since the accidents of sickness, of madness, or of sleep make things appear other unto us than they seem unto the healthy, unto the wise, and to the waking, is it not likely that our right seat and natural humours have also wherewith to give a being unto things, having reference unto their condition, and to appropriate them to itself, as do inordinate humours? And our health, as capable to give them his visage as sickness? Why hath not the temperate man some form of the objects relative unto himself as the intemperate, and shall not he likewise imprint his character in them? The distasted[169] impute wallowishness[170] unto wine; the healthy, good taste; and the thirsty, briskness, relish, and delicacy.

Now our condition appropriating things unto itself and transforming them to its own humour, we know no more how things are in sooth and truth. For *nothing comes unto us but falsified and altered by our senses.* Either the compass, the quadrant, or the ruler are crooked: all proportions drawn by them, and all the buildings erected by their measure, are also necessarily defective and imperfect. The uncertainty of our senses yields whatever they produce also uncertain.

> *Denique ut in fabrica, si prava est regula prima,*
> *Normaque si fallax rectis regionibus exit,*
> *Et libella aliqua si ex parte claudicat hilum,*
> *Omnia mendose fieri, atque obstipa necessum est,*
> *Prava, cubantia, prona, supina, atque absona tecta,*
> *Iam ruere ut quædam videantur velle, ruantque*
> *Prodita iudiciis fallacibus omnia primis.*
> *Hic igitur ratio tibi rerum prava necesse est,*
> *Falsaque sit falsis quæcunque a sensibus orta est.*
> As in building if the first rule be to blame,
> And the deceitful squire err from right forms and frame,
> If any instrument want any jot of weight,
> All must needs faulty be, and stooping in their height,
> The building naught, absurd, upward and downward bended,
> As if they meant to fall, and fall as they intended;
> And all this as betrayed by judgements foremost laid.
> Of things the reason therefore needs must faulty be
> And false, which from false senses drawes its pedigree.[171]

As for the rest, who shall be a competent judge in these differences? As we said in controversies of religion that we must have a judge inclined to neither party and free from partiality or affection, which is hardly to be had among Christians, so happeneth it in this. For if he be old, he cannot judge of age's sense, himself being a party in this controversy. And so if he be young, healthy, sick, sleeping, or waking, it is all one. We had need of somebody void and exempted from all these qualities that without any preoccupation of judgement might judge of these propositions as indifferent unto him; by which account we should have a judge that were no man.

To judge of the appearances that we receive of subjects,[172] we had need have a judicatory instrument; to verify this instrument, we should have demonstration; and to approve demonstration, an instrument: thus are we ever turning round. Since the senses cannot determine our disputation, themselves being so full of uncertainty, it must then be reason. And no reason can be established without another reason: then are we ever going back unto infinity.

Our fantasy[173] doth not apply itself to strange things but is rather conceived by the interposition of senses; and senses cannot comprehend a strange subject, nay, not so much as their own passions. And so, nor the fantasy nor the appearance is the subject's but rather the passions only, and sufferance of the sense; which passion and subject are diverse things. Therefore, *who judgeth by appearances judgeth by a thing different from the subject.*

And to say that the senses' passions refer the quality of strange subjects by resemblance unto the soul, how can the soul and the understanding rest assured of that resemblance, having of itself no commerce with foreign subjects? Even as he that knows not *Socrates*, seeing his picture, cannot say that it resembleth him.

And would a man judge by appearances, be it by all, it is impossible, for by their contrarieties and differences they hinder one another, as we see by experience. May it be that some choice appearances rule and direct the others? This choice must be verified by another choice, the second by a third; and so shall we never make an end.

In few, *there is no constant existence, neither of our being nor of the objects.* And we, and our judgement, and all mortal things else do uncessantly roll, turn, and pass away. Thus can nothing be certainly established, nor of the one nor of the other, both the judging and the judged being in continual alteration and motion.

We have no communication with being,[174] for every human nature is ever in the middle between being born and dying, giving nothing of itself but an obscure appearance and shadow, and an uncertain and weak opinion. And if perhaps you fix your thought to take its being, it would be even as if one should go about to poyson[175] the water: for how much the more he shall close and press that which by its own nature is ever gliding, so much the more he shall lose what he would hold and fasten. Thus, seeing all things are subject to pass from one change to another, reason, which therein seeketh a real subsistence, finds herself deceived, as unable to apprehend anything subsistent and permanent; forsomuch as each thing either commeth to a being and is not yet altogether, or beginneth to die before it be born.

Plato said that bodies had never an existence but indeed a birth, supposing that *Homer* made the *Ocean* Father and *Thetis* Mother of the gods, thereby to show us that all things are in continual motion, change, and variation. As he sayeth, a common opinion amongst all the philosophers before his time, only *Parmenides* excepted, who denied any motion to be in things, of whose power he maketh no small account. *Pythagoras*, that each thing or matter was ever gliding and labile. The Stoics affirm there is no present time and that which we call present is but conjoining and assembling of future time and past. *Heraclitus* averreth that no man ever entered twice in one same river.

Epicarmus avoucheth that who erewhile borrowed any money doth not now owe it, and that he who yesternight was bidden to dinner this day cometh today unbidden, since they are no more themselves but are become others. And that one mortal substance could not twice be found in one self[176] state. For, by the suddenness and lightness of change, sometimes it wasteth and othertimes it reassembleth; now it comes, and now it goes. In such sort that he who beginneth to be born never comes to the perfection of being. For this being born cometh never to an end, nor ever stayeth as being at an end, but after the seed proceedeth continually in change and alteration from one to another. As of man's seed there is first made a shapeless fruit in the mother's womb, then a shapen child; then, being out of the womb, a sucking babe; afterward he becometh a lad; then consequently a stripling[177]; then a full-grown man; then an old man; and in the end an aged, decrepit man. So that age and subsequent generation goeth ever undoing and wasting the precedent.

Mutat enim mundi naturam totius ætas,
Ex alioque alius status excipere omnia debet,

Nec manet illa sui similis res, omnia migrant,
Omnia commutat natura et vertere cogit.
Of th'universal world, age doth the nature change,
And all things from one state must to another range,
No one thing like itself remains, all things do pass,
Nature doth change, and drive to change, each thing that was.[178]

And when we others do foolishly fear a kind of death, when as we
have already passed and daily pass so many others. For not only (as
Heraclitus said) the death of fire is a generation of air, and the death
of air a generation of water; but also we may most evidently see it in
ourselves. The flower of age dyeth, fadeth, and fleeteth, when age
comes upon us, and youth endeth in the flower of a full-grown man's
age; childhood in youth; and the first age dyeth in infancy. And yesterday endeth in this day, and today shall die in tomorrow. *And
nothing remaineth or ever continueth in one state.*

For, to prove it, if we should ever continue one and the same, how
is it then that now we rejoice at one thing, and now at another? How
comes it to pass, we love things contrary, or we hate them, or we love
them, or we blame them? How is it that we have different affections,
holding no more the same sense in the same thought? For it is not
likely that without alteration we should take other passions, and
What admitteth alterations, continueth not the same, and if it be not
one self-same, then it is not; but rather with being all one, the simple
being doth also change, ever becoming other from other. And by
consequence nature's senses are deceived and lie falsely, taking what
appeareth for what is, for want of truly-knowing what it is that is.

But then what is it, that is indeed? That which is eternal: that is
to say, that which never had birth, nor ever shall have end; and to
which no time can bring change or cause alteration. For time is a
fleeting thing, and which appeareth as in a shadow, with the matter
ever gliding, always fluent, without ever being stable or permanent.
To whom rightly belong these terms, *Before* and *After*, and it *Hath
been* or *Shall be.* Which at first sight doth manifestly show that it is
not a thing which is; for it were great sottishness[179] and apparent

falsehood to say that that is which is not yet in being, or that already hath ceased from being. And concerning these words, *Present, Instant, Even-now,* by which it seems that especially we uphold and principally ground the intelligence of time, reason discovering the same doth forthwith destroy it; for presently it severeth it asunder and divideth it into future and past-time, as willing to see it necessarily parted in two.

As much happeneth unto nature which is measured, according unto time which measureth her. For no more is there anything in her that remaineth or is subsistent; rather all things in her are either born, or ready to be born, or dying. By means whereof, it were a sin to say of God, who is the only that is, that he was or shall be. For these words are declinations,[180] passages, or vicissitudes of that which cannot last nor continue in being. Wherefore we must conclude *that only God is, not according to any measure of time, but according to an immovable and unmoving eternity, not measured by time nor subject to any declination; before whom nothing is, nor nothing shall be after, nor more new or more recent; but a real being, which by one only* Now *or* Present *filleth the* Ever, *and there is nothing that truly is but he alone.* Without saying he hath been or he shall be— without beginning and sans ending.[181]

To this so religious conclusion of a heathen man I will only add this word, taken from a testimony of the same condition, for an end of this long and period of this tedious discourse, which might well furnish me with endless matter. *Oh, what a vile and abject thing is man* (sayeth he) *unless he raise himself above humanity!*[182]

Observe here a notable speech and a profitable desire, but likewise absurd. For to make the handful greater than the hand, and the embraced greater than the arm, and to hope to straddle more than our legs' length, is impossible and monstrous. Nor that man should mount over and above himself or humanity; for he cannot see but with his own eyes, nor take hold but with his own arm.

He shall raise himself up, if it please God extraordinarily to lend him His helping hand. He may elevate himself by forsaking and renouncing his own means and suffering himself to be elevated and raised by mere[183] heavenly means.

It is for our Christian faith, not for his Stoic virtue, to pretend or aspire to this divine metamorphosis or miraculous transmutation.

We Taste Nothing Purely

2.20

THE WEAKNESS of our condition causeth that things in their natural simplicity and purity cannot fall into our use. The elements we enjoy are altered, metals likewise, yea gold must be empared[1] with some other stuff to make it fit for our service.

Nor virtue so simple which *Ariston, Pyrrho,* and Stoics made the end of their life hath been able to do no good without composition,[2] nor the Cyrenaic sensuality or Aristippian voluptuousness.[3] *Of the pleasures and goods we have, there is none exempted from some mixture of evil and incommodity.*[4]

> ——*medio de fonte leporum*
> *Surgit amari aliquid, quod in ipsis floribus angat.*
> From middle spring of sweets some bitter springs,
> Which in the very flower smartly stings.[5]

Our exceeding voluptuousness[6] hath some air of groaning and wailing. Would you not say it dyeth with anguish? Yea, when we forge its image in her excellency, we deck it with epithets of sickish and dolorous qualities: languor, effeminacy, weakness, fainting, and *Morbidezza,*[7] a great testimony of their consanguinity and consubstantiality.[8]

Excessive joy hath more severity than jollity; extreme and full content, more settledness than cheerfulness. *Ipsa felicitas, se nisi temperat, premit. Felicity itself, unless it temper itself, distempers us.*[9] Ease consumeth us.

It is that which an old Greek verse sayeth of such a sense: "The gods sell us all the goods they give us." That is to say, they give us not one pure and perfect, and that which we buy not with the price of some evil. Travell[10] and pleasure, most unlike in nature, are notwithstanding followed together by a kind I wot not what natural conjunction. *Socrates* sayeth that some god attempted to huddle up together and confound sorrow and voluptuousness, but being unable to effect it, he bethought himself to couple them together, at least by the tail.

Metrodorus said that in sadness there is some alloy of pleasure. I know not whether he meant anything else, but I imagine that for one to inure himself to melancholy, there is some kind of purpose of consent and mutual delight; I mean besides ambition, which may also be joined unto it. There is some shadow of delicacy and quaintness which smileth and fawneth upon us, even in the lap of melancholy. Are there not some complexions[11] that of it make their nourishment?[12]

——*est quædam flere voluptas.*
It is some pleasure yet
With tears our cheeks to wet.[13]

And one *Attalus* in *Seneca* sayeth the remembrance of our last friends[14] is as pleasing to us as bitterness in wine that is over old—

Minister veteris puer falerni
Ingere mi calices amariores:
Sir boy, my servitor of good old wine,
Bring me my cup thereof bitter, but fine.[15]

—and as of sweetly-sour apples.

Nature discovereth this confusion unto us: Painters are of opinion that *the motions and wrinkles in the face which serve to weep serve also to laugh.* Verily, before one or other be determined to express which, behold the pictures success; you are in doubt toward which one inclineth. And the extremity of laughing intermingles itself with tears. *Nullum sine auctoramento malum est. There is no evil without some obligation.*[16]

When I imagine man fraughted with all the commodities may be wished—let us suppose all his several members were for ever possessed with a pleasure like unto that of generation, even in the highest point that may be—I find him to sink under the burden of his ease and perceive him altogether unable to bear so pure, so constant, and so universal a sensuality.[17] Truly, he flies when he is even upon the nick[18] and naturally hasteneth to escape it, as from a step whereon he cannot stay or contain himself, and feareth to sink into it.

When I religiously confess myself unto myself, I find the best good I have hath some vicious taint.[19] And I fear that *Plato* in his purest virtue (I that am as sincere and loyal an esteemer thereof, and of the virtues of such a stamp, as any other can possibly be), if he had nearly listened unto it (and sure he listened very near), he would therein have heard some harsh tune of human mixture, but an obscure tune, and only sensible unto himself. *Man all in all is but a botching and parti-coloured work.*[20]

The very laws of justice cannot subsist without some commixture of injustice. And *Plato* sayeth, *They undertake to cut off Hydra's heads that pretend to remove all incommodities and inconveniences from the laws. Omne magnum exemplum habet aliquid ex iniquo, quod contra singulos utilitate publica rependitur. Every great example hath some touch of injustice, which is requited by the common good against particulars*, sayeth *Tacitus.*[21]

It is likewise true that for the use of life and service of public society there may be excess in the purity and perspicuity of our spirits. This piercing brightness hath overmuch subtlety and curiosity. They should be made heavy and dull to make them the more obedient to example and practice, and they must be thickened and obscured to proportion them to this shady and terrestrial life. Therefore are vulgar and less-wire-drawn[22] wits found to be more fit and happy in the conduct of affairs. And the exquisite and high-raised opinions of philosophy, unapt and unfit to exercise. This sharp vivacity of the spirit, and this supple and restless volubility,[23] troubleth our negotiations. Human enterprises should be managed more grossly and superficially and have a good and great part of them left for the rights of fortune. Affairs need not be sifted so nicely and so profoundly. A man loseth himself about the considerations of so many contrary lusters and diverse forms. *Volutantibus res inter se pugnantes, obtorpuerant animi. Their minds were astonished while they revolved things so different.*[24]

It is that which our elders report of *Simonides*: because his imagination concerning the question *Hieron* the King had made unto him[25] (which the better to answer he had diverse days allowed him to think of it) presented sundry subtle and sharp considerations unto him, doubting which might be the likeliest, he altogether despaireth of the truth.

Whosoever searcheth all the circumstances and embraceth all the consequences thereof, hindereth his election. *A mean engine*[26] *doth equally conduct and sufficeth for the executions of great and little weights.* It is commonly seen that the best husbands[27] and the thriftiest are those who cannot tell how they are so, and that these cunning arithmeticians[28] do seldom thrive by it. I know a notable pratler[29] and an excellent blazoner[30] of all sorts of husbandry and thrift who hath most piteously let ten thousand pound sterling a year pass from him. I know another who sayeth he consulteth better than any man of his council, and there cannot be a properer man to see unto, or of more sufficiency. Notwithstanding, when he cometh to any execution, his own servants find he is far otherwise. This I say without mentioning or accounting his ill luck.

Of a Monstrous Child

THIS DISCOURSE shall pass single,[1] for I leave it to physicians to treat of. I saw two days since a child whom two men and a nurse (which named themselves to be his father, his uncle, and his aunt) carried about with intent to get some money with the sight of him, by reason of his strangeness. In all the rest he was as other children are. He stood upon his feet, went,[2] and prattled in a manner as all others of his age. He would never take nourishment but by his nurse's breast; and what in my presence was offered to be put in his mouth, he chewed a little, and put it all out again. His puling[3] differed somewhat from others. He was just fourteen months old.

Under his paps[4] he was fastened and joined to another child but had no head, and who had the conduit of his back[5] stopped, the rest whole. One of his arms was shorter than the other and was by accident broken at their birth. They were joined face to face, and as if a little child would embrace another somewhat bigger. The joining and space whereat they were closed together was but four inches broad or thereabouts; in such sort that if you thrust up the imperfect child, you might see under the other's navel. And the seam was between the paps and his navel. The navel of the imperfect one could not be seen, but all the rest of his belly might. Thus, what of the imperfect one was not joined, as arms, buttocks, thighs, and legs, did hang and shake upon the other, whose length reached to the middle-leg of the other perfect. His nurse told me he made water by both privities. The members of the little one were nourished, living, and in the same state as the others, except only they were less and thinner.

This double body[6] and these different members having reference to one only head might serve for a favorable prognostication[7] to our king, to maintain the factions and differing parties of this our kingdom under a unity of the laws.[8] But lest the success should prove it contrary, it is not amiss to let him run his course. For in things already past there need no divination. *Ut quum facta sunt, tum ad conjecturam aliquid interpretatione revocantur. So as when they are done, they then by some construction should be revoked to conjecture.*[9] As it is reported of *Epimenides*, who ever divined contrary.[10]

I come now from seeing of a shepherd at *Medoc*, of thirty years of age or thereabouts, who had no sign at all of genitorie[11] parts. But where they should be are three little holes by which his water doth continually trill from him.

Those which we call monsters are not so with God, who in the immensity of his work seeth the infinity of forms therein contained. And it may be thought that any figure doth amaze us hath relation unto some other figure of the same kind, although unknown unto man. *From out his all-seeing wisdom proceedeth nothing but good, common, regular, and orderly; but we neither see the sorting nor conceive the relation. Quod crebro videt, non miratur, etiam si, cur fiat, nescit. Quod ante non videt, id, si evenerit, ostendum esse censet. That which he often seeth, he doth not wonder at, though he know not why it is done. But if that happen which he never saw before, he thinks it some portentous wonder.*[12]

We call that against nature which cometh against custom. There is nothing, whatsoever it be, that is not according to her.[13] Let therefore this universal and natural reason chase from us the error and expel the astonishment which novelty breedeth and strangeness causeth in us.

Of Repenting

OTHERS fashion man; I repeat him and represent a particular one, but ill made and whom, were I to form a new, he should be far other than he is. But he is now made.

And though the lines of my picture change and vary, yet lose they not themselves. The world runs all on wheels. All things therein move without intermission; yea, the earth, the rocks of *Caucasus*, and the pyramids of *Ægypt*, both with the public and their own motion.[1] *Constancy itself is nothing but a languishing and wavering dance.*

I cannot settle my object. It goeth so unquietly and staggering, with a natural drunkenness. I take it in this plight, as it is at the instant I amuse myself about it. I describe not the essence but the passage. Not a passage from age to age, or, as the people reckon, from seven years to seven, but from day to day, from minute to minute. My history must be fitted to the present. I may soon change, not only fortune but intention. It is a counter-roule[2] of diverse and variable accidents and irresolute imaginations, and sometimes contrary: whether it be that myself am other, or that I apprehend subjects by other circumstances and considerations. Howsoever, I may perhaps gainsay[3] myself, but truth (as *Demades* said) I never gainsay. Were my mind settled, I would not essay but resolve myself.[4] It is still a prentise[5] and a probationer.

I propose a mean life and without luster; 'tis all one. They fasten all moral philosophy as well to a popular and private life, as to one of richer stuff. *Every man beareth the whole stamp of human condition.*

Authors communicate themselves unto the world by some special and strange mark; I the first by my general disposition, as *Michel de Montaigne*, not as a grammarian, or a poet, or a lawyer. If the world complain I speak too much of myself, I complain, it speaks no more of itself.

But is it reason that, being so private in use, I should pretend to make myself public in knowledge? Or is it reason I should produce into the world, where fashion and art have such sway and command, the raw and simple effects of nature, and of a nature as yet exceeding weak? *To write books without learning, is it not to make a wall without stone or such like thing?* Conceits[6] of music are directed by art, mine by hap.[7]

Yet have I this according to learning, that never man handled subject he understood or knew better than I do this I have undertaken, being therein the cunningest man alive. Secondly, that never man waded further into his matter, nor more distinctly sifted the parts and dependences of it, nor arrived more exactly and fully to the end he proposed unto it. To finish the same, I have need of naught but faithfulness, which is therein as sincere and pure as may be found. I speak truth, not my belly-full, but as much as I dare; and I dare the more the more I grow into years, for it seemeth custom alloweth old age more liberty to babble and indiscretion to talk of itself. It cannot herein be as in trades, where the craftsman and his work do often differ. Being a man of so sound and honest conversation, writ he so foolishly? Are such learned writings come from a man of so weak a conversation? Who hath but an ordinary conceit and writeth excellently, one may say his capacity is borrowed, not of himself. A skilful man is not skilful in all things; but a sufficient man is sufficient everywhere, even unto ignorance.

Here my books and myself march together and keep one pace. Elsewhere one may commend or condemn the work, without the workman; here not: who toucheth one, toucheth the other. He who shall judge of it without knowing him, shall wrong himself more than me; he that knows it hath wholly satisfied me. Happy beyond my merit, if I get this only portion of public approbation, as I may cause men of understanding to think I had been able to make use and benefit of learning, had I been endowed with any, and deserved better help of memory.

Excuse we here what I often say, that I seldom repent myself and that my conscience is contented with itself, not of an angel's or a horse's consciences but as of a man's conscience. Adding ever this clause, not of ceremony but of true and essential submission: that *I speak enquiring and doubting, merely and simply referring myself from resolution unto common and lawful opinions.* I teach not; I report.

No vice is absolutely vice which offendeth not, and a sound judgement accuseth not. For the deformity and incommodity thereof is so palpable as peradventure they have reason who say it is chiefly produced by sottishness[8] and brought forth by ignorance. So hard is it to imagine one should know it without hating it.

Malice sucks up the greatest part of her own venom and therewith empoisoneth herself. Vice leaveth, as an ulcer in the flesh, a repentance in the soul, which still scratcheth and bloodieth itself. For reason effaceth other griefs and sorrows but engendereth those of repentance, the more irksome because inwards, as the cold and heat of agues is more offensive than that which comes outward. I account vice (but each according to their measure) not only those which reason disallows and nature condemns but such as men's opinion hath forged as false and erroneous, if laws and custom authorize the same.

In like manner, there is no goodness but gladdeth an honest disposition. There is truly I wot not what kind of congratulation of well doing which rejoiceth us in ourselves, and a generous jollity that accompanieth a good conscience. A mind courageously vicious may happily arm itself with security, but she shall never munite[9] herself with this self-joying delight and satisfaction. It is no small pleasure for one to feel himself preserved from the contagion of an age so infected as ours, and to say to himself, "Could a man enter and see even into my soul, yet should he not find me guilty, either of the affliction or ruin of anybody; nor culpable of envy or revenge; nor of public offence against the laws; nor tainted with innovation, trouble, or sedition; nor spotted with falsifying of my word. And although the liberty of times allowed and taught it every man, yet could I never be induced to touch the goods or dive into the purse of any *French* man, and have always lived upon mine own, as well in time of war as of peace; nor did I ever make use of any poor man's labor without reward."[10] These testimonies of an unspotted conscience are very pleasing, which natural joy is a great benefit unto us, and the only payment never faileth us.

To ground the recompense of virtuous actions upon the approbation of others is to undertake a most uncertain or troubled foundation. Namely in an age so corrupt and times so ignorant as this is, *the vulgar people's good opinion is injurious.* Whom trust you in seeing what is commendable? God keep me from being an honest man, according to the description I daily see made of honour, each one by himself. *Quæ fuerant vitia, mores sunt. What erst were vices are now grown fashions.*[11]

Some of my friends have sometimes attempted to school me roundly and sift me plainly, either of their own motion or invited by me, as to an office[12] which to a well-composed mind, both in profit and lovingness, exceedeth all the duties of sincere amity. Such have I ever entertained with open arms of courtesy and kind acknowledgement. But now to speak from my conscience, I often found so much false measure in their reproaches and praises that I had not greatly erred if I had rather erred than done well after their fashion.

Such as we especially who live a private life, not exposed to any gaze but our own, ought in our hearts establish a touchstone and thereto touch our deeds and try our actions and, accordingly, now cherish and now chastise ourselves. I have my own laws and tribunal to judge of me whither I address myself more than anywhere else. I restrain my actions according to others but extend them according to myself. None but your self knows rightly whether you be demisse[13] and cruel, or loyal and devout. Others see you not, but guess you by uncertain conjectures. They see not so much your nature as your art. Adhere not then to their opinion, but hold unto your own. *Tuo tibi iudicio est utendum. Virtutis et viciorum graue ipsius conscientiæ pondus est: qua sublata, iacent omnia. You must use your own judgement. The weight of the very conscience of vice and virtues is heavy: take that away, and all is down.*[14]

But whereas it is said that repentance nearly[15] followeth sin seemeth not to imply sin placed in his rich array, which lodgeth in us as in his proper mansion. One may disavow and disclaim vices that surprise us and whereto our passions transport us. But those which by long habit are rooted in a strong and anchored in a powerful will are not subject to contradiction. *Repentance is but a denying of our will and an opposition of our fantasies*, which diverts us here and there. It makes some disavow his former virtue and continency.

Quæ mens est hodie, cur eadem non puero fuit,
Velcur his animis incolumes non redeunt genæ?
Why was not in a youth same mind as now?
Or why bears not this mind a youthful brow?[16]

That is an exquisite life which even in his own private keepeth itself in awe and order. Everyone may play the juggler[17] and represent an honest man upon the stage. But within, and in bosom, where all things are lawful, where all is concealed—to keep a due rule or formal decorum, that's the point. The next degree is to be so in one's own home and in his ordinary actions, whereof we are to give account to nobody, wherein is no study nor art. And therefore *Byas*,[18] describing the perfect state of a family, whereof (sayeth he) the master be such inwardly by himself as he is outwardly, for fear of the laws and respect of men's speeches. And it was a worthy saying of *Julius Drusus* to those workmen, which for three thousand crowns offered so to reform his house that his neighbours should no more overlook into it. "I will give you six thousand" (said he), "and contrive it so that on all sides every man may look into it." The custom of *Agesilaus* is remembered with honour, who in his travail was wont to take up his lodging in churches, that the people and gods themselves might pry into his private actions. Some have been admirable to the world, in whom nor his wife nor his servant ever noted anything remarkable. *Few men have been admired of their familiars.*[19]

No man hath been a prophet, not only in his house but in his own country, sayeth the experience of histories. Even so in things of nought.[20] And in this base example is the image of greatness discerned. In my climate of *Gascoigne*[21] they deem it a jest to see me in print. The further the knowledge which is taken of me is from my home, of so much more worth am I. In *Guienne*[22] I pay printers; in other places they pay me. Upon this accident they ground who, living and present, keep close-lurking to purchase credit when they shall be dead and absent.[23] I had rather have less.[24] And I cast not myself into the world but for the portion I draw from it. That done, I quit it.

The people attend on such a man with wonderment from a public act unto his own doors. Together with his robes he leaves-off his part; falling so much the lower, by how much higher he was mounted. View him within there, all is turbulent, disordered, and vile. And were order and formality found in him, a lively, impartial, and well-sorted judgement is required to perceive and fully to discern him in these base and private actions. Considering that order is but a dumpish and drowsy virtue. To gain a battle, perform an ambassage,[25] and govern a people are noble and worthy actions. To chide, laugh, sell, pay, love, hate, and mildly and justly to converse both with his own and with himself; not to relent, and not gainsay himself, are things more rare, more difficult, and less remarkable.[26]

Retired lives sustain that way, whatever some say, offices as much or more crabbed and extended than other lives do. And private men (sayeth *Aristotle*) serve virtue more hardly[27] and more highly attend her than those which are magistrates or placed in authority. We prepare ourselves unto eminent occasions, more for glory than for conscience. *The nearest way to come unto glory were to do that for conscience which we do for glory*. And me seemeth the virtue of *Alexander* representeth much less vigor in her large theater than that of *Socrates* in his base and obscure exercitation.[28] I easily conceive *Socrates* in the room of *Alexander*; *Alexander* in that of *Socrates*, I cannot. If any ask the one what he can do, he will answer, *Conquer the world*. Let the same question be demanded of the other, he will say, *lead my life conformably to its natural condition*—a science much more generous, more important, and more lawful.

The worth of the mind consisteth not in going high but in marching orderly. Her greatness is not exercised in greatness; in mediocrity, it is. As those which judge and touch us inwardly make no great account of the brightness of our public actions, and see they are but streaks and points of clear water, surging from a bottom otherwise slimy and full of mud; so those who judge us by this gay outward appearance conclude the same of our inward constitution and cannot couple popular faculties as theirs are unto these other faculties which amaze them so far from their level. So do we attribute savage shapes and oughly[29] forms unto devils. As who doth not ascribe high-raised eye-brows, open nostrils, a stern frightful visage, and a huge body unto *Tamburlane*, as is the form or shape of the imagination we have fore-conceived by the bruite[30] of his name? Had any heretofore showed me *Erasmus*, I could hardly have been induced to think but whatsoever he had said to his boy or host had been adages and apothegms. We imagine much more fitly an artificer[31] upon his close stool[32] or on his wife than a great judge, reverend for his carriage and regardful for his sufficiency. We think that from those high thrones they should not abase themselves so low as to live.

As vicious minds are often incited to do well by some strange impulsion, so are virtuous spirits moved to do ill. They must then be judged by their settled estate, when they are near themselves and, as we say, at home, if at any time they be so; or when they are nearest unto rest and in their natural seat.

Natural inclinations are by institution[33] helped and strengthened, but they neither change nor exceed. A thousand natures in my time have athwart a contrary discipline escaped toward virtue or toward vice.

> *Sic ubi desuetæ silvis in carcere clausæ,*
> *Mansuevere feræ, et vultus posuere minaces,*
> *Atque hominem didicere pati, si torrida paruus*
> *Venit in ora cruor, redeunt rabiesque furorque,*

Admonitæque tument gustato sanguine fauces,
Fervet, et a trepido vix abstinet ira magistro.
So when wild beasts, disused from the wood,
Fierce looks laid-down, grow tame, closed in a cage,
Taught to bear man, if then a little blood
Touch their hot lips, fury returns and rage;
Their jaws by taste admonished swell with veins,
Rage boils, and from faint keeper scarce abstains.[34]

These original qualities are not grubbed[35] out, they are but covered and hidden. The Latin tongue is to me in a manner natural; I understand it better than French. But it is now forty years, I have not made use of it to speak nor much to write. Yet in some extreme emotions and sudden passions, wherein I have twice or thrice fallen since my years of discretion—and namely one, when my father, being in perfect health, fell all along upon me in a swoon—I have ever, even from my very heart, uttered my first words in Latin; Nature rushing and by force expressing itself, against so long a custom. The like example is alleged of diverse others.

Those which in my time have attempted to correct the fashions[36] in the world by new opinions reform the vices of appearance; those of essence they leave untouched, if they increase not. And their increase is much to be feared. We willingly protract all other well-doing upon these external reformations, of less cost and of greater merit; whereby we satisfy good-cheap[37] other natural, consubstantial, and intestine[38] vices.

Look a little into the course of our experience. There is no man (if he listen to himself) that doth not discover in himself a peculiar form of his, a swaying[39] form, which wrestleth against the institution[40] and against the tempests of passions which are contrary unto him. As for me, I feel not myself much agitated by a shock; I commonly find myself in mine own place, as are sluggish and lumpish bodies. If I am not close and near unto myself, I am never far-off. My debauches or excesses transport me not much. There is nothing extreme and strange, yet have I sound fits and vigorous lusts.

The true condemnation, and which toucheth the common fashion of our men, is that their very retreat[41] is full of corruption and filth. The idea of their amendment blurred and deformed; their repentance crazed and faulty, very near as much as their sin. Some, either because they are so fast and naturally joined unto vice or through custom, have lost all sense of its ugliness. To others (of whose rank I am) vice is burthenous,[42] but they counter-balance it with pleasure or other occasions, and suffer it and at a certain rate lend themselves unto it, though basely and viciously. Yet might happily[43] so remote a disposition of measure be imagined, where with justice, the pleasure might excuse the offence, as we say of profit. Not only being accidental and out of sin, as in thefts, but even in the very exercise of it, as in the acquaintance or copulation with women, where the provocation is so violent and, as they say, sometime unresistable.[44]

In a town of a kinsman of mine, the other day being in *Armignac*, I saw a country man, commonly surnamed the Thief, who himself reported his life to have been thus. Being born a beggar and perceiving that to get his bread by the sweat of his brow and labour of his hands would never sufficiently arm him against penury, he resolved to become a thief; and in that trade had employed all his youth, safely, by means of his bodily strength. For he ever made up harvest and vintage in other men's grounds, but so far off and in so great heaps that it was beyond imagination one man should in one night carry away so much upon his shoulders. And was so careful to equal the prey and disperse the mischief he did that the spoil was of less import to every particular man. He is now in old years indifferently rich; for a man of his condition (God-a-mercy his trade) which he is not ashamed to confess openly. And to reconcile himself with God, he affirmeth to be daily ready with his gettings and other good turns to satisfy the posterity of those he hath heretofore wronged or robbed; which if himself be not of ability to perform (for he cannot do all at once), he will charge his heirs withal, according to the knowledge he hath of the wrongs by him done to every man. By this description, be it true or false, he respecteth theft as a dishonest and unlawful action and hateth the same, yet less than pinching want.[45]

He repents but simply, for in regard it was so counter-balanced and recompensed, he repenteth not. That is not that habit which incorporates us unto vice and confirmeth our understanding in it; nor is it that boisterous wind which by violent blasts dazzleth and troubleth our minds, and at that time confounds and overwhelms both us, our judgement, and all, into the power of vice.

What I do is ordinarily full and complete, and I march (as we say) all in one piece. I have not many motions that hide themselves and slink away from my reason, or which very near are not guided by the consent of all my parts without division or intestine sedition. My judgement hath the whole blame or commendation, and the blame it hath once, it hath ever. For, almost from its birth, it hath been one of the same inclination, course, and force. And in matters of general opinions, even from my infancy, I ranged myself to the point I was to hold.

Some sins there are outrageous, violent, and sudden; leave we them. But those other sins, so often reassumed, determined, and advised upon, whether they be of complexion,[46] or of profession and calling, I cannot conceive how they should so long be settled in one same courage,[47] unless the reason and conscience of the sinner were thereunto inwardly privy and constantly willing. And how to imagine or fashion the repentance thereof which, he[48] vaunteth, doth sometimes visit him, seemeth somewhat hard unto me.

I am not of *Pythagoras'* sect, that men take a new soul when, to receive oracles, they approach the images of gods, unless he would say with all that it must be a strange one, new and lent him for the time, our own, giving so little sign of purification and cleanness worthy of that office.

They do altogether against the Stoical precepts, which appoint us to correct the imperfections and vices we find in ourselves, but withal forbid us to disturb the quiet of our mind. They make us believe they feel great remorse and are inwardly much displeased with sin. But of amendment, correction, or intermission, they show us none. *Surely there can be no perfect health, where the disease is not perfectly removed.* Were repentance put in the scale of the balance, it would weigh down sin. *I find no humour so easy to be counterfeited as devotion.* If one conform not his life and conditions to it, her essence is abstruse and concealed, her appearance gentle and stately.

For my part, I may in general wish to be other than I am; I may condemn and mislike my universal form; I may beseech God to grant me an undefiled reformation and excuse my natural weakness. But me seemeth I ought not to term this repentance, no more than the displeasure of being neither angel nor *Cato*.[49] My actions are squared to what I am and conformed to my condition. I cannot do better. And *repentance doth not properly concern what is not in our power; sorrow doth.* I may imagine infinite dispositions of a higher pitch and better governed than mine, yet do I nothing better my faculties; no more than mine arm becometh stronger or my wit more excellent by conceiving some others to be so. If to suppose and wish a more nobler working than ours might produce the repentance of our own, we should then repent us of our most innocent actions. Forsomuch as we judge that in a more excellent nature, they had been directed with greater perfection and dignity, and ourselves would do the like.

When I consult with my age of my youth's proceedings, I find that commonly (according to my opinion) I managed them in order. This is all my resistance is able to perform. I flatter not myself; in like circumstances, I should ever be the same. It is not a spot, but a whole dye that stains me. I acknowledge no repentance . . . [that] is superficial, mean, and ceremonious. It must touch me on all sides before I can term it repentance. It must pinch my entrails and afflict them as deeply and thoroughly, as God himself beholds me.

When in negotiating, many good fortunes have slipped me for want of good discretion yet did my projects make good choice, according to the occurrences presented unto them. Their manner is ever to take the easier and surer side. I find that in my former deliberations I proceeded, after my rules, discretely, for the subject's state propounded to me; and in like occasions would proceed alike a hundred years hence. I respect[50] not what now it is, but what it was when I consulted of it.

The consequence of all designs consists in the seasons; occasions pass, and matters change uncessantly. I have in my time run into some gross, absurd, and important errors; not for want of good advice but of good hap. There are secret and indivinable parts in the objects men do handle, especially in the nature of men; and mute conditions without show and sometimes unknown of the very possessors produced and stirred up by sudden occasions. If my wit could neither find nor presage[51] them, I am not offended with it; the function thereof is contained within its own limits. If the success[52] beat me and favour the side I refused, there is no remedy; I fall not out with myself; I accuse my fortune, not my endeavour. That's not called repentance.

Phocion had given the Athenians some counsel which was not followed; the matter, against his opinion, succeeding happily. "How now, *Phocion*" (quoth one), "art thou pleased the matter hath thrived so well?" "Yea" (said he), "and I am glad of it, yet repent not the advice I gave."

When any of my friends come to me for counsel, I bestow it frankly and clearly, not (as well nigh all the world doth) wavering at the hazard of the matter, whereby the contrary of my meaning may happen, that so they may justly find fault with my advice. For which I care not greatly. For they shall do me wrong, and it became not me to refuse them that duty.

I have nobody to blame for my faults or misfortunes but myself. For in effect I seldom use the advice of others, unless it be for compliment's sake and where I have need of instruction or knowledge of the fact. Marry, in things wherein nought but judgement is to be employed, strange reasons may serve to sustain but not to divert me. I lend a favourable and courteous ear unto them all. But (to my remembrance) I never believed any but mine own. With me they are but flies and moathes[53] which distract my will. I little regard mine own opinions, other men's I esteem as little. Fortune pays me accordingly. If I take no counsel, I give as little. I am not much sought after for it and less credited when I give it. Neither know I any enterprise, either private or public, that my advice hath directed and brought to conclusion. Even those whom fortune had some way tied thereunto have more willingly admitted the direction of others' conceits than mine. As one that am as jealous of the rights of my quiet as of those of my authority, I would rather have it thus. Where leaving me,[54] they jump with my profession, which is wholly to settle and contain me in myself. It is a pleasure unto me to be disinterested of other men's affairs and disengaged from their contentions.

When suits or businesses be over-past, howsoever it be, I grieve little at them. For the imagination that they must necessarily happen so puts me out of pain: behold them in the course of the universe and enchained in Stoical causes. Your fancy cannot by wish or imagination remove one point of them, but the whole order of things must reverse both what is past and what is to come.

Moreover, I hate that accidental repentance which old age brings with it. He that in ancient times said he was beholden to years because they had rid him of voluptuousness was not of mine opinion. I shall never give impuissance[55] thanks for any good it can do me. *Nec tam aversa vnquam videbitur ab opere suo prouidentia, ut debilitas inter optima inuenta sit. Nor shall foresight ever be seen so averse from her own work that weakness be found to be one of the best things.*[56] Our appetites are rare in old age; the blow over-passed, a deep sacietie[57] seizeth upon us. Therein I see no conscience. Fretting care and weakness imprint in us an effeminate and drowsy virtue. We must not suffer ourselves so fully to be carried into natural alterations as to corrupt or adulterate our judgement by them. Youth and pleasure have not heretofore prevailed so much over me but I could ever (even in the midst of sensualities) discern the ugly face of sin; nor can the distaste which years bring on me at this instant keep me from discerning that of voluptuousness in vice. Now I am no longer in it, I judge of it as if I were still there.

I, who lively and attentively examine my reason, find it to be the same that possessed me in my most dissolute and licentious age, unless perhaps they,[58] being enfeebled and impaired by years, do make some difference. And [I] find that what delight it refuseth to afford me in regard of my bodily health, it would no more deny me than in times past, for the health of my soul. To see it out of combat, I hold it not the more courageous. My temptations are so mortified and crazed as they are not worthy of its oppositions. Holding but my hand before me, I becalm them. Should one present that former concupiscence unto it, I fear it would be of less power to sustain it than heretofore it hath been. I see in it by itself no increase of judgement nor access of brightness; what it now judgeth, it did then. Wherefore if there be any amendment,[59] 'tis but diseased.

Oh miserable kind of remedy, to be beholden unto sickness for our health. It is not for our mishap but for the good success of our judgement to perform this office. Crosses and afflictions make me do nothing but curse them; they are for people that cannot be awaked but by the whip. The course of my reason is the nimbler in prosperity. It is much more distracted and busied in the digesting of mischiefs than of delights. I see much clearer in fair weather. Health forewarneth me, as with more pleasure, so to better purpose than sickness. I approached the nearest I could unto amendment and regularity when I should have enjoyed the same. I should be ashamed and vexed that the misery and mishap of my old age could exceed the health, attention, and vigor of my youth, and that I should be esteemed, not for what I have been, but for what I am left to be.

The happy life (in my opinion), not (as said *Antisthenes*) the happy death, is it that makes man's happiness in this world. I have not preposterously[60] busied myself to tie the tail of a philosopher unto the head and body of a varlet;[61] nor that this paltry end should disavow and belie the fairest, soundest, and longest part of my life. I will present myself and make a general muster of my whole, everywhere uniformly. Were I to live again, it should be as I have already lived. I neither deplore what is past nor dread what is to come. And if I be not deceived, the inward parts have nearly resembled the outward. It is one of the chiefest points wherein I am beholden to fortune that, in the course of my body's estate, each thing hath been carried in season. I have seen the leaves, the blossoms, and the fruit; and now see the drooping and withering of it—happily, because naturally. I bear my present miseries the more gently because they are in their prime, and with greater favour make me remember the long happiness of my former life.

In like manner, my discretion[62] may well be of like proportion in the one and the other time; but sure it was of much more performance, and had a better grace, being fresh, jolly, and full of spirit than now that it is worn, decrepit, and toilsome.

I therefore renounce these casual and dolorous reformations.

God must touch our hearts; our conscience must amend of itself and not by reinforcement of our reason nor by the enfeebling of our appetites.[63] Voluptuousness in itself is neither pale nor discoloured, to be discerned by bleary and troubled eyes. We should affect[64] temperance and chastity for itself and for God's cause, who hath ordained them unto us; that which Catars[65] bestow upon us and which I am beholden to my colic for is neither temperance nor chastity. A man cannot boast of contemning or combating sensuality if he see her not or know not her grace, her force, and most attractive beauties.

I know them both and therefore may speak it. But methinks our souls in age are subject unto more importunate diseases and imperfections than they are in youth. I said so, being young, when my beardless chin was upbraided me.[66] And I say it again, now that my gray beard gives me authority. We entitle "wisdom" the frowardness[67] of our humours and the distaste of present things. But in truth we abandon not vices so much as we change them, and, in mine opinion, for the worse. Besides a silly and ruinous pride, cumbersome tattle,[68] wayward and unsociable humors, superstition, and a ridiculous carking for[69] wealth when the use of it is well-nigh lost, I find the more envy, injustice, and lewdness in it. It sets more wrinkles in our minds than on our foreheads; nor are there any spirits, or very rare ones, which in growing old taste not sourly and mustily.[70] Man marcheth entirely towards his increase and decrease.

View but the wisdom of *Socrates* and diverse circumstances of his condemnation, I dare say he something lent himself unto it by prevarication, of purpose[71]—being so near and at the age of seventy to endure the benumbing of his spirit's richest pace, and the dimming of his accustomed brightness.

What *Metamorphoses* have I seen it[72] daily make in diverse of mine acquaintances? It is a powerful malady which naturally and imperceptibly glideth into us. There is required great provision of study, heed, and precaution to avoid the imperfections wherewith it chargeth us, or at least to weaken their further progress. I find that notwithstanding all my entrenchings,[73] by little and little it[74] getteth ground upon me. I hold out as long as I can but know not whither at length it will bring me. Hap what hap will, I am pleased the world knows from what height I tumbled.

Of Three Commerces or Societies[1]

WE MUST not cleave so fast unto our humours and dispositions. Our chiefest sufficiency is to apply ourselves to diverse fashions. It is a being, but not a life, to be tied and bound by necessity to one only course. The goodliest minds are those that have most variety and pliableness in them. Behold an honourable testimony of old *Cato*: *Huic versatile ingenium sic pariter ad omnia fuit, ut natum ad id vnum diceres, quodcumque ageret. He had a wit so turnable to all things alike, as one would say he had been only born for that he went about to do.*[2]

Were I to dress myself after mine own manner, there is no fashion so good whereto I would be so affected or tied as not to know how to leave and loose it. *Life is a motion unequal, irregular, and multiform.* It is not to be the friend (less the master) but the slave of oneself to follow incessantly and be so addicted to his inclinations as he cannot stray from them nor wrest them. This I say now, as being extremely pestered with the importunity of my mind, forsomuch as she cannot amuse herself but whereon it is busied, nor employ itself but bent and whole. How light soever the subject is one gives it, it willingly amplifieth and wire-draws[3] the same, even unto the highest pitch of toil. Its idleness is therefore a painful trade unto me and offensive to my health. Most wits have need of extravagant stuff to un-benumb and exercise themselves; mine hath need of it rather to settle and continue itself. *Vitia otii negotio discucienda sunt. The vices of idleness should be shaken off with business.*[4] For the most laborious care and principal study of it is to study itself.

Books are one of those businesses that seduce it[5] from study. At the first thoughts that present themselves, it rouseth up and makes proof of all the vigor it hath. It exerciseth its function sometimes toward force, sometimes toward order and comeliness; it rangeth, moderates, and fortifieth. It hath of itself to awaken the faculties of it. Nature having given it, as unto all other, matter of its own for advantage, subjects fit enough whereon to devise and determine.

Meditation is a large and powerful study to such as vigorously can taste and employ themselves therein. I had rather forge than furnish my mind. There is no office or occupation either weaker or stronger than that of entertaining of one's thoughts according to the mind, whatsoever it be. The greatest make it their vacation.[6] *Quibus viuere est cogitare, to whom it is all one to live and to meditate.*[7] Nature hath also favoured it with this privilege, that there is nothing we can do so long, nor action whereso we give ourselves more ordinarily and easily. It is the work of gods (sayeth Aristotle) whence both their happiness and ours proceedeth. Reading serves me especially to awake my conceit[8] by diverse objects to busy my judgement, not my memory.

Few entertainments,[9] then, stay me without vigour and force. 'Tis true that courtesy and beauty possess me, as much or more, than weight and depth. And because I slumber in all other communications and lend but the superficial parts of my attention unto them, it often befalleth me in such kind of weak and absurd discourses (discourses of countenance[10]) to blurt out and answer ridiculous toys and fond absurdities, unworthy a child, or willfully to hold my peace, therewithal more foolishly and incivilly. I have a kind of raving, fanciful behaviour that retireth me into myself and, on the other side, a gross and childish ignorance of many ordinary things. By means of which two qualities, I have in my days committed five or six as sottish tricks as any one whosoever, which to my derogation may be reported.

But to follow my purpose, this harsh complexion[11] of mine makes me nice[12] in conversing with men (whom I must pick and cull out for the nonce[13]) and unfit for common actions. We live and negotiate with the people. If their behaviour importune us, if we disdain to lend ourselves to base and vulgar spirits, which often are as regular as those of a finer mould—and *all wisdom is foolish that is not conformed to common insipience*[14]—we are no longer to intermeddle either with our or other men's affairs, and both [in] public and private forsake[15] such kind of people.

The least wrested[16] and most natural proceedings of our mind are the fairest; the best occupations, those which are least forced. Good God, how good an office doth wisdom unto those whose desires she squareth according to[17] their power! There is no science[18] more profitable. *As one may* was the burden[19] and favoured saying of *Socrates*: a sentence of great substance. We must address and stay our desires to things most easy and nearest. Is it not a fond-peevish humour in me to disagree from a thousand to whom my fortune joineth me, without whom I cannot live, to adhere unto one or two that are out of my commerce and conversation, or rather to a fantastical conceit or fanciful desire for a thing I cannot obtain? My soft behaviours and mild manners, enemies to all sharpness and foes to all bitterness, may easily have discharged me from envy and contention. To be beloved, I say not; but not to be hated, never did man give more occasion. But the coldness of my conversation hath with reason robbed me of the good will of many, which may be excused if they interpret the same to other or worse sense.

I am most capable of getting rare amities[20] and continuing exquisite acquaintances. Forsomuch as with so greedy hunger I snatch at such acquaintances as answer my taste and square with my humour. I so greedily produce and head-long cast myself upon them that I do not easily miss to cleave unto them, and where I light on, to make a steady impression. I have often made happy and successful trial of it. In vulgar[21] worldly friendships, I am somewhat cold and barren, for my proceeding is not natural if not unresisted and with hoised-full sails.[22] Moreover, my fortune having inured and allured me, even from my infancy, to one sole-singular and perfect amity, hath verily, in some sort, distasted me from others; and over-deeply imprinted in my fantasy that it is a beast sociable and for company and not of troupe,[23] as said an ancient writer. So that it is naturally a pain unto me to communicate myself by halves and with modification, and

[with] that servile or suspicious wisdom which in the conversation of these numerous and imperfect amities is ordained and proposed unto us; prescribed in these days especially, *Wherein one cannot speak of the world but dangerously or falsely.*

Yet I see that who (as I do) makes for his end the commodities of his life (I mean essential commodities) must avoid as a plague these difficulties and quaintness of humour. I should commend a high-raised mind that could both bend and discharge itself; that wherever her fortune might transport her, she might continue constant; that could discourse with her neighbour of all matters, as of her building, of her hunting, and of any quarrel,[24] and entertain with delight a carpenter or a gardener. I envy those which can be familiar with the meanest of their followers and vouchsafe to contract friendship and frame discourse with their own servants.

Nor do I like the advice of *Plato*, ever to speak imperiously unto our attendants without blithness and sance[25] any familiarity, be it to men or women servants. For besides my reason, it is inhumanity and injustice to attribute so much unto that prerogative of fortune. And the government where less inequality is permitted between the servant and master is, in my conceit, the more indifferent.[26]

Some others study to rouse and raise their mind, but I to abase and prostrate mine. It is not faulty but in extension.[27]

Narras et genus Æaci,
Et pugnata sacro bella sub Ilio,
Quo Chium pretio cadum
Mercemur, quis aquam temperet ignibus,
Quo præbente domum, et quota
Pelignis caream frigoribus, taces.
You tell of *Æacus* the pedigree,
The wars at sacred *Troy,* you do display.
You tell not at what price a hog's head we
May buy of the best wine; who shall allay
Wine-fire with water; at whose house to hold;
At what o'clock I may be kept from cold.[28]

Even as the Lacedemonian[29] valour had need of moderation and of sweet and pleasing sounds of flutes to flatter and allay it in time of war, lest it should run head-long into rashness and fury, whereas all other nations use commonly piercing sounds and strong shouts, which violently excite and enflame their soldiers courage; so think I (against ordinary custom) that in the employment of our spirit,[30] we have for the most part more need of lead than wings, of coldness and quiet than of heat and agitation. Above all, in my mind, *The only way to play the fool well is to seem wise among fools*, to speak as though one's tongue were ever bent to *favellar in punta di forchetta, To syllabize or speak mincingly.*[31] One must lend himself unto those he is with and sometimes affect ignorance. Set force and subtlety aside; in common employments 'tis enough to reserve order. Drag yourself even close to the ground, if they will have it so.

The learned stumble willingly on this block, making continual muster and open show of their skill and dispersing their books[32] abroad. And have in these days so filled the closets[33] and possessed the ears of ladies that if they retain not their[34] substance, at least they have their countenance.[35] Using in all sorts of discourse and subject, how base or popular soever, a new, an affected, and learned fashion of speaking and writing.

> *Hoc sermone pauent, hoc iram, gaudia, curas,*
> *Hoc cuncta effundunt animi secreta, quid ultra?*
> *Concumbunt docte.*
> They in this language fear, in this they fashion
> Their joys, their cares, their rage, their inward passion;
> What more? They learned are in copulation.[36]

And allege *Plato* and Saint *Thomas* for things which the first man they meet would decide as well and stand for as good a witness. Such learning as could not enter into their mind hath stayed on their tongues.

If the well-born[37] will give any credit unto me, they shall be pleased to make their own and natural riches to prevail and be of worth. They hide and shroud their forms under foreign and borrowed beauties: *It is great simplicity for anybody to smother and conceal his own brightness, to shine with a borrowed light.* They are buried and entombed under the art of *CAPSULA TOTÆ.*[38] It is because they do not sufficiently know themselves. The world contains nothing of more beauty; it is for them to honour arts and to beautify embellishment. What need they more than to live beloved and honoured? They have and know but too much in that matter. There needs but a little rousing and enflaming of the faculties that are in them. When I see them[39] meddling with rhetoric, with law, and with logic and such like trash, so vain and unprofitable for their use, I enter into fear that those who advise them to such things do it that they may have more law to govern or colour them under that pretence. For what other excuse can I devise for them? It is sufficient that without us they may frame or roll the grace of their eyes unto cheerfulness, unto severity, and unto mildness; and season a *No* with frowardness,[40] with doubt, and with favour; and require not an interpreter in discourses made for their service. With this learning they command without control and over-rule both regents and schools.[41]

Yet if it offend them to yield us any preeminence and would for curiosity's sake have part in books also, poesy is a study fit for their purpose; being a wanton, amusing, subtle, disguised, and prattling art, all in delight, all in show, like to themselves. They may also select diverse commodities out of history. In moral philosophy, they may take the discourses which enable them to judge of our humours and censure of our conditions and to avoid our guiles and treacheries; to moderate their liberty; lengthen the delights of life; gently to bear the inconstancy of a servant,[42] the peevishness or rudeness of a husband, the importunity of years, the unwelcome of wrinkles, and such like mind-troubling accidents. Lo, here the most and greatest share of learning I would assign them.

There are some particular, retired, and close dispositions. My essential form is fit for communication and proper for production; I am all outward and in appearance, born for society and unto friendship. The solitude I love and commend is especially but to retire my affections and redeem my thoughts unto myself, to restrain and close up—not my steps but my desires and my cares, resigning all foreign solicitude and trouble and mortally shunning all manner of servitude and obligation, and not so much the throng of men as the importunity of affairs. Local solitariness[43] (to say truth) doth rather extend and enlarge me outwardly; I give myself to state-business and to the world more willingly when I am all alone. At the Court[44] and in press of people, I close and slink into mine own skin. Assemblies thrust me again into myself. And I never entertain myself so fondly, so licentiously, and so particularly, as in places of respect and ceremonious discretion. Our follies make me not laugh, but our wisdoms do.

Of mine own complexion,[45] I am no enemy to the agitations and stirrings of our courts; I have there past great part of my life and am inured to be merry in great assemblies, so it be by intermission[46] and suitable to my humor. But this tenderness and coyness of judgement (whereof I speak) doth perforce tie me unto solitariness. Yea, even in mine own house, in the midst of a numerous family and most frequented houses, I see people more than a good many but seldom such as I love to converse or communicate withal. And there I reserve, both for myself and others, an unaccustomed liberty. Making truce with ceremonies, assistance, and envitings,[47] and such other troublesome ordinances of our courtesies (oh, servile custom and importunate manner); there every man demeaneth[48] himself as he pleaseth and entertaineth what his thoughts affect, whereas I keep myself silent, meditating, and close, without offence to my guests or friends.

The men whose familiarity and society I hunt after are those which are called honest, virtuous, and sufficient; the image of whom doth distaste and divert me from others. It is (being rightly taken) the rarest of our forms and a form or fashion chiefly due unto nature. The end or scope of this commerce is principally and simply familiarity, conference, and frequentation[49]: the exercise of minds, without other fruit. In our discourses, all subjects are alike to me. I care not though they want either weight or depth; grace and pertinency are never wanting; all therein is tainted with a ripe and constant judgement and commixed with goodness, liberty, cheerfulness, and kindness. It is not only in the subject of laws and affairs of princes that our spirit showeth its beauty, grace, and vigor; it showeth them as much in private conferences. I know my people by their very silence and smiling, and peradventure discover them better at a table than sitting in serious counsel. *Hippomachus* said he discerned good wrestlers but by seeing them march through a street.

If learning vouchsafe[50] to step into our talk, she shall not be refused, yet must not she be stern, mastering, imperious, and importunate, as commonly she is, but assistant and docile of herself. Therein we seek for nothing but recreation and pastime; when we shall look to be instructed, taught, and resolved, we will go seek and sue to her in her throne. Let her if she please keep from us at that time. For, as commodious and pleasing as she is, I presume that for a need we could spare her presence and do our business well enough without her. Wits well born, soundly bred, and exercised in the practise and commerce of men become gracious and plausible of themselves. Art is but the check-roll[51] and register of the productions uttered and conceits produced by them.[52]

The company of fair and society of honest women is likewise a sweet commerce for me. *Nam nos quoque oculos eruditos habemus. For we also have learned eyes.*[53] If the mind have not so much to solace herself as in the former, the corporal senses, whose part is more in the second, bring it to a proportion near unto the other, although in mine opinion not equal. But it is a society wherein it behooveth a man somewhat to stand upon his guard and especially those that are of a strong constitution and whose body can do much, as in me. In my youth I heated myself therein and was very violent and endured all the rages and furious assaults which poets say happen to those who without order or discretion abandon themselves over-loosely and riotously unto it.[54] True it is indeed that the same lash hath since stood me instead of an instruction.[55]

Quicumque Argolica de classe Capharea fugit,
Semper ab Euboicis vela retorquet aquis.

> Greek sailors that *Capharean* rocks did fly,
> From the *Euboean* seas their sails still ply.[56]

It is folly to fasten all one's thoughts upon it and with a furious and indiscreet affection to engage himself unto it. But on the other side, to meddle with it without love or bond of affection, as comedians[57] do, to play a common part of age and manners, without ought[58] of their own but bare-conned[59] words, is verily a provision for one's safety, and yet but a cowardly one, as is that of him who would forgo his honour, his profit, or his pleasure for fear of danger. For it is certain that the practisers of such courses cannot hope for any fruit able to move or satisfy a worthy mind. One must very earnestly have desired that whereof he would enjoy an absolute delight. I mean, though fortune should unjustly favour their intention, which often happeneth because there is no woman, how deformed or unhandsome soever, but thinks herself lovely, amiable, and praiseworthy, either for her age, her hair, or gate (for there are generally no more fair than foul ones). And the *Brachmanian*[60] maids wanting other commendations, by proclamation for that purpose, made show of their matrimonial parts unto the people assembled, to see if thereby at least they might get them husbands.

By consequence there is not one of them, but upon the first oath one maketh to serve her, will very easily be persuaded to think well of herself. Now this common treason and ordinary protestations of men in these days must needs produce the effects, experience already discovereth, which is that either they join together and cast away themselves on themselves to avoid us; or on their side follow also the example we give them, acting their part of the play, without passion, without care, and without love, lending themselves to this intercourse.[61] *Neque affectui suo aut alieno obnoxiæ. Neither liable to their own nor other folks' affection.*[62] Thinking, according to *Lysias'* persuasions in *Plato*, they may so much the more profitably and commodiously yield unto us by how much less we love them. Wherein it will happen as in comedies: the spectators shall have as much or more pleasure as the comedians.

For my part, I no more acknowledge *Venus* without *Cupid* than a motherhood without an offspring.[63] They are things which inter-lend and inter-owe one another[64] their essence. Thus doth this coz-ening rebound on him that useth it and, as it costs him little, so gets he not much by it. Those which made *Venus* a goddess have respected that her principal beauty was incorporeal and spiritual; but she[65] whom these kind of people hunt after is not so much as human nor also brutal.[66] But such as wild beasts would not have her so filthy and terrestrial. We see that imagination enflames them, and desire or lust urgeth them before the body. We see in one and other sex, even in whole herds, choice and distinctions in their affections, and amongst themselves acquaintances of long continued good will and liking. And even those to whom age denieth bodily strength do yet bray, neigh, roar, skip, and wince for love. Before the deed we see them full of hope and heat, and when the body hath played his part, even tickle and tingle themselves with the sweetness of that remem-brance; some of them swell with pride at parting from it; others, all weary and glutted, ring out songs of glee and triumph. Who makes no more of it but to discharge his body of some natural necessity hath no cause to trouble others with so curious a preparation. *It is no food for a greedy and clownish hunger.*

As one that would not be accounted better than I am, thus much I will display of my youth's wanton errors. Not only for the danger of one's health that follows that game (yet could I not avoid two, though light and cursory, assaults) but also for contempt, I have not much been given to mercenary and common acquaintances.[67] I have coveted to set an edge on that sensual pleasure by difficulty, by de-sire, and for some glory; and liked *Tiberius* his fashions, who in his amours was swayed as much by modesty and nobleness as by any other quality. And *Flora's*[68] humour, who would prostitute herself to none worse than dictators, consuls, or senators, and took delight in the dignity and greatness of her lovers, doth somewhat suit with mine. Surely glittering pearls and silken clothes add something unto it, and so do titles, nobility, and a worthy train.

Besides which, I made high esteem of the mind, yet so as the body might not justly be found fault withal. For, to speak my conscience, if either of the two beauties were necessarily to be wanting, I would rather have chosen to want the mental, whose use is to be employed in better things. But in the subject of love, a subject that chiefly hath reference unto the two senses of seeing and touching, something may be done without the graces of the mind, but little or nothing without the corporal.

Beauty is the true availful advantage of women. It is so peculiarly theirs that ours, though it require some features and different allurements, is not in her right cue[69] or true bias, unless confused with theirs, childish and beardless.[70] It is reported that such as serve the great Turk under the title of beauty (whereof the number is infinite) are dismissed at furthest when they once come to the age of two and twenty years. *Discourse, discretion, together with the offices of true amity, are better found amongst men and therefore govern they the world's affairs.*

These two commerces or societies[71] are accidental and depending of others: the one is troublesome and tedious for its rarity; the other withers with old age; nor could they have sufficiently provided for my life's necessities. That of books, which is the third, is much more solid-sure and much more ours; some other advantages it yieldeth to the two former, but hath for her share constancy and the facility of her service. This accosteth and secondeth all my course, and everywhere assisteth me. It comforts me in age and solaceth me in solitariness. It easeth me of the burden of a wearisome sloth, and at all times rids me of tedious companies. It abateth the edge of fretting sorrow, on condition it be not extreme and over-insolent. *To divert me from any importunate imagination or insinuating conceit, there is no better way then to have recourse unto books:* with ease they allure me to them, and with facility they remove them[72] all. And though they perceive I neither frequent nor seek them, but wanting other more essential, lively, and more natural commodities, they never mutiny or murmur at me; but still entertain me with one and self-same visage.

He may well walk a foot that leads his horse by the bridle, sayeth the proverb. And our *James,* king of *Naples* and *Sicily,* who being fair, young, healthy, and in good plight, caused himself to be carried abroad in a plain wagon or skreene,[73] lying upon an homely pillow of course feathers, clothed in a suit of homespun gray and a bonnet of the same, yet royally attended on by a gallant troupe of nobles, of litters, coaches, and of all sorts of choice led-horses, a number of gentlemen and officers, represented a tender and wavering austerity. *The sick man is not to be moaned that hath his health*[74] *in his sleeve.* In the experience and use of this sentence,[75] which is most true, consisteth all the commodity I reap of books. In effect, I make no other use of them than those who know them not. I enjoy them, as a miser doth his gold, to know that I may enjoy them when I list; my mind is settled and satisfied with the right of possession.

I never travel without books, nor in peace nor in war. Yet do I pass many days and months without using them. It shall be anon, say I, or tomorrow, or when I please; in the meanwhile, the time runs away and passeth without hurting me. For it is wonderful, what repose I take and how I continue in this consideration that they are at my elbow to delight me when time shall serve, and in acknowledging what assistance they give unto my life. This is the best munition I have found in this human peregrination,[76] and I extremely bewail those men of understanding that want[77] the same. I accept with better will all other kinds of amusements, how slight soever, forsomuch as this cannot fail me.

At home I betake me somewhat the oftener to my library, whence all at once I command and survey all my household. It is seated in the chief entry of my house; thence I behold under me my garden, my base court, my yard, and look even into most rooms of my house. There, without order, without method, and by piecemeals I turn over and ransack now one book, and now another. Sometimes I muse and rave; and walking up and down, I indite and enregister[78] these my humors, these my conceits.

It is placed on the third story of a tower. The lower-most is my chapel; the second a chamber with other lodgings, where I often lie because I would be alone. Above it is a great wardrobe. It was in times past the most unprofitable place of all my house. There I pass the greatest part of my life's days and wear out most hours of the day. I am never there a-nights. Next unto it is a handsome neat cabinet,[79] able and large enough to receive fire in winter and very pleasantly windowed. And if I feared not care more than cost (care which drives and diverts me from all business), I might easily join a convenient gallery of a hundred paces long and twelve broad, on each side of it and upon one floor, having already, for some other purpose, found all the walls raised unto a convenient height. Each retired place requireth a walk.[80] My thoughts are prone to sleep, if I sit long. My mind goes not alone, as if legs did move it.[81] Those that study without books are all in the same case.[82]

The form of it is round and hath no flat side but what serveth for my table and chair; in which bending or circling manner, at one look it offereth me the full sight of all my books, set round about upon shelves or decks, five ranks one upon another. It hath three bay windows of a far-extending, rich, and unresisted prospect[83] and is in diameter sixteen paces void.[84]

In winter I am less continually there; for my house (as the name of it importeth[85]) is perched upon an over-peering hillock and hath no part more subject to all weathers than this, which pleaseth me the more both because the access unto it is somewhat troublesome and remote, and for the benefit of the exercise; which is to be respected and that I may the better seclude myself from company and keep encroachers from me. There is my seat that is my throne. I endeavour to make my rule therein absolute and to sequester that only corner from the community of wife, of children, and of acquaintance. Elsewhere I have but a verbal authority of confused essence. Miserable in my mind is he who, in his own home, hath nowhere to be to himself, where he may particularly court[86] and at his pleasure hide or withdraw himself. Ambition payeth her followers well to keep them still in open view, as a statue in some conspicuous place. *Magna servitus est magna fortuna. A great fortune is a great bondage.*[87] They cannot be private so much as at their privy.[88] I have deemed nothing so rude in the austerity of the life which our churchmen[89] affect as that in some of their companies they institute a perpetual society of place and a numerous assistance amongst them in anything they do. And [I] deem it somewhat more tolerable to be ever alone than never be able to be so.

If any say to me it is a kind of vilifying the Muses to use them only for sport and recreation, he wots not as I do what worth pleasure, sport, and pastime is of. I had well-nigh termed all other ends ridiculous. I live from hand to mouth, and, with reverence be it spoken, I live but to myself; there end all my designs.

Being young, I studied for ostentation; then, a little to enable myself and become wiser; now, for delight and recreation—never for gain. A vain conceit and lavish humour I had after this kind of stuff,[90] not only to provide for my need, but somewhat further to adorn and embellish myself withal; I have since partly left it.

Books have and contain diverse pleasing qualities to those that can duly choose them. But *no good without pains, no roses with out prickles.* It is a pleasure not absolutely pure and neat, no more than all others; it hath his inconveniences attending on it, and sometimes weighty ones. The mind is therein exercised, but the body (the care whereof I have not yet forgotten) remaineth therewhilst without action, and is wasted and ensorrowed. I know no excess more hurtful for me, nor more to be avoided by me in this declining age.

Lo, here my three most favoured and particular employments. I speak not of those I owe of duty to the world.

Of Diverting or Diversion

I WAS ONCE employed in comforting of a truly afflicted lady: the greatest part of their[1] discourses [of mourning] are artificial and ceremonious.

> *Uberibus semper lachrimis, semperque paratis.*
> *In statione sua, atque expectantibus illam,*
> *Quo iubeat manare modo.*
> With plenteous tears, still ready in their stand,
> Expecting still their mistresses' command,
> How they must flow, when they must go.[2]

Men do but ill in opposing themselves against this passion, for opposition doth but incense and engage them more to sorrow and quietness. *The disease is exasperated by the jealousy of debate.* In matters of common discourse, we see that what I have spoken without heed or care, if one come to contest with me about it, I stiffly maintain and make good mine own, much more if it be a thing wherein I am interested.

Besides, in so doing, you enter but rudely into your matter, whereas a physician's first entertainment of his patient should be gracious, cheerful, and pleasing. *An ugly and froward[3] physician wrought never any good effect.* On the contrary, then, we must at first assist and smooth their laments and witness some approbation and excuse thereof. By which means you get credit to go on, and by an easy and insensible inclination you fall into more firm and serious discourses and fit for their amendment.

I, who desired chiefly to gull the assistants[4] that had their eyes cast on me, meant to salve their mischief.[5] I verily find by experience that I have but an ill and unfruitful vein to persuade. I present my reasons either too sharp, or too dry, or too stirringly, or too carelessly. After I had for awhile applied myself to her torment, I attempted not to cure it by strong and lively reasons, either because I want[6] them or because I supposed I might otherwise effect my purpose the better. Nor did I cull out the several fashions of comfort prescribed by philosophy: that the thing lamented is not ill, as *Cleanthes* [says]; or but a little ill, as the Peripatetics; that to lament is neither just nor commendable, as *Chrisippus*; nor this of *Epicurus*, most agreeing with my manner, to translate the conceit of irksome into delightsome things; nor to make a load of all this mass,[7] dispensing the same as one hath occasion, as *Cicero*. But fair and softly declining our discourses, and by degrees bending them unto subjects more near, then a little more remote, even as she more or less inclined to me. I unperceivably removed those doleful humours from her so that, as long as I was with her, so long I kept her in cheerful countenance and untroubled fashion, wherein I used diversion. Those which in the same service succeeded me found her no whit amended: the reason was, I had not yet driven my wedge[8] to the root.

I have peradventure elsewhere glanced at some kinds of public diversions. And the military customs used by *Pericles* in the Peloponnesian war and a thousand others elsewhere, to divert or withdraw the army of an enemy from their own country, is too frequent in histories.

It was an ingenious diverting, wherewith the Lord of *Himbercourt* saved both himself and others in the town of *Liege*, into which the Duke of *Burgundy*, who beleaguered the same, had caused him to enter to perform the covenant of their accorded yielding. The inhabitants thereof, to provide for it, assembled by night and began to mutiny against their former agreement, determining upon this advantage to set upon the negotiators, now in their power. He, perceiving their intent and noise of this shower ready to fall upon him and the danger his lodging was in, forthwith rushed out upon them two citizens (whereof he had diverse with him), furnished with most plausible and new offers to be propounded to their counsel but indeed forged at that instant to serve his turn withal and to amuse[9] them. These two stayed the first-approaching storm and carried this incensed Hydra-headed-monster multitude back to the townhouse to hear their charge and accordingly to determine of it. The conclusion was short, when, lo, a second tempest came rushing on, more furiously enraged than the former; to whom he immediately dispatched four new and semblable[10] intercessors,[11] with protestations that now they were in earnest to propose and declare new and far more ample conditions unto them, wholly to their content and satisfaction. Whereby this disordered route was again drawn to their conclave and senate house. In sum, he, by such a dispensation of amusements diverting their head-long fury and dissipating the same with vain and frivolous consultations, at length lulled them into so secure a sleep that he gained the day, which was his chiefest drift and only aimed scope.

This other story is also of the same predicament.[12] *Atalanta*, a maid of rare surpassing beauty and of a wondrous-strange disposition, to rid herself from the importunate pursuit of a thousand amorous suitors who solicited her for marriage, prescribed this law unto them: that she would accept of him that should equal her in running, on condition those she should overcome might lose their lives. Some there were found who deemed this prize worthy the hazard and who incurred the penalty of so cruel a match.

Hippomenes, coming to make his assay after the rest, devoutly addressed himself to the divine protectress of all amorous delights,[13] earnestly invoking her assistance; who gently listening to his hearty prayers, furnished him with three golden apples and taught him how to use them. The scope of the race being plain, according as *Hippomenes* perceived his swift-footed mistress to approach his heels, he let fall (as at unawares[14]) one of his apples. The heedless maiden, gazing and wondering at the alluring beauty of it, failed not to turn and take it up.

Obstupuit virgo, nitidique cupidine pomi,
Dectinat cursus, aurumque volubile tollit.
The maid amaz'd, desiring that fair gold,
Turns by her course, takes it up as it rolled.[15]

The like he did (at his need) with the second and third, until by this digressing and diverting, the goal and advantage of the course was judged his.

When physicians cannot purge the rheum, they divert and remove the same unto some less dangerous part. I also perceive it to be the most ordinary receite[16] for the mind's diseases. *Ab ducendus etiam non nunquam animus est ad alia studia, solicitudines, curas, negotia: Loci denique mutatione, tanquam ægroti non conualescentes, sæpe curandus est. Our mind also is sometimes to be diverted to other studies, cogitations, cares, and businesses; and lastly to be cured by chance of place, as sick folks use that otherwise cannot get health.*[17] One makes it seldom to shock mischiefs with direct resistance. One makes it neither bear nor break, but shun or divert the blow.

This other lesson is too high and over-hard. It is for them of the first rank, merely to stay upon the thing itself, to examine, and judge it. It belongeth to one only *Socrates* to accost and entertain death with an undaunted ordinary visage, to become familiar and play with it. He seeketh for no comfort out of this thing itself. To die seemeth unto him a natural and indifferent accident. Thereon he wishly[18] fixeth his sight and thereon he resolveth without looking elsewhere.

Hegesias his disciples, who with hunger starved themselves to death, incensed thereunto with the persuading discourses of his lessons and that so thick[19] as King *Ptolomy* forbade him any longer to entertain his school with such murderous precepts. Those considered not death in itself; they judge it not. This was not the limit of their thoughts; they run on and aim at another being.

Those poor creatures we see on scaffolds, fraught with an earnest to heavens-raised devotion, therein to the uttermost of their power, employing all their senses—their ears attentive to such instructions as preachers give them and wringing hands heaved up to heaven;

with heart-proceeding voice, uttering devout prayers, with fervent and continual ruth-moving[20] motion—do verily what in such an unavoidable exigent[21] is commendable and convenient. One may well commend their religion, but not properly their constancy. They shun the brunt; they divert their consideration from death, as we use to dandle and busy children, when we would lance them or let them blood.[22] I have seen some who, if by fortune they chanced to cast their eyes towards the dreadful preparations of death which were round about them, fall into trances, and with fury cast their cogitations[23] elsewhere. We teach those that are to pass over some steepy down-fall[24] or dreadful abyss to shut or turn aside their eyes.

Subrius Flavius, being by the appointment of *Nero* to be put to death by the hands of *Niger*, both chief commanders in war; when he was brought unto the place where the execution should be performed, seeing the pit *Niger* had caused to be digged for him uneven and unhandsomely made. "*Nor is this pit*" (quoth he to the soldiers that stood about him), "*according to the true discipline of war.*" And to *Niger*, who willed him to hold his head steady, "*I wish thou wouldst strike as steadily.*" He guessed right, for *Niger*'s arm trembling, he had diverse blows at him before be could strike it off. This man seemed to have fixed his thoughts surely and directly on the matter.

He that dies in the fury of a battle, with weapons in hand, thinks not then on death and neither feeleth nor considereth the same; the heat of the fight transports him. An honest man of my acquaintance, falling down in a single combat and feeling himself stabbed nine or ten times by his enemy, was called unto by the bystanders to call on God and remember his conscience. But he told me after that, albeit those voices came unto his ears, they had no whit moved him and that he thought on nothing but how to discharge and revenge himself. In which combat he vanquished and slew his adversary.

He who brought *L. Sillanus* his condemnation did much for him, in that when he heard him answer he was prepared to die but not by the hands of base villains, ran upon him with his soldiers to force him; against whom obstinately defending himself (though unarmed) with fists and feet, he was slain in the conflict, dispersing with a ready and rebellious choler the painful sense of a long and fore-prepared death to which he was assigned.

We ever think on somewhat else: either the hope of a better life doth settle and support us, or the confidence of our children's worth, or the future glory of our name, or the avoiding of these lives' mischiefs, or the revenge hanging over their heads that have caused and procured our death:

> *Spero equidem mediis, si quid pia numina possunt,*
> *Supplcia hausurum scopulis, et nomine Dido*
> *Sæpe vocaturum.*
> *Audiam, et hæc manes veniet mihi fama sub imos.*
> I hope, if powers of heaven have any power,
> On rock he shall be punished, at that hour
> He oft on *Dido's* name, shall pitiless exclaim.
> This shall I hear, and this report shall to me in my grave resort.[25]

Xenophon sacrificed with a crown on his head, when one came to tell him the death of his son *Gryllus* in the battle of *Mantinea*. At the first hearing whereof he cast his crown to the ground; but finding upon better relation how valiantly he died, he took it up and put it on his head again.

Epicurus also at his death comforted himself in the eternity and worth of his writings. *Omnes clari et nobilitati labores fiunt tolerabiles. All glorious and honourable labours are made tolerable.* And the same wound and the same toil (sayeth *Xenophon*) toucheth not a general of an army as it doth a private soldier. *Epaminondas* took his death much the more cheerfully, being informed that the victory remained on his side. *Hæc sunt solatia, hæc fomenta summorum dolorum. These are the comforts, these the eases of most grievous pains.*[26] And such other like circumstances amuse, divert, and remove us from the consideration of the thing in itself.

Even the arguments of philosophy at each clap[27] wrest and turn the matter aside and scarcely wipe away the scab thereof. The first man of the first philosophical school and superintendent of the rest, that great *Zeno*, against death cried out: *No evil is honourable; death is; therefore is death no evil.* Against drunkenness, *No man entrusts his secrets to a drunkard; every one to the wise; therefore the wise will not be drunk.* Is this to hit the white?[28] I love to see that these principal wits cannot rid themselves of our company. As perfect and absolute as they would be, they are still but gross and simple men.

Revenge is a sweet-pleasing passion, of a great and natural impression. I perceive it well, albeit I have made no trial of it. To divert of late a young prince[29] from it, I told him not he was to offer the one side of his cheek to him who had struck him on the other in regard of charity; nor displayed I unto him the tragical events poesy bestoweth upon that passion. There I left him and strove to make him taste the beauty of a contrary image: the honour, the favour, and the good will he should acquire by gentleness and goodness. I diverted him to ambition. Behold how they deal in such cases.

If your affection in love be over-powerful, disperse or dissipate the same, say they. And they say true, for I have often, with profit made trial of it. Break it by the virtue of several desires, of which one may be regent or chief master, if you please; but for fear it should misuse and tyrannize you, weaken it with dividing, and protract it with diverting the same.

> *Cum morosa vago singultiet inguine vena,*
> *Coniicito humorem collectum in corpora quæque.*
> When raging lust excites a panting tumor,
> To diverse parts send that collected humor.[30]

And look to it in time, lest it vex you, if it have once seized on you.

> *Si non prima novis conturbes vulnera plagis,*
> *Volgiuagaque vagus Venere ante recentia cures.*
> Unless the first wounds with new wounds you mix,
> And, ranging, cure the fresh with common tricks.[31]

I was once nearly touched with a heavy displeasure,[32] according to my complexion,[33] and yet more just than heavy. I had peradventure lost myself in it had I only relied upon mine own strength. Needing a vehement diversion to withdraw me from it, I did by art and study make myself a lover, whereto my age assisted me. Love discharged and diverted me from the inconvenience, which good will and amity had caused in me.

So is it in all things else. A sharp conceit possesseth and a violent imagination holdeth me; I find it a shorter course to alter and divert than to tame and vanquish the same. If I cannot substitute a contrary unto it, at least I present another unto it. *Change ever easeth, variety dissolveth, and shifting dissipateth.* If I cannot buckle with[34] it, I slip from it; and in shunning it, I stray and double from it. Shifting of place, exercise, and company, I save myself amid the throng of other studies and amusements, where it loseth my track, and so I slip away.

Nature proceedeth thus by the benefit of inconstancy. For the time it hath bestowed on us, as a sovereign physician of our passions, chiefly obtains his purpose that way: when fraughting[35] our conceits with other and different affairs, it dissolveth and corrupteth[36] that first apprehension, how forcible soever it be. A wise man seeth little less his friend dying at the end of five and twenty years than at the beginning of the first year.[37] And according to *Epicurus*, nothing less, for he ascribed no qualification of perplexities either to the foresight[38] or antiquity of them. But so many other cogitations cross this that it languisheth and in the end groweth weary.

To divert the inclination of vulgar reports, *Alcibiades* cut off his fair dog's ears and tail and so drove him into the marketplace, that giving this subject of prattle to the people, they might not meddle with his other actions. I have also seen some women, who to divert the opinions and conjectures of the babbling people and to divert the fond tattling of some, did by counterfeit and dissembled affections overshadow and cloak true affections. Amongst which I have noted some who, in dissembling and counterfeiting, have suffered themselves to be entrapped wittingly and in good earnest, quitting their true and original humor for the feigned.[39] Of whom I learn that such as find themselves well seated are very fools to yield unto that mask. The common greetings and public entertainments being reserved unto that set or appointed servant, believe[40] there is little sufficiency in him if in the end he usurp not your room and send you unto his. This is properly to cut out and stitch up a shoe for another to put on.

A little thing doth divert and turn us, for a small thing holds us. We do not much respect subjects in gross and alone; they are circumstances or small and superficial images that move and touch us, and vain rinds which rebound from subjects.[41]

> *Folliculos ut nunc teretes æstate cicadæ*
> *Linguunt.*
> As grasshoppers in summer now forsake
> The round-grown sheafs, which they in time should take.[42]

Plutarch himself bewails his daughter by the fopperies of her childhood. The remembrance of a farewell, of an action, of a particular grace, or of a last commendation afflict us. *Caesar's* gown disquieted all *Rome*, which his death had not done. The very sound of names, which gingleth[43] in our ears as, "*Oh, my poor master*"; or, "*Alas, my dear friend*"; "*Oh, my good father*"; or, "*Alas, my sweet daughter.*" When such like repetitions pinch me, and that I look more nearly to them, I find them but grammatical laments. The word and the tune wound me—even as preachers' exclamations do often move their auditory[44] more than their reasons,[45] and as the pitiful groan of a beast yearneth us, though it be killed for our use—without poising[46] or entering therewhilst into the true and massy[47] essence of my subject.

> *His se stimulis dolor ipse lacessit.*
> Grief by these provocations,
> Puts itself in more passions.[48]

They are the foundations of our mourning.

The obstinacy of the stone,[49] namely in the yard,[50] hath some times for three or four days together so stopped my urine and brought me so near death's door that it had been mere folly in me to hope, nay to desire, to avoid the same, considering what cruel pangs that painful plight did seize me with. Oh, how cunning a master in the murdering art or hangman's trade was that good Emperor,[51] who caused malefactors' yards to be fast-tied that so he might make them die for want of pissing. In which tears finding myself, I considered by how slight causes and frivolous objects imagination nourished in me the grief to lose my life; with what atoms the consequence and difficulty of my dislodging was contrived in my mind; to what idle conceits and frivolous cogitations we give place in so weighty a case or important affair. A dog, a horse, a hare, a glass, and whatnot were counted in my loss. To others, their ambitious hopes, their purse, their learning—in my mind as sottishly.[52] I view death carelessly when I behold it universally as the end of life. I overwhelm and contemn it thus in great; by retail, it spoils and proules[53] me.[54] The tears of a lackey,[55] the distributing of my cast suits,[56] the touch of a known hand, an ordinary consolation doth disconsolate and entender me.[57]

So do the plaints and fables of trouble vex our minds, and the wailing laments of *Dido* and *Ariadne* passionate[58] even those that believe them not in *Virgil* nor in *Catullus*. It is an argument of an obstinate nature and indurate[59] heart not to be moved therewith; as for a wonder, they report of *Polemon*, who was not so much as appalled at the biting of a dog who took away the brawn or calf of his leg. And no wisdom goeth so far as by due judgement to conceive aright the evident cause of a sorrow and grief too lively and wholly. That it suffer or admit no accession [except] by presence, when eyes and ears have their share therein, parts that cannot be agitated but by vain accidents.[60]

Is it reason that even arts should serve their purposes, and make their profit of our imbecility and natural blockishness?[61] An orator, (sayeth Rhetoric), in the play of his pleading, shall be moved at the sound of his own voice and by his feigned agitations, and suffer himself to be cozened by the passion he representeth. Imprinting a lively and essential sorrow by the juggling[62] he acteth, to transfer it into the judges, whom of the two it concerneth less. As the persons hired at our funerals who, to aid the ceremony of mourning, make sale of their tears by measure and of their sorrow by weight. For although they strive to act it in a borrowed form, yet by habituating and ordering their countenance, it is certain they are often wholly transported into it and entertain the impression of a true and unfeigned melancholy.

I assisted amongst diverse others of his friends to convey the dead corpse of the Lord of *Grammont* from the siege of *Lafere*, where he was untimely slain, to *Soissons*. I noted that everywhere as we passed along we filled with lamentations and tears all the people we met by the only show of our convoy's mourning attire, for the deceased man's name was not so much as known or heard of about those quarters.

Quintilian reporteth to have seen comedians[63] so far engaged in a sorrowful part that they wept after being come to their lodgings; and of himself, that having undertaken to move a certain passion in another, he had found himself surprised, not only with shedding of tears but with a paleness of countenance and behaviour of a man truly dejected with grief.[64]

In a country near our mountains, the women say and unsay, weep and laugh with one breath, as *Martin* the priest.[65] For as for their lost husbands they entreat their waymentings[66] by repetition of the good and graceful parts they were endowed with, therewithal under one they make public relation of those imperfections; to work, as it were, some recompense unto themselves and transchange their pity unto disdain; with a much better grace than we who, when we lose a late acquaintance, strive to load him with new and forged praises and to make him far other now that we are deprived of his sight than he seemed to be when we enjoyed and beheld him. As if mourning were an instructing party,[67] or tears cleared our understanding by washing the same. I renounce from this time forward all the favourable testimonies any man shall afford me, not because I shall deserve them but because I shall be dead.

If one demand that fellow what interest he hath in such a siege, *"The interest of example" (will he say), "and common obedience of the prince;* I nor look nor pretend any benefit thereby; and of glory I know how small a portion cometh to the share of a private man, such as I am. I have neither passion nor quarrel in the matter." Yet the next day shall you see him all changed, and chafing, boiling, and blushing with rage in his rank of battle, ready for the assault. It is the glaring reflecting of so much steel, the flashing thundering of the cannon, the clang of trumpets, and the rattling of drums that have infused this new fury and rancor in his swelling veins.

A frivolous cause, will you say. How a cause? There needeth none to excite our mind: a doting humour without body, without substance overswayeth and tosseth it up and down. Let me think of building castles in *Spain*, my imagination will forge me commodities and afford me means and delights wherewith my mind is really tickled and essentially gladded. How often do we pester our spirits with anger or sadness by such shadows and entangle ourselves into fantastical passions which alter both our mind and body? What astonished, flearing,[68] and confused mumps and mows[69] doth this dotage stir up in our visages! What skippings[70] and agitations of members and voice! Seems it not by this man, alone, that he hath false visions of a multitude of other men with whom he doth negotiate, or some inward goblin that torments him?

Inquire of yourself, where is the object of this alteration? Is there anything but us in nature, except subsisting nullity, over whom it hath any power?

Because *Cambyses* dreamed that his brother should be King of *Persia*, he put him to death—a brother whom he loved and ever trusted. *Aristodemus*, King of the *Messenians*, killed himself upon a conceit he took of some ill presage[71] by I know not what howling of his dogs. And King *Midas* did as much, being troubled and vexed by a certain unpleasing dream of his own. It is the right way to prize one's life at the right worth of it, to forgo it for a dream.[72]

Hear, notwithstanding, our mind triumph over the body's weak-nesses and misery, in that it[73] is the prey and mark[74] of all wrongs and alterations to feed on and aim at. It hath surely much reason to speak of it.

> *O prima infælix fingenti terra Prometheo?*
> *Ille parum cauti pectoris egit opus.*
> *Corpora disponens, mentem non vidit in arte?*
> *Recta animi primum debuit esse via.*
> Unhappy earth first by *Prometheus* formed,
> Who of small providence a work performed.
> He, framing bodies, saw in art no mind;
> The mind's way first should rightly be assign'd.[75]

Upon Some Verses of Virgil
(selections) 3.5

I HATE a wayward and sad disposition that glideth over the pleasures of his life, and fastens and feeds on miseries. As flies that cannot cleave to smooth and sleek bodies, but seize and hold on rugged
and uneven places. Or as cupping-glasses[1] that affect and suck none
but the worst blood. For my part I am resoluted to dare speak whatsoever I dare do. And am displeased with thoughts not to be published. The worst of my actions or conditions seem not so ugly unto
me as I find it both ugly and base not to dare to avouch them. *Every
one is wary in the confession; we should be as heedy[2] in the action.* The
boldness of offending is somewhat recompensed and restrained by
the boldness of confessing.

Even from their [women's] infancy we frame them to the sports of
love. Their instruction, behaviour, attire, grace, learning, and all
their words aimeth only at love, respects only affection. Their nurses
and their keepers imprint no other thing in them than the loveliness
of love, were it but by continually presenting the same unto them to
distaste them of it.[3] My daughter (all the children I have) is of the age
wherein the laws excuse[4] the forwardest[5] to marry. She is of a slow,[6]
nice, and mild complexion, and hath accordingly been brought up
by her mother in a retired and particular manner: so that she beginneth but now to put off childish simplicity.

She was one day reading a *French* book before me. An obscene word [7] came in her way (more bawdy in sound than in effect, it signi-fieth the name of a tree and another thing).The woman that looks to her staid her presently and somewhat churlishly making her step over[8] the same. I let her alone because I would not cross their rules, for I meddle nothing with this government: women's policy hath a mystical proceeding; we must be content to leave it to them. But if I be not deceived, the conversation of twenty lackeys could not in six months have settled in her thoughts the understanding, the use, and consequences of the sound belonging to those filthy syllables as did that good old woman by her check and interdiction.

Motus doceri gaudet Ionicos
Natura virgo, et frangitur artubus
Iam nunc, et incestos amores
De tenero meditatur ungui.
Maids marriage-ripe straight to be taught delight
Ionique dances, fram'd by art aright
In every joint, and ev'n from their first hair
Incestuous loves in meditation bear.[9]

Let them somewhat dispense with ceremonies, let them fall into free liberty of speech; we are but children, we are but gulls in respect of them about any such subject. Hear them relate how we sue, how we woo, how we solicit, and how we entertain them, they will soon give you to understand that we can say, that we can do, and that we can bring them nothing but what they already knew and had long before digested without us. May it be (as *Plato* sayeth) because they have one time or other been themselves wanton, licentious, and am-orous lads?[10]

Besides the fear of God and the reward of so rare a glory, which should incite them to preserve themselves, the corruption of our age enforceth them unto it. And were I in their clothes, there is nothing but I would rather do than commit my reputation into so dangerous hands. In my time the pleasure of reporting and blabbing what one hath done (a pleasure not much short of the act itself in sweetness) was only allowed to such as had some assured, trusty, and singular friend. Whereas nowadays the ordinary entertainments and familiar discourses of meetings and at tables are the boastings of favors received, graces obtained, and secret liberalities of ladies. Verily, it is too great an objection and argueth a baseness of heart so fiercely to suffer those tender, dainty, delicious joys to be persecuted, pelted, and foraged by persons so ungrateful, so undiscreet, and so giddy-headed.

This our immoderate and lawless exasperation against this vice proceedeth and is bred of jealousy, the most vain and turbulent infirmity that may afflict man's mind.

> *Quis vetat apposito lumen de lumine sumi?*
> *Dent licet assidue, nil tamen inde perit.*
> To borrow light of light, who would deny?
> Though still they give, nothing is lost thereby.[11]

That[12] and envy her sister are (in mine opinion) the fondest[13] of the troupe. Of the latter, I cannot say much: a passion which how effectual and powerful soever they set forth, of her good favour she meddleth not with me. As for the other, I know it only by sight. Beasts have some feeling of it: the shepherd *Cratis*, being fallen in love with a she-goat, her buck for jealousy beat out his brains as he lay asleep. We have raised to the highest strain the excess of this moody fever, after the example of some barbarous nations. The best disciplined have therewith been tainted, it is reason, but not carried away by it:

> *Ense maritali nemo conf[o]ssus adulter,*
> *Purpureo stygias sanguine tinxit aquas.*
> With husband's sword yet no adulter[14] slain,
> With purple blood did Stygian waters stain.[15]

Lucullus, Caesar, Pompey, Anthony, Cato, and diverse other gallant men were cuckolds and knew it, though they made no stir about it. There was in all that time but one gullish coxcomb Lepidus that died with the anguish of it.

> *Ah tum te miserum malique fati,*
> *Quæm attractis pedibus patente porta.*
> *Percurrent mugilesque raphanique.*
> Ah, thee, then wretched, of accursed fate
> Whom fish-wives, radish-wives of base estate,
> Shall scoffing over-run in open gate.[16]

And the god of our poet's,[17] when he surprised one of his companions napping with his wife, was contented but to shame them:

> *Atque aliquis de Diis non tristibus optat,*
> *Sic fieri turpis.*
> Some of the merrier gods doth wish in heart,
> To share their shame, of pleasure to take part.[18]

And yet forbeareth not to be enflamed with the gentle dalliances and amorous blandishments she offereth him, complaining that for so slight a matter he should distrust her to him dear-dear affection:

> *Quid causas petis ex alto? fiducia cessit*
> *Quo tibi Diva mei?*
> So far why fetch you your plea's pedigree?
> Whither is fled the trust you had in me?[19]

And which is more, she becomes a suitor to him in the behalf of a bastard of hers,

> *Arma rogo genitrix nato.*
> A mother for a son, I crave,
> An armor he of you may have.[20]

Which is freely granted her. And *Vulcan* speaks honourably of *Aeneas*:

> *Arma acri facienda viro.*
> An armor must be hammered-out,
> For one of courage stern and stout.[21]

In truth with an humanity more than human. And which excess of goodness by my consent shall only be left to the gods:

> *Nec divis homines componier æquum est.*
> Nor is it meet that men with gods
> Should be compar'd, there is such odds.[22]

As for the confusion of children,[23] besides that the gravest lawmakers appoint and affect it in their commonwealths, it concerneth not women, with whom this passion is I wot not how in some sort better placed, fitter seated.[24]

> *Sæpe etiam Iuno maxima cælicolum*
> *Coniugis inculpa flagravit quotidiana.*
> Ev'n *Juno*, chief of goddesses oft-time,
> Hath grown hot at her husband's daily crime.[25]

When jealousy once seizeth on these silly, weak, and unresisting souls, 'tis pitiful to see how cruelly it tormenteth, insultingly it tyrranizeth them. It insinuateth itself under colour of friendship, but after it once possesseth them, the same causes which served for a ground of good will serve for the foundation of mortal hatred. *Of all the mind's diseases, that is it, whereto most things serve for sustenance and fewest for remedy.* The virtue, courage, health, merit, and reputation of their husbands are the firebrands of their despite and motives of their rage.

> *Nullæ sunt inimicitiæ nisi amoris acerbæ.*
> No enmities so bitter prove
> And sharp as those which spring of love.[26]

244 · MICHEL DE MONTAIGNE

This consuming fever blemisheth and corrupteth all that otherwise is good and goodly in them. And how chaste or good a housewife soever a jealous woman is, there is no action of hers but tasteth of sharpness and smacks of importunity.[27] It is a furious perturbation, a moody agitation, which throws them into extremities altogether contrary to the cause. The success of one *Octavius* in *Rome* was strange who, having lain with and enjoyed the love of *Pontia Posthumia*, increased his affection by enjoying her and instantly sued to marry her. But being unable to persuade her, his extreme passionate love precipitated him into effects of a most cruel, mortal, and inexorable hatred; whereupon he killed her. Likewise, the ordinary *symptoms* or passions of this other amorous disease are intestine hates, sly *monopolies*, close conspiracies,

> *Notumque, furens quid fœmina possit.*
> It is known what a woman may,
> Whose raging passions have no stay.[28]

and a raging spite, which so much the more fretteth itself by being forced to excuse itself under pretense of good will.

Now the duty of chastity hath a large extension and far-reaching compass. Is it their will we would have them to bridle? That's a part very pliable and active; it is very nimble and quick-rolling to be stayed. What if dreams do sometimes engage them too far, as they cannot dissemble nor deny them? It lieth not in them (nor perhaps in Chastity itself, seeing she is a female) to shield themselves from concupiscence and avoid desiring. If only their will interest and engage us, where and in what case are we? Imagine what great throng of men there would be, in pursuit of this privilege, with winged-speed (though without eyes and without tongue) to be conveyed upon the point of every woman that would buy him.[29]

The Scythian women were wont to thrust out the eyes of all their slaves and prisoners taken in war, thereby to make more free and private use of them.

Oh what a furious advantage is opportunity! He that should demand of me what the chief or first part in love is, I would answer, *To know how to take fit time*; even so the second, and likewise the third. It is a point which may do all in all.

I have often wanted fortune but sometimes also enterprise. God shield him from harm that can yet mock himself with it. In this age more rashness is required, which our youths excuse under colour of heat.[30] But should our women look nearer unto it, they might find how it rather proceedeth of contempt. I superstitiously feared to offend, and what I love, I willingly respect. Besides that, who depriveth this merchandise of reverence defaceth all luster of it. I love that a man should therein somewhat play the child, the dastard, and the servant. If not altogether in this, yet in some other things I have some airs or motives of the sottish bashfulness whereof *Plutarch* speaketh, and the course of my life hath diversely been wounded and tainted by it: a quality very ill-beseeming my universal form.[31] And *what is there amongst us but sedition and jarring?* Mine eyes be as tender to bear a refusal as to refuse; and it doth so much trouble me to be troublesome to others that, where occasions force me or duty compelleth me to try the will of anyone, be it in doubtful things or of cost unto him, I do it but faintly and much against my will. But if it be for mine own private business (though *Homer* say most truly that in *an indigent or needy man, bashfulness is but a fond*[32] *virtue*), I commonly substitute a third party who may blush in my room.[33] And direct them that employ me with like difficulty, so that it hath sometimes befallen me *to have the will to deny when I had not power to refuse.*

It is then folly to go about to bridle women of a desire so fervent and so natural in them. And when I hear them brag to have so virgin-like a will and cold mind, I but laugh and mock at them. They recoil too far backward. If it be a toothless beldam or decrepit grandam, or a young dry, tisicke[34] starveling, if it be not altogether credible, they have at least some colour or appearance to say it. But those which stir about and have a little breath left them mar but their market with such stuff. Forsomuch as *inconsiderate excuses are no better than accusations.* As a gentleman my neighbour, who was suspected of insufficiency,[35]

Languidior tenera cui pendens sicula beta,
Nunquam se mediam sustulit ad tunicam,[36]

to justify himself,[37] three or four days after his marriage, swore confidently that the night before he had performed twenty courses,[38]
which oath hath since served to convince[39] him of mere ignorance
and to divorce him from his wife. Besides, this allegation is of no
great worth, for *there is nor continency nor virtue where no resistance
is to the contrary.* It is true, may one say, but I am not ready to yield.
The saints themselves speak so. This is understood of such as boast
in good earnest of their coldness and insensibility and would be
credited with a serious countenance. For when it is from an affected
look (where the eyes give words the lie) and from the faltering speech
of their profession (which ever works against the wool[40]), I allow of
it. I am a duteous servant unto plainness, simplicity, and liberty, but
there is no remedy if it be not merely plain, simple, or infantine;[41] it
is fond, inept, and unseemly for ladies in this commerce: it presently
inclineth and bendeth to impudency. Their disguisings, their figures, and dissimulations cozen none but fools. Their lying sitteth in
the chair of honour; it is a by-way which by a false postern[42] leads us
unto truth.

If we cannot contain their imaginations, what require we of them?
The effects? Many there be who are free from all strangers' communication, by which chastity may be corrupted and honesty defiled.

Illud sæpe facit, quod sine teste facit.
What she doth with no witness to it,
She often may be found to do it.[43]

And *those whom we fear least are peradventure most to be feared*; their
secret sins are the worst.

Offendor mæcha simpliciore minus.
Pleas'd with a whore's simplicity,
Offended with her nicety.[44]

There are effects which without impurity may lose them their pudicity,[45] and which is more, without their knowledge. *Obstetrix virginis cuiusdam integritatem manu velut explorans, sive malevolentia, sive inscitia, suve casu, dum inspicit, per didit. A midwife searching with her finger into a certain maiden's virginity, either for ill will or of unskilfulness or by chance, whilst she seeks and looks into it, she lost and spoiled it.* Some one hath lost or wronged her virginity in looking or searching for it; some other killed the same in playing with it.[46]

We are not able precisely to circumscribe them the actions we forbid them. Our law must be conceived under general and uncertain terms. The very idea we forge unto their chastity is ridiculous. For amongst the extremest examples or patterns I have of it, it is *Fatua*, the wife of *Faunus*, who after she was married would never suffer herself to be seen of any man whatsoever. And *Hieron's* wife, that never felt[47] her husband's stinking breath, supposing it to be a quality peculiar and common to all men. It were necessary that to satisfy and please us they should become insensible and invisible.

Now let us confess that the knot of the judgement of this duty[48] consisteth principally in the will. There have been husbands who have endured this accident[49] not only without reproach and offence against their wives but with singular acknowledgement, obligation, and commendation to their virtue. Someone that more esteemed her honesty than she loved her life hath prostituted the same unto the lawless lust and raging sensuality of a mortal hateful enemy, thereby to save her husband's life; and hath done that for him which she never could have been induced to do for herself. This is no place to extend these examples: they are too high and over-rich to be presented in this luster; let us therefore reserve them for a nobler seat.

But to give you some examples of a more vulgar stamp, are there not women daily seen amongst us who, for the only profit of their husbands and by their express order and brokage,[50] make sale of their honesty? And in old times *Phaulius* the *Argian* through ambition offered his[51] to King *Philip*. Even as that *Galba*, who bestowed a supper on *Mecenas*, perceiving him and his wife begin to bandy eye-tricks and signs, of civility shrunk down upon his cushion, as one oppressed with sleep, to give better scope unto their love, which he avouched as prettily.[52] For at that instant a servant of his, presuming to lay hands on the plate which was on the table, he cried outright unto him: "*How now varlet? Seest thou not I sleep only for Mecenas?*"

One may be of loose behaviour yet of purer will and better reformed than another who frameth herself to a precise appearance. As some are seen complain because they vowed chastity before years of discretion or knowledge, so have I seen others unfeignedly bewail and truly lament that they were vowed to licentiousness and dissoluteness before the age of judgement and distinction. The parents' lewdness may be the cause of it, or the force of impulsive necessity, which is a shrewd counselor and a violent persuader. Though chastity were in the East Indies of singular esteem, yet the custom permitted that a married wife might freely betake herself to what man soever did present her an elephant, and that with some glory to have been valued at so high a rate.

Phedon the philosopher, of a noble house, after the taking of his country, *Elides*, professed to prostitute the beauty of his youth to all comers, so long as it should continue, for money to live with and bear his charges. And *Solon* was the first of *Greece* (say some) who, by his laws, gave women liberty by the price of their honesty to provide for their necessities, a custom which *Herodotus* reporteth to have been entertained before him in diverse commonwealths.

And moreover, what fruit yield this careful vexation?[53] For what justice soever be in this passion, yet should we note whether it harry us unto our profit or no.[54] Thinks any man that he can ring them[55] by his industry?

> *Pone seram, cohibe; sed quis custodiet ipsos*
> *Custodes? cauta est, et ab illis incipit uxor.*
> Keep her with lock and key, but from her who shall keep
> Her keepers? She begins with them, her wits so deep.[56]

What advantage sufficeth them not, in this so skilfull age?
Curiosity is everywhere vicious but herein pernicious. It is mere

folly for one to seek to be resolved of a doubt or search into a mischief for which there is no remedy but makes it worse, but festereth the same. The reproach whereof is increased and chiefly published by jealousy; the revenge whereof doth more wound and disgrace our children than it helpeth or graceth us. You waste away and die in pursuit of so concealed a mystery, of so obscure a verification.

Whereunto how piteously have they arrived who in my time have attained their purpose? If the accuser or intelligencer[57] present not withal the remedy and his assistance, his office is injurious, his intelligence harmful, and which better deserveth a stab than doth a lie. We flout him no less that toileth to prevent it than laugh at him that is a cuckold and knows it not. *The character of cuckoldry is perpetual; on whom it once fasteneth, it holdeth forever.* The punishment bewrayeth[58] it more than the fault. It is a goodly sight to draw our private misfortunes from out the shadow of oblivion or the dungeon of doubt for to blazon[59] and proclaim them on tragical stages, and misfortunes which pinch us not but by relation. For (as the saying is) she is a good wife and that a good marriage not that is so indeed, but whereof no man speaketh. We ought to be wittily-wary to avoid this irksome, this tedious, and unprofitable knowledge. The Romans were accustomed, when they returned from any journey, to send home before and give their wives notice of their coming, that so they might not surprise them. And therefore hath a certain nation instituted the priest to open the way unto the bridegroom on the wedding day, thereby to take from him the doubt and curiosity of searching in this first attempt whether she come a pure virgin to him or be broken and tainted with any former love.

"But the world speaks of it." I know a hundred cuckolds, which are so honestly and little undecently. An honest man and a gallant spirit is moaned[60] but not disesteemed by it. Cause your virtue to suppress your mishap that honest-minded men may blame the occasion and curse the cause; that he which offends you may tremble with only thinking of it. And moreover, what man is scot-free, or who is not spoken of in this sense, from the meanest unto the highest?

——tot qui legionibus imperitauit,
Et melior quam tu multis fuit, improbe, rebus.
He that so many bands of men commanded,
Thy better much, sir knave, was much like branded.[61]

Seest thou not how many honest men, even in thy presence, are spoken of and touched with this reproach? Imagine, then, they will be as bold with thee and say as much of thee elsewhere. For no man is spared. "And even ladies will scoff and prattle of it." And what do they nowadays more willingly flout at than at any well-composed and peaceable marriage? There is none of you all but hath made one cuckold or other: now nature stood ever on this point—*Kæ me Ile kæ thee*—and ever ready to be even, always on recompenses and vicissitude of things, and to give as good as one brings. The long-continued frequency of this accident should by this time have seasoned the bitter taste thereof; it is almost become a custom.

Oh, miserable passion, which hath also this mischief, to be incommunicable.

Fors etiam nostris invidit quæstibus aures.
Fortune ev'n ears envied,
To hear us when we cried.[62]

For to what friend dare you entrust your grievances, who, if he laugh not at them, will not make use of them, as a direction and instruction to take a share of the quarry or booty to himself? As well the sourness and inconveniences as the sweetness and pleasures incident to marriage are secretly concealed by the wiser sort. And amongst other importunate conditions belonging to wedlock, this one, unto a babbling fellow as I am, is of the chiefest: that tyrannous custom makes it uncomely and hurtful for a man to communicate with anyone all he knows and thinks of it.

To give women advice to distaste them from jealousy were but time lost or labour spent in vain. Their essence is so infected with suspicion, with vanity and curiosity, that we may not hope to cure them by any lawful mean. They often recover of this infirmity by a form of health, much more to be feared than the disease itself. For even as some enchantment cannot rid away an evil but with laying it on another, so when they lose it they transfer and bestow this malady on their husbands.

And to say truth, I wot not whether a man can endure anything at their hands worse than jealousy. Of all their conditions it is most dangerous, as the head of all their members. *Pittacus* said that *every man had one imperfection or other: his wife's curst pate*[63] *was his*; and but for that, he should esteem himself most happy. It must needs be a weighty inconvenience, wherewith so just, so wise, and worthy a man felt the state of his whole life distempered. What shall we petty fellows do then?

The senate of *Marseilles* had reason to grant and enroll his request who demanded leave to kill himself, thereby to free and exempt himself from his wife's tempestuous scolding humor; for *it is an evil that is never clean rid away but by removing the whole piece* and hath no other composition of worth but flight or sufferance—both too-too hard, God knows. And in my conceit, he understood it right that said *a good marriage might be made between a blind woman and a deaf man.*

———

What *Virgil* sayeth of *Venus* and *Vulcan*, *Lucretius* had more suitably said it of a secretly-stolen enjoying between her and *Mars*,

>   ——*belli fera mœnera Mauors*
> *Armipotens regit, in gremium qui sæpe tuum se*
> *Rejicit, æterno devinctus vulnere amoris:*
> *Pascit amore avidos inhians in te Dea visus,*
> *Eque tuo pendet resupini spiritus ore:*
> *Hunc tu Diua tuo recubantem corpore sancto*
> *Circumfusa super, suaveis ex ore loquelas*
> *Funde.*

Mars, mighty arm'd, rules the fierce feats of arms,
Yet often casts himself into thine arms,
Oblig'd thereto by endless wounds of love,
Gaping on thee feeds greedy sight with love,
His breath hangs at thy mouth who upward lies,
Goddess thou circling him, while he so lies,
With thy celestial body, speeches sweet
Pour from thy mouth (as any Nectar sweet).

When I consider this, *rejicit, pascit, inhians, molli, fovet, medullas, labefacta, pendet, percurrit*, and this noble *circumfusa*, mother of gentle *infusus*, I am vexed at these small points and verbal allusions which since have sprung up. To those well-meaning people there needed no sharp encounter or witty equivocation: their speech is altogether full and massie,[64] with a natural and constant vigor. They are all epigram, not only tail but head, stomach, and feet. There is nothing forced, nothing wrested, nothing limping; all marcheth with like tenor. *Contextus totus virilis est, non sunt circa flosculos occupati. The whole composition or text is manly; they are not Bee-busied about rhetoric flowers.*[65] This is not a soft quaint eloquence and only without offence; it is sinnowy, material, and solid; not so much delighting, as filling and ravishing; and ravisheth most the strongest wits, the wittiest conceits. When I behold these gallant[66] forms of expressing, so lively, so nimble, so deep, I say not "This is to speak well" but "to think well." It is the quaintness[67] or liveliness of the conceit that elevateth and puffs up the words. *Pectus est quod disertum facit: It is a man's own breast that makes him eloquent.* Our people term judgement, language; and full conceptions, fine words.

Well, then, leaving books aside and speaking more materially and simply, when all is done I find that *love is nothing else but an insatiate thirst of enjoying a greedily desired subject.*[68] Nor *Venus* that good housewife other than a tickling delight of emptying one's semenary[69] vessels, as is the pleasure which nature giveth us to discharge other parts, which becometh faulty by immoderation and defective by indiscretion. To *Socrates, love is an appetite of generation by the intermission*[70] *of beauty.* Now considering oftentimes the ridiculous tickling or titillation of this pleasure, the absurd, giddy, and hare-brained motions wherewith it tosseth *Zeno* and agitates *Cratippus*,[71] that unadvised rage that furious and with cruelty enflamed visage in love's lustful and sweetest effects; and then a grave, stern, severe, surly countenance in so fond-fond an action that one hath pell-mell[72] lodged our joys and filths together; and that the supremest voluptuousness both ravisheth and plaineth,[73] as doth sorrow. I believe that which *Plato* says to be true, that *man was made by the gods for them to toy and play withal.*

> *quænam ista iocandi,*
> ——*Sævitia?*
> What cruelty is this, so set on jesting is?[74]

And that nature in mockery left us the most troublesome of our actions, the most common, thereby to equal us and without distinction to set the foolish and the wise, us and beasts, all in one rank; no barrel better hearing.[75] When I imagine the most contemplative and discreetly wise men in these terms in that humour,[76] I hold him for a cozener, for a cheater to seem either studiously contemplative or discreetly wise. *It is the foulness of the peacock's feet which doth abate his pride and stoop his gloating-eyed tail*:

> ——*ridentem dicere verum,*
> *Quid vetat?*
> What should forbid thee sooth to say,
> Yet be as merry as we may.[77]

Those which in plays refuse serious opinions do, as one reporteth, like unto him who dreadeth to adore the image of a saint if it want a cover, an apron, or a tabernacle.

We feed full well and drink like beasts, but they are not actions that hinder the offices of our mind. In those we hold good our advantage over them, whereas this[78] brings each other[79] thought under subjection, and by its imperious authority makes brutish and dulleth all *Plato's* philosophy and divinity; and yet he complains not of it. In all other things you may observe decorum and maintain some decency; all other operations admit some rules of honesty. This cannot only be imagined but vicious or ridiculous. See whether for example sake you can but find a wise or discreet proceeding in it. *Alexander* said that he knew himself mortal chiefly by this action and by sleeping. Sleep doth stifle and suppresseth the faculties of our soul; and that[80] both devoureth and dissipates them. Surely it is an argument not only of our original corruption but a badge of our vanity and deformity.

On the one side Nature urgeth us unto it, having thereunto combined, yea fastened, the most noble, the most profitable, and the most sensually pleasing of all her functions; and on the other suffereth us to accuse, to condemn, and to shun it as insolent, as dishonest, and as lewd, to blush at it, and allow, yea, and to commend abstinence. *Are not we most brutish to term that work beastly which begets and which maketh us?*

Most people have concurred in diverse ceremonies of religion, as sacrifices, luminaries, fastings, incensings, offerings, and amongst others, in condemning of this action. All opinions agree in that, besides the so far-extended use of circumcision. We have peradventure reason to blame ourselves for making so foolish a production as man and to entitle both the deed and parts thereto belonging shameful. (Mine are properly so at this instant.)

The *Esseniens*,[81] of whom *Pliny* speaketh, maintained themselves a long time without nurses or swaddling-clothes, by the arrival of strangers that came to their shores who, seconding their fond humor, did often visit them—a whole nation hazarding rather to consume[82] than engage themselves to feminine embracements and rather lose the succession of all men than forge one. They report that *Zeno* never dealt with woman but once in all his life, which he did for civility, lest he should over-obstinately seem to contemn the sex.

Each one avoideth to see a man born, but all run hastily to see him die. To destroy him we seek a spacious field and a full light; but to construct him, we hide ourselves in some dark corner and work as close[83] as we may. It is our duty to conceal ourselves in making him; it is our glory and the original of many virtues to destroy him, being framed. The one is a manifest injury, the other a great favor; for *Aristotle* sayeth that in a certain phrase where he was born, to bonifie[84] or benefit was as much to say as to kill one. The Athenians, to equal the disgrace of these two actions, being to cleanse the isle of *Delos* and justify themselves unto *Apollo*, forbade within that precinct all burial and births. *Nostri nosmet pœnitet. We are weary of ourselves.*[85]

There are some nations that, when they are eating, they cover themselues. I know a lady (yea, one of the greatest) who is of opinion that to chew is an unseemly thing which much impaireth their grace and beauty; and therefore by her will she never comes abroad with an appetite. And a man that cannot endure one should see him eat, and shunneth all company more when he filleth than when he emptieth himself.

In the Turkish empire there are many who, to excel the rest, will not be seen when they are feeding and who make but one meal in a week; who mangle their face and cut their limbs; and who never speak to anybody: who think to honour their nature by disnaturing themselves, oh fanatical people that prize themselves by their contempt and mend by their impairing. What monstrous beast is this that makes himself a horror to himself, whom his delights displease, who ties himself unto misfortune?

Some there are that conceal their life—

Exilioque domos et dulcia limina mutant,
They change for banishment,
The places that might best content.[86]

—and steal it from the sight of other men; that eschew health and shun mirth as hateful qualities and harmful. Not only diverse sects, but many people curse their birth and bless their death. Some there be that abhor the glorious sun and adore the hideous darkness.

We are not ingenious but to our own vexation; it is the true food of our spirit's force, a dangerous and most unruly implement.

O miseri quorum gaudia crimen habent.
O miserable they,
Whose joy in fault we lay.[87]

Alas, poor silly man, thou hast but too-too many necessary and unavoidable incommodities, without increasing them by thine own invention and are sufficiently wretched of condition without any art. Thou aboundest in real and essential deformities and need not forge any by imagination. Dost thou find thyself too well at ease, unless the moiety of thine ease molest thee? Findest thou to have supplied or discharged all necessary offices whereto nature engageth thee and that she is idle in thee, if thou bind not thyself unto new offices? Thou fearest not to offend her universal and undoubted laws and art moved at thine own partial and fantastical ones. And by how much more particular, uncertain, and contradicted they are, the more endeavours thou bestowest that way. The positive orders of thy parish tie thee; those of the world do nothing concern thee. Run but a little over the examples of this consideration; thy life is full of them.

The verses of these two poets,[88] handling lasciviousness so sparingly and so discreetly as they do, in my conceit seem to discover and display it nearer. Ladies cover their bosom with networke,[89] priests many sacred things with a veil, and painters shadow their works to give them the more luster and to add more grace unto them. And they say that the streaks of the sun and force of the wind are much more violent by reflection than by a direct line. The Egyptian answered him wisely that asked him what he had hidden under his cloak. It is (quoth he) *hidden under my cloak that thou mayest not know what it is.* But there are certain other things which men conceal to show them.

Hear this fellow more open.

Et nudam pressi corpus ad usque meum.
My body I applied,
Even to her naked side.[90]

Methinks he baffles[91] me. Let *Martial* at his pleasure tuck up *Venus*, he makes her not by much appear so wholly. *He that speaks all he knows doth cloy and distaste us.* Who feareth to express himself leadeth our conceit to imagine more than happily he conceiveth. There is treason in this kind of modesty, and chiefly as these do, in opening us so fair a path unto imagination. Both the action and description should taste of purloining.

The love[92] of the Spaniards and of the Italians pleaseth me by how much more respective and fearful it is, the more nicely close and closely nice it is.[93] I wot not who in ancient time wished his throat were as long as a crane's neck that so he might the longer and more leisurely taste what he swallowed. That wish were more to purpose in this sudden and violent pleasure, namely in such natures as mine, who am faulty in suddenness. To stay her fleeting and delay her with preambles with them all serveth for favour, all is construed to be a recompense, a wink, a cast of the eye, a bowing, a word, or a sign; a beck is as good as a dew guard.[94] *He that could dine with the smoke of roast-meat, might he not live at a cheap rate? would he not soon be rich?* It is a passion that commixeth with small store of solid essence, great quantity of doting vanity and febricitant[95] raving; it must therefore be requited and served with the like. Let us teach ladies to know how to prevail, highly to esteem themselves, to amuse, to circumvent, and cozen us. We make our last charge the first; we show ourselves right French men. Ever rash, ever headlong, wiredrawing[96] their[97] favours and installing them by retail: each one,[98] even unto miserable old age, finds some list's end,[99] according to his worth and merit.

He who hath no jouissance[100] but in enjoying, who shoots not but to hit the mark, who loves not hunting but for the prey; it belongs not to him to intermeddle with our school. *The more steps and degrees there are, the more delight and honour is there on the top.* We should be pleased to be brought unto it, as unto stately palaces, by diverse porches, several passages, long and pleasant galleries, and well-contrived turnings. This dispensation would in the end redound to our benefit; we should stay on it and longer love to lie at rack and manger.[101] For these snatches and away[102] mar the grace of it. Take away hope and desire, we grow faint in our courses; we come but lagging after.

Our mastery and absolute possession is infinitely to be feared of them. After they have wholly yielded themselves to the mercy of our faith and constancy, they have hazarded something. They are rare and difficult virtues: so soon as they are ours, we are no longer theirs.

> ——*postquam cupidæ mentis satiata libido est,*
> *Verba nihil metuere, nihil periuria curant.*
> The lust of greedy mind once satisfied,
> They fear no words, nor reke[103] oaths falsified.[104]

And *Thrasonides*, a young Grecian, was so religiously amorous of his love that, having after much suit gained his mistress' heart and favour, he refused to enjoy her, least by that jouissance he might or quench or satisfie or languish that burning flame and restless heat wherewith he gloried and so pleasingly fed himself.

Things far-fetched and dearly bought are good for ladies. It is the dear price makes viands[105] savour the better. See but how the form of salutations which is peculiar unto our nation doth by its facility bastardize the grace of kisses, which *Socrates* sayeth to be of that consequence, weight, and danger to ravish and steal our hearts. It is an unpleasing and injurious custom unto ladies that they must afford their lips to any man that hath but three lackeys following him, how unhandsome and loathsome soever he be:

> *Cuius livida naribus caninis,*
> *Dependet glacies, rigetque barba:*
> *Centum occurrere malo culilingis.*

From whose dog nostrils black-blue ice depends,
Whose beard frost-hardened stands on bristled ends, &c.[106]

Nor do we ourselves gain much by it. For as the world is divided into four parts, so for four fair ones, we must kiss fifty foul. And to a nice or tender stomach, as are those of mine age, one ill kiss doth surpay[107] one good.

In *Italy* they are passionate and languishing suitors to very common and mercenary women, and thus they defend and excuse themselves, saying, *That even in enjoying there be certain degrees* and that by humble services they will endeavour to obtain that which is the most absolutely perfect. *They sell but their bodies; their wills cannot be put to sale;* that is too free and too much its own. So say these, that it is the will they attempt, and they have reason. It is the will one must serve and most solicit. I abhor to imagine mine[108] a body void of affection. And me seemeth, this frenzy hath some affinity with that boy's fond humor who for pure love would wantonize with that fair image of *Venus* which *Praxiteles* had made, or of that furious Egyptian who lusted after a dead woman's corpse which he was embalming and stitching up; which was the occasion of the law that afterward was made in *Egypt*, that the bodies of fair, young, and nobly-born women should be kept three days before they should be delivered into the hands of those who had the charge to provide for their funerals and burials. *Periander* did more miraculously: who extended his conjugal affection (more regular and lawful) unto the enjoying of *Melissa* his deceased wife.

Seems it not to be a lunatic humor in the Moon,[109] being otherwise unable to enjoy *Endymion* her favorite darling, to lull him in a sweet slumber for many months together and feed herself with the jouissance of a boy that stirred not but in a dream?

I say likewise that *a man loveth a body without a soul when he loveth a body without his consent and desire.* All enjoyings are not alike. There are some ethicke,[110] faint, and languishing ones. A thousand causes besides affection and good will may obtain us this grant of women. It is no sufficient testimony of true affection; therein may lurk treason, as elsewhere. They sometime go but faintly to work[111] and as they say with one buttock:

> *Tanquam thura merumque parent;*
> As though they did dispense
> Pure wine and frankincense.
> *Absentem marmoreamue putes.*
> Of marble you would think she were,
> Or that she were not present there.[112]

I know some that would rather lend that than their coach and who impart not themselves but that way.[113] You must also mark whether your company pleaseth them for some other respect or for that end only, as of a lusty-strong groom of a stable; as also in what rank and at what rate you are there lodged or valued.

> ——*tibi si datur uni*
> *Quo lapide illa diem candidiore notet.*
> If it afforded be to thee alone,
> Whereby she counts that day of all days one.[114]

What if she eat your bread with the sauce of a more pleasing imagination?

> *Te tenet, absentes alios suspirat amores.*
> Thee she retains, yet sigheth she
> For other loves that absent be.[115]

What? Have we not seen some in our days to have made use of this action for the execution of a most horrible revenge, by that means murdering and empoisoning (as one did) a very honest woman?

Such as know *Italy* will never wonder if for this subject I seek for no examples elsewhere. For the said nation may in that point be termed regent[116] of the world. They have commonly more fair women and fewer foul than we, but in rare and excellent beauties I think we match them. The like I judge of their wits. Of the vulgar sort they have evidently many more. Blockishness is without all comparison more rare amongst them; but for singular wits, and of the highest pitch, we are no whit behind them. Were I to extend this comparison, I might (methinks) say, touching valor, that on the other side it is in regard of them popular and natural amongst us. But in their hands one may sometimes finde it so complete and vigorous that it exceedeth all the most forcible examples we have of it.

The marriages of that country are in this somewhat defective. Their custom doth generally impose so severe observances and slavish laws upon wives that the remotest acquaintance with a stranger is amongst them as capital as the nearest. Which law causeth that all approaches prove necessarily substantial; and seeing all commeth to one reckoning with them, they have an easy choice. And have they broken down their hedges? Believe it, they will have fire: *Luxuria ipsis vinculis, sicut fera bestia, irritata, deinde emissa*: Luxury[117] *is like a wild beast, first made fiercer with tying and then let loose.*[118] They must have the reins given them a little.

> *Vidi ego nuper equum contra sua frena tenacem*
> *Ore reluctante fulminis ire modo.*
> I saw, spite of his bit, a resty[119] colt
> Run head-strong headlong like a thunder bolt.[120]

One allayeth the desire of company by giving it some liberty.

It is a commendable custom with our nation that our children are entertained in noble houses, there as in a school of nobility to be trained and brought up as pages. And 'tis said to be a kind of discourtesy to refuse it a gentleman. I have observed (for, *so many houses, so many several forms and orders*) that such ladies as have gone about to give their waiting women the most austere rules have not had the best success. There is required more than ordinary moderation: a great part of their government must be left to the conduct of their discretion. For when all comes to all, no discipline can bridle them in each point. True it is that she who escapeth safe and unpolluted from out the school of freedom giveth more confidence of herself than she who cometh sound out of the school of severity and restraint.

Our forefathers framed their daughters' countenances unto shamefastness and fear (their inclinations and desires always alike); we, unto assurance. We understand not the matter. That belongeth to the Sarmatian wenches, who by their laws may lie with no man except with their own hands they have before killed another man in war.

To me that have no right but by the ears,[121] it sufficeth if they retain me to be of their counsel, following the privilege of mine age. I then advise both them and us to embrace abstinence, but if this season be too much against it, at least modesty and discretion. For, as *Aristippus* (speaking to some young men who blushed to see him go into a bawdy house) said, *the fault was not in entering but in not coming out again.* She that will not exempt her conscience, let her exempt her name: though the substance be not of worth, yet let the appearance hold still good.

I love gradation and prolonging in the distribution of their favours. *Plato* showeth that in all kinds of love, facility and readiness is forbidden to defendants. 'Tis a trick of greediness which it behooveth them to cloak with their art, so rashly and fond-hardily to yield themselves in gross. In their distributions of favours, holding a regular and moderate course, they much better deceive our desires and conceal theirs. Let them ever be flying before us: I mean even those that intend to be overtaken. As the Scythians are wont, though they seem to run away, they beat us more and sooner put us to rout. Verily, according to the law which Nature giveth them, it is not fit for them to will and desire; their part is to bear, to obey, and to consent. Therefore hath nature bestowed a perpetual capacity; on us a seld[122] and uncertain ability. They have always their hour that they may ever be ready to let us enter. And whereas she hath willed our appetites should make apparent show and declaration, she caused theirs to be concealed and inward and hath furnished them with parts unfit for ostentation and only for defence.[123]

Such pranks as this we must leave to the Amazonian liberty. *Alex-*

ander the great, marching through *Hyrcania*, *Thalestris*, queen of the Amazons, came to meet him with three hundred lances[124] of her sex, all well mounted and completely armed, having left the residue of a great army that followed her beyond the neighbouring mountains. And thus aloud, that all might hear, she bespake him that the far-resounding fame of his victories and matchless valour had brought her thither to see him and to offer him her meanes and forces for the advancing and furthering of his enterprises. And finding him so fair, so young, and strong, she, who was perfectly accomplished in all his qualities, advised him to lie with her that so there might be born of the most valiant woman in the world and only valiant man then living, some great and rare creature for posterity. *Alexander* thanked her for the rest; but to take leisure for her last demand's accomplishment, he stayed thirteen days in that place, during which he reveled with as much glee and feasted with as great jollity as possibly could be devised, in honour and favour of so courageous a princess.

We are well-nigh in all things partial and corrupted judges of their action, as no doubt they are of ours. I allow of truth as well when it hurts me as when it helps me. It is a foul disorder that so often urgeth them unto change and hinders them from settling their affection on any one subject, as we see in this goddess, to whom they impute so many changes and several friends. But withal, *it is against the nature of love not to be violent, and against the condition of violence to be constant.* And those who wonder at it, exclaim against it, and in women search for the causes of this infirmity as incredible and unnatural— why see they not how often, without any amazement and exclaiming, themselves are possessed and infected with it? It might happily seem more strange to find any constant stay in them. It is not a passion merely corporeal. *If no end be found in coveteousness, nor limit in ambition, assure yourself there is nor end nor limit in lechery.* It yet continueth after satiety: nor can any man prescribe [its] end or constant satisfaction; it ever goeth on beyond its possession, beyond its bounds.

And inconstancy be peradventure in some sort more pardonable in them than in us. They may readily allege against us our ready inclination unto daily variety and new ware. And secondly allege without us that they buy a pig in a poke. *Ione*,[125] queen of *Naples*, caused *Andreosse*[126] her first husband to be strangled and hanged out of the bars of his window with a cord of silk and gold woven with her own hands because in bed-business she found neither his members nor endeavours answerable the hope she had conceived of him, by viewing his stature, beauty, youth, and disposition, by which she had formerly been surprised and abused. That action[127] hath in it more violence than passion, so that on their part at least necessity is ever provided for; on our behalf it may happen otherwise.[128]

Therefore *Plato* by his laws did very wisely establish that before marriages, the better to decide its opportunity, competent judges might be appointed to make view of young men which pretended the same, all naked: and of maidens but to the waist. In making trial of us, they happily[129] find us not worthy their choice:

> *Experta latus, madidoque simillima loro*
> *Inguina, nec lassa stare coacta manu.*
> *Deserit imbelles thalamos.*[130]

It is not sufficient that will keepe a level course: weaknesse and incapacity may lawfully break wedlock:

> *Et querendum aliunde foret neruosius illud,*
> *Quod posset Zonam soluere virgineam.*[131]

Why not? And according to measure, an amorous intelligence, more licencious and more active?

> *Si blando nequeat superesse labori.*
> If it cannot out last, labor with pleasure past.[132]

But is it not great impudency to bring our imperfections and weakness in place where we desire to please and leave good report and commendation behind us? For the little I now stand in need of,

———*ad unum.*
Mollis opus.
Unable to hold out, one only busy bout,[133]

I would not importune anyone, whom I am to reverence and fear.

———*fuge suspicari,*
Cuius undenum trepidavit ætas
Claudere lustrum.
Him of suspicion clear,
Whom age hath brought well neare
To five and fifty year.[134]

Nature should have been pleased to have made this age miserable without making it also ridiculous. I hate to see one, for an inch of wretched vigor which enflames him but thrice a week, take on and swagger as fiercely as if he had some great and lawful day's work in his belly: a right blast or puff of wind. And admire his itching, so quick and nimble, all in a moment to be lubberly,[135] squat, and benumbed. This appetite should only belong to the blossom of a prime youth. Trust not unto it,[136] though you see it second that indefatigable, full, constant and swelling heat that is in you. For truly it will leave you at the best and when you shall most stand in need of it. Send it rather to some tender, irresolute, and ignorant guirle,[137] which yet trembleth for fear of the rod and that will blush at it,

Indum sanguineo veluti violaverit ostro,
Si quis ebur, vel mista rubent ubi lilia, multa
Alba rosa.
As if the Indian ivory one should taint
With bloody scarlet grain, or lilies' paint,
White intermixed with red, with roses over-spread.[138]

Who can stay until the next morrow and not die for shame, the disdain of those love-sparkling eyes, privy to his faintness,[139] das-tardise[140] and impertinency,

> *El taciti fecere tamen convitia vultus.*
> The face though silent, yet silent upbraid it,[141]

he never felt the sweet contentment and the sense-moving earnest-ness to have beaten and tarnished them by the vigorous exercise of an officious and active night. When I have perceived any of them weary of me, I have not presently accused her lightness but made question whether I had not more reason to quarrel with nature for handling me so unlawfully and uncivilly—

> *Si non longa satis, si non bene mentula crassa:*
> *Nimirum sapiunt videntque parvam*
> *Matronæ quoque mentulam illibenter.*[142]

—and to my exceeding hurt.

Each of my pieces are equally mine, one as another: and no other doth more properly make me a man than this. My whole portraiture I universally owe unto the world. The wisdom and reach of my les-son is all in truth, in liberty, in essence; disdaining in the catalogue of my true duties, these easy, faint, ordinary, and provincial rules; all natural, constant, and general, whereof civility and ceremony are daughters, but bastards.

We shall easily have the vices of appearance when we shall have had those of essence.[143] When we have done with these, we run upon others, if we find need of running. For there is danger that we devise new offices, to excuse our negligence toward natural offices and to confound them. That it is so, we see that in places where faults are crimes, crimes are but faults. That among nations, where laws of seemliness[144] are more rare and slack, the primitive lawes of common reason are better observed, the innumerable multitude of so mani-fold duties stifling, languishing, and dispersing our care. The apply-ing of ourselves unto sleight matters, withdraweth us from such as be just. Oh how easy and plausible a course do these superficial men undertake, in respect of ours. These are but shadows under which we shroud wherewith we pay one another. But we pay not but rather heap debt on debt, unto that great and dreadful Judge who tucks up our clouts and rags from about our privy parts and is not squeamish to view all-over, even to our most inward and secret deformities—a beneficial decency of our maidenly bashfulness, could it debar him of this tainted discovery.

To conclude, he that could recover or un-besot man from so scrupulous and verbal a superstition should not much prejudice the world. *Our life consisteth partly in folly and partly in wisdom.* He that writes of it but reverently and regularly omits the better moiety of it. I excuse me not unto myself, and if I did, I would rather excuse my excuses than any fault else of mine. I excuse myself of certain humors, which in number I hold stronger than those which are on my side. In consideration of which, I will say thus much more (for I desire to please all men, though it be a hard matter, *Esse unum hominem accommodatum ad tantam morum, ac sermonum et voluntatum varietatem. That one man should be appliable to so great variety of manners, speeches, and dispositions*[145]) that they are not to blame me for what I cause authorities received and approved of many ages to utter: and that it is not reason they should for want of rhyme deny me the dispensation which even some of our churchmen usurp and enjoy in this season. Whereof behold here two, and of the most pert and cocket[146] amongst them:

Rimula, dispeream, ni mono qramma tua est.[147]
Un vit d'ami la contente et bien traite.[148]

How many others more?

I love modesty, nor is it from judgement that I have made choice of this kind of scandalous speech: 'tis nature hath chosen the same for me. I commend it no more than all forms contrary unto received custom; only I excuse it, and by circumstances as well general as particular would qualify the imputation. Well, let us proceed.

Whence commeth also the usurpation of sovereign authority which you assume unto yourselves, over those that favour you to their cost and prejudice—

Si furtiua dedit nigra munuscula nocte.
If she have giv'n by night,
The stolen gift of delight.[149]

—that you should immediately invest withal the interest, the coldness, and a wedlock authority? It is a free bargain: why do you not undertake it on those terms you would have them to keep? *There is no prescription upon voluntary things.*[150]

It is against form, yet it is true that I have in my time managed this match (so far as the nature of it would allow) with as much conscience as any other whatsoever and not without some colour of justice; and have given them no further testimony of mine affection than I sincerely felt, and have lively displayed unto them the declination, vigor, and birth of the same, with the fits and deferring of it. *A man cannot always keep an even pace*, nor ever go to it alike. I have been so sparing to promise that (as I think) I have paid more than either I promised or was due. They have found me faithful even to the service of their inconstancy—I say an inconstancy avowed and sometimes multiplied. I never broke with them as long as I had any hold, were it but by a threads-end; and whatsoever occasion they have given me by their fickleness, I never fell off unto contempt and hatred. For such famliarities, though I attain them on most shameful conditions, yet do they bind me unto some constant good will. I have sometimes given them a taste of choler and indiscreet impatience, upon occasions of their wiles, sleights, close-conveyances, controversies, and contestations between us; for, by complexion, I am subject to hasty and rash motions which often impeach my traffic and mar my bargains, though but mean and of small worth. Have they desired to essay the liberty of my judgement, I never dissembled to give them fatherly counsel and biting advice, and shewed myself ready to scratch them where they itched. If I have given them cause to complain of me, it hath been most for finding a love in me, in respect of our modern fashion, foolishly conscientious. I have religiously kept my word in things that I might easily have been dispensed with. They then yielded sometimes with reputation and under conditions which they would easily suffer to be infringed by the conqueror. I have more than once made pleasure in her greatest efforts strike sail unto the interest of their honor. And where reason urged me, armed them against me so that they guided themselves more safely and severely by my prescriptions, if they once freely yielded unto them, than they could have done by their own.

I have as much as I could endeavored to take on myself the charge and hazard of our appointments,[151] thereby to discharge them from all imputation, and ever contrived our meetings in most hard, strange, and unsuspected manner, to be the less mistrusted and (in my seeming) the more accessible. They are opened, especially in those parts, where they suppose themselves most concealed. *Things least feared are least defended and observed.* You may more securely dare what no man thinks you would dare, which by difficulty becometh easy.

Never had man his approaches more impertinently genital.[152] This way to love is more according to discipline. But how ridiculous unto our people and of how small effect, who better knows than I? Yet will I not repent me of it; I have no more to lose by the matter.

> ——*me tabula sacer*
> *Votiva paries, indicat uvida,*
> *Suspendisse potenti*
> *Vestimenta maris Deo.*
> By tables of the vows which I did owe
> Fastened thereto the sacred wall doth show;
> I have hung up my garments water-wet,
> Unto that God whose power on seas is great.[153]

It is now high time to speak plainly of it. But even as to another, I would perhaps say, "My friend thou dotest; the love of thy times hath small affinity with faith and honesty."

———*hæc si tu postules*
Ratione certa facere, nihilo plus agas,
Quam si des operam; ut cum ratione insanias.
If this you would by reason certain make,
You do no more, than if the pains you take
To be stark-mad, and yet to think it reason fit.[154]

And yet if I were to begin anew, it should be by the very same path and progress, how fruitless soever it might prove unto me. *Insufficiency and sottishness are commendable in a discommendable action.* As much as I separate myself from their humor in that, so much I approach unto mine own.

Moreover, I did never suffer myself to be wholly given over to that sport; I therewith pleased but forgot not myself. I ever kept that little understanding and discretion which nature hath bestowed on me, for their service and mine: some motion towards it, but no dotage. My conscience also was engaged therein, even unto incontinency and excess but never unto ingratitude, treason, malice or cruelty. I bought not the pleasure of this vice at all rates and was content with its own and simple cost. *Nullum intra se vitium est. There is no vice contained in itself.*[155]

I hate almost alike a crouching dull laziness and a toilsome and thorny working. The one pincheth, the other dulleth me. I love wounds as much as bruises, and blood wipes as well as dry-blows.[156] I had in the practise of this solace, when I was fitter for it, an even moderation between these two extremities. Love is a vigilant, lively, and blithe agitation: I was neither troubled nor tormented with it, but heated and distempered by it. There we must make a stay; it is only hurtful unto fools.

A young man demanded of the philosopher *Panetius* whether it would beseem a wise man to be in love. *Let wise men alone* (quoth he), *but for thee and me that are not so, it were best not to engage ourselves into so stirring and violent a humour, which makes us slaves to others and contemptible unto ourselves.*[157] He said true, for we ought not entrust a matter so dangerous unto a mind that hath not wherewith to sustain the approaches of it, nor effectually to quail the speech of *Agesilaus, that wisdom and love cannot liue together*. It is a vain occupation ('tis true), unseemly, shameful, and lawless. But using it in this manner, I esteem it wholesome and fit to rouse a dull spirit and a heavy body; and as a physician experienced, I would prescrib the same unto a man of my complexion and form, as soon as any other receipt[158] to keep him awake and in strength when he is well in years, and delay him from the grippings of old age. As long as we are but in the suburbs of it and that our pulse yet beateth,

> *Dum nona canities, dum prima et recta senectus,*
> *Dum superest Lachesi quod torqueat, et pedibus me*
> *Porto meis, nullo dextram subeunte bacillo.*
> While hoary haires are new, and old-age fresh and straight,
> While *Lachesis* hath yet to spin, while I my weight
> Bear on my feet, and stand, without staff in my hand.[159]

We had need to be solicited and tickled by some biting agitation as this is. See but what youth, vigor, and jollity it restored unto wise *Anacreon*. And *Socrates*, when he was elder than I am, speaking of an amourous object: "Leaning" (says he) "shoulder to shoulder, and approaching my head unto his, as we were both together looking upon a book, I felt, in truth, a sudden tingling or prickling in my shoulder, like the biting of some beast, which more then five days after tickled me, whereby a continual itching glided into my heart." But a casual touch, and that but in a shoulder, to enflame, to distemper, and to distract a mind enfeebled, tamed, and cooled through age; and of all human minds the most reformed. And why not I pray you? *Socrates* was but a man and would neither be nor seem to be other.

Philosophy contends not against natural delights, so that due measure be joined therewith and alloweth the moderation, not the shunning, of them. The efforts of her resistance are employed against strange and bastard or lawless ones. She sayeth that *the body's appetites ought not to be increased by the mind*. And wittily adviseth us that we should not excite our hunger by satiety; not to stuff instead of filling our bellies; to avoid all jouissance that may bring us to want; and shun all meat and drink which may make us hungry or thirsty. As in the service of love, she appoints us to take an object that only may satisfy the body's need without once moving the mind, which is not there to have any doing but only to follow and simply to assist the body.

But have I not reason to think that these precepts, which (in mine opinion are elsewhere somewhat rigorous) have reference unto a body which doth his office; and that a dejected one, as a weakened stomach, may be excused if he cherish and sustain the same by art, and by the intercourse of fancy to restore [to] it the desires, the delights, and blithnesse which of itself it hath lost?

May we not say that there is nothing in us during this earthly prison, simply corporal or purely spiritual, and that injuriously we dismember a living man? That there is reason we should carry ourselves in the use of pleasure, at least as favourably as we do in the pangs of grief? For example, it[160] was vehement even unto perfection in the souls of saints, by repentance. The body had naturally a part therein, by the right of their combination, and yet might have but little share in the cause. And were not contented that it should simply follow and assist the afflicted soul; they have tormented the body itself with convenient and sharp punishments, to the end that, one with the other, the body and the soul might avie[161] plunge man into sorrow, so much the more saving by how much the more smarting.

In like case, in corporal pleasures, is it not injustice to quell and cool the mind and say it must thereunto be entrained,[162] as unto a forced bond or servile necessity? She should rather hatch and cherish them[163] and offer and invite itself unto them, the charge of swaying rightly belonging to her. Even as, in my conceit, it is her part in her proper delights to inspire and infuse into the body all sense or feeling which his condition may bear, and endeavor that they may be both sweet and healthy for him. For, as they say, t'is good reason that the body follow not his appetites to the mind's prejudice or domage.[164] But why is it not likewise reason that the mind should not follow hers to the body's danger and hurt?

I have no other passion that keeps me in breath. What avarice, ambition, quarrels, suits in law, or other contentions work an effect in others who, as myself, have no assigned vocation or certain leisure, love would perform more commodiously. It would restore me the vigilancy, sobriety, grace, and care of my person and assure my countenance against the wrinkled frowns of age (those deformed and wretched frowns) which else would blemish and deface the same. It would reduce me to serious, to sound and wise studies, whereby I might procure more love and purchase more estimation. It would purge my mind from despair of itself and of its use, acquainting the same again with itself. It would divert me from thousands of irksome tedious thoughts, and melancholy carking[165] cares, wherewith the doting idleness and crazed condition of our age doth charge and comber[166] us. It would restore and heat, though but in a dream, the blood which nature forsaketh. It would uphold the drooping chin and somewhat strengthen or lengthen the shrunken sinnowes,[167] decayed vigor, and dulled lives-blitheness[168] of silly-wretched man, who gallops apace to his ruin.

But I am not ignorant how hard a matter it is to attain to such a commodity.[169] Through weakness and long experience our taste is grown more tender, more choice, and more exquisite. We challenge most when we bring least; we are most desirous to choose when we least deserve to be accepted. And knowing ourselves to be such, we are less hardy and more distrustful. Nothing can assure us to be beloved, seeing our condition and their quality. I am ashamed to be in the company of this green, blooming, and boiling youth.

Cuius in indomito constantior inguine nervus,
Quam nova collibus arbor inhæret.[170]

Why should we present our wretchedness amid this their jollity?

Possint ut iuvenes visere fervidi
Multo non sine risu,
Dilapsam in cineres facem.

That hot young men may go and see,
Not without sport and merry glee,
Their fire-brands turn'd to ashes be.[171]

They have both strength and reason on their side: let us give them place; we have no longer hold fast.[172]

This bloom of budding beauty loves not to be handled by such numbed and so clumsy hands, nor would it be dealt with by the means or material of ordinary stuff. For, as that ancient philosopher answered one that mocked him because he could not obtain the favour of a youngling whom he suingly pursued: *My friend* (quoth he) *the hook bites not at such fresh cheese.*[173]

It is a commerce needing relation and mutual correspondency. Other pleasures that we receive may be requited by recompenses of different nature, but this cannot be repaid but with the very same kind of coin. Verily, the pleasure I do others in this sport doth more sweetly tickle my imagination than that is done unto me. Now if no generous mind can receive pleasure where he returneth none, it is a base mind that would have all duty and delights to feed with conference those under whose charge he remaineth. There is no beauty nor favour nor familiarity so exquisite which a gallant mind should desire at this rate. Now if women can do us no good but in pity, I had much rather not to live at all than to live by alms. I would I had the privilege to demand of them in the same style I have heard some beg in *Italy*: *Fate beno per voi. Do some good for yourself*; or after the manner that *Cyrus* exhorted his soldiers: *Whosoever loveth me, let him follow me.*[174]

Consort yourself, will some say to me, with those of your own condition, whom the company of like fortune will yield of more easy access. Oh sottish and wallowish composition![175]

——*nolo*
Barbam vellere mortito leoni.
I will not pull (though not afeard),
When he is dead a Lion's beard.[176]

Xenophon useth for an objection and accusation against *Menon* that in his love he dealt with fading objects. I take more sensual pleasure by only viewing the mutual, even-proportioned, and delicate commixture of two young beauties, or only to consider the same in mine imagination, than if myself should be second in a lumpish, sad, and disproportioned conjunction. I resign such distasted and fantastical appetites unto the Emperour *Galba*, who meddled with none but cast, worn, hard-old flesh; and to that poor slave:

> *O ego di' faciant talem te cernere possim,*
> *Charaque mutatis oscula ferre comis,*
> *Amplectique meis corpus non pingue lacertis.*
> Gods grant I may behold thee in such case,
> And kiss thy chang'd locks with my dearest grace,
> And with mine arms thy limbs not fat embrace.[177]

And amongst blemishing-deformities, I deem artificial and forced beauty to be of the chiefest. *Emonez*, a young lad of *Chios*, supposing by gorgeous attires to purchase the beauty which nature denied him, came to the philosopher *Arcesilaus* and asked of him *whether a wise man could be in love or no. Yes, marry* (quoth he), *so it were not with a painted and sophisticate beauty as thine is.* The foulness of an old known woman is in my seeming not so aged or so ill-favoured as one that's painted and sleeked.

Shall I boldly speak it, and not have my throat cut for my labour? *Love is not properly nor naturally in season but in the age next unto infancy.*

> *Quam si puellarum insereres choro,*
> *Mille sagaces falleret hospites,*
> *Discrimen obscurum, solutis*
> *Crinibus, ambiguoque vultu.*
> Whom if you should in crew of wenches place,
> With hair loose-hanging, and ambiguous face,

Strangely the undiscern'd distinction might
Deceive a thousand strangers of sharpe sight.[178]

No more is perfect beauty. For whereas *Homer* extends it until such time as the chin begins to bud, *Plato* himself hath noted the same for very rare. And the cause for which the sophister *Dion* termed youth's budding hairs *Aristogitons* and *Harmodii* is notoriously known.[179] In manhood I find it already to be somewhat out of date, much more in old age:

*Importunus enim transvolat aridas
Qærcus.*
Importune[180] love doth over-fly
The oaks with withered old-age dry.[181]

And *Margaret* Queen of *Navarre* lengthens much (like a woman) the privilege of women: *ordaining thirty yeares to be the season for them to change the title of fair into good.*

The shorter possession we allow it[182] over our lives, the better for us. Behold its behaviour: it is a princock boy.[183] Who in his school knows not how far one proceeds against all order? *Study, exercise, custom, and practice are paths to insufficiency;* there novices bear all the sway: *Amor ordinem nescit. Love knows or keeps no order.* Surely its course hath more garb[184] when it is commixed with unadvisedness and trouble; faults and contrary successes give it edge and grace. So it be eager and hungry, it little importeth whether it be prudent. Observe but how he staggers, stumbleth, and fooleth; you fetter and shackle him when you guide him by art and discretion, and you force his sacred liberty when you submit him to those bearded, grim, and tough-hard hands.

Moreover, I often hear them[185] display this intelligence as absolutely spiritual, disdaining to draw into consideration the interest which all the senses have in the same. All serveth to the purpose. But I may say that I have often seen some of us excuse the weakness of their minds in favour of their corporal beauties; but I never saw them yet that, in behalf of the mind's-beauties, how sound and ripe soever they were, would afford an helping hand unto a body that never so little falleth into declination. Why doth not some one of them long to produce that noble Socratical brood, or breed that precious gem between the body and the mind, purchasing with the price of her thighs a philosophical and spiritual breed and intelligence, which is the highest rate she can possibly value them at? *Plato* appointeth in his *Laws* that he who performeth a notable and worthy exploit in war during the time of that expedition should not be denied a kiss or refused any other amorous favour, of whomsoever he shall please to desire it, without respect either of his ill-favouredness, deformity, or age. What he deemeth so just and allowable in commendation of military valour may not the same be thought as lawful in commendation of some other worth? And why is not one of them possessed with the humor to preoccupate[186] on her companions the glory of this chaste love? Chaste I may well say:

> ——*nam si quando ad prælia ventum est,*
> *Ut quondam stipulis magnus sine viribus ignis*
> *In cassum furit.*
> If once it come to handy-gripes[187] as great,
> But force-less fire in stubble; so his heat
> Rageth amain,[188] but all in vain.[189]

Vices smothered in one's thought are not of the worst.

To conclude this notable commentary, escaped from me by a flux of babbling, a flux sometimes as violent as hurtful—

> *Ut missum sponsi furtivo munere malum,*
> *Procurrit casto virginis e gremio:*
> *Quod miseræ oblitæ molli sub veste locatum,*
> *Dum adventu matris prosilit, excutitur,*
> *Atque illud prono præceps agitur decursu,*
> *Huic manat tristi conscius ore rubor.*
> As when some fruit by stealth sent from her friend,

From chaste lap of a virgin doth descend,
Which by her, under her soft apron plast,[190]
Starting at mother's coming thence is cast;
And trilling down in haste doth headlong go,
A guilty blush in her sad face doth flow.[191]

—*I say that both male and female are cast in one same mold; instruction and custom excepted, there is no great difference between them.* *Plato* calleth them both indifferently to the society of all studies, exercises, charges, and functions of war and peace, in his commonwealth. And the philosopher *Antisthenes* took away all distinction between their virtue and ours. It is much more easy to accuse the one sex than to excuse the other. It is that which some say proverbially: *Ill may the kiln call the oven burnt-tail.*[192]

Of Coaches

IT IS EASY to verify that excellent authors, writing of causes, do not only make use of those which they imagine true but eftsoons[1] of such as themselves believe not, always provided they have some invention and beauty. They speak sufficiently, truly, and profitably, if they speak ingeniously. We cannot assure ourselves of the chief cause: we huddle up a many together, to see whether by chance it shall be found in that number:

> *Namque unam dicere causam,*
> *Non satis est, verum plures, unde una tamen sit.*
> Enough it is not one cause to devise,
> But more, whereof that one may yet arise.[2]

Will you demand of me, whence this custom ariseth to bless and say "God help" to those that sneeze? We produce three sorts of wind: that issuing from below is too undecent; that from the mouth implieth some reproach of gourmandise;[3] the third is sneezing. And because it cometh from the head and is without imputation, we thus kindly entertain it. Smile not at this subtlety; it is (as some say) *Aristotle's*.

Me seemeth to have read in *Plutarch* (who of all the authors I know, hath best commixed art with nature and coupled judgement with learning), where he yieldeth a reason why those which travel by sea do sometimes feel such qualms and risings of the stomach, saying that it proceedeth of a kind of fear, having found out some reason by which he proveth that fear may cause such an effect. Myself, who am much subject unto it, know well that this cause doth nothing concern me. And I know it, not by argument but by necessary experience. Without alleging what some have told me, that the like doth often happen unto beasts, namely unto swine, when they are farthest from apprehending any danger; and what an acquaintance of mine hath assured me of himself and who is greatly subject unto it that twice or thrice in a tempestuous storm, being surprised with exceeding fear, all manner of desire or inclination to vomit had left him. As to that ancient good fellow: *Peius vexabat quam ut periculum mihi succurreret. I was worse vexed than that danger could help me.*[4] I never apprehended fear upon the water, nor anywhere else (yet have I often had just cause offered me, if death itself may give it), which either might trouble or astonie[5] me.

It proceedeth sometimes as well from want of judgement, as from lack of courage. All the dangers I have had have been when mine eyes were wide open and my sight clear, sound, and perfect. For *even to fear, courage is required*. It hath sometimes steaded me, in respect of others, to direct and keep my flight in order, that so it might be, if not without fear, at least without dismay and astonishment. Indeed, it[6] was moved but not amazed nor distracted.

Undaunted minds march further and represent flight,[7] not only temperate, settled, and sound but also fierce and bold. Report we that which *Alcibiades* relateth of *Socrates* his companion in arms. "I found" (sayeth he) "after the rout and discomfiture of our army, both him and *Lachez* in the last rank of those that ran away, and with all safety and leisure considered him, for I was mounted upon an excellent good horse and he on foot, and so had we combated all day. I noted first how in respect of[8] *Lachez*, he showed both discreet judgement and undaunted resolution; then I observed the undismayed bravery of his march, nothing different from his ordinary pace, his look orderly and constant, duly observing and heedily judging whatever passed round about him—sometimes viewing the one, and sometimes looking on the other, both friends and enemies, with so composed a manner that he seemed to encourage the one and menace the other, signifying that whosoever should attempt his life must purchase the same or his blood at a high-valued rate. And thus they both saved themselves; for men do not willingly grapple with these but follow such as show or fear or dismay." Lo, hear the testimony of that renowned captain, who teacheth us what we daily find by experience, that there is nothing doth sooner cast us into dangers than an inconsiderate greediness to avoid them. *Quo timoris minus est, eo minus ferme periculi est. The less fear there is most commonly, the less danger there is.*[9]

Our people is to blame to say such a one feareth death, when it would signify that he thinks on it and doth foresee the same. Foresight doth equally belong as well to that which concerneth us in good as touch us in evil. *To consider and judge danger is in some sort not to be daunted at it.*

I do not find myself sufficiently strong to withstand the blow and violence of this passion of fear, or of any other impetuosity.[10] Were I once therewith vanquished and deterred, I could never safely recover myself. He that should make my mind forgo her footing could never bring her unto her place again. She doth over lively sound and over deeply search into herself. And therefore never suffers the wound which pierced the same, to be thoroughly cured and consolidated. It hath been happy for me that no infirmity could ever yet displace her. I oppose and present myself in the best ward[11] I have, against all charges and assaults that beset me. Thus the first that should bear me away would make me unrecoverable. I encounter not two:[12] which way soever spoil should enter my hold, there am I open and remedilessly drowned.

Epicurus sayeth that *a wise man can never pass from one state to its contrary.* I have some opinion answering his sentence, that *he who hath once been a very fool shall at no time prove very wise.*

God sends my cold answerable to my clothes and passions answering the means I have to endure them. Nature having discovered me on one side hath covered me on the other. Having disarmed me of strength, she hath armed me with insensibility and a regular or soft apprehension.

I cannot long endure (and less could in my youth) to ride either in coach or litter,[13] or to go in a boat. Both in the city and country, I hate all manner of riding but a-horse-back. And can less endure a litter than a coach, and by the same reason, more easily a rough agitation upon the water, whence commonly proceedeth fear, than the soft stirring a man shall feel in calm weather. By the same easy gentle motion which the oars give, conveying the boat under us, I wot not how, I feel both my head intoxicated and my stomach distempered, as I cannot likewise abide a shaking stool under me. When as either the sail or the gliding course of the water doth equally carry us away, or that we are but towed, that gently gliding and even agitation doth no whit distemper or hurt me. It is an interrupted and broken motion that offends me, and more when it is languishing. I am not able to display[14] its form. Physicians have taught me to bind and gird myself with a napkin or swathe round about the lower part of my belly as a remedy for this accident; which as yet I have not tried, being accustomed to wrestle and withstand such defects as are in me and tame them by myself.

Were my memory sufficiently informed of them, I would not think my time lost here to set down the infinite variety which histories present unto us of the use of coaches in the service of war, diverse according to the nations and different according to the ages: to my seeming of great effect and necessity. So that it is wondrously strange how we have lost all true knowledge of them. I will only allege this, that even lately in our father's time, the Hungarians did very availefully[15] bring them into fashion and profitably set them a work against the Turks, every one of them containing a targeteer[16] and a musketeer with a certain number of harquebuses or calivers,[17] ready charged and so ranged that they might make good use of them, and all over covered with a pavesado[18] after the manner of a galliotte.[19] They made the front of their battle with three thousand such coaches, and after the cannon had played, caused them to discharge and shoot off this volley of small shot upon their enemies, before they should know or feel what the rest of the forces could do, which was no small advancement. Or if not this, they mainly drove those coaches amid the thickest of their enemies' squadrons with purpose to break, disroute,[20] and make way through them. Besides the benefit and help they might make of them in any suspicious or dangerous place, to flank their troupes marching from place to place or in haste to encompass, to embarricado,[21] to cover, or fortify any lodgment or quarter.

In my time a gentleman of quality in one of our frontiers, unwieldy and so burly of body that he could find no horse able to bear his weight and having a quarrel or deadly feud in hand, was wont to travel up and down in a coach made after this fashion and found much ease and good in it. But leave we these warlike coaches. As if their nullity were not sufficiently known by better tokens, the last kings of our first race[22] were wont to travel in chariots drawn by four oxen.

Mark Antony was the first that caused himself, accompanied with a minstrel harlot, to be drawn by lions fitted to a coach. So did *Heliogabalus* after him, naming himself *Cybele*, the mother of the gods; and also by tigers, counterfeiting god *Bacchus*; who sometimes would also be drawn in a coach by two stags, and another time by four mastiff dogs, and by four naked wenches, causing himself to be drawn by them in pomp and state, he being all naked. The Emperour *Firmus* made his coach to be drawn by ostriches of exceeding greatness, so that he rather seemed to fly than to roll on wheels.

The strangeness of these inventions doth bring this other thing unto my fantasy: that it is a kind of pusillanimity in monarchs, and a testimony that they do not sufficiently know what they are, when they labour to show their worth and endeavour to appear unto the world, by excessive and intolerable expenses. A thing which in a strange country might somewhat be excused, but among his native subjects, where he swayeth all in all, he draweth from his dignity the extremest degree of honour that he may possibly attain unto. As for a gentleman, in his own private house to apparel himself richly and curiously, I deem it a matter vain and superfluous; his house, his household, his train, and his kitchen do sufficiently answer for him.

The counsel which *Isocrates* giveth to his king (in my conceit) seemeth to carry some reason: when he willeth him to be richly stored and stately adorned with movables and household-stuff,[23] forsomuch as it is an expense of continuance and which descendeth even to his posterity or heirs. And to avoid all magnificences which presently vanish both from custom and memory.

I loved when I was a younger brother to set myself forth and be gay in clothes, though I wanted other necessaries, and it became me well. There are some on whose backs their rich robes weep, or as we say, their rich clothes are lined with heavy debts. We have diverse strange tales of our ancient kings' frugality about their own persons and in their gifts—great and far-renowned kings both in credit, in valour, and in fortune. *Demosthenes* mainly combats the law of his city, who assigned their public money to be employed about the stately setting forth of their plays and feasts; he willeth that their magnificence should be seen in the quantity of tall ships well manned and appointed, and armies well furnished.

And they have reason to accuse *Theophrastus*, who in his book of riches established a contrary opinion and upholdeth such a quality of expenses to be the true fruit of wealth and plenty. They are pleasures (sayeth *Aristotle*) that only touch the vulgar and basest communality,[24] which as soon as a man is satisfied with them vanish out of mind, and whereof no man of sound judgement or gravity can make any esteem. The employment of it, as more profitable, just, and durable would seem more royal, worthy, and commendable about ports, havens, fortifications, and walls; in sumptuous buildings, in churches, hospitals, colleges, mending of highways and streets, and such like monuments, in which things Pope *Gregory* the Thirteenth shall leave aye-lasting[25] and commendable memory unto his name, and wherein our Queen *Catherine*[26] should witness unto succeeding ages her natural liberality and exceeding bounty, if her means were answerable to her affection. Fortune hath much spited me to hinder the structure and break off the finishing of our new-bridge[27] in our great city and before my death to deprive me of all hope to see the great necessity of it set forward again.

Moreover, it appeareth unto subjects, spectators of these triumphs, that they have a show made them of their own riches and that they are feasted at their proper charges. For the people do easily presume of their kings, as we do of our servants, that they should take care plenteously to provide us of whatsoever we stand in need of but that on their behalf they should no way lay hands on it. And therefore the Emperor *Galba*, sitting at supper, having taken pleasure to hear a musician play and sing before him, sent for his casket,[28] out of which be took a handful of crowns and put them into his hand with these words: *Take this, not as a gift of the public money but of mine own private store.* So is it, that it often cometh to pass that the common people have reason to grudge and that their eyes are fed with that which ... should feed their belly.

Liberality itself in a sovereign hand is not in her own luster; private men have more right and may challenge more interest in her. For taking the matter exactly as it is, *a king hath nothing that is properly his own; he oweth even himself to others.*

Authority is not given in favour of the authorising but rather in favour of the authorised. A superior is never created for his own profit but rather for the benefit of the inferiour, and a physician is instituted for the sick, not for himself. All magistracy, even as each art, rejecteth her end out of herself.[29] *Nulla ars in se versatur. No art is all in itself.*[30]

Wherefore the governours[31] and overseers of princes' childhood or minority who so earnestly endeavour to imprint this virtue of bounty and liberality in them and teach them not to refuse anything and esteem nothing so well employed, as what they shall give (an instruction which in my days I have seen in great credit) either they prefer and respect more their own profit than their masters, or else they understand not aright to whom they speak. It is too easy a matter to imprint liberality in him that hath wherewith plenteously to satisfy what be desireth at other men's charges. And his estimation being directed not according to the measure of the present but according to the quality of his means that exerciseth the same, it cometh to prove vain in so puissant[32] hands. They are found to be prodigal before they be liberal. Therefore is it but of small commendation, in respect of other royal virtues, and the only [one] (as said the tyrant *Dionysius*) that agreed and squared well with tyranny itself. I would rather teach him the verse of the ancient labourer,

> Not whole sacks, but by the hand
> A man should sow his seed in the land.[33]

That whosoever will reap any commodity by it must sow with his hand and not pour out of the sack; that *corn must be discreetly scattered and not lavishly dispersed;* and that being to give, or to say better, to pay and restore to such a multitude of people, according as they have deserved, he ought to be a loyal, faithful, and advised distributor thereof. If the liberality of a prince be without heedy[34] discretion and measure, I would rather have him covetous and sparing.

Princely virtue seemeth to consist most in justice; and of all parts of justice, that doth best and most belong to kings which accompanieth liberality. For they have it particularly reserved to their charge, whereas all other justice they happily exercise the same by the intermission[35] of others. *Immoderate bounty is a weak mean to acquire them good will*; for it rejecteth more people than it obtaineth: *Quo in plures usus sis, minus in multos uti possis. Quid autem est stultius, quam, quod libenter facias, curare ut id diutius facere non possis? The more you have used it to many, the less may you use it to many more. And what is more fond[36] than what you willingly would do, to provide you can no longer do it?*[37] And if it be employed without respect of merit, it shameth him that receiveth the same and is received without grace. Some tyrants have been sacrificed to the people's hatred by the very hands of those whom they had rashly preferred and wrongfully advanced; such kind of men meaning to assure the possession of goods unlawfully and indirectly gotten, if they show to hold in contempt and hatred him from whom they held them and, in that, combine themselves unto the vulgar judgement and common opinion.

The subjects of a prince rashly excessive in his gifts become impudently excessive in begging; they adhere not unto reason but unto example. Verily, we have often just cause to blush for our impudency. We are overpaid according to justice, when the recompense equalleth our service: for do we not owe a kind of natural duty to our princes? If he bear our charge, he doth over much; it sufficeth if he assist it. The overplus[38] is called a benefit which cannot be exacted, for the very name of liberality implieth liberty. After our fashion, we have never done: what is received is no more reckoned of; only future liberality is loved. Wherefore *the more a prince doth exhaust himself in giving, the more friends he impoverisheth.* How should he satisfy intemperate desires which increase according as they are replenished? *Who so hath his mind on taking, hath it no more on what he hath taken.* Covetousness hath nothing so proper as to be ungrateful.

The example of *Cyrus* shall not ill fit this place for the behoof[39] of our kings of these days as a touch-stone, to know whether their gifts be well or ill employed and make them perceive how much more happily that emperour did wound and oppress[40] them than they do. Whereby they are afterward forced to exact and borrow of their unknown subjects, and rather of such as they have wronged and aggrieved than of those they have enriched and done good unto; and receive no aids, where anything is gratitude except the name.

Croesus upbraided him[41] with his lavish bounty and calculated what his treasure would amount unto if he were more sparing and close-handed. A desire surprised him[42] to justify his liberality, and dispatching letters over all parts of his dominions to such great men of his estate whom he had particularly advanced, entreated every one to assist him with as much money as they could for an urgent necessity of his and presently to send it him by declaration. When all these count-books or notes were brought him, each of his friends supposing that it sufficed not to offer him no more than they had received of his bounteous liberality but adding much of their own unto it, it was found that the said sum amounted unto much more than the niggardly sparing of *Croesus*. Whereupon *Cyrus* said, *I am no less greedy of riches than other princes, but I am rather a better husband of them. You see with what small venter[43] I have purchased the unvaluable treasure of so many friends, and how much more faithful*

treasurers they are to me than mercenary men would be, without obli-
gation and without affection; and my exchequer or treasury better
placed than in paltry coffers, by which I draw upon me the hate, the
envy, and the contempt of other princes.

The ancient emperours were wont to draw some excuse for the
superfluity of their sports and public show, for so much as their authority did in some sort depend (at least in appearance) from the
will of the Roman people, which from all ages was accustomed to be
flattered by such kinds of spectacles and excess. But they were particular ones who had bred this custom to gratify their con-citizens[44]
and fellows, especially with their purse, by such profusion and magnificence. It was clean altered when the masters and chief rulers
came once to imitate the same. *Pecuniarum translatio a iustis domi-
nis ad alienos non debet liberalis videri. The passing of money from
right owners to strangers should seem liberality.*[45]

Philip, because his son endeavored by gifts to purchase the good
will of the Macedonians, by a letter seemed to be displeased and
chided him in this manner: *What? Wouldst thou have thy subjects to
account thee for their purse-bearer and not repute thee for their king?
Wilt thou frequent and practice them? Then do it with the benefits of
thy virtue, not with those of thy coffers.*[46]

Yet was it a goodly thing to cause a great quantity of great trees,
all branchy and green, to be far brought and planted in plots[47] yielding nothing but dry gravel, representing a wild shady forest, divided
in due seemly proportion. And the first day to put into the same a
thousand ostriches, a thousand stags, a thousand wild boars, and a
thousand bucks, yielding them over to be hunted and killed by the
common people; the next morrow in the presence of all the assembly
to cause a hundred great lions, a hundred leopards, and three hundred huge bears to be baited and tugged in pieces;[48] and for the third
day, in bloody manner and good earnest, to make three hundred
couple of gladiators or fencers to combat and murder one another, as
did the Emperour *Probus*.[49]

It was also a goodly show to see those wondrous huge amphitheaters all enchased[50] with rich marble, on the outside curiously

wrought with carved statues and all the inner side glittering with precious and rare embellishments—

Baltheus en gemmis, en illita porticus auro.
A belt beset with gems behold,
Behold a walk bedawb'd with gold.[51]

—all the sides round about that great void, replenished and environed from the ground unto the very top with three or four score ranks of steps and seats, likewise all of marble covered with fair cushions—

——*exeat, inquit,*
Si pudor est, et de pulvino surgat equestri,
Cuius res legi non sufficit.
If shame there be, let him be gone, he cries,
And from his knightly cushion let him rise,
Whose substance to the law doth not suffice.[52]

—where might conveniently be placed a hundred thousand men and all sit at ease. And the plain ground-work of it, where sports were to be acted,[53] first by art to cause the same to open and chap[54] in sunder with gaps and cranishes[55] representing hollow caverns which vomited out the beasts appointed for the spectacle; that ended, immediately to overflow it all with a main deep sea, fraught with store of sea-monsters and other strange fishes, all over-laid with goodly tall ships, ready rigged and appointed to represent a sea-fight; and thirdly, suddenly to make it smooth and dry again for the combat of gladiators; and fourthly, being forthwith cleansed, to strew it over with vermillion and storax[56] instead of gravel, for the erecting of a solemn banket[57] for all that infinite number of people: the last act of one only[58] day.

——*quoties nos descendentis arenæ*
Vidimus in partes, ruptaque voragine terræ

Emersisse feras, et iisdem sæpe latebris
Aurea cum croceo creverunt arbuta libro.
Nec solum nobis silvestria cernere monstra
Contigit, æquoreos ego cum certantibus ursis
Spectavi vitulos, et equorum nomine dignum,
Sed deforme pecus.
How oft have we beheld wild beasts appear
From broken gulfs of earth, upon some part
Of sand that did not sink? how often there
And thence did golden boughs oresaffron'd[59] start?
Nor only saw we monsters of the wood,
But I have seen sea-calves whom bears withstood
And such a kind of beast as might be named
A horse,[60] but in most foul proportion framed.[61]

They have sometimes caused an high steepy mountain to arise in the midst of the said amphitheaters, all over-spread with fruitful and flourishing trees of all sorts, on the top whereof gushed out streams of water, as from out the source of a purling[62] spring. Other times they have produced therein a great tall ship floating up and down which of itself opened and split asunder, and after it had disgorged from out its bulk four or five hundred wild beasts to be baited, it closed and vanished away of itself, without any visible help. Sometimes from out the bottom of it, they caused streaks and purlings[63] of sweet water to spout up, bubbling to the highest top of the frame and gently watering, sprinkling, and refreshing that infinite multitude. To keep and cover themselves from the violence of the weather, they caused that huge compass to be all over-spread, sometimes with purple sails all curiously wrought with the needle, sometimes of silk and of some other colour, and in the twinkling of an eye, as they pleased, they displayed and spread, or drew and pulled them in again.

Quamuis non modico caleant spectacula sole
Vela reducuntur cum venit Hermogenes.

Though fervent sun make't hot to see a play,
When linen thieves come, sails are kept away.[64]

The nets likewise, which they used to put before the people, to save them from the harm and violence of the baited beasts, were woven with gold.

auro quoque torta refulgent
Retia.
Nets with gold interlaced,
Their shows with glittering graced.[65]

If anything be excusable in such lavish excess, it is where the invention and strangeness breedeth admiration,[66] and not the costly charge.

Even in those vanities we may plainly perceive how fertile and happy those former ages were of other manner of wits than ours are. It happeneth of this kind of fertility, as of all other productions of Nature. We may not say what Nature employed than the utmost of her power. We go not, but rather creep and stagger here and there; we go our pace.[67] I imagine our knowledge to be weak in all senses: *we neither discern far-forward, nor see much backward*. It embraceth little and liveth not long. It is short, both in extension of time and in ampleness of matter or invention.

Vixere fortes ante Agamemnona
Multi, sed omnes illachrymabiles
Urgentur, ignotique longa
Nocte.
Before great *Agamemnon* and the rest,
Many liv'd valiant, yet are all supprest,
Unmoan'd, unknown, in dark oblivion's nest.[68]
Et supera bellum Troianum et funera Troiæ,
Multi alias alii quoque res cecinere poetæ.
Beside the Trojan war, *Troy's* funeral night,
Of other things did other poets write.[69]

And *Solon's* narration, concerning what he had learned of the *Egyptian* priests of their states long-life, and manner how to learn and preserve strange or foreign histories, in mine opinion is not a testimony to be refused in this consideration. *Si interminatam in omnes partes magnitudinem regionum videremus, et temporum, in quam se inijciens animus et intendens, ita late longeque peregrinatur, ut nullam oram ultimi videat, in qua possit insistere: in hæc immensitate infinita, vis innumerabilium appareret formarum.* If we behold an unlimited greatness on all sides both of regions and times, whereupon the mind casting itself and intentive doth travel far and near so as it sees no bounds of what is last whereon it may insist; in this infinite immensity there would appear a multitude of innumerable forms.[70]

If whatsoever hath come unto us by report of what is past were true and known of anybody, it would be less than nothing in respect of that which is unknown. And even of this image of the world which, whilst we live therein, glideth and passeth away, how wretched, weak, and how short is the knowledge of the most curious? Not only of the particular events which fortune often maketh exemplary and of consequence but of the state of mighty commonwealths, large monarchies, and renowned nations, there escapeth our knowledge a hundred times more than cometh unto our notice. We keep a coyle[71] and wonder at the miraculous invention of our artillery and amazed at the rare device of printing; when as unknown to us, other men and another end of the world named *China* knew and had perfect use of both a thousand years before. *If we saw as much of this vast world as we see but a least part of it, it is very likely we should perceive a perpetual multiplicity and ever-rolling vicissitude of forms. Therein is nothing singular and nothing rare, if regard be had unto nature, or to say better, if relation be had unto our knowledge,* which is a weak foundation of our rules and which doth commonly present us a right-false image of things. How vainly do we nowadays conclude the declination and decrepitude of the world by the fond arguments we draw from our own weakness, drooping, and declination:

Iamque adeo afecta est ætas, affectaque tellus.
And now both age and land
So sick affected stand.[72]

And as vainly did another conclude its birth and youth by the vigour
he perceiveth in the wits of his time, abounding in novelties and inventions of diverse arts:

Verum ut opinor, habet nouitatem, summa recensque
Natura est mundi, neque pridem exordia cepit:
Quare etiam quædam nunc artes expoliuntur,
Nunc etiam augescunt, nunc addita navigiis sunt
Multa.
But all this world is new, as I suppose,
World's nature fresh, nor lately it arose:
Whereby some arts refined are in fashion,
And many things now to our navigation
Are added, daily grown to augmentation.[73]

Our world hath of late discovered another (and who can warrant
us whether it be the last of his brethren, since both the *Daemons*, the
Sibyls, and all we have hitherto been ignorant of this?) no less large,
fully-peopled, all-things-yielding and mighty in strength than ours,
nevertheless so new and infantine[74] that he is yet to learn his A. B. C.
It is not yet full fifty years that he knew neither letters, nor weight,
nor measures, nor apparel, nor corn, nor vines. But was all naked,
simply-pure, in Nature's lap, and lived but with such means and food
as his mother-nurse afforded him. If we conclude aright of our end,
and the foresaid poet of the infancy of his age, this late-world shall
but come to light when ours shall fall into darkness. The whole universe shall fall into a palsy or convultion of sinnowes;[75] one member
shall be maimed or shrunken, another nimble and in good plight.

I fear that by our contagion we shall directly have furthered his[76]
declination and hastened his ruin, and that we shall too dearly have

sold him our opinions, our new-fangles, and our arts. It was an unpolluted, harmless, infant world; yet have we not whipped and submitted the same unto our discipline or schooled him by the advantage of our valour or natural forces, nor have we instructed him by our justice and integrity, nor subdued by our magnanimity. Most of their answers and a number of the negotiations we have had with them witness that they were nothing short of us, not beholding to us for any excellency of natural wit or perspicuity concerning pertinency.

The wonderful, or as I may call it, amazement-breeding magnificence of the never-like seen cities of *Cuzco* and *Mexico*, and amongst infinite such like things, the admirable garden of that King, where all the trees, the fruits, the herbs, and plants, according to the order and greatness they have in a garden, were most artificially framed in gold; as also in his cabinet, all the living creatures that his country or his seas produced were cast in gold; and the exquisite beauty of their works, in precious stones, in feathers, in cotton, and in painting, show that they yielded as little unto us in cunning and industry. But concerning unfeigned devotion, awful observance of laws, unspotted integrity, bounteous liberality, due loyalty, and free liberty, it hath greatly availed us that we had not so much as they: by which advantage they have lost, cast-away, sold, undone, and betrayed themselves.

Touching hardiness and undaunted courage and as for matchless constancy, unmoved assuredness, and undismayed resolution against pain, smarting, famine, and death itself, I will not fear to oppose the examples which I may easily find amongst them to the most famous ancient examples we may with all our industry discover in all the annals and memories of our known old world. For, as for those which have subdued them, let them lay aside the wiles, the policies, and stratagems which they have employed to cozen, to cony-catch,[77] and to circumvent them; and the just astonishment which those nations might justly conceive, by seeing so unexpected an arrival of bearded men, diverse in language, in habit, in religion, in behaviour, in form, in countenance, and from a part of the world so distant and where they never heard any habitation was, mounted upon great and unknown monsters, against those who had never so much as seen any horse and less any beast whatsoever apt to bear or taught to carry either man or burden; covered with a shining and hard skin and armed with slicing-keen weapons and glittering armour, against them who, for the wonder of the glistering of a looking-glass or of a plain knife, would have changed or given inestimable riches in gold, precious stones, and pearls; and who had neither the skill nor the matter wherewith at any leisure they could have pierced our steel; to which you may add the flashing-fire and thundering roar of shot and harquebuses, able to quell and daunt even *Cæsar* himself, had he been so suddenly surprised and as little experienced as they were; and thus to come unto and assault silly-naked people, saving where the invention of weaving of cotton cloth was known and used; for the most altogether unarmed, except some bows, stones, staves, and wooden bucklers;[78] unsuspecting poor people, surprised under colour of amity and well-meaning faith, over-taken by the curiosity to see strange and unknown things: I say, take this disparity from the conquerors, and you deprive them of all the occasions and cause of so many unexpected victories.

When I consider that stern-untamed obstinacy and undaunted vehemence, wherewith so many thousands of men, of women, and of children, do so infinite times present themselves unto inevitable dangers for the defence of their gods and liberty, [and] this generous obstinacy to endure all extremities, all difficulties, and death, more easily and willingly than basely to yield unto their domination, of whom they have so abominably been abused—some of them choosing rather to starve with hunger and fasting, being taken, than to accept food at their enemies' hands, so basely victorious—I perceive that whosoever had undertaken them man to man, without odds of arms, of experience, or of number, should have had as dangerous a war, or perhaps more, as any we see amongst us.

Why did not so glorious a conquest happen under *Alexander*, or during the time of the ancient Greeks and Romans? Or why befell not so great a change and alteration of empires and people under

such hands as would gently have polished, reformed, and uncivi-
lized, what in them they deemed to be barbarous and rude or would
have nourished and fostered those good seeds, which nature had
there brought forth, adding not only to the manuring of their
grounds and ornaments of their cities such arts as we had, and that
no further then had been necessary for them, but therewithal joining unto the original virtues of the country those of the ancient Grecians and Romans? What reparation and what reformation would
all that far-spreading world have found, if the examples, demeanors,
and policies wherewith we first presented them had called and allured those uncorrupted nations to the admiration and imitation of
virtue and had established between them and us a brotherly society
and mutual correspondency? How easy a matter had it been, profitably to reform and Christianly to instruct minds yet so pure and
new, so willing to be taught, being for the most part endowed with
so docile, so apt and so yielding natural beginnings? Whereas, contrariwise, we have made use of their ignorance and inexperience to
draw them more easily unto treason, fraud, luxury, avarice, and all
manner of inhumanity and cruelty, by the example of our life and
pattern of our customs. Who ever raised the service of merchandise
and benefit of traffic to so high a rate? So many goodly cities ransacked and razed; so many nations destroyed and made desolate; so
infinite millions of harmless people of all sexes, states, and ages,
massacred, ravaged, and put to the sword; and the richest, the fairest,
and the best part of the world topsy-turvied,[79] ruined, and defaced
for the traffic of pearls and pepper. Oh mechanical victories! Oh
base conquest! Never did blind ambition, never did greedy revenge,
public wrongs, or general enmities, so moodily enrage and so passionately incense men against men unto so horrible hostilities,
bloody dissipation, and miserable calamities.

Certain Spaniards coasting alongst the sea in search of mines,
fortuned to land in a very fertile, pleasant, and well-peopled country, unto the inhabitants whereof they declared their intent and
showed their accustomed persuasions saying that they were quiet
and well-meaning men, coming from far-countries, being sent from

the king of *Castile*, the greatest King of the habitable earth, unto whom the Pope, representing God on earth, had given the principality of all the *Indies*; that if they would become tributaries to him, they should be most kindly used and courteously entreated.[80] They required of them victuals for their nourishment and some gold for the behoof[81] of certain physical experiments. Moreover, they declared unto them the believing in one only God and the truth of our religion, which they persuaded them to embrace, adding thereto some minatory[82] threats.

Whose answer was this: That *happily they might be quiet and well meaning, but their countenance showed them to be otherwise. As concerning their King, since he seemed to beg, he showed to be poor and needy. And for the Pope, who had made that distribution, he expressed himself a man loving dissention, in going about to give unto a third man a thing which was not his own, so to make it questionable and litigious amongst the ancient possessors of it. As for victuals, they should have part of their store. And for gold, they had but little and that it was a thing they made very small account of, as merely unprofitable for the service of their life; whereas all their care was but how to pass it happily and pleasantly; and therefore, what quantity soever they should find, that only excepted which was employed about the service of their gods, they might boldly take it. As touching one only God, the discourse of him had very well pleased them: but they would by no means change their religion, under which they had for so long time lived so happily and that they were not accustomed to take any counsel but of their friends and acquaintance. As concerning their menaces, it was a sign of want of judgement to threaten those whose nature, condition, power, and means was to them unknown. And therefore they should with all speed hasten to avoid their dominions, forsomuch as they were wont to admit or take in good part the kindnesses and remonstrances of armed people, namely, of strangers; otherwise they would deal with them as they had done with such others, showing them the heads of certain men sticking upon stakes about their city, which had lately been executed.*

Lo, here an example of the stammering of this infancy. But so it is, neither in this nor in infinite other places, where the Spaniards found not the merchandise they sought for, neither made stay or attempted any violence whatsoever other commodity the place yielded: witness my Cannibals.[83]

Of two the most mighty and glorious monarchs of that world and peradventure of all our western parts, kings over so many kings: the last they deposed and overcame. He of *Peru*, having by them been taken in a battle and set at so excessive a ransom that it exceedeth all belief and that truly paid, and by his conversation having given them apparent signs of a free, liberal, undaunted, and constant courage, and declared to be of a pure, noble, and well-composed understanding, a humour possessed the conquerors, after they had most insolently exacted from him a million, three hundred five and twenty thousand, and five hundred weights[84] of gold; besides the silver and other precious things, which amounted to no less a sum (so that their horses were all shod of massive gold), to discover (what disloyalty or treachery soever it might cost them) what the remainder of this king's treasure might be and without controlment enjoy whatever he might have hidden or concealed from them. Which to compass, they forged a false accusation and proof against him that he practised to raise his provinces and intended to induce his subjects to some insurrection so to procure his liberty. Whereupon, by the very judgement of those who had complotted this forgery and treason against him, he was condemned to be publicly hanged and strangled, having first made him to redeem the torment of being burned alive by the baptism[85] which at the instant of his execution in charity they bestowed upon him. A horrible and the like never heard-of accident, which nevertheless he undismayedly endured with an unmoved manner and truly-royal gravity, without ever contradicting himself either in countenance or speech. And then, somewhat to mitigate and circumvent those silly unsuspecting people, amazed and astonished at so strange a spectacle, they counterfeited a great mourning and lamentation for his death and appointed his funerals to be solemnly and sumptuously celebrated.

The other King, of *Mexico*, having a long time manfully defended his besieged city, and in the tedious siege showed whatever pinching-

sufferance and resolute-perseverance can effect, if ever any courageous prince or war-like people showed the same; and his disastrous
success having delivered him alive into his enemies' hands, upon
conditions to be used as beseemed a king; who during the time of his
imprisonment, did never make the least show of any thing unworthy
that glorious title. After which victory, the Spaniards, not finding
that quantity of gold they had promised themselves, when they had
ransacked and ranged all corners, they by means of the cruelest tortures and horriblest torments they could possibly devise, began to
wrest and draw some more from such prisoners as they had in keeping. But unable to profit any thing that way, finding stronger hearts
than their torments, they in the end fell to such moody outrages,
that contrary to all law of nations and against their solemn vows and
promises, they condemned the king himself and one of the chiefest
princes of his court, to the rack, one in presence of another. The
prince, environed round with hot burning coals, being overcome
with the exceeding torment, at last in most piteous sort turning his
dreary eyes toward his master, as if he asked mercy of him for that he
could endure no longer. The king, fixing rigorously and fiercely his
looks upon him, seeming to upbraid him with his remissness and
pusillanimity,[86] with a stern and settled voice, uttered these few
words unto him: *What, supposest thou I am in a cold bath? Am I at
more ease than thou art?* Whereat the silly[87] wretch immediately
fainted under the torture and yielded up the ghost. The king, half
roasted, was carried away, not so much for pity (for what ruth could
ever enter so barbarous minds, who upon the surmised information
of some odd piece or vessel of gold they intended to get, would broil
a man before their eyes, and not a man only, but a king, so great in
fortune and so renowned in desert?), but forsomuch as his un-
matched constancy did more and more make their inhumane cruelty ashamed. They afterward hanged him because he had
courageously attempted by arms to deliver himself out of so long
captivity and miserable subjection, where he ended his wretched life,
worthy an high-minded and never-daunted prince.

At another time, in one same fire, they caused to be burned all alive four hundred common men, and three score principal lords of a province whom by the fortune of war they had taken prisoners.

These narrations we have out of their own books, for they do not only avouch but vauntingly publish them.[88] *May it be they do it for a testimony of their justice or zeal toward their religion?* Verily, they are ways over-different and enemies to so sacred an end. Had they proposed unto themselves to enlarge and propagate our religion, they would have considered that it is not amplified by possession of lands but of men; and would have been satisfied with such slaughters as the necessity of war bringeth, without indifferently adding thereunto so bloody a butchery as upon savage beasts and so universal as fire or sword could ever attain unto, having purposely preserved no more than so many miserable bond-slaves, as they deemed might suffice for the digging, working, and service of their mines. So that divers of their chieftains have been executed to death, even in the places they had conquered, by the appointment of the kings of *Castile*, justly offended at the seld-seen[89] horror of their barbarous demeanours and well nigh all disesteemed, contemned, and hated. God hath meritoriously permitted that many of their great pillages and ill-gotten goods have either been swallowed up by the revenging seas in transporting them, or consumed by the intestine[90] wars and civil broils, wherewith themselves have devoured one another; and the greatest part of them have been overwhelmed and buried in the bowels of the earth, in the very places they found them, without any fruit of their victory.

Touching the objection which some make that the receipt, namely in the hands of so thrifty, wary, and wise a prince,[91] doth so little answer the fore-conceived hope which was given unto his predecessors and the said former abundance of riches they met withal at the first discovery of this new-found world (for although they bring home great quantity of gold and silver, we perceive the same to be nothing, in respect of what might be expected thence), it may be answered that the use of money was there altogether unknown and, consequently, that all their gold was gathered together, serving to no other purpose than for show, state, and ornament, as a moveable[92] reserved from father to son by many puissant kings who exhausted all their mines to collect so huge a heap of vessels or statues for the ornament of their temples and embellishing of their palaces; whereas all our gold is employed in commerce and traffic between man and man. We mince and alter it into a thousand forms; we spend, we scatter, and disperse the same to several uses. Suppose our kings should thus gather and heap up all the gold they might for many ages hoard up together and keep it close and untouched.

Those of the kingdom of *Mexico* were somewhat more encivilized[93] and better artists than other nations of that world. And as we do, so judged they, that this universe was near his end and took the desolation we brought amongst them as an infallible sign of it. They believed the state of the world to be divided into five ages and in the life of five succeeding suns, whereof four had already ended their course or time, and the same which now shined upon them was the fifth and last. The first perished together with all other creatures, by an universal inundation of waters. The second by the fall of the heavens upon us, which stifled and overwhelmed every living thing; to which age they affirm the giants to have been and showed the Spaniards certain bones of them, according to whose proportion the stature of men came to be, of the height of twenty handfuls. The third was consumed by a violent fire, which burned and destroyed all. The fourth by a whirling emotion of the air and winds, which with the violent fury of itself removed and overthrew divers high mountains; saying that men died not of it but were transformed into Munkeis.[94] (*Oh what impressions doth not the weakness of man's belief admit!*) After the consummation of this fourth sun, the world continued five and twenty years in perpetual darkness, in the fifteenth of which one man and one woman were created who renewed the race of mankind. Ten years after, upon a certain day, the sun appeared as newly created, from which day beginneth ever since the calculation of their years. On the third day of whose creation died their ancient gods, their new ones have day by day been born since. In what manner this last sun shall perish, my author could not learn of them. But their number of this fourth change doth jump and meet with that great conjunction of the stars which eight hundred and odd years since, according to the astrologians' supposition, produced diverse great alterations and strange novelties in the world.

Concerning the proud pomp and glorious magnificence, by occasion of which I am fallen into this discourse, nor *Greece* nor *Rome* nor *Ægypt* can (be it in profit or difficulty or nobility) equal or compare sundry and diverse of their works. The cawcie[95] or highway which is yet to be seen in *Peru*, erected by the kings of that country, stretching from the city of *Quito* unto that of *Cusco* (containing three hundred leagues in length) straight, even and fine, and twenty paces in breadth, curiously paved, raised on both sides with goodly, high masonry-walls, all alongst which, on the inner side, there are two continual running streams, pleasantly beset with beauteous trees, which they call *molly*. In framing of which, where they met any mountains or rocks, they have cut, raised, and levelled them and filled all below places with lime and stone. At the end of every day's journey, as stations, there are built stately great palaces, plenteously stored with all manner of victuals, apparel, and arms, as well for daily wayfaring men as for such armies that might happen to pass that way.

In the estimation of which work I have especially considered the difficulty which in that place is particularly to be remembered. For they built with no stones that were less than ten foot square. They had no other means to carry or transport them than by mere strength of arms to draw and drag the carriage they needed; they had not so much as the art to make scaffolds, nor knew other device than to raise so much earth or rubbish against their building according as the work riseth, and afterward to take it away again.

But return we to our coaches. Instead of them and of all other carrying beasts, they caused themselves to be carried by men, and upon their shoulders. This last king of *Peru*, the same day he was taken, was thus carried upon rafters or beams of massive gold, sitting in a fair chair of state, likewise all of gold, in the middle of his battaile.[96] Look how many of his porters as were slain to make him fall (for all their endeavour was to take him alive) so many others, and as it were avie,[97] took and underwent presently the place of the dead so that they could never be brought down or made to fall, what slaughter so ever was made of those kind of people, until such time as a horseman furiously ran to take him by some part of his body and so pulled him to the ground.

Of the Lame or Cripple

TWO OR three years are now past since the year hath been short-ened ten days in *France*.[1] Oh, how many changes are like to ensue this reformation! It was a right removing of Heaven and Earth to-gether, yet nothing removeth from its own place: my neighbours find the season of their feed and harvest time, the opportunity of their affairs, their lucky and unlucky days, to answer just those sea-sons to which they had from all ages assigned them. Neither was the error heretofore perceived, nor is the reformation now discerned in our use. So much uncertainty is there in all things: so gross, so ob-scure, and so dull is our understanding.

Some are of opinion this reformation might have been redressed after a less incommodious manner, subtracting according to the ex-ample of *Augustus*, for some years, the bissextile[2] or leap day, which in some sort is but a day of hindrance and trouble, until they might more exactly have satisfied the debt; which by this late reformation is not done. For we are yet some days in arrearages.[3] And if by such a mean we might provide for times to come, appointing that after the revolution of such or such a number of years that extraordinary day might for ever be eclipsed, so that our misreckoning should not henceforward exceed four and twenty hours.

We have no other computation of time but years. The world hath used them so many ages; and yet is it a measure we have not until this day perfectly established. And such, as we daily doubt, what form other nations have diversely given the same and which was the true use of it. And what if, some say, that the heavens in growing old com-press themselves towards us and cast us into an uncertainty of hours and days? And as *Plutarch* sayeth of months that even in his days, astrology could not yet limit[4] the motion of the moon? Are not we then well holp-up[5] to keep a register of things past?

I was even now plodding[6] (as often I do) upon this, what free and gadding[7] instrument human reason is. I ordinarily see that men, in matters proposed them, do more willingly amuse and busy themselves in seeking out the reasons than in searching out the truth of them. They omit presuppositions but curiously examine consequences. They leave things and run to causes. Oh, conceited discoursers!

The knowledge of causes doth only concern Him, who hath the conduct of things, not us that have but the sufferance of them, and who according to our need, without entering into their beginning and essence, have perfectly the full and absolute use of them. Nor is wine more pleasant unto him that knows the first faculties[8] of it. Contrariwise, both the body and the mind interrupt and alter the right which they have of the world's use and of themselves, commixing therewith the opinion of learning.[9] The effects concern us but the means nothing at all. To determine and distribute belongeth to superiority and regency, as accepting to subjection and apprenticeship. Let us reassume our custom.[10]

They commonly begin thus: *How is such a thing done?* Whereas they should say: *Is such a thing done?* Our discourse is capable to frame a hundred other worlds and find the beginnings and contexture of them. It needeth neither matter nor ground. Let it but run on; it will as well build upon emptiness as upon fullness, and with inanity as with matter.

> *Dare pondus idonea fumo.*
> That things which vanish straight
> In smoke, should yet bear weight.[11]

I find that we should say most times: *There is no such thing.* And I would often employ this answer, but I dare not, for they cry it is a defeature[12] produced by ignorance and weakness of spirit. And I must commonly juggle[13] for company's sake to treat of idle subjects and frivolous discourses which I believe nothing at all. Since truly, it is a rude and quarelous[14] humour flatly to deny a proposition. And few miss[15] (especially in things hard to be persuaded) to affirm that they have seen it or to allege such witnesses as their authority shall stay our contradiction. According to which use, we know the foundation and means of a thousand things that never were. And the world is in a thousand questions descanted[16] and bandied to and fro; the pro and contra of which is merely false. *Ita finitima sunt falsa veris, ut in præcipitem locum non debeat se sapiens committere. Falsehood is so near neighbour to truth that a wise man should not put himself upon a slippery downfall.*[17]

Truth and falsehood have both alike countenances, their port,[18] *their taste, and their proceedings semblable.*[19] We behold them with one same eye. I observe that we are not only slow in defending ourselves from deceit, but that we seek and sue to embrace it. We love to meddle and entangle ourselves with vanity, as conformable unto our being.[20]

I have seen the birth of diverse miracles in my days. Although they be smothered in the first growth, we omit not to foresee the course they would have taken had they lived their full age. The matter is to find the end of the clue;[21] that found, one may wind off[22] what he list. *And there is a further distance from nothing to the least thing in the world than between that and the greatest.*

Now the first that are embrued[23] with the beginning of strangeness, coming to publish their history, find by the oppositions made against them where the difficulty of persuasion lodgeth, and go about with some false patch to botch up[24] those places. Besides that, *Insita hominibus libidine alendi de industria rumores. Men having a natural desire to nourish reports.*[25] We naturally make it a matter of conscience to restore what hath been lent us, without some usury and accession of our increase.[26] *A particular error doth first breed a public error.* And when his turn commeth, *a public error begetteth a particular error.* So goeth all this vast frame, from hand to hand, confounding and composing itself in such sort that the furthest-abiding[27] testimony is better instructed of it than the nearest, and the last informed better persuaded than the first. It is a natural progress. For whosoever believeth anything thinks it a deed of charity to persuade it unto another; which, that he may the better effect, he feareth not to add something of his own invention thereunto, so far as he seeth necessary in his discourse to supply the resistance and defect he imagineth to be in another's conception.

Myself, who make an especial matter of conscience to lie and care not greatly to add credit or authority to what I say, perceive nevertheless by the discourses I have in hand that being earnested,[28] either by the resistance of another or by the earnestness[29] of my narration, I swell and amplify my subject by my voice, motions, vigor, and force of words, as also by extension and amplification, not without some prejudice to the naked truth. But yet I do it upon condition that to the first that brings me home again and enquireth for the bare and simple truth at my hands, I suddenly give over my hold and without exaggeration, emphasis, or amplification, I yield both myself and it unto him. A lively, earnest, and ready speech as mine is easily transported unto hyperboles.

There is nothing whereunto men are ordinarily more prone than to give way to their opinions. Wherever usual means fail us, we add commandment, force, fire, and sword. It is not without some ill fortune to come to that pass that the multitude of believers, in a throng where fools do in number so far exceed the wise, should be the best touchstone of truth. *Quasi vero quidquam sit tam valde, quam nil sapere vulgare. Sanitatis patrocinium est, insanientium turba. As though anything were so common as to have no wit.*[30] *The multitude of them that are mad is a defence for them that are in their wits.*[31] It is a hard matter for a man to resolve his judgement against common opinions. The first persuasion taken from the very subject seizeth on the simple; whence under the authority of the number and antiquity of testimonies, it extends itself on the wiser sort. As for me, in a matter which I could not believe being reported by one, I should never credit the same, though affirmed by a hundred. And I judge not opinions by years.

It is not long since one of our princes, in whom the gout had spoiled a gentle disposition and blithe composition,[32] suffered himself so far to be persuaded or misled by the report made unto him of the wondrous deeds of a priest who by way of charms, spells, and gestures cured all diseases that he undertook a long-tedious journey to find him out, and by the virtue of his apprehension did so persuade and for certain hours so lull his legs asleep that for a while he brought them to do him that service which for a long time they had forgotten. Had fortune heaped five or six like accidents one in the neck of another, they had doubtless been able to bring this miracle into nature. Whereas afterward there was so much simplicity and so little skill found in the architect of these works that he was deemed unworthy of any punishment. As likewise should be done with most such-like things were they thoroughly known in their nature. *Miramur ex intervallo fallentia. We wonder at those things that deceive us by distance.*[33] Our sight doth in such sort often represent us a far-off with strange images, which vanish in approaching nearer. *Nunquam ad liquidum fama perducitur. Fame is never brought to be clear.*[34]

It is a wonder to see how from many vain beginnings and frivolous causes so famous impressions do ordinarily arise and ensue. Even that hindereth the information of them. For whilst a man endeavoureth to find out causes, forcible and weighty ends, and worthy so great a name, he loseth the true and essential. They are so little that they escape our sight. And verily a right wise, heedy,[35] and subtle inquisitor is required in such questings, impartial and not preoccupated.[36] All these miracles and strange events are until this day hidden from me. I have seen no such monster, or more express wonder in this world, than myself. *With time and custom a man doth acquaint and inure himself to all strangeness.* But the more I frequent and know myself, the more my deformity astonieth[37] me, and the less I understand myself.

The chiefest privilege to produce and advance such accidents is reserved unto fortune. Travelling yesterday thorough a village within two leagues of my house, I found the place yet warm of a miracle that was but newly failed and discovered, wherewith all the country thereabout[38] had for many months been amused and abused; and diverse bordering provinces began to listen unto it, and several troupes of all qualities[39] ceased not thick and threefold to flock thither. A young man of that town undertook one night in his own house (never dreaming of any knavery) to counterfeit the voice of a spirit or ghost but only for sport to make himself merry for that present. Which succeeding better than be had imagined, to make the jest extend further and himself the merrier, he made a country maiden acquainted with his device who, because she was both seely and harmless, consented to be secret and to second him. In the end they got another and were now three, all of one age and like sufficiency. And from private spirit-talking they began with hideous voices to cry and roar aloud, and in and about churches biding themselves under the chief altar, speaking but by night, forbidding any light to be set up. From speeches tending the world's subversion and threatening of the day of judgement (which are the subjects by whose authority and abusive reverence imposture and illusion is more easily lurked), they proceeded to certain visions and strange gestures, so foolish and ridiculous, that there is scarce any thing more gross and absurd used among children in their childish sports. Suppose, I pray you, that fortune would have seconded this harmless device or juggling trick, who knoweth how far it would have extended and to what it would have grown? The poor seely[40] three devils are now in prison and may happily ere long pay dear for their common sottishness.[41] And I wot not whether some cheverell[42] judge or other will be avenged of them for his.[43] It is manifestly seen in this, which now is discovered. As also in diverse other things of like quality, exceeding our knowledge, I am of opinion that we uphold our judgement as well to reject as to receive.[44]

Many abuses are engendered into the world, or, to speak more boldly, all the abuses of the world are engendered upon this, that we are taught to fear to make profession of our ignorance and are bound to accept and allow all that we cannot refute. We speak of all things by precepts and resolution. The stile[45] of *Rome* did bear that even the same that a witness deposed because he had seen it with his own eyes and that which a judge ordained of his most assured knowledge was conceived in this form of speech, *It seemeth so unto me.* I am drawn to hate likely things when men go about to set them down as infallible. I love these words or phrases which mollify and moderate the temerity of our propositions: *It may be; Peradventure; In some sort; Some; It is said; I think*; and such like. And had I been to instruct children, I would so often have put this manner of answering in their mouth, enquiring and not resolving—*What means it? I understand it not; It may well bee; Is it true?*—that they should rather have kept the form of learners until three score years of age than present themselves doctors at ten, as many do. *Whosoever will be cured of ignorance must confess the same. Iris is the daughter of Thaumantis.*[46] *Admiration*[47] *is the ground of all philosophy, inquisition the progress, ignorance the end.* Yea, but there is some kind of ignorance strong and generous that for honor and courage is nothing beholding to knowledge, an ignorance, which to conceive rightly, there is required no less learning than to conceive true learning.[48]

Being young, I saw a law case which *Corras*, a counsellor of *Toulouse*, caused to be printed of a strange accident of two men who presented themselves one for another. I remember (and I remember nothing else so well) that methought he proved his imposture, whom he condemned as guilty, so wondrous-strange and so far exceeding both our knowledge and his own who was judge, that I found much boldness in the sentence which had condemned him to be hanged.[49] Let us receive some form of sentence that may say, *The Court understands nothing of it*, more freely and ingenuously than did the *Areopagites* who, finding themselves urged and entangled in a case they could not well clear or determine, appointed the parties to come again and appear before them a hundred years after.

The witches about my country[50] are in hazard of their life upon the opinion of every new author[51] that may come to give their dreams a body.[52] To apply such examples as the Holy Word of God offereth us of such things (assured and irrefragable[53] examples) and join them to our modern events, since we neither see the causes nor means of them, some other better wit than ours is thereunto required. Peradventure it appertaineth to that only most-mighty testimony[54] to tell us: "This here, and that there, and not this other are of them."[55] God must be believed, and good reason he should be so. Yet is there not one amongst us that will be amazed at his own narration (and he ought necessarily to be astonished at it, if he be not out of his wits) whether he employ it about others matters or against himself.[56]

I am plain and homely and take hold on the main point and on that which is most likely, avoiding ancient reproaches. *Maiorem fidem homines adhibent iis quæ non intelligunt. Cupidine humani ingenii libentius obscura creduntur. Men give more credit to things they understand not.*[57] *Things obscure are more willingly believed through a strange desire of man's wit.*[58] I see that men will be angry and am forbid to doubt of it[59] upon pain of execrable injuries. A new manner of persuading! *Mercy for God's sake.* My belief is not carried away with blows. Let them tyrannize over such as accuse their opinion of falsehood; I only accuse mine[60] of difficulty and boldness. And equally to them I condemn the opposite affirmation, if not so imperiously.

He that with bravery and by commandment will establish his discourse declareth his reason to be weak. For a verbal and scholastical altercation . . . , they have as much appearance as their contradictors.[61] *Videantur sane, non affirmentur modo. Indeed let them seem, so they be not avouched.*[62] But in the effectual consequence they draw from it, these have great odds.

To kill men, there is required a bright-shining and clear light.[63] And our life is over-real and essential to warrant their supernatural and fantastical accidents.[64] As for drugs and poisons, they are out of my element; they are homicides, and of the worst kind. In which nevertheless, it is said, that one must not always rely upon the mere confession of those people, for they have sometimes been seen to accuse themselves, to have made away men which were both sound and living.[65]

In these other extravagant accusations, I should easily say that it sufficeth what commendations soever he hath, a man be believed in such things as are human; but of such as are beyond his conception and of a supernatural effect, he ought then only be believed when a supernatural approbation hath authorized him.[66] That privilege it hath pleased God to give some of our testimonies ought not to be vilified or slightly communicated. Mine ears are full of a thousand such tales. Three saw him such a day in the east; three saw him the next day in the west, at such an hour, in such a place, and thus and thus attired. Verily, in such a case I could not believe myself. How much more natural and more likely do I find it that two men should lie than one in twelve hours pass with the winds from east to west? How much more natural that our understanding may by the volubility of our loose-capering mind be transported from his place than that one of us should by a strange spirit, in flesh and bone, be carried upon a broom through the tunnel of a chimney?

Let us, who are perpetually tossed to and fro with domestical[67] and our own illusions, not seek for foreign and unknown illusions. I deem it a matter pardonable not to believe a wonder, so far forth at least as one may divert and exclude the verification by no miraculous way. And I follow Saint *Augustine*'s opinion, that *a man were better bend towards doubt than incline towards certainty in matters of difficult trial and dangerous belief.*

Some years are now past that I travelled through the country of a sovereign prince who, in favour of me and to abate my incredulity, did me the grace, in his own presence and in a particular place, to make me see ten or twelve prisoners of that kind, and amongst others an old beldam witch, a true and perfect sorceress, both by her ugliness and deformity and such a one as long before was most famous in that profession. I saw both proofs, witnesses, voluntary confessions, and some other insensible marks about this miserable old woman; I inquired and talked with her a long time, with the greatest heed and attention I could; yet am I not easily carried away by preoccupation.[68] In the end, and in conscience, I should rather have appointed them Eleborum than Hemlock.[69] *Captisque res magis mentibus, quam consceleratis similis visa. The matter seemed liker to minds captivate*[70] *than guilty.*[71] Law hath her own corrections for such diseases.

Touching the oppositions and arguments that honest men have made unto me, both there and often elsewhere, I have found none that tie me and that admit not always a more likely solution than their conclusions. True it is, that proofs and reasons grounded upon the fact and experience I untie not, for indeed they have no end; but often cut them, as *Alexander* did his knot.[72] When all is done, it is an over-valuing of one's conjectures, by them to cause a man to be burned alive.

It is reported by diverse examples (and *Prœstantius* sayeth of his father) that being in a slumber much more deeply than in a full-sound sleep, he dreamed and verily thought himself to be a mare and served certain soldiers for a sumpter-horse[73] and was indeed what he imagined to be. If sorcerers dream thus materially, if dreams may sometimes be thus incorporated into effects, I cannot possibly believe that our will should therefore be bound to the laws and justice; which I say, as one who am neither a judge nor a counsellor unto kings and furthest from any such worthiness, but rather a man of the common stamp and both by my deeds and sayings born and vowed to the obedience of public reason. He that should register my humours to the prejudice of the simplest law or opinion or custom of his village should greatly wrong himself and injure me as much. For in what I say, I gape for[74] no other certainty but that such was then my thought, a tumultuous and wavering thought.

It is by way of discourse that I speak of all, and of nothing by way of advise. *Nec me pudet, ut istos, fateri nescire quod resciam. Nor am I ashamed, as they are, to confess I know not that which I do not know.*[75] I would not be so hardy to speak if of duty I ought to be believed; and so I answered a great man who blamed the sharpness and contention of my exhortations: "When I see you bent and prepared on one side, with all the endeavour I can, I will propose the contrary unto you, to resolve and enlighten your judgement, not to subdue or bind the same. God hath your hearts in his hands, and He will furnish you with choice. I am not so malapert[76] as to desire that my opinions alone should give sway to a matter of such importance. My fortune hath not raised them to so powerful and deep conclusions."

Truly, I have not only a great number of complexions[77] but an infinite many of opinions from which, had I a son of mine own, I would dissuade him and willingly make him to distaste them.[78] What if the truest [opinions] are not ever the most commodious for[79] man, he being of so strange and untamed a composition?

Whether it be to the purpose or from the purpose, it is no great matter. It is a common proverb in *Italy* that *He knows not the perfect pleasure of* Venus *that hath not lain with a limping woman.* Either fortune or some particular accident have long since brought this bysaying in the people's mouth; and it is as well spoken of men as of women. For the queen of the Amazons answered the Scythian that wooed her to loves-embracements: *The crooked man doth it best.*[80] In that feminine commonwealth of theirs, to avoid the domination of men, they were wont in their infancy to maim them, both in their arms and legs and other limbs, that might any way advantage their strength over them and make only that use of them that we in our world make of women.

I would have said that the loose or disjointed motion of a limping or crook-backed woman might add some new kind of pleasure unto that business or sweet sin and some unassayed[81] sensual sweetness to such as make trial of it. But I have lately learnt that even ancient philosophy hath decided the matter. Who sayeth that the legs and thighs of the crooked-backed or halting-lame, by reason of their imperfection, not receiving the nourishment due unto them, it followeth that the genital parts that are above them are more full better nourished and more vigorous. Or else that, such a defect having the exercise, such as are therewith possessed do less waste [their] strength and consume their virtue and so much the stronger and fuller they come to *Venus'* sports. Which is also the reason why the Græcians described their women-weavers to be more hot and earnestly-luxurious[82] than other women: because of their sitting-trade, without any violent exercise of the body. What cannot we dispute of according to that rate? I might likewise say of these that the same stirring which their labour, so sitting, doth give them, doth rouse and solicit them, as the jogging and shaking of their coaches doth our ladies.

Do not these examples fit that whereof I spake in the beginning? That our reasons do often anticipate the effect and have the extension of their jurisdiction so infinite that they judge and exercise themselves in inanity and to a not-being?[83] Besides the flexibility of our invention to frame reasons unto all manner of dreams, our imagination is likewise found easy to receive impressions from falsehood by very frivolous appearances. For by the only authority of the ancient and public use of this word or phrase,[84] I have heretofore persuaded myself to have received more pleasure of a woman in that she was not straight, and have accounted her crookedness in the number of her graces.

Torquato Tasso,[85] in the comparison he makes between *Italy* and *France*, reporteth to have noted that we commonly have more slender and spiny legs than the Italian gentlemen, and imputeth the cause unto our continual riding and sitting on horseback; which is the very same from which *Suetonius* draweth another clean contrary conclusion. For he sayeth that *Germanicus* had by the frequent use of this exercise brought his to be very big. *There is nothing so supple and wandering as our understanding.* It is like to *Theramenes'* shoe, fit for all feet.[86] It is double and diverse, and so are matters diverse and double. "Give me a drachma of silver," said a Cynic philosopher unto *Antigonus*. "It is not the present of a king," answered he. "Give me then a talent." "It is not gift for a Cynic," quoth he.

> *Seu plures calor ille vias, et cæca relaxat*
> *Spiramenta, novas veniat qua succus in herbas:*
> *Seu durat magis, et venas astringit hiantes,*
> *Ne tenues pluviæ, rapidive potentia solis*
> *Acrior, aut Boreæ penetrabile frigus adurat.*
> Whether the heat lays open holes unseen,
> Whereby the sap may pass to herbs fresh-green:
> Or rather hardens and binds gaping veins,
> Lest sharp power of hot sun, or thinning rains
> Or piercing North-cold blast,
> Should scorch, consume, and waste.[87]

Ogni medaglia ha il suo riverscio. Each outside hath his inside, say-eth the Italian.[88] Lo, why *Clitomachus* was wont to say that *Carneades* had surmounted the labours of *Hercules*, because be had exacted consent from men[89]—that is to say, opinion and temerity to judge. This fantasia[90] of *Carneades*, so vigorous (as I imagine), pro-ceeded anciently from the impudency of those who make profession to know and from their excessive self-overweening.[91]

Aesop was set to sale[92] together with two other slaves. A chap-man[93] inquired of the first what he could do: he, to endear himself, answered: mountains and wonders and what not, for he knew and could do all things. The second answered even so for himself and more too. But when he came to *Aesop* and demanded of him what he could do, "Nothing" (said he). "For these two have forestalled all, and know and can do all things, and have left nothing for me."

So hath it happened in the school of philosophy. The rashness of those who ascribed the capacity of all things to man's wit, through spite and emulation, produced this opinion in others that human wit was not capable of anything.[94] Some hold the same extremity in ignorance that others hold in knowledge. To the end none may deny that man is not immoderate in all and everywhere, and hath no other sentence or arrest than that of necessity and impuissance[95] to proceed further.[96]

Of Experience
(selections)

3.13

THERE is no desire more natural than that of knowledge. We attempt all means that may bring us unto it. When reason fails us, we employ experience—

> *Per varios usus artem experientia fecit,*
> *Exemplo monstrante viam.*
> By diverse proofs experience art hath bred,
> Whilst one by one the way examples led.[1]

—which is a mean by much more weak and vile. But truth is of so great consequence that we ought not disdain any induction that may bring us unto it. *Reason hath so many shapes that we know not which to take hold of. Experience hath as many.* The consequence we seek to draw from the conference of events is unsure because they are ever dissemblable.[2] No quality is so universal in this surface of things as variety and diversity.

The Greeks, the Latins, and we use for the most express examples of similitude that of eggs. Some have nevertheless been found, especially one in *Delphos*, that knew marks of difference between eggs and never took one for another; and having diverse hens, could rightly judge which had laid the egg.

Dissimilitude doth of itself insinuate into our works; no art can come near unto similitude. Neither *Perozet*[3] nor any other card-maker can so industriously smooth or whiten the backside of his cards but some cunning gamester will distinguish them, only by seeing some other player handle or shuffle them. Resemblance doth not

17

318 · MICHEL DE MONTAIGNE
318 · MICHEL DE MONTAIGNE

so much make one as difference maketh another. Nature hath bound herself to make nothing that should not be dissemblable.

Yet doth not the opinion of that man greatly please me that supposed by the multitude of laws to curb the authority of judges in cutting out their morsels.[4] He perceived not that there is as much liberty and extension in the interpretation of laws as in their fashion.[5] And those but mock themselves who think to diminish our debates and stay them by calling us to the express word of the sacred Bible. Because our spirit finds not the field less spacious to control and check the sense of others than to represent his own. And as if there were as little courage and sharpness to gloss[6] as to invent.

We see how far he was deceived. For we have in *France* more laws than all the world besides—yea, more than were needful to govern all the worlds imagined by *Epicurus:*[7] *Ut olim flagitiis, sic nunc legibus laboramus. As in times past we were sick of offenses, so now are we of laws.*[8] And we have given our judges so large a scope to moot, to opinionate, to suppose, and decide that there was never so powerful and so licentious a liberty. What have our lawmakers gained with choosing a hundred thousand kinds of particular cases and add[ing] as many laws unto them? That number hath no proportion with the infinite diversity of human accidents. The multiplying of our inventions shall never come to the variation of examples. Add a hundred times as many unto them; yet shall it not follow that, of events to come, there be any one found that in all this infinite number of selected and enregistered events shall meet with one to which he may so exactly join and match it. But some circumstance and diversity will remain that may require a diverse consideration of judgement. There is but little relation between our actions that are in perpetual mutation and the fixed and unmoveable laws. The most to be desired are the rarest, the simplest, and most general. And yet I believe it were better to have none at all than so infinite a number as we have.

Nature gives them[9] ever more happy than those we give ourselves. Witness the image of the golden age that poets feign and the state wherein we see diverse nations to live which have no other.[10] Some there are who to decide any controversy that may rise amongst them will choose for judge the first man that by chance shall travel alongst their mountains. Others that upon a market day will name some one amongst themselves who in the place without more wrangling shall determine all their questions. What danger would ensue if the wisest should so decide ours, according to occurrences and at first sight, without being tied to examples and consequences? *Let every foot have his own shoe. Ferdinando*, King of *Spain*, sending certain colonies into the *Indies*, provided wisely that no lawyers or students of the laws should be carried thither for fear lest controversies, suits, or processes should people that new-found world. As a science that of her own nature engendereth altercation and division, judging with *Plato* that *lawyers and physicians are an ill provision for any country.*

Wherefore is it that our common language, so easy to be understood in all other matters, becometh so obscure, so harsh, and so hard to be understood in law cases, bills, contracts, indentures, citations, wills, and testaments? And that he who so plainly expresseth himself whatever he speak or writ of any other subject, in law matters finds no manner or way to declare himself or his meaning that admits not some doubt or contradiction? Unless it be that the princes of this art, applying themselves with a particular attention to invent and choose strange, choice, and solemn words and frame artificial cunning clauses, have so plodded and poised every syllable, canvassed and sifted so exquisitely every seam and quiddity,[11] that they are now so entangled and so confounded in the infinity of figures and so several-small partitions that they can no more come within the compass of any order or prescription or certain understanding. *Confusum est quidquid usque in pulverem sectum est. Whatsoever is sliced into very powder is confused.*[12]

Whosoever hath seen children labouring to reduce a mass of quicksilver to a certain number? The more they press and work the same and strive to force it to their will, so much more they provoke the liberty of that generous metal which scorneth their art and scatteringly disperseth itself beyond all imagination. Even so of lawyers who, in subdividing their subtleties or quiddities, teach men to multiply doubts; and by extending and diversifying difficulties, they lengthen and amplify, they scatter and disperse them. In sowing and retailing[13] of questions, they make the world to fructify and abound in uncertainty, in quarrels, in suits, and in controversies, as the ground the more it is crumbled, broken, and deeply removed or grubbed up becometh so much more fertile. *Difficultatem facit doctrina. Learning breeds difficulty.*[14]

We found many doubts in *Ulpian*, we find more in *Bartolus* and *Baldus*.[15] The trace of this innumerable diversity of opinions should never have been used to adorn posterity and have it put in her head[16] but rather have been utterly razed out.

I know not what to say to it, but this is seen by experience that so many interpretations dissipate and confound all truth. *Aristotle* hath written to be understood; which if he could not, much less shall another not so learned as he was, and a third than he who treateth his own imagination. We open the matter and spill it in distempering[17] it. Of one subject we make a thousand, and, in multiplying and subdividing, we fall again into the infinity of *Epicurus* his atoms. It was never seen that two men judged alike of one same thing. And it is impossible to see two opinions exactly semblable, not only in diverse men but in any one same man at several hours. I commonly find something to doubt of where the commentary happily never deigned to touch as deeming it so plain. I stumble sometimes as much in an even, smooth path as some horses that I know who oftener trip in a fair plain way than in a rough and stony.

Who would not say that glosses increase doubts and ignorance, since no book is to be seen, whether divine or profane, commonly read of all men, whose interpretation dims or tarnisheth not the difficulty? The hundredth commentary sends him to his succeeder more thorny and more crabbed than the first found him. When agreed we amongest ourselves to say this book is perfect, there's now nothing to be said against it?

This is best seen in our French-peddling[18] law. Authority of law is given to infinite doctors, to infinite arrests,[19] and to as many interpretations. Find we for all that any end of need of interpreters? Is there any advancement or progress towards tranquility seen therein?

Have we now less need of advocates and judges than when this huge mass of law was yet in her first infancy? Clean contrary, we obscure and bury understanding. We discover it no more but at the mercy of so many courts, barres,[20] or plea-benches.

Men mis-acknowledge the natural infirmity of their mind. She doth but quest and firret,[21] and uncessantly goeth turning, winding, building, and entangling herself in her own work, as do our silkworms, and therein stifleth herself. *Mus in pice. A mouse in pitch.*[22] He supposeth to note a far-off I wot-not-what appearance of clearness and imaginary truth; but whilst he runneth unto it, so many lets[23] and difficulties cross his way, so many impeachments and new questings start up, that they stray loose and besot him. Not much otherwise than it fortuned to *Aesop's* dogs, who far-off discovering some show of a dead body to float upon the sea and being unable to approach the same, undertook to drink up all the water that so they might dry up the passage, and were all stifled.[24] To which answereth that which one *Crates* said of *Heraclitus* his compositions, that they needed a reader who should be a cunning swimmer, lest the depth and weight of his learning should drown and swallow him up.

It is nothing but a particular weakness that makes us contented with that which others or we ourselves have found in this pursuit of knowledge. A more sufficient man will not be pleased therewith. There is a place for a follower, yea, and for ourselves, and *more ways to the wood than one.*[25] There is no end in our inquisitions. Our end is in the other world. It is a sign his wits grow short when he is pleased, or a sign of weariness. No generous spirit stays and relies upon himself; he ever pretendeth[26] and goeth beyond his strength. He hath some vagaries beyond his effects. If he advance not himself, press, settle, shock, turn, wind, and front himself, he is but half alive. His pursuits are termless and formless. His nourishment is admiration,[27] questing, and ambiguity. Which *Apollo* declared sufficiently, always speaking ambiguously, obscurely, and obliquely unto us, not feeding, but busying and amusing us. It is an irregular uncertain motion, perpetual, patternless, and without end. His inventions enflame, follow, and interproduce one another.

322 · MICHEL DE MONTAIGNE

Ainsi voit-on en un ruisseau coulant,
Sans fin l'une eau, apres l'autre roulant,
Et tout de rang, d'un eternel conduit,
L'une suit l'autre, et l'une l'autre fuit.
Par cette-ci, celle-là est poussée,
Et cette-ci, par l'autre est devancée:
Tousiours l'eau va dans l'eau, et tousiours est ce
Même ruisseau, et tousiours eau diverse.
As in a running river we behold
How one wave after th' other still is rolled,
And all along as it doth endless rise,
Th' one th' other follow, th' one from th' other flies.
By this wave, that is driv'n, and this again,
By th' other is set forward all a-main:
Water in water still, one river still,
Yet diverse waters still that river fill.[28]

There's more ado to interpret interpretations than to interpret things, and more books upon books than upon any other subject. We do but inter-gloss ourselves.[29] All swarmeth with commentaries; of authors, their is great penury. Is not the chiefest and most famous knowledge of our ages to know how to understand the wise? Is it not the common and last scope of our study? Our opinions are grafted one upon another. The first serveth as a stock[30] to the second; the second to the third. Thus we ascend from step to step. Whence it followeth that the highest-mounted hath often more honour than merit. For he is got-up but one inch above the shoulders of the last save one.

———

It is in the hands of custom to give our life what form it pleaseth; in that it can do all in all. It is the drink of *Circe's,* diversifieth our nature as she thinks good. How many nations near-bordering upon us imagine the fear of the sereine or night-calm[31] to be but a jest, which so apparently doth blast and hurt us? and whereof our mariners, our watermen, and our countrymen make but a laughing stock? You make a German sick if you lay him upon a mattress, as you distemper[32] an Italian upon a featherbed, and a Frenchman to lay him in a bed without curtains or lodge him in a chamber without a fire. A Spaniard cannot well brook to feed after our fashion, nor we endure to drink as the Swizzers.[33]

A German pleased me well at *Augusta*[34] to rail against the incommodity of our chimneys, using the same reasons or arguments that we ordinarily employ in condemning their stoves. For, to say truth, the same close-smothered heat and the smell of that oft-heated matter whereof they are composed fumeth in the heads of such as are not accustomed unto them; not so with me. But on the other side, that heat being equally dispersed, constant, and universal, without flame or blazing, without smoke, and without that wind which the tunnels of our chimneys bring us, may many ways be compared unto ours.

Why do we not imitate the Romans' architecture? It is reported that in ancient times they made no fire in their houses, but without[35] and at the foot of them; whence by tunnels, which were conveyed through their thickest walls and contrived near and about all such places as they would have warmed, so that the heat was conveyed into every part of the house. Which I have seen manifestly described in some place of *Seneca*, though I cannot well remember where.

This German, hearing me commend the beauties and commodities of his city (which truly deserveth great commendation), began to pity me because I was shortly to go from it. And the first inconvenience he urged me withal was the heaviness in the head, which chimneys in other places would cause me. He had heard some other body complain of it and therefore alleged the same against me, being wont by custom to perceive it in such as came to him. All heat coming from fire doth weaken and dull me. Yet said *Evenus* that fire was the best sauce of life. I rather allow and embrace any other manner or way to escape cold.

We fear our wines when they are low, whereas in *Portugal*, the fume of it is counted delicious and is the drink of princes.[36]

To conclude, each several nation hath diverse customs, fashions, and usages which, to some others, are not only unknown and strange, but savage, barbarous, and wondrous.

What shall we do unto that people that admit no witness except printed, that will not believe men if not printed in books, nor credit truth unless it be of competent age? We dignify our fopperies when we put them to the press. It is another manner of weight for him to say, "I have seen it" than if you say, "I have heard it reported." But I, who misbelieve no more the mouth than the hand of men, and know that *men write as indiscreetly as they speak unadvisedly*, and esteem of this present age as of another past, allege as willingly a friend of mine as *Aulus Gellius* or *Macrobius*, and what myself have seen as that they have written. And as they account virtue to be nothing greater by being longer, so deem I truth to be nothing wiser by being more aged. I often say it is mere folly that makes us run after strange and scholastical[37] examples. The fertility of them is now equal unto that of *Homer* and *Plato's* times. But is it not that we rather seek the honour of allegations than the truth of discourses? As if it were more to borrow our proofs from out the shop of *Vascosane* or *Plantin*[38] than from that we daily see in our village. Or verily, that we have not the wit to blanch, sift-out, or make that to prevail which passeth before us, and forcibly judge of it to draw the same into example. For if we say that authority fails us to add credit unto our testimony, we speak from the purpose. For so much as in my conceit could we but find out their true light, Nature's greatest miracles and the most wonderful examples, namely upon the subject of human actions, may be drawn and formed from most ordinary, most common, and most known things.

Now concerning my subject, omitting the examples I know by books, and that which *Aristotle* speaketh of *Andron of Argos*, that he would travel all over the scorching sands of *Libya* without drinking, a gentleman who hath worthily acquitted himself of many honourable charges reported where I was that, in the parching heat of summer, he had travelled from *Madrid* to *Lisbon* without ever drinking. His age respected, he is in very good and healthy plight and hath nothing extraordinary in the course or custom of his life, saving (as himself hath told me) that he can very well continue two or three months, yea, a whole year, without any manner of beverage. He sometimes finds himself thirsty but lets it pass, and holds that it is an appetite which will easily and of itself languish away; and if he drink at any time, it is more for a caprice or humor than for any need or pleasure.

Lo, here one of another key. It is not long since that I found one of the wisest men of *France* (among those of no mean fortune), studying hard in the corner of a great hall, which for that purpose was hung about with tapestry and round about him a disordered rabble of his servants, grooms, and lackeys, prattling, playing, and hoyting.[39] Who told me (as *Seneca* in a manner sayeth of himself) that he learned and profited much by that burly-burly or tintimare,[40] as if, beaten with that confused noise, he did so much the better re-call and close himself into himself for serious contemplation, and that the said tempestuous rumours[41] did strike and repercuss his thoughts inward. Whilst he was a scholar in *Padua*, his study was ever placed so near the jangling of bells, the rattling of coaches, and rumbling tumults of the marketplace that for the service of his study, he was fain[42] not only to frame and inure himself to contemn but to make good use of that turbulent noise. *Socrates* answered *Alcibiades*, who wondered how he could endure the continual tittle-tattle and uncessant scolding of his wife: "Even as those who are accustomed to hear the ordinary creaking of the squeaking wheels of wells." Myself am clean contrary, for I have a tender brain and easy to take snuff in the nose or to be transported.[43] If my mind be busy alone, the least stirring, yea the buzzing of a fly, doth trouble and distemper the same.

Seneca in his youth, having earnestly undertaken to follow the example of *Sextius*,[44] to feed on nothing that were taken dead, could with pleasure (as himself averreth) live so a whole year. And left it only because he would not be suspected to borrow this rule from some new religions that instituted the same. He therewithal followed some precepts of *Attalus*,[45] not to lie upon any kind of carpets or bedding that would yield under one; and until he grew very aged, he never used but such as were very hard and unyielding to the body. What the custom of his days makes him account rudeness,[46] ours makes us esteem wantonness.[47]

Behold the difference between my varlet's life and mine. The Indians have nothing further from my form and strength. Well I wot that I have heretofore taken boys from begging and that went roguing up and down to serve me, hoping to do some good upon them who have within a little while after left me, my fare, and my livery, only that they might without control or check follow their former idle, loitering life. One of which I found not long since gathering of mussels in a common sink[48] for his dinner; whom (do what I could) I was never able, neither with entreaty to reclaim nor by threatening, to withdraw from the sweetness he found in want and delight he felt in roguing laziness. Even vagabonding rogues, as well as rich men, have their magnificences and voluptuousness and (as some say) their dignities, pre-eminences, and politic orders.

They are effects of custom and use, and *what is bred in the bone will never out of the flesh*.[49] Both which have power to inure and fashion us, not only to what form they please (therefore, say the wise, ought we to be addressed to the best, and it will immediately seem easy unto us), but also to change and variation, which is the noblest and most profitable of their apprentisages.[50] The best of my corporal complexions[51] is that I am flexible and little opiniative.[52] I have certain inclinations, more proper and ordinary, and more pleasing, than others. But with small ado and without compulsion, I can easily leave them and embrace the contrary. A young man should trouble his rules to stir up his vigor and take heed he suffer not the same to grow faint, sluggish, or reasty.[53] For there is no course of life so weak and sottish as that which is managed by order, method, and discipline.

Death intermedleth and everywhere confounds itself with our life. Declination doth preoccupate her hour and insinuate itself into the very course of our advancement. I have pictures of mine own that were drawn when I was five and twenty and others being thirty years of age, which I often compare with such as were made by me as I am now at this instant. How many times do I say, I am no more myself. How much is my present image further from those than from that of my decease? It is an over-great abuse unto Nature to drag and hurry her so far that she must be forced to give us over and abandon our conduct, our eyes, our teeth, our legs, and the rest to the mercy of a foreign help and begged assistance, and to put ourselves into the hands of art,[54] weary to follow us.

I am not over-much or greedily desirous of sallets[55] or of fruits, except melons. My father hated all manner of sauces; I love them all. Over-much eating doth hurt and distemper me, but for the quality I have yet no certain knowledge that any meat offends me; I never observe either a full or waned moon, nor make a difference between the springtime or autumn. There are certain inconstant and unknown motions in us. For (by way of example) I have heretofore found radish-roots to be very good for me, then very hurtful, and now again very well agreeing with my stomach. In diverse other things I feel my appetite to change and my stomach to diversify from time to time. I have altered my course of drinking, sometimes from white to claret wine, and then from claret to white again. I am very friand[56] and gluttonous of fish, and keep my shroving[57] days upon fish days, and my feasts upon fasting-days. I believe as some others do, that fish is of lighter digestion than flesh. As I make it a conscience to eat flesh upon a fish day, so doth my taste to eat fish and flesh together.[58] The diversity between them seems to me over-distant.

———

Myself, who but grovel on the ground, hate that kind of inhuman wisdom which would make us disdainful and enemies of the body's reformation. I deem it an equal injustice either to take natural sensualities against the heart or to take them too near the heart.[59] *Xerxes* was a ninny-hammer[60] who, enwrapped and given to all human voluptuousness, proposed rewards for those that should devise such as he had never heard of. And he is not much behind him in sottishness that goes about to abridge those which nature hath devised for him. One should neither follow nor avoid them but receive them. I receive them somewhat more amply and graciously and rather am contented to follow natural inclination. We need not exaggerate their inanity; it will sufficiently be felt and doth sufficiently produce itself. God-a-mercy our weak, crazed, and joy-diminishing spirit,[61] which makes us distaste both them and himself. He[62] treateth both himself and whatsoever he receiveth, sometimes forward and other times backward, according as himself is either insatiate, vagabond, newfangled, or variable.

> *Sincerum est nisi vas, quodcunque infundis accescit.*
> In no sweet vessel all you pour,
> In such a vessel soon will sour.[63]

Myself, who brag so curiously to embrace and particularly to allow the commodities of life, whensoever I look precisely into it, I find nothing therein but wind. But what? We are nothing but wind. And the very wind also, more wisely than we, loveth to bluster and to be in agitation, and is pleased with his own offices, without desiring stability or solidity, qualities that be not his own.

The mere pleasures of imagination, as well as displeasure (say some), are the greatest, as the balance of *Critolaus* did express.[64] It is no wonder: she[65] composeth them at her pleasure and cuts them out of the whole cloth. I see daily some notable precedents of it and peradventure to be desired. But I, that am of a commixed condition, homely and plain, cannot so thoroughly bite on that only and so simple object, but shall grossly and carelessly give myself over to the present delights of the general and human law, intellectually sensible and sensibly intellectual. The *Cyrenaic* philosophers[66] are of the opinion that as griefs, so corporal pleasures, are more powerful and, as double, so more just.

There are some (as *Aristotle* sayeth) who with a savage kind of stupidity will seem distasteful or squeamish of them.[67] Some others

I know that do it out of ambition. Why renounce they not also breathing? Why live they not of their own and refuse light because it cometh of gratuity and costs them neither invention nor vigor? That *Mars* or *Pallas* or *Mercury* should nourish them to see instead of *Ceres*, *Venus*, or *Bacchus*.[68] Will they not seek for the quadrature[69] of the circle, even upon their wives?[70] I hate that we should be commanded to have our minds in the clouds whilst our bodies are sitting at the table. Yet would I not have the mind to be fastened thereunto, nor wallow upon it, nor lie along thereon; but apply itself and sit at it. *Aristippus* defended but the body, as if we had no soul; *Zeno* embraced but the soul, as if we had no body. Both viciously. *Pythagoras* (say they) hath followed a philosophy, all in contemplation; *Socrates* altogether in manners and in action; *Plato* hath found a mediocrity[71] between both. But they say so by way of discourse, for the true temperature is found in *Socrates*, and *Plato* is more *Socratical* than *Pythagorical*, and it becomes him best.

When I dance, I dance; and when I sleep, I sleep. And when I am solitary walking in a fair orchard, if my thoughts have a while entertained themselves with strange occurrences, I do another while bring them to walk with me in the orchard and to be partakers of the pleasure of that solitariness and of myself. Nature hath like a kind mother observed this, that such actions as she for our necessities hath enjoined unto us should also be voluptuous[72] unto us; and doth not only by reason but also by appetite invite us unto them. It were injustice to corrupt her rules.

When I behold *Cæsar* and *Alexander* in the thickest of their wondrous-great labours, so absolutely to enjoy human and corporal pleasures, I say not that they release thereby their mind but rather strengthen the same, submitting by vigor of courage their violent occupation and laborious thoughts to the customary use of ordinary life. Wise had they been had they believed that that was their ordinary vocation, and this their extraordinary.[73]

What egregious fools are we? "He hath passed his life in idleness," say we; "Alas I have done nothing this day." What, have you not lived? It is not only the fundamental but the noblest of your occupations. "Had I been placed or thought fit for the managing of great affairs, I would have showed what I could have performed." *Have you known how to meditate and manage your life? You have accomplished the greatest work of all.* For a man to show and exploit himself, nature hath no need of fortune; she equally shows herself upon all grounds, in all suits, before and behind, as it were without curtains, welt or guard.[74] *Have you known how to compose your manners? You have done more than he who hath composed books.* Have you known how to take rest? You have done more than he who hath taken empires and cities. *The glorious masterpiece of man is to live to the purpose.* All other things, as to reign, to govern, to hoard up treasure, to thrive, and to build are for the most part but appendixes[75] and supporters thereunto.

It is to me a great pleasure to see a general of an army at the foot of a breach which ere long intendeth to charge or enter, all whole, undistracted, and carelessly to prepare himself, whilst he sits at dinner with his friends about him, to talk of any matter. And I am delighted to see *Brutus*, having both heaven and earth conspired against him and the liberty of *Rome*, by stealth to take some hours of the night from his other cares and walking of the round in all security to read, to note, and to abbreviate *Polybius*. It is for base and petty minds, dulled and overwhelmed with the weight of affairs, to be ignorant how to leave them and not to know how to free themselves from them, nor how to leave and take them again:

> *O fortes peioraque passi,*
> *Mecum sæpe viri, nunc vino pellite curas,*
> *Cras ingens iterabimus æquor.*
> Valiant compeers, who oft have worse endured
> With me, let now with wine your cares be cured:
> Tomorrow we again
> Will launch into the main.[76]

Whether it be in jest or earnest that the *Sorbonical* or theological wines and their feasts or gaudy[77] days are now come to be proverbially jested at, I think there is some reason that by how much more profitably and seriously they have bestowed the morning in the exercise of their schools, so much more commodiously and pleasantly should they dine at noon.[78] A clear conscience to have well employed and industriously spent the other hours is a perfect seasoning and savory condiment of tables. So have wise men lived. And that inimitable contention unto virtue which so amazeth us in both *Catos*, their so strictly-severe humour, even unto importunity, hath thus mildly submitted itself and taken pleasure in the laws of human condition, and in *Venus* and *Bacchus*, according to their sect's precepts, which require a perfectly wise man to be fully-expert and skilful in the true use of sensualities as in all other duties or devoires[79] belonging to life. *Cui cor sapiat, ei et sapiat palatus. Let his palate be savory, whose heart is savory.*[80]

Easy-yielding and facility doth in my conceit greatly honour and is best befitting a magnanimous and noble mind. *Epaminondas* thought it no scorn to thrust himself amongst the boys of his city and dance with them, yea and to sing and play, and with attention busy himself were it in things that might derogate from the honor and reputation of his glorious victories and from the perfect reformation of manners that was in him. And amongst so infinite admirable actions of *Scipio* the grandfather, a man worthy to be esteemed of heavenly race, nothing addeth so much grace unto him as to see him carelessly to dally and childishly to trifle in gathering and choosing of cockle-shells and play at cob-castle[81] along the seashore with his friend *Lælius*. And if it were foul weather, amusing and solacing himself to represent in writing and comedies the most popular and base actions of men. And having his head continually busied with that wonderful enterprise against *Hannibal* and *Africa*, yet he still visited the schools in *Sicily*, and frequented the lectures of philosophy, arming his enemies' teeth at *Rome* with envy and spite. Nor any thing more remarkable in *Socrates* than, when being old and crazed, he would spare so much time as to be instructed in the art of dancing and playing upon instruments, and thought the time well bestowed.

Who notwithstanding hath been seen to continue a whole day and night in an ecstasy or trance, yea ever standing on his feet, in presence of all the Greek army, as it were surprised and ravished by some deep and mind-distracting thought. He hath been noted to be the first amongst so infinite valiant men in the army, headlong to rush out to help and bring off *Alcibiades*, engaged and enthronged by his enemies; to cover him with his body; and, by main force of arms and courage, bring him off from the rout. And in the *Delian* battle to save and disingage *Xenophon*, who was beaten from his horse. And in the midst of all the Athenian people wounded, as it were, with so unworthy a spectacle, headlong present himself the first man to recover *Theramenes*, from out the hands of the officers and satellites, of the Thirty Tyrants of *Athens*, who were leading him to his death; and never desisted from his bold attempt until he met with *Theramenes* himself, though he were followed and assisted with two more. He hath been seen (provoked thereunto by a matchless beauty, wherewith he was richly endowed by nature) at any time of need to maintain a severe continency.[82] He hath continually been noted to march to the wars on foot; to break the ice with his bare feet; to wear one same garment in summer and winter; to exceed all his companions in patience of any labour or travel; to eat no more or otherwise at any banquet than at his ordinary.

He hath been seen seven and twenty years together with one same undismayed countenance, patiently to bear and endure hunger, poverty, the indocility and stubbornness of his children, the forwardness and scratchings of his wife; and in the end malicious detraction, tyranny, imprisonment, shackles, and poison. But was that man invited to drink to him by duty of civility? He was also the man of the army, to whom the advantage thereof remained. And yet he refused not, nor disdained to play for nuts with children, nor to run with them upon a hobby-horse, wherein he had a very good grace. *For all actions* (sayeth philosophy) *do equally beseem well and honour a wise man.* We have good ground and reason, and should never be weary to present the image of this incomparable man unto all patterns and form of perfections. There are very few examples of life absolutely full and pure, and our instruction is greatly wronged in that it hath certain weak, defective, and unperfect forms proposed unto it, scarcely good for any good use, which divert and draw us back and may rather be termed corrupters than correctors.

Man is easily deceived. One may more easily go by the sides, where extremity serveth as a bound, as a stay and as a guide, than by the mid-way, which is open and wide, and more according unto art than according unto nature; but therewithal less nobly and with less commendation. *The greatness of the mind is not so much to draw up and hale forward as to know how to range, direct, and circumscribe itself.* It holdeth for great whatever is sufficient and showeth her height in loving mean things better than eminent. *There is nothing so goodly, so fair, and so lawful as to play the man well and duly, nor science so hard and difficult as to know how to live this life well.* And of all the infirmities we have the most savage is to despise our being.

Whoso will sequester or distract his mind, let him hardily do it, if he can, at what time his body is not well at ease, thereby to discharge it from that contagion; and elsewhere contrary, that she may assist and favour him[83] and not refuse to be partaker of his natural pleasures and continually[84] be pleased with them, adding thereunto, if she be the wiser, moderation, lest through indiscretion they might be confounded with displeasure. *Intemperance is the plague of sensuality; and temperance is not her scourge but rather her seasoning.* Eudoxus,[85] who thereon established his chief felicity,[86] and his companions, that raised the same to so high a pitch, by means of temperance, which in them was very singular and exemplar, savoured the same in her most gracious sweetness.

I enjoin my mind with a look equally regular to behold both sorrow and voluptuousness:[87] *Eodem enim vitio est effusio animi in lætitia, quo in dolore contractio. As faulty is the enlarging of the mind in mirth as the contracting it in grief;*[88] and equally constant, but the one merrily and the other severely, and according to that she may bring unto it, to be as careful to extinguish the one as diligent to quench the other. *To have a perfect insight into a good draws with it an absolute insight into evil.* And sorrow hath in her tender beginning something that is unavoidable, and voluptuousness in her excessive end something that is evitable.[89] *Plato* coupleth them together and would have it to be the equal office of fortitude to combat against sorrows and fight against the immoderate and charming blandishments of sensuality. They are two fountains: at which whoso draweth whence, when, and as much as he needeth—be it a city, be it a man, be it a beast—he is very happy. The first must be taken for physic[90] and necessity, and more sparingly; the second for thirst, but not unto drunkenness. *Pain, voluptuousness, love, and hate are the first passions a child feeleth; if reason approach, and they apply themselves unto it, that is virtue.*

I have a dictionary[91] severally[92] and wholly to myself. I "pass the time" when it is foul and incommodious; when it is fair and good, I will not pass it; I run it over again and take hold of it. *A man should run the bad and settle himself in the good.* This vulgar phrase of "pass time" and "to pass the time" represents the custom of those wise men who think to have no better account of their life than to pass it over and escape it; to pass it over and bawk[93] it, and so much as in them lieth to ignore and avoid it, as a thing of an irksome, tedious, and to-be-disdained quality. But I know it to be otherwise and find it to be both priseable[94] and commodious, yea in her last declination, where I hold it. And Nature hath put the same into our hands, furnished with such and so favourable circumstances that, if it press and molest us, or if unprofitably it escape us, we must blame ourselves. *Stulti vita ingrata est, trepida est, tota in futurum fertur. A fool's life is all pleasant, all fearful, all fond of the future.*[95] I therefore prepare and compose myself to forgo and lose it without grudging, but a thing that is losable and transitory by its own condition; not as troublesome and importunate. Nor beseems it a man not to be grieved when he dieth, except they be such as please themselves to live still. There is a kind of husbandry in knowing how to enjoy it. I enjoy it double to others, for *the measure in jouissance*[96] *dependeth more or less on the application we lend it.* Especially at this instant, that I perceive mine to be short in time, I will extend it in weight; I will stay the readiness of her flight by the promptitude of my hold-

fast by it,[97] and by the vigor of custom[98] recompense the haste of her
fleeting. According as the possession of life is more short, I must endeavour to make it more profound and full.

Other men feel the sweetness of a contentment and prosperity; I
feel it as well as they, but it is not in passing and gliding. Yet should
it be studied, tasted, and ruminated, thereby to yield Him condign[99]
thanks, that it pleased to grant the same unto us. They enjoy other
pleasures as that of sleep, without knowing them. To the end that
sleep should not dully and unfeelingly escape me and that I might
better taste and be acquainted with it, I have heretofore found it
good to be troubled and interrupted in the same. I have a kind of
contentment to consult with myself, which consultation I do not
superficially run over but considerately sound the same and apply
my reason to entertain and receive it, which is now become forward,
peevish, and distasted. Do I find myself in some quiet mood? Is
there any sensuality that tickles me? I do not suffer the same to busy
itself or dally about my senses but associate my mind unto it. Not to
engage or plunge itself therein but therein to take delight; not to lose
but therein to find itself. And for her part,[100] I employ her to view
herself in that prosperous estate, to ponder and esteem the good fortune she hath and to amplify the same. She measureth how much
she is beholding unto God for that she is at rest with her conscience
and free from other intestine[101] passions, and hath her body in her
natural disposition, orderly and competently enjoying certain flattering and effeminate functions with which it pleaseth him of his
grace to recompense the griefs, wherewith his justice at his pleasure
smiteth us. Oh how availful[102] is it unto her to be so seated that,
wherever she casteth her eyes, the heavens are calm round about her;
and no desire, no fear, or doubt troubleth the air before her; here is
no difficulty, either past or present or to come, over which her imagination passeth not without offence.

This consideration takes a great lustre from the comparison of different conditions. Thus do I in a thousand shapes propose unto myself those whom either fortune or their own error doth transport and
torment. And these nearer, who so slackly and incuriously receive

their good fortune. They are men which indeed "pass their time";
they overpass the present and that which they possess, thereby to
serve their hopes with shadows and vain images which fancy sets
before them—

> *Morte oblita quales fama est volitare figuras*
> *Aut quæ sopitos deludunt somnia sensus.*
> Such walking shapes we say, when men are dead,
> Dreams, whereby sleeping senses are mis-led.[103]

—which hasten and prolong their flight, according as they are followed. The fruit and scope of their pursuit is to pursue. As *Alexander* said, that *the end of his travel was to travel.*

> *Nil actum credens cum quid superesset agendum.*
> Who thought that nought was done,
> When ought remain'd undone.[104]

As for me, then, I love my life and cherish it, such as it hath
pleased God to grant it us. I desire not he should speak of the necessity of eating and drinking.[105] And I would think to offend no less
excusably in desiring it should have it double. *Sapiens divitiarum
naturalium quæsitor acerrimus. A wise man is a most eager and earnest searcher of those things that are natural.*[106] Not that we should
sustain ourselves by only putting a little of that drug into our mouth
wherewith *Epimenides* was wont to allay hunger and yet maintained
himself. Nor that we should insensibly[107] produce children at our
fingers' ends or at our heels but rather (speaking with reverence) that
we might with pleasure and voluptuousness produce them both at
our heels' and fingers' ends. Nor that the body should be void of desire and without tickling-delight. They are ungrateful and impious
complaints. I cheerfully and thankfully and with a good heart accept what nature hath created for me, and am therewith well pleased
and am proud of it. Great wrong is offered unto that great and all-

puissant Giver, to refuse his gift, which is so absolutely good, and disanull or disfigure the same, since he made it perfectly good. *Omnia quæ secundum naturam sunt; estimatione digna sunt. All things that are according to nature are worthy to be esteemed.*[108]

Of philosophy's opinions, I more willingly embrace those which are the most solid, that is to say, such as are most human and most ours. My discourses are suitable to my manners, low and humble. She[109] then brings forth a child well-pleasing me when she betakes herself to her quiddities and ergos to persuade us that it is a barbarous alliance to marry what is divine with that which is terrestrial; wed reasonable with unreasonable; combine severe with indulgent; and couple honest with unhonest; that voluptuousness is a brutal quality, unworthy the taste of a wise man.[110] The only pleasure he draws from the enjoying of a fair young bride is the delight of his conscience, by performing an action according unto order, as to put on his boots for a profitable riding. Oh that his followers had no more right or sinews or pith or juice at the dis-maidening of their wives than they have in his lessons.[111]

It is not that which *Socrates*, both his[112] and our master, sayeth. He valueth rightly as he ought corporal voluptuousness, but he preferreth that of the mind, as having more force, more constancy, facility, variety, and dignity. This, according to him, goeth nothing alone—he is not so fantastical—but only first. For him, temperance is a moderatrix[113] and not an adversary of sensualities.[114]

Nature is a gentle guide, yet not more gentle than prudent and just. *Intrandum est in rerum naturam, et penitus quid ea postulet, pervidendum. We must enter into the nature of things and thoroughly see what she inwardly requires.*[115] I quest after her track; we have confounded her with artificial traces. And that Academical and Peripatetical[116] *summum bonum* or sovereign felicity, which is to live according to her rules, by this reason becometh difficult to be limited and hard to be expounded. And that of the Stoics, cousin-german[117] to the other, which is to yield unto nature.

Is it not an error to esteem some actions less worthy forsomuch as they are necessary? Yet shall they never remove out of my head that it is not a most convenient marriage to wed pleasure unto necessity, with which (sayeth an ancient writer) the gods do ever complot and consent. To what end do we by a divorce dismember a frame contexted with so mutual, coherent, and brotherly correspondency? Contrariwise, let us repair and renew the same by interchangeable offices: that the spirit may awake and quicken the dull heaviness of the body, and the body stay the lightness of the spirit, and settle and fix the same. *Qui velut summum bonum, laudat animæ naturam, et tanquam malum, naturam carnis accusat, profecto et animam carnaliter appetit, et carne incarnaliter fugit, quoniam id vanitate sentit humana, non veritate divina. He that praiseth the nature of the soul as his principal good and accuseth the nature of the flesh as evil assuredly he both carnally affecteth the soul and carnally escheweth the flesh, since he is of this mind not by divine verity but human vanity.*[118]

There is no part or parcel unworthy of our care in that present which God hath bestowed upon us; we are accountable even for the least hair of it. And it is no commission for fashion-sake for any man to direct man according to his condition; it is express, natural, and principal, and the Creator hath seriously and severely given the same unto us. Only authority is of force with men of common reach and understanding and is of more weight in a strange language. But here let us charge again. *Stultitiæ proprium quis non dixerit, ignave et contumaciter facere quæ facienda sunt: et alio corpus impellere, alio animum, distrahique inter diversissimos motus? Who will not call it a property of folly to do slothfully and frowardly*[119] *what is to be done, and one way to drive the body and another way the mind, and himself to be distracted into most diverse motions?*[120]

Which, the better to see, let such a man one day tell you the amusements and imaginations which he puts into his own head and for which he diverteth his thoughts from a good repast and bewaileth the hour he employeth in feeding himself. You shall find there is nothing so wallowish in all the messes of your table, as is that goodly entertainment of the mind—*It were often better for us to be sound asleep than awake unto that we do*—and you shall find that his discourses and intentions are not worth your meanest dish. Suppose they were the entrancings of *Archimedes* himself, and what of that? There touch not nor do I blend with that rabble or rascality of men as we are, nor with that vanity of desires and cogitations which divert us. Only those venerable minds which through a fervency of devotion and earnestness of religion elevated to a constant and conscientious meditation of heavenly-divine things, and which by the violence of a lively and virtue of a vehement hope, preoccupating the use of eternal soul-saving nourishment, the final end, only stay, and last scope of Christian desires—the only constant delight and incorruptible pleasure—disdain to rely on our necessitous, fleeting, and ambiguous commodities, and easily resign the care and use of sensual and temporal feeding unto the body. It is a privileged study. Super-celestial opinions and under-terrestrial manners are things that amongst us I have ever seen to be of singular accord.[121]

Æsop, that famous man, saw his master piss as he was walking. "What" (said he), "must we not &c.[122] when we are running?" *Let us husband time as well as we can. Yet shall we employ much of it, both idly and ill.* As if our mind had not other hours enough to do her business, without disassociating herself from the body in that little space which she needeth for her necessity.

They will be exempted from them and escape man.[123] It is mere folly: instead of transforming themselves into angels, they transchange themselves into beasts; in lieu of advancing, they abase themselves. Such transcending humours affright me as much as steepy, high, and inaccessible places. And I find nothing so hard to be digested in *Socrates* his life as his ecstasies and communication with *dæmons*, nothing so human in *Plato* as that for which they say he is called divine. And of our sciences those which are raised and extolled for the highest seem to me the most basest and terrestrial. I find nothing so humble and mortal in *Alexander's* life as his conceits about his immortalization. *Philotas* by his answer quipped at him very pleasantly and wittily. He had by a letter congratulated with him and rejoiced that the oracle of *Jupiter Hammon* had placed him amongst the gods; to whom he answered that, in respect and consideration of him, he was very glad;[124] but yet there was some cause those men should be pitied that were to live with a man and obey him who outwent others and would not be contented with the state and condition of mortal man.

> ——*Diis te minorem quod geris, imperas.*
> Since thou less than the gods
> Bear'st thee, thou rul'st with odds.[125]

The quaint inscription wherewith the Athenians honored the coming of *Pompey* into their city agreeth well and is conformable to my meaning.

> *D'autant es tu Dieu, comme*
> *Tu te recognois homme.*
> So far a God thou may'st accounted be
> As thou a man dost re-acknowledge thee.[126]

It is an absolute perfection and as it were divine for a man to know how to enjoy his being loyally. We seek for other conditions because we understand not the use of ours, and go out of ourselves forsomuch as we know not what abiding there is. *We may long enough get upon stilts for be we upon them, yet must we go with our own legs. And sit we upon the highest throne of the world, yet sit we upon our own tail.*

The best and most commendable lives, and best pleasing me, are (in my conceit) those which with order are fitted and with *decorum* are ranged to the common mould and human model, but without wonder or extravagancy. Now hath old age need to be handled more tenderly. Let us recommend it unto that god who is the protector of health and fountain of all wisdom, but blithe and social:[127]

> *Frui paratis et valido mihi*
> *Latoe dones, et precor integra*

Cum mente, nec turpem senectam,
Degere, nec cithara carentem.
Apollo grant, enjoy in health I may
That I have got, and with sound mind, I pray;
Nor that I may with shame spend my old years,
Nor wanting music to delight mine ears.[128]

Selected Bibliography

PRIMARY SOURCES

Cotgrave, Randle. *A Dictionarie of the French and English Tongves.* London, 1611.

Florio, John. *Firste Fruites.* London, 1578.

——. *Qveen Anna's New World of Words, Or Dictionarie of the* Italian *and* English *tongues, Collected, and newly much augmented by Iohn Florio, Reader of the Italian vnto the Soueraigne* Maiestie *of ANNA, Crowned Queene of* England, Scotland, France, and Ireland, *&c. . . .* London, 1611.

——. *Second Frutes.* London, 1591.

——. *A Worlde of* Wordes, *Or Most copious, and exact* Dictionarie *in* Italian and English, collected by *Iohn Florio.* London, 1598.

Montaigne, Michel de. *The Complete Essays of Montaigne.* Translated by Donald M. Frame. Stanford, CA: Stanford University Press, 1958.

——. *Les Essais.* Edited by Denis Bjaï, Bénédicte Boudou, Jean Céard, and Isabelle Pantin. Paris: Librairie Générale Française, 2001.

——. *The Essayes or Morall, Politike and Millitarie Discourses of Lo[rd]: Michaell de Montaigne.* Translated by John Florio. London, 1603.

——. *The Essays of Michel de Montaigne.* Translated by M. A. Screech. London: Penguin Press, 1991.

Shakespeare, William. *The Norton Shakespeare.* Edited by Stephen Greenblat. New York: W. W. Norton, 2008, second edition.

SECONDARY SOURCES

Acheson, Arthur. *Shakespeare's Lost Years in London 1586–1592.* New York: Brentano's, 1920.

Bakewell, Sarah. *How to Live, or, A Life of Montaigne in One Question and Twenty Attempts at an Answer.* New York: Other Press, 2011.

Bate, Jonathan. *The Soul of the Age: The Life, Mind, and World of William Shakespeare.* New York: Viking, 2008.

Boutcher, Warren Vincent. "Florio's Montaigne: Translation and Pragmatic Humanism in the Sixteenth Century." PhD dissertation, University of Cambridge, 1991.

Bradbrook, Muriel. *The School of Night.* Cambridge: Cambridge University Press, 1936.

Bullough, Geoffrey, ed. *Narrative and Dramatic Sources of Shakespeare*, 8 vols. New York: Columbia University Press, 1961–1975.

Burke, Peter. *Montaigne.* Oxford University Press, 1981.

Cave, Terence. *The Cornucopian Text: Problems of Writing in the French Renaissance.* Oxford University Press, 1979).

——. *How to Read Montaigne.* London: Granta, 2007.

Chambrun, Clara Longworth de. *Giovanni Florio.* Paris: Payot, 1921.

——. *Shakespeare Actor-Poet.* New York and London: D. Appleton and Company, 1927.

Desan, Philippe, ed. *Dictionnaire de Michel de Montaigne.* Paris: Champion, 2007.

Engle, Lars. "Shame and Reflection in Montaigne and Shakespeare." *Shakespeare Survey* 63 (2010): 249–61.

——. "Sovereign Cruelty in Montaigne and *King Lear.*" In *Shakespearean International Yearbook 6: Special section, Shakespeare and Montaigne revisited.* Edited by Graham Bradshaw, Thomas Bishop, and Peter Holbrook, 119–39. Aldershot: Ashgate Publishing Limited, 2006.

Frame, Donald M. *Montaigne: A Biography.* London: Hamish Hamilton, 1965.

Frampton, Saul. *When I Am Playing with My Cat, How Do I Know She Is Not Playing with Me?: Montaigne and Being in Touch with Life*. New York: Pantheon Books, 2011.

Friedrich, Hugo. *Montaigne*, Edited by Philippe Desan. Translated by Dawn Eng. Berkeley: University of California Press, 1991. Translation of the 1949 German edition.

Gillespie, Stuart. *Shakespeare's Books: A Dictionary of Shakespeare Sources*. London: The Athlone Press, 2001.

Grady, Hugh. *Shakespeare, Machiavelli, and Montaigne: Power and Subjectivity from* Richard II *to* Hamlet. Oxford University Press, 2002.

Hamlin, William M. "Florio's Montaigne and the Tyrany of 'Custome': Appropriation, Ideology, and Early English Readership of the *Essayes*." *Renaissance Quarterly* 63 (2010): 491–544.

——. "The Shakespeare-Montaigne-Sextus Nexus: A Case Study in Early Modern Reading." In *The Shakespearean International Yearbook 6: Special section, Shakespeare and Montaigne revisited*. Edited by Graham Bradshaw, Thomas Bishop, and Peter Holbrook, 21–36. Aldershot: Ashgate Publishing Limited, 2006.

Henderson, W. B. Drayton. "Montaigne's *Apologie of Raymond Sebond* and *King Lear*." *Shakespeare Association Bulletin* 14 (1939): 209–25 and 15 (1940): 40–56..

Jeanneret, Michel. *Perpetual Motion: Transforming Shapes in the Renaissance, from da Vinci to Montaigne*. Translated by Nidra Poller. Baltimore: Johns Hopkins University Press, 2001. Translation of the 1997 French edition.

Maguin, Jean Marie, and Kapitaniak, Pierre, eds. *Shakespeare et Montaigne: Vers un Nouvel Humanisme*. Paris: Société Française Shakespeare, 2003.

Matthiessen, F. O. *Translation: An Elizabethan Art*. Cambridge, MA: Harvard University Press, 1931.

McFarlane, D., and Maclean, Ian, eds. *Montaigne: Essays in Memory of Richard Sayce*. Oxford: Clarendon, 1982.

Muir, Kenneth. *The Sources of Shakespeare's Plays*. New Haven, CT: Yale University Press, 1978.

Oxford English Dictionary. 2nd ed. 20 vols. Oxford University Press, 1989.

Quint, David. *Montaigne and the Quality of Mercy: Ethical and Political Themes in the* Essais. Princeton University Press, 1998.

Salingar, Leo. "*King Lear,* Montaigne and Harsnett." *The Aligarh Journal of English Studies* 8 (1983): 124–66.

Scholar, Richard. *Montaigne and the Art of Free-Thinking.* Oxford: Peter Lang, 2010.

Starobinski, Jean. *Montaigne in Motion.* Translated by Arthur Goldhammer. University of Chicago Press, 1985. Translation of the 1982 French edition.

Taylor, George Coffin. *Shakespeare's Debt to Montaigne.* Cambridge, MA: Harvard University Press, 1925.

Wyatt, Michael. *The Italian Encounter with Tudor England: A Cultural Politics of Translation.* Cambridge: Cambridge University Press, 2005.

Yates, Frances. *John Florio: The Life of an Italian in Shakespeare's England.* New York: Octagon Books, 1968. Reprint of 1934 edition.

———. *A Study of* Love's Labour's Lost. Cambridge: Cambridge University Press, 1936.

Appendix: Floriolegium

1. Life in itself is neither good nor evil; it is the place of good or evil according as you prepare it for them. (1.20/1.19)

> *For there is nothing either good or bad but thinking makes it so.*
> *(Hamlet, II.ii.244–45)*

2. To conclude, they are inimaginable effects to him that hath not tasted them, and which makes me wonderfully to honor the answer of that young soldier to *Cyrus*, who enquiring of him what he would take for a horse with which he had lately gained the prize of a race, and whether he would change him for a kingdom. (1.28/1.27)

> *A horse! A horse! My kingdom for a horse!*
> *(Richard III, V.vii.7)*

3. It is a nation, would I answer *Plato*, that hath no kind of traffic, no knowledge of letters, no intelligence of numbers, no name of magistrate, nor of politic superiority; no use of service, of riches, or of poverty; no contracts, no successions, no dividences, no occupation but idle; no respect of kindred, but common; no apparel, but natural; no manuring of lands, no use of wine, corn, or metal. The very words that import lying, falsehood, treason, dissimulation, covetousness, envy, detraction, and pardon were never heard of amongst them. (1.31/1.30)

> *I'th'commonwealth I would by contraries*
> *Execute all things. For no kind of traffic*

Would I admit, no name of magistrate;
Letters should not be known; riches, poverty,
And use of service, none; contract, succession,
Bourn, bound of land, tilth, vineyard, none;
No use of metal, corn, or wine, or oil;
No occupation, all men idle, all;
And women too—but innocent and pure;
No sovereignty—

. . . . . .

All things in common nature should produce
Without sweat or endeavour. Treason, felony,
Sword, pike, knife, gun, or need of any engine,
Would I not have; but nature should bring forth
Of it own kind all foison, all abundance,
To feed my innocent people.

(*The Tempest*, II.i.147–56; 159–64)

4. The first fit of an ague or the first guird that the gout gives him, what avail his goodly titles of majesty? (1.42)

O be sick, great greatness,
And bid thy ceremony give thee cure.
Think'st thou the fiery fever will go out
With titles blown from adulation?

(*Henry V*, IV.i.233–36)

5. Methinks that considering the weakness of our life, and seeing the infinite number of ordinary rocks and natural dangers it is subject unto, we should not so soon as we come into the world allot so great a share thereof unto unprofitable wantonness in youth, ill-breeding idleness, and slow-learning prentissage. (1.57)

The heartache and the thousand natural shocks
That flesh is heir to.

(Hamlet, III.i.64–65)

6. Nature willeth that in all things alike there be also like relation. (2.12)

The mightiest space in fortune nature brings
To join like likes and kiss like native things.
(All's Well That Ends Well, I.i.205–6)

7. Truly, when I consider man all naked (yea, be it in that sex which seemeth to have and challenge the greatest share of eye-pleasing beauty) and view his defects, his natural subjection, and manifold imperfections, I find we have had much more reason to hide and cover our nakedness than any creature else. We may be excused for borrowing those which nature had therein favored more than us with their beauties, to adorn us and under their spoils of wool, of hair, of feathers, and of silk to shroud us. (2.12)

Is man no more than this? Consider him well. Thou owest the
worm no silk, the beast no hide, the sheep no wool, that cat no
perfume. Ha! here's three on's are sophisticated! Thou art the
thing itself; unaccommodated man is no more but such a poor,
bare, forked animal as thou art. Off, off, you lendings! come un-
button here.

(King Lear, III.iv.95–101)

8. When I religiously confess myself unto myself, I find the best good I have hath some vicious taint. And I fear that *Plato* in his purest virtue (I that am as sincere and loyal an esteemer thereof, and of the virtues of such a stamp, as any other can possibly be), if he had nearly listened unto it (and sure he listened very near), he would

therein have heard some harsh tune of human mixture, but an obscure tune, and only sensible unto himself. *Man all in all is but a
botching and parti-coloured work.* (2.20)

> *The web of our life is of a mingled yarn, good and ill together. Our
> virtues would be proud if our faults whipped them not, and our
> crimes would despair if they were not cherished by our virtues.*
> *(All's Well That Ends Well, IV.iii.69–72)*

> *Bid the dishonest man mend himself: if he mend, he is no longer
> dishonest; if he cannot, let the botcher mend him. Anything
> that's mended is but patched. Virtue that transgresses is but
> patched with sin, and sin that amends is but patched with virtue.*
> *(Twelfth Night, I.v.38–45)*

9. *Quintilian* reporteth to have seen comedians so far engaged in a
sorrowful part that they wept after being come to their lodgings;
and of himself, that having undertaken to move a certain passion in
another, he had found himself surprised, not only with shedding of
tears but with a paleness of countenance and behaviour of a man
truly dejected with grief. (3.4)

> *Seems, madam? Nay, it* is. *I know not "seems."*
> *'Tis not alone my inky cloak, good-mother,*
> *Nor customary suits of solemn black,*
> *Nor windy suspiration of forced breath,*
> *No, nor the fruitful river in the eye,*
> *Nor the dejected haviour of the visage,*
> *Together with all forms, moods, shows of grief,*
> *That can denote me truly. These indeed "seem,"*
> *For they are actions that a man might play;*
> *But I have that within which passeth show—*
> *These but the trappings and the suits of woe.*

> *(I.ii.76–86)*

10. And I wot not whether some cheverell judge or other will be avenged of them for his [foolishness]. It is manifestly seen in this, which now is discovered. As also in diverse other things of like quality, exceeding our knowledge, I am of opinion that we uphold our judgement as well to reject as to receive. (3.11)

A sentence is but a cheverel glove to a good wit, how quickly the wrong side may be turned outward.

(Twelfth Night, III.i.10–12)

Notes

Abbreviations Used

Céard: Michel de Montaigne, *Les Essais.*

Cotgrave: Randle Cotgrave, *A Dictionarie of the French and English Tongves.*

Essayes: Michel de Montaigne, *The Essayes or Morall, Politike and Millitarie Discourses of Lo[rd]: Michaell de Montaigne.*

Frame: Michel de Montaigne, *The Complete Essays of Montaigne.*

OED: *Oxford English Dictionary.*

QAWW: John Florio, *Qveen Anna's New World of Words, Or Dictionarie of the* Italian *and* English *tongues, Collected, and newly much augmented by Iohn Florio, Reader of the Italian vnto the Soueraigne* Maiestie *of ANNA, Crowned Queene of* England, Scotland, France, and Ireland, *&c. . . .*

Screech: Michel de Montaigne, *The Essays of Michel de Montaigne.*

WW: John Florio, *A Worlde of* Wordes, *Or Most copious, and exact* Dictionarie *in Italian and* English, collected by *Iohn Florio.*

DEDICATORY POEM

1. In the version of the poem in the 1613 edition of the *Essayes*, the dedication reads: "*To my deare brother and friend* M. IOHN FLORIO, *one of the Gentlemen of hir Maiesties most* Royall Priuie Chamber." There is a similar dedication to a poem in *Cotgrave*: "*To my deare friend and brother M. Iohn Florio*, one of the Gentlemen of hir Maiesties most Royall Priuy-chamber." In addition to confirming Florio's status at court, these dedications reveal—in the minds of many critics—the recognition that Florio was married to Daniel's sister, hence not only "friend" but also "brother."

2. *Amass of humors* a collection of moods, spirits, styles. Grounded in the system of the second-century AD Greek physician Galen, humoral theory sought to explain human personality by means of four humors or bodily fluids that had corresponding traits: blood (sanguine), phlegm (phlegmatic), yellow bile (choleric), and black bile (melancholic). The healthy person had all four humors in balance.

3. *Conceit* central metaphor, design, plan.

4. *Shadowed in leaves* represented, albeit murkily, in the pages of books.

5. *And wherein ... this doubtful center of the right* In this difficult set of lines, Daniel seems to suggest that very few books help the questing soul approach the truth. Montaigne's book is one that, though reaching truth is still "doubtful," helps get the reader closer to the target or bull's-eye ("center of the right") than most. Thanks to Will Hamlin for help with this gloss.

6. Up until this point of the stanza, "his" has referred to Montaigne. Now Daniel is praising Florio for "his studious care" in making Montaigne's *"transpassage"* into English ("our speech") so smooth that the *Essayes* seem "as if born here."

7. *Free* native, enfranchised.

8. *B'invassal'd* to be envassaled—that is, reduced to subjection, servitude, or subservience.

9. *Commercement* business or social dealings.

10. Daniel—in alluding to the form of the essay as "a troubled frame confus'dly set"—seems to understand what Montaigne said about the genre in "Of Friendship" (1.27 in Florio): "And what are these my compositions in truth, other than antique works, and monstrous bodies, patched and huddled-up together of diverse members, without any certain or well-ordered figure, having neither order, dependency, or proportion but casual and framed by chance?"

11. *H'is* he is.

12. *Might spare to tax th'unapt conveyances* Daniel warns critics not to find fault with the vehicles ("unapt conveyances") that bring us Montaigne's important ideas ("rich pieces and extracts of man"). These "conveyances" could be Florio's translations but probably allude instead to Montaigne's complicated form, his "troubled frame confus'dly set." Thanks to Will Hamlin for help with this gloss.

13. *Both work and frame* both Montaigne and Florio.

14. In Plutarch's *Alcibiades*, Alcibiades asks his schoolmaster for a copy of Homer. When the schoolmaster says he does not have one, Alcibiades hits him for his lack of such an important book. In his own time, Daniel suggests, "they unblest who letters do profess / And have him [Montaigne] not" deserve even greater disapprobation, even "more sound blows."

TO THE COURTEOUS READER

1. *Freehold* right, entitlement.

2. Because vernacular translations would undermine humanist classical education; because the translators were largely Protestant and thus a threat to the medieval scholasticism of the universities; and because of the fear that pagan writings, spread through the vernacular, would undermine Christian teachings. See Yates, *John Florio*, 223.

3. *Impeach or empaire* hindrance or impairment.

4. *Nolano* "The Nolan" was Giordano Bruno's nickname for himself. The philosopher and polymath came from the town of Nola, near Naples. He was a friend of Florio, and the two spent time together at the French ambassador's house in London from 1583 to 1585.

5. In this section, Florio is entertaining imagined questions ("Why, ...") and answering them ("Yea," "Nay"). He addresses a claim that there are some things that should not be known and that translators thus should not be making available through translation. His response is that no matter what translators do, human knowledge is limited; only God knows all things.

6. *Best* best translators.

7. *Ficinus* Marsilio Ficino (1433–1499) translated many of the classic texts of the ancient world from Greek to Latin.

8. *Altiloquence* high speech. Interestingly, the *OED*'s first recorded use of this word is 1731.

9. *Featness* elegance, shapeliness, fitness.

10. Terence the Roman playwright (ca. 195–ca. 159 BC) put into Latin many of the Greek comedies of Menander (ca. 342–ca. 291 BC), most of whose plays are now lost.

11. *My peerless dear-dearest and never sufficiently commended friend* A reference to Matthew Gwinne, a Welsh doctor who, Florio tells us in the

"Epistle Dedicatorie" to volume I of the *Essayes*, tracked down (and probably translated) the "Latin Prose" and "Greek, Latin, Italian, or French poesie [that] should cross my way."

12. *Ferdillant, legier* "Ferdillant" is probably a typo for "fretillant" (see *Cotgrave*: "*Fretiller*. To move, wag, stir often, stand on no ground; to wriggle, frig, tickle, itch, lust to be at it"); "legier" means, like "léger," light, airy, playful.

13. If anyone complains that the *Essayes* have a "disjointed, broken, and gadding style; and that many times they answer not his titles and have no coherence together," Florio sends him or her to "the ninth chapter of the third book, folio 596" ("Of Vanitie") of his edition for Montaigne's answer: "Forsomuch as the often breaking of my chapters I so much used in the beginning of my book seemed to interrupt attention before it be conceived, disdaining for so little a while to collect and there seat itself, I have betaken myself to frame them longer, as requiring proposition and assigned leisure. In such an occupation he to whom you will not grant one hour, you will allow him nothing. And you do nought for him for whom you do but in doing some other thing. Sithence peradventure I am particularly tied and precisely vowed to speak by halves, to speak confusedly, to speak discrepantly" (III.ix.596).

14. *Eftsoones* moreover, again.

15. *Capital in sense mistaking* fatally wrong, in error.

16. Florio is describing the multiple versions of Montaigne's *Essais* that he consulted in making his translation and claiming that they are at least partly to blame for the errors in his 1603 edition. According to Will Hamlin, whose *Montaigne's English Journey* (Oxford University Press, 2013) breaks new ground in accounting for the production and reception of Florio's book, a table of errata is indeed at the back of "about three quarters" of the copies of the *Essayes'* first printing.

17. *Littletonians* Claudius Hollyband's *French Littleton* was a book of grammar and dialogues published in 1566.

THAT TO PHILOSOPHIZE IS TO LEARN HOW TO DIE

1. See Cicero, *Tusculanae disputationes*, I.xxx.74–I.xxxi.75.

2. *Severally* separately, individually.

3. *Apprentisage* apprenticeship, beginning, trial run.

4. *In fine* in the end, ultimately.

5. *Give ear unto him* listen to him.

6. Seneca, *Epistulae morales*, 117.30.

7. *Person* ... personate role ... play.

8. In this difficult passage—made more so by Florio—Montaigne is argu-
    ing for a virtuous pleasure or "voluptuousness" that is more long-lasting,
    substantial, and indeed pleasurable than the "baser sensuality" that we
    usually connect to the term.

9. *Incommodities* disadvantages.

10. *Jouissance* enjoyment.

11. *It* virtue.

12. Montaigne continues the argument that—in spite of what some may
    claim—the pursuit of virtue is itself pleasurable.

13. *Lot-pot* an urn from which lots are shaken or drawn (*OED*); Florio's is
    the first entry.

14. *Aye* ever.

15. Horace, *Odes*, II.iii.25.

16. *Starting-hole* hiding place for a hunted animal.

17. Cicero, *De finibus*, I.xviii.60.

18. Horace, *Odes*, III.i.18–21.

19. Claudian, *In Rufinum*, II.137.

20. *Cariere* highway, road.

21. Lucretius, *De rerum natura*, IV.472.

22. *Periphrasis* circumlocution.

23. Until the sixteenth century in France—and the eighteenth century in
    England—the new year dated from around Easter (March 25 in Eng-
    land). Dating the year from January 1 started in France in 1567, in Eng-
    land not until 1752 (though Scotland partially shifted to the so-called
    Gregorian calendar in 1600).

24. Montaigne lived only twenty years more, dying in 1592 at fifty-nine.

25. *Bedrell* bedridden.

26. *Mathusalem* Methuselah, the oldest person mentioned in the Old Tes-
    tament. Montaigne suggests that people delude themselves into think-
    ing they can live longer lives by thinking about Methuselah.

27. *Twenty years* another twenty years.

28. *Seely* foolish, simple, silly.

29. *Renoune* renown, fame.

30. *Register them* make a list of them.

31. Horace, *Odes*, II.xiii.13–14.

32. *Whilome* formerly, once.

33. *Chocke* violent knock, shock.

34. Henry II was killed in a tournament in 1559; his ancestor Philip, who never ruled, was killed by a pig.

35. *Eschilus* Aeschylus, Greek playwright of fifth century BC.

36. *Captain Saint Martin* Montaigne's younger brother Arnaud—lord of Saint-Martin—was born in 1541 and died in this freakish fashion at twenty-seven (not twenty-three).

37. Horace, *Epistles*, II.ii.126–28.

38. Horace, *Odes*, III.ii.14–17.

39. *Cuirace* cuirass, steel piece of armor.

40. Propertius, *Elegies*, IV.xviii.25.

41. *Shapen* misshapen.

42. Horace, *Epistles*, I.iv.13–14.

43. Catullus, *Epigrams*, LXVIII.16.

44. Lucretius, *De rerum natura*, III.915.

45. *She* death.

46. Seneca, *Epistulae morales*, XCI.16.

47. Horace, *Odes*, II.xvi.17–18.

48. *Accrease* increase.

49. *Ta'ne* taken.

50. Lucretius, *De rerum natura*, III.898–99.

51. *Hie* hasten, go quickly. Virgil, *Aeneid*, IV.88–89.

52. Ovid, *Amores*, II.x.36.

53. Lucretius, *De rerum natura*, III.900–1.

54. *O're* o'er, over.

55. Silius Italicus, *The Punic War*, XI.li–liv.

56. *Moiety* half.

57. Pseudo-Gallus, *Elegies*, I.16.

58. *Dost thou think to be alive then?* in other words, "Do you consider yourself alive *now*?"; see Seneca, *Epistula morales*, LXXVII.18. The Roman

emperor was Caligula.

59. Horace, *Odes*, III.iii.3–6.

60. *She* the soul.

61. *Gyves* shackles, especially for the leg.

62. Horace, *Epistles*, I.xvi.76–79.

63. *Moaned* regretted, lamented.

64. *Cark* to have burdens, pains, anxiety.

65. What follows—until page 33—should be considered a speech of Nature, based on Nature's soliloquy in Lucretius, *De rerum natura*, III.

66. Lucretius, *De rerum natura*, II.76, 79.

67. Seneca, *Hercules furens*, III.874–75.

68. Manilius, *Astronomica*, IV.xvi.

69. Lucretius, *De rerum natura*, III.938.

70. Ibid., III.941–42.

71. See Shakespeare, *Hamlet*: "for there is nothing either good or bad, but thinking makes it so" (II.ii.244–45).

72. Manilius, *Astronomica*, I.522–23.

73. Florio has "commoditie" but Montaigne has "*comedie*," and the theatrical metaphor is clear here.

74. Lucretius, *De rerum natura*, III.1080.

75. Virgil, *Georgics*, II.402.

76. Lucretius, *De rerum natura*, III.944–45.

77. Ibid., III.1090–91.

78. Ibid., III.885–87.

79. Ibid., III.919, 922.

80. Ibid., III.926–27.

81. Ibid., III.972–73.

82. Ibid., III.968.

83. Ibid., II.578–80.

84. *Ell* a measurement based on the length of the arm; see Latin, *ulna*.

85. *He* your last day.

86. *Behold here … mother nature* This marks the end of Nature's speech and the return of Montaigne's narrative.

87. *She* death.

88. *Seely* foolish, simple, silly.

89. *Equipage* a group of attendants—in this case, mourners.

IT IS FOLLY TO REFER TRUTH OR FALSEHOOD
TO OUR SUFFICIENCY

1. Cicero, *Academica*, II.xii.38.

2. *Gudgeons* those who will take and swallow any bait; thus, credulous, gullible people.

3. *Sottish* foolish.

4. Horace, *Epistles*, II.ii.208–9.

5. *Seely* foolish, simple, silly.

6. That is, my limited knowledge is not a result of an absence of curiosity.

7. *Science* knowledge.

8. Lucretius, *De rerum natura*, II.1037–38, 1033–36.

9. Ibid., VI.674–77.

10. Cicero, *De natura deorum*, II.xxxviii.96.

11. *Leave them in suspense* suspend disbelief.

12. *That which is against the course of nature* according to Christian theology, a miracle.

13. *Froysard* Jean Froissard (ca. 1337–ca. 1405), a medieval French writer of chronicles; see *Screech*, 202n7.

14. *Them* funeral rites.

15. *Cousoned* cozened, deceived.

16. See Jean Bouchet, *Annales of Acquitaine* (Poitiers, 1567), 21–30, esp. 25–26.

17. *Canker* cancer.

18. *Assistant* eyewitness.

19. Saint Augustine, *City of God*, XXII.viii.

20. Cicero, *Tusculanae disputationes*, I.xxi.49.

21. *Troubles of religion* a reminder that Montaigne wrote during—and was deeply affected by—the wars of religion in sixteenth-century France between the Protestants (called Huguenots) and Catholics. Although a committed Catholic, Montaigne reveals in his essays a desire to make sense of these deep-seated and violent conflicts.

OF FRIENDSHIP

1. *Proceeding of a painter's work I have* the method of a painter whom I employ.

2. *Boscage* "The pictorial representation of wooded landscape; also, a decorative design imitating branches and foliage" (*OED*).

3. *Crotesko* a grotesque; a monstrous and fantastic kind of painting.

4. Horace, *Ars Poetica*, 4.

5. *Table* tablet or board on which a picture is painted; the picture itself. See Shakespeare, *All's Well That Ends Well*: "To see him every hour, to sit and draw / His arched brows, his hawking eye, his curls, / In our heart's table" (I.i.88–90).

6. *Steven de la Boitie* Montaigne's friend and soul mate, Étienne de La Boétie (1530–1563).

7. *Not long of him* not because of him.

8. *Edict of January* Also called the Edict of Saint-Germain, this royal proclamation of January 1562 allowed Protestants the right to preach without persecution for the first time.

9. *Intestine war* internecine, civil war.

10. Paris: Fédéric Morel, 1571.

11. Aristotle, *Nicomachean Ethics*, VIII.i.

12. *Amities* friendships.

13. *Venerian* erotic.

14. *Happly* by chance.

15. *Unbeseeming* unbecoming.

16. *Enterbearing* carrying mutually. In this difficult passage Montaigne discusses nations in which children would kill parents, and others in which parents would kill children, as a way of avoiding the burdens each would cause the other; the only way for one to survive is to destroy the other. The friendship he is discussing, on the other hand, never yields such burdens.

17. Diogenes Laertius, *Life of Empedocles*, II.81.

18. Plutarch, translated by Jacques Amyot, *De l'amitie fraternelle*, 82E.

19. *Dividence* division.

20. Horace, *Odes*, II.ii.5–6.

21. Catullus, *Epigrams*, LXVIIIa.17–18.

22. Ariosto, *Orlando Furioso*, X.vii.

23. *Jouissance* enjoyment, pleasure.

24. *Pitch* slope, height, trajectory (in falconry).

25. *Greek licence* homosexuality.

26. Cicero, *Tusculanae disputationes*, IV.xxxiii.70.

27. *The Academy* the school of Plato.

28. *Son of Venus* Cupid, Eros.

29. *A false image of corporal generation* a false image generated from the body by lust, instead of a true one born from the soul.

30. *Difficile knowledge* difficult to know.

31. *Mistress* strong(er) force.

32. *Availful* useful.

33. *Comfortable* salutary, wholesome, beneficial.

34. *Demisness* humbleness, lowliness.

35. Montaigne is still discussing homosexual friendship-love, emptied of most of its erotic components and thus thought of as "sacred and divine" except by tyrants and common people.

36. Cicero, *Tusculanae disputationes*, IV.xxxiv.72.

37. Cicero, *De amicitia*, XX.74.

38. *Mediatrix* mediator.

39. *Remiss* diluted, diminished, languid.

40. *Preallable* preliminary.

41. *Semblable* equal.

42. *His* Gracchus's.

43. *Mistress* powerful, masterful.

44. See Aristotle, *Nicomachean Ethics*, IX.x.

45. *Accrease* increase.

46. Aristotle, *Nicomachean Ethics*, IX.viii.

47. *Alonely* sole, only.

48. See Shakespeare, *Richard III*: "A horse! a horse! my kingdom for a horse!" (V.vii.7).

49. *Wards* interior mechanisms, usually of a lock.

50. *In confederacies which hold but by one end* in relationships—unlike the ideal friendship that he is discussing—that are connected by only a

small part. As an example of these simpler "confederacies," Montaigne goes on to mention doctor-patient and lawyer-client relationships.

51. *Muleteer* mule driver.

52. Terence, *Heautontimorumenos*, I.i.28.

53. Montaigne has "*preud'homie*," which, according to *Cotgrave*, means "courage, valour, prowesse; loyaltie, faithfulnesse; honestie, sinceritie, integritie; good dealing, true meaning."

54. *Seld* seldom.

55. Horace, *Satires*, I.v.44.

56. Terence, *Heautontimorumenos*, I.i.97–98.

57. Horace, *Odes*, II.xvii.5–9.

58. *Saying* the French suggests "missing" rather than "saying." Montaigne claims that he misses his friend, regardless of what he is doing or saying, and his friend would have similarly missed him.

59. Horace, *Odes*, I.xxiv.1–2.

60. Catullus, *Epigrams*, LXV.9–11.

61. Montaigne evidently planned to publish La Boétie's *Discours de la servitude volontaire* [*On Voluntary Servitude*] here. But because it had been published in part in 1574 and in full in 1576, and had been co-opted for Protestant purposes, he decided to leave it out.

62. *Interested* "toucht in honor, or reputation"; see *WW*, "*Interessato*."

63. *Wire-drawn* elongated, drawn out.

64. *Born at Venice than at Sarlac* La Boétie was born at Sarlac (Sarlat), a village in Périgord (Nord). Venice was famous, at least partly, in Montaigne's day for being an unusually tolerant state, founded on law and reason and removed from the factionalism of sixteenth-century France, which Montaigne goes on to characterize as full of "changes, innovations, new-fangles, and hurly-burlies."

65. In editions of the *Essays* published in Montaigne's lifetime, the next essay, "Nine and Twenty Sonnets of *Steven de la Boétie*, to the Lady of *Grammont*," included the sonnets. Although presumably an edition of these sonnets was published between 1588 and 1592, it has never been found.

OF THE CANNIBALS

1. Vice Admiral Nicolas Durand de Villegaignon (1510–1571) established the French colony of France Antarctique, near Rio de Janeiro, Brazil, in

1557, as a haven for French Protestants (Huguenots) and Swiss Calvinists. Its main bastion, Fort Coligny, was destroyed by the Portuguese in 1560, and the French were completely expelled in 1567.

2. *Sithence* since.

3. *Mare-Maggiore* the Black Sea.

4. Plato, *Timaeus*, 21e–22a, 24e–25f.

5. Virgil, *Aeneid*, III.414, 416–17.

6. *Soria* Syria; *Negroponte* the Greek island of Euboea; *Beotia* Boetia or Voiotia, the regional unit of Greece that contains Thebes.

7. Horace, *Ars Poetica*, 65–66.

8. *Febricitant* feverish.

9. *Rents and domains* farms and arable lands.

10. As Montaigne suggests, Aristotle's book of wonders, *On Marvellous Things Heard*, was almost certainly not written by Aristotle.

11. The same man "I have had long time dwelling with me" whom Montaigne mentioned early in the essay.

12. *Scantling* scant thing, scrap.

13. *Where* "that nation" referred to previously—the home of the Brazilian Indians.

14. *Those* those things altered by European agriculture and civilization.

15. *Those . . . these* the unadorned nature of Brazil ("those") as opposed to the altered forms of nature in Europe ("these").

16. *They are even savage . . . wonderfully ashamed* see the debate between Perdita and Polixenes in Shakespeare, *Winter's Tale*, IV.4.87–103.

17. *Un-hanted* unhaunted, solitary.

18. Propertius, *Elegies*, I.ii.10–12.

19. *Least birdlet* smallest bird.

20. *Seely* foolish, simple, silly.

21. Plato, *Laws*, X.889a.

22. *Genuitie* ingenuousness, simplicity. This is the only example of the word in the *OED*.

23. *Dividences* partitions, shares of goods; see *WW*: "*Partigione*, a partition, a diuidence, a separation, a share, a part" (260).

24. *Manuring* fertilizing.

25. *"It is a nation ... amongst them"*: see Shakespeare, *The Tempest*, II.1.145–66. This is the clearest example of Shakespeare's borrowing from Montaigne. But see note 49 below.

26. Virgil, *Georgics*, II.20.

27. *Steepie* steep.

28. *Champaine* a level, open field.

29. *Steadeth them as a flank* provides them with a (structural) side to the building.

30. *Riving* breaking apart.

31. *Several* own.

32. *From* apart from.

33. *Pledge carouses* they drink often and fully.

34. *Corianders confected* preserved coriander.

35. *Wallowish* insipid, tasteless; see *WW*: "*Disapito*, vnsauorie, tasting of nothing, wallowish" (104).

36. *Auditory* audience.

37. *For their restraint* Montaigne has "*pour leur refrein*"—"as their refrain."

38. *French league* a little over two miles.

39. *Sufficiency* capacity, limitation.

40. *Cony-catch* deceive or dupe.

41. *Broaches* boar spears.

42. *Rowts* routs.

43. *Portugales* Portuguese.

44. *Smartful* painful.

45. *Mammockes* shreds, broken pieces.

46. Juvenal, *Satires*, XV.93–94.

47. *Availful to* availing, in aid of, useful to.

48. Montaigne is referring to the supposed magical and medical properties of corpses and "mummies." See Shakespeare, *Othello*, Othello's description of his mother's handkerchief, "dyed in mummy which the skilful / Conserved of maidens' hearts" (III.iv.72–73).

49. Kenji Go—in "Montaigne's 'Cannibals' and *The Tempest* Revisited," *Studies in Philology* 109.4 (2012): 455–73—has convincingly argued that the next two paragraphs ("But there was never any opinion ... brings

them into the world") are the almost unrecognized source of the second part of Gonzalo's speech in Shakespeare, *The Tempest*, II.1.159–64.

50. *Ubertie* fertility, copiousness, abundance.

51. *Enlarge their limits* expand their boundaries, push back their frontiers.

52. *Enter-call* mutually call, call each other.

53. *Remissely* weakly.

54. *Danted* daunted, subdued, controlled.

55. Claudian, *De sexto consulatu Honorii*, 248–49.

56. *Porterly-rascal* one who bears burdens, like a porter.

57. *Disposition* agility.

58. Seneca, *De providentia*, II.6–10.

59. *Salamine* Salamis, the site of a famous naval battle, won by the Greeks over the Persians in 480 BC.

60. *Politikely* in a politic manner.

61. *A mean and indifferent course* a middle way.

62. *An invention* an idea, a topic.

63. *Mowes* frowns, grimaces.

64. *Awful* full of awe and terror (toward the rule of custom).

65. *Canzonet* the Italian *canzonetta*, a sixteenth-century vocal form; see *QAWW*: "*canzonétta*, a canzonet or dittie."

66. *Anacreontike* Anacreontic, like the poetry of Anacreon (582 BC–485 BC), the ancient Greek poet. An edition of his poetry was published in Paris by Henri Estienne in 1554.

67. *Terminations* word endings.

68. *Cozened by a desire of new-fangled novelties* This phrase is especially interesting since this essay is the one quoted in Shakespeare's *The Tempest*. Compare Caliban—ironically, the "Indian" and "cannibal" of the play—who criticizes Stephano and Trinculo for focusing on the "frippery," "trash," and "luggage" of Prospero's wardrobe instead of on the murder of the magus (IV.1.222, 224, 229).

69. *Roane* Rouen. In 1562, Rouen, the capital city of Normandy, in the north of France, was retaken by royalist Protestant forces.

70. *Swizzers* Swiss Guard.

71. *Whereby they call men but a moiety of men from others* they speak of men as halves—"moieties"—of each other.

OF THE INEQUALITY THAT IS BETWEEN US

1. Plutarch, "Que les bêtes brutes usent de la raison," 992d, translated by Jacques Amyot (1572), 274.

2. Terence, *Phormio*, V.iii.7.

3. Juvenal, *Satires*, VIII.57–59.

4. *Furniture* harness.

5. *Cranes* jesses, straps used in hawking.

6. *Cheapen a horse* bargain or haggle over a horse.

7. *Abroad* uncovered, open to view.

8. *Crupper* saddle strap.

9. Horace, *Satires*, I.ii.86–89.

10. *Pattins* thick-soled shoes, wooden clogs.

11. *The Base is no part of his stature* the base—or plinth—is not part of the statue. See Seneca, *Epistulae morales*, LXXVI.31.

12. *His shirt* his undershirt.

13. Horace, *Satires*, II.vii.83–88.

14. Plautus, *Trinummus*, II.ii.84.

15. *bark . . . bark* complain . . . body's outer shell.

16. Lucretius, *De rerum natura*, II.16–19.

17. *Several* separate, distinct, apart.

18. *Dissemblance* difference.

19. *Interlude-players* actors in interludes or plays.

20. *Porterly-hirelings* vulgar, uncouth hired servants.

21. Lucretius, *De rerum natura*, IV.1126–28. Florio has "heat" for "sweat."

22. *Seely* foolish, simple, silly.

23. Seneca, *Epistulae morales*, CXIX.12, CXV.9.

24. *Maires officers* chief municipal officers.

25. Horace, *Odes*, II.xvi.9–12.

26. Lucretius, *De rerum natura*, II.48–51.

27. *Ague . . . megrim* fever . . . migraine headache.

28. *Lowting-curtzies or putting-off of hats* deferential curtsies or doffing of hats—in other words, acts of ceremonial deference.

29. *Enchased* enclosed, encased (with)

30. *Pangs . . . colic* shooting pains . . . sharp pains in the belly.

31. Lucretius, *De rerum natura*, II.34–36.

32. *Alexander* Alexander the Great (356–323 BC).

33. *Close-stool* chamber pot.

34. *Assays* attempts.

35. *Eftsoones* recently.

36. Persius, *Satires*, II.37–38.

37. Terence, *Heautontimorumenos*, I.ii.21–22.

38. *Foments* fomentations, soothing applications to a sore or wound; see *WW*: "*Fomentatione*, a fomentation, a comforting, a feeding with any plaisters applied to the stomacke, a strengthening with any cordials. Also a nourishment laid to the body to comfort and warme it" (135); *sore-sight* blurred vision, blindness. This passage suggests that material possessions help the tormented, lustful, or unhealthy person as much as a lotion or an unguent can help a bad case of gout or pictures can soothe the blind—that is, not at all.

39. Horace, *Epistles*, I.ii.47–52.

40. Plato, *Laws*, II.661.C–D.

41. *Guird* sudden blow or spasm of pain.

42. See Shakespeare, *Henry V*: "O be sick, great greatness, / And bid thy ceremony give thee cure. / Think'st thou the fiery fever will go out / With titles blown from adulation?" (IV.i.233–36).

43. Tibullus, *Elegies*, I.ii.71.

44. Horace, *Epistles*, I.xii.5–6.

45. Lucretius, *De rerum natura*, V.1127–28.

46. King Hieron—who plays a substantial role in this essay—was the subject of *Hieron*, written by Xenophon (ca. 430–354 BC), about a debate on kingship between Hiero, the tyrant of Syracuse, and the lyric poet Simonides. Xenophon's *Cyropaedia*, or *Education of Cyrus*, was a favorite text of Sir Philip Sidney and other Renaissance humanists.

47. *They* kings.

48. Ovid, *Amores*, II.xix.25–26.

49. In Montaigne, "*enfans de c[h]oeur*"—choirboys. Florio's version makes little sense.

50. *Tasteless* lacking taste, insipid.

51. Once again, Shakespeare's *Henry V* seems pertinent. Prince Hal has rev-

eled in his recent past—explored in parts 1 and 2 of *Henry IV*—in the "base and popular kind of life" with Falstaff, and King Henry disguises himself on the eve of the Battle of Agincourt to see what his soldiers think of him and the war.

52. Horace, *Odes*, III.xxix.12–15.

53. *Seraille* seraglio, harem.

54. *Falkners* falconers.

55. Plato, *Gorgias*, 469c.

56. *To have a score of find-faults, pick-thanks, and controllers about his close-stool* to have twenty faultfinders, sycophants/flatterers, and stewards around him while he goes to the toilet. (Shakespeare's Malvolio, from *Twelfth Night*, could be called a "controller.")

57. *Cales … Sienna* Casale … Siena—sites of two battles between the armies of Henri II, king of France, and those of Charles V, Holy Roman Emperor, in 1555.

58. The Duke of Venice is also known as the Doge.

59. Seneca, *Epistulae morales*, XXII.11.

60. The next few paragraphs are imagined thoughts of Hieron, though neither Montaigne nor Florio provides quotation marks.

61. *Will-he or nill-he* willy-nilly, like it or not.

62. *Low-lowting curtzie* low-bowing curtsy.

63. Seneca, *Thyestes*, 206–7.

64. *Sithence* since.

65. This is the end of Hieron's remarks.

66. See Plutarch, "Banquet des sept sages," 154E, translated by Jacques Amyot (1572), 155.

67. See Plutarch, *Life of Pyrrhus*, XIV.

68. Lucretius, *De rerum natura*, V.1432–33.

69. *Exclude* conclude.

70. Cornelius Nepos, *Life of Pomponius Atticus*, XI.6.

OF AGE

1. *Receive* accept.

2. *Continuance* duration, span.

3. Montaigne rejects the notion of a normal life span being the biblical "three-score years and ten"; see *Screech*, 366n1.

4. *Might do it* might achieve these extra years of life.

5. *Fond-goodly* fine, pretty, self-flattering.

6. See Regan's comment to Lear in Shakespeare, *King Lear*: "O, sir, you are old; / Nature in you stands on the very verge / Of her confine" (II. iv.139–41).

7. *Ages* centuries.

8. *Cariere* career, life's journey.

9. *We are very forward* we have lived a long time.

10. *Charge of judgement* the office of judge.

11. *Dispensed* released.

12. *Sejourning* sojourning—in other words, retirement.

13. *Three score* sixty.

14. *Appearance* appearance of reason.

15. Montaigne is funnier—and cruder—here. Florio converts "*la place d'une gouttière*"—the position of a gutter—into "cottage or farm."

16. *Delphinate* Dauphiné, a former province of southeastern France, whose historical capital was Grenoble. What follows is a French proverb from that region.

17. Lucretius, *De rerum natura*, III.451–53.

18. *Sensible* perceptible.

19. See Shakespeare, *Hamlet*: "The heartache and the thousand natural shocks / That flesh is heir to—" (III.i.64–65).

20. *Prentissage* apprenticeship.

OF THE INCONSTANCY OF OUR ACTIONS

1. *Let* hindrance, impediment.

2. *Charge* office, his time in power.

3. *Sithence* since.

4. Publius Cyrus, quoted in Aulus Gellius, *Attic Nights*, XVII.xiv.4.

5. *Contexture* fabric.

6. Judging a man by his parts would yield a closer approximation to the truth of his being than judging him by his whole self.

7. Horace, *Epistles*, I.i.98–99.

8. *That beast that takes the colour of the place wherein it is laid* the chameleon.

9. Horace, *Satires*, II.vii.82. The metaphor is that of a puppet or marionette.

10. *Hulling* floating or being driven by the wind on the hull alone, without a sail.

11. Lucretius, *De rerum natura*, III.1057–59. Human beings constantly search for answers beyond themselves, hoping to abandon their individual burdens.

12. Homer, *Odyssey*, XVIII. 136–37; cited by Saint Augustine in *City of God*, V.viii. The meaning is difficult but seems to suggest that human minds and spirits are as bright, fertile, and powerful as the sunlight sent from heaven.

13. *Deformity* inconsistency. The Agrigentines lived for pleasure, as if they would die tomorrow, and built for posterity, as if they would live forever.

14. Diogenes Laertius, *Life of Empedocles*, VIII.63.

15. *Force* rape.

16. *Upon easier composition* much more easily; that is, she only seemed to be chaste like Lucrece.

17. Horace, *Epistles*, II.ii.36. *Spright* spirit, heart.

18. *Said he unto him* said the soldier to Lucullus.

19. Horace, *Epistles*, II.ii.39–40.

20. *Mahomet* Mahomet or Mehmed II (1432–1481) was a sultan of the Ottoman Empire.

21. *Rated* berated.

22. *Ianizers* Janissaries, part of the Turkish infantry.

23. *Justification* self-justification.

24. *Meacocke* coward.

25. *Change copy* a changeable, fickle person.

26. *Froward* going counter to what is asked or reasonable; perverse, contrary, or contentious.

27. *Liberal* generous, free-spending.

28. *Distinguo* I make a distinction; see *Screech*: "A term used in formal debates to reject or modify an opponent's assertion" (377n11).

29. *Conclude a man to be valiant* proves that a man is brave.

30. *Seely* foolish, simple, silly.

31. *Milk-sop* a weak, ineffectual, cowardly person (usually a boy or man).

32. *Suit* lawsuit.

33. *Infancy* Florio misreads; Montaigne has "*infamie.*" The idea is that some people are cowardly about small matters (infamy, personal slights) and brave about large matters (poverty).

34. *Barber's razor* barber-surgeon's scalpel.

35. *Constant* brave.

36. *Cimbrians and Celtiberians* The Cimbrians were a Germanic tribe who fought the Romans in the second century BC. The Celtiberians were Celtic-speaking people from the Iberian peninsula in the last centuries BC.

37. Cicero, *Tusculanae disputationes*, II.xxvii.65.

38. *In species* of only one kind.

39. *Demisse* abject, base.

40. *Pusillanimity* cowardice.

41. Cicero, *Tusculanae disputationes*, IV.xxxvii.79. Alexander murdered his best friend, Clitus, when he was drunk. See Shakespeare, *Henry V*: "Alexander, God knows, and / you know, in his rages, and his furies, and his / wraths, and his cholers, and his moods, and his / displeasures, and his indignations, and also being a little / intoxicates in his prains, did, in his ales and / his angers, look you, kill his best friend, Cleitus" (IV. vii.27–32).

42. Cicero, *Paradoxa stoicorum*, V.i.34.

43. *Way* path, direction.

44. *Imprease* impresa, motto, crest. *Our good Talbot* John Talbot, the first Earl of Shrewsbury (1384–1453), was a famous fifteenth-century English soldier who died at Castillon (near Montaigne) at the end of the Hundred Years' War between England and France. This impresa—and Talbot—are also invoked in a prefatory sonnet to Book III of Florio's *Montaigne*. Written by "Il Candido" (usually thought to be Florio's friend Matthew Gwinne), the poem is addressed to Lady Elizabeth Grey, whose maiden name was Elizabeth Talbot. John Talbot was a quintessential English and Shakespearean hero. Thomas Nashe, almost certainly alluding to part 1 of Shakespeare's *Henry VI*, commented en-

thusiastically in his *Pierce Pennilesse* (1592), "How would it have joyed brave Talbot (the terror of the French) to thinke that after he had lyne two hundred yeares in his Tombe, hee should triumphe againe on the Stage, and have his bones newe embalmed with the teares of ten thousand spectators at least, (at severall times) who, in the Tragedian that represents his person, imagine they behold him fresh bleeding" (sig. F3). Montaigne's praise for this "terror of the French" is based in local pride. Bordeaux sided with England in the war, and there is still a monument to Talbot in Castillon. Montaigne identifies himself here as a Gascon rather than as a Frenchman. Many thanks to Saul Frampton for help with this note; see also *Céard*, 542n9.

45. That is, a vision of the whole life is essential before one can put the parts together.

46. See Cicero, *De senecute*, VII.2, and Erasmus, *Apophthegmatum opus*, VIII.xxvi.

47. Seneca, *Epistulae morales*, CXX.22.

48. *Sith* since.

49. Venus instills the qualities of a "ruthless soldier" in the heart of the youngest women, still "in their mothers' laps."

50. *Yonker* young nobleman or gentleman; see Tibullus, *Elegies*, II.i.75–76.

A CUSTOM OF THE ISLE OF *CEA*

1. *Isle of Cea* Cea, also known as Ceos or Kea, is a Greek island in the Cyclades archipelago. The allusion to the island and its "custom" comes at the end of the essay. This essay, which catalogs reasons for suicide throughout history, has obvious connections to Shakespeare's Roman plays. It is especially relevant to *Antony and Cleopatra*, which explicitly treats suicide as a superior option to being caught and paraded as an emblem of triumph for the conqueror.

2. *Philosophate* to philosophize. Florio's usage is the earliest recorded example in the *OED*.

3. *Fantastiquize* a variant of *fantasticize*, "to throw oneself into fantastic or strange attitudes." This is the only *OED* citation for either word.

4. *Cathedral master* professor of the *cathèdre*, or university chair.

5. *Cathedral* master, professor.

6. *Armed hand* armed band, army.

7. *Lacedemonians* Spartans.

8. *Varlet* scoundrel, rogue, rascal.

9. *Groundot* almost certainly a typo for "ground" or "groundplot." Montaigne's parallelism is clear: "*de terre pour y vivre, mais de terre pour y mourir*" (*Céard*, 560).

10. *Boiocatus* Boiocalus, the leader of a German tribe, who turned against the Romans in AD 59; see Tacitus, *Annales*, 13.55.56.

11. Seneca, *Thebaid*, I.i.151–53.

12. *Receipt* remedy.

13. *Charge* cost, expense.

14. *Physic* medicine, cure.

15. *Mediane* the median vein of the arm—used for the routine bloodletting alluded to just above.

16. *Mortify* kill.

17. *Podagrees* gouty, filled with gout.

18. The gist of this difficult passage is that the happy wise man can kill himself and the miserable fool can cling to existence as long as they are both acting "according unto nature."

19. *"All hail, Diogenes"* "Good health to you, Diogenes."

20. Virgil, *Aeneid*, IV.434–36.

21. Both Regulus and Cato were Romans who fought in the Punic Wars against Carthage (third and second centuries BC). Saint Augustine, in *City of God*, I.xxii and xxiv, expressed a similar preference for Regulus.

22. *Holme-trees* holly trees.

23. Horace, *Odes*, IV.iv.57–60.

24. Seneca, *Phoenissae* (or *Thebaid*), 190–92.

25. Martial, *Epigrams*, XI.lvi.15–16.

26. Horace, *Odes*, III.iii.7–8.

27. Martial, *Epigrams*, II.lxxx.2.

28. Lucan, *Pharsalia*, VII.104–7.

29. *The hate of life / And seeing-light* . . . the hate of life and the light of day.

30. Lucretius, *De rerum natura*, III.79–82.

31. *In fine* in the end, finally.

32. *To be made of a man an angel* to be made an angel out of a man.

33. Lucretius, *De rerum natura*, III.862–64.

34. In other words, a reasonable exit or exodus. This was an expression attributed to the Stoics and especially to the philosopher Zeno.

35. *Provided for it* put a stop to it.

36. *Halters* ropes, nooses.

37. *Receipt* remedy.

38. *Fencer* the translation of "gladiator" into "fencer" shifts the battle from a Roman "arena" to a more contemporary jousting "list."

39. From Justus Lipsius, *Saturnalium sermonum libri*, II.xxii.

40. Seneca, *Epistulae morales*, LXX.6–7.

41. *Joseph* Titus Flavius Josephus (37–ca. AD 100) was a Roman Jewish historian.

42. *Opiniate* to stick firmly to an opinion.

43. *Battle of Serisolles* The battle of Ceresole, fought in 1544 between the French and the forces of both Spain and the Holy Roman Empire, was part of the Italian War of 1542–1546. The battle was won by the French. "The Lord of *Anguien*"—François de Vendôme, Count of Enghien— was ultimately the successful leader of the battle.

44. Seneca, *Epistulae morales*, XIII.11–13.

45. Virgil, *Aeneid*, XI.425–27.

46. *Seneca, those only … mind* as acceptable motives for suicide, Seneca allows only those that chronically disturb and distract the mind.

47. *Ward* protect.

48. *Gosa* Gozo, near Malta.

49. *Caliver* light musket, harquebus.

50. *Gaols* jails.

51. *Prease* crowd, throng.

52. *By* through.

53. A strange passage suggesting that sexual violence against women is the worst violence "committed against conscience" because women, against their will, cannot help but derive some pleasure from the horrible act.

54. *A wise author of these days and namely a Parisian* See *Screech*: "Allusion to some conteur, not a theologian" (401n37); and *Céard*: "Henri Estienne dans son *Apologie pour Hérodote*, XV, 'Des larcins de notre temps'" (571n7).

55. *These cruelties* violent acts against women.

56. *Advertisement* in the French, "*avertissement*"; so, advice, warning. In this confusing passage, Montaigne seems to be praising the wise words of Marot that follow.

57. From an epigram of Clément Marot (1496–1544), "D'ouy et nenny," I.lxix.

58. *His taking* his being captured.

59. *Minachetuen* Ninachetuen.

60. *Engaged their life* sacrificed their lives.

61. *Inward with Augustus* a close friend of Augustus. This refers to Fulvius, not his wife.

62. *He* Fulvius.

63. *Sithence* since.

64. *Inconvenience* an error by Florio. Montaigne has "*incontinance*." Fulvius's wife is acknowledging her inability to contain her tongue—her verbal incontinence.

65. *Diverse* many people.

66. Montaigne's version is less bleak: the suicides come an hour before encountering the enemies (*furent à une heure près de voir les ennemis*, [*Céard*, 575]). In Florio, "some lived an hour after they had seen their enemies" take their town and incur the miseries that "at so high a rate they had sought to eschew."

67. *There* from Capoa.

68. *Arrested* stopped. Taurea Jubellius is accosting Fulvius.

69. *Brought to a very narrow pinch* in a great deal of difficulty, hard-pressed.

70. *Warrant* ensure.

71. *Give back* retreat.

72. Montaigne is suggesting that although the mass suicides and murders seem worse than those of individuals, they actually are less so because a group passion and enthusiasm possessed the individual wills ("*l'ardeur de la société ravissant les particuliers jugements*" [*Céard*, 576]). There is a kind of unity of judgment lacking in individual suicides.

73. *Enterred* interred, buried.

74. *These late-discovered Indies* not the West Indies but Orissa, a state on the east coast of India. This is the story of the Juggernaut, an idol of Krishna,

dragged throughout the town in a carriage, under whose wheels pilgrims would throw themselves; see *OED*, *Juggernaut*, 1.

75. *Mammocks* scraps, shreds, torn pieces.

76. *Moldered* crumbled, decayed, turned to dust.

77. *The death of this Bishop* the bishop of Soissons.

78. *Amusing one part of it* holding or occupying part of his feeling.

79. *Appay* pay.

80. *Hiperborean* In Greek mythology, the Hyperboreans lived to the north of Thrace, beyond the boreas—the north wind. Their climate was thus perfect—breezeless and sunny every hour of the day. In addition, there was no old age or disease, and beautiful music, accompanied by the voices of lovely maidens, played constantly. Perhaps Gonzalo had Hyperborea in mind—as well as the land of Montaigne's Brazilian Indians—when he was thinking of his perfect commonwealth. See "Of the Cannibals," note 25.

81. *Grieving-smart* unbearable pain.

82. *Most excusable incitations* most excusable motives (for suicide).

OF THE AFFECTION OF FATHERS TO THEIR CHILDREN

1. Madame d'Estissac was a friend and neighbor of Montaigne, whose son Charles traveled with Montaigne to Italy in 1580–1581.

2. *This enterprise* the writing of the *Essays*.

3. *Carking* troubling, anxious.

4. *Descant* to make comments or observations (with a connotation of song); see Shakespeare, *Richard III*: "Why, I in this weak piping time of peace / Have no delight to pass away the time, / Unless to spy my shadow in the sun / And descant on mine own deformity" (I.i.24–27).

5. *Forwardness* direction.

6. *It* affection.

7. *Profitable* here and throughout the essay, "profitable" means "useful."

8. *Common laws* laws of Nature, instincts.

9. *Distasted* blunted.

10. *Propensions* propensities.

11. *Perokitoes* parakeets.

12. *Babbles* baubles, trinkets, toys.

13. *It is mere injustice . . . necessaries* compare Edmund's forged letter, supposedly written by Edgar, in Shakespeare, *King Lear*, I.ii.45–52.

14. *Covetism* covetousness, avarice, desire to possess wealth and riches.

15. *Discourse* reason.

16. *Long of* because of.

17. *Suingly sought* sought after, as by a suitor.

18. Terence, *Adelphi*, I.i.40–42.

19. *And were my desire frustrate* and even if my hopes for her were frustrated.

20. *Discipline* method or system of discipline.

21. Livy, *The History of Rome*, XXVIII.xxviii.1.

22. *Breed* offspring.

23. Tasso, *Jerusalem Delivered*, X.xxxix.6–8.

24. *Muleasses, King of Thunes* Muley-Hassan, the king of Tunis. ·

25. *Venerian* sexual.

26. *His* his family.

27. Horace, *Epistles*, I.i.8–9. *Breed a skoffe* give birth to a contemptuous insult.

28. *Betimes* early.

29. *Us* us younger people.

30. *They . . . them* parents . . . children.

31. *Rheume* watery, mucous secretions (*OED*).

32. *Degenerate* In Shakespeare's *King Lear*, this word is used twice to refer to the unnatural behavior of Goneril: once by her father, Lear (I.iv.229), and once by her husband, Albany (IV.ii.44).

33. This is a reversal of Machiavelli's famous dictum that a prince should be feared rather than loved; see *The Prince*, XVII.

34. *Impuissance* impotence.

35. *Carke* trouble, turbulence, anxiety.

36. *Boulster* stuffed pillow.

37. That is, if a servant is foolish enough to devote himself to this master, he will eventually turn on him in suspicion.

38. Terence, *Adelphi*, IV.ii.9.

39. *Scholastical* purely academic.

40. Throughout this paragraph, the pronouns "he" and "him" continue to refer to "the most boisterous and tempestuous master of *France*" mentioned above.

41. *Frowardness* contrariness, contentiousness, going against what is reasonable.

42. *Might and main* utmost power.

43. That is, wives do not consider their actions free if they come with their husbands' consent.

44. *More hardly* less easily.

45. *Cunny-catching* trickery, deception.

46. *Tumultuary* tumultuous.

47. *Thirling* "flying like something hurled; darting; whirling" (*OED*).

48. *Haply* perhaps, by chance.

49. *It* friendship.

50. *Mine own people* my family.

51. *Jointer* jointure, joint possession.

52. *Work the deed* do the job.

53. *Dilated* expanded, extended.

54. *Substitutions* entails, lines of succession.

55. *Infant-spirits* childish minds.

56. *Fantasies* fancies.

57. *Febricitant* feverish.

58. The law in question is the Salic law, which plays such a large part early in Shakespeare's *Henry V*.

59. *Their* women's.

60. *To go* to walk.

61. *This kind* written, verbal progeny—"what we engender by the mind."

62. Montaigne's elaborate metaphor concerns Heliodorus of Emesa (third century AD), probably a bishop of Tricca and the author of the *Aethiopica* (*An Ethiopian History*), a Greek romance translated into French by Jacques Amyot in 1547 and into English by Thomas Underdowne in 1569. In this section, Montaigne is discussing the immortality bestowed not only on parents by having children but on authors by writing books. Thus, the "daughter" here is the *Aethiopica*.

63. *Highly-esteemed issues* his burned books.

64. *Together* at the same time.

65. *Bare* bore, carried.

66. *This* this book: the *Essays*.

67. *Statuary* sculptor.

68. Ovid, *Metamorphoses*, X.283–84.

AN APOLOGY OF *RAYMOND SEBOND*

1. *Heavens'-cope* the canopy or vault of the heavens.

2. *The three conditions* those that swim, fly, walk.

3. *This notable author* Plato.

4. A classic example of Florio's "Englishing." Montaigne has "*les Basques et les Troglodytes*" (*Céard*, 711).

5. Lucretius, *De rerum natura*, V.1059–61.

6. *Treat* negotiate, bargain.

7. Lucretius, *De rerum natura*, V.1030–31.

8. Tasso, *Aminta*, II.iii.140–41.

9. *Despite* to show contempt for.

10. *Vacations* vocations, occupations.

11. Virgil, *Georgics*, IV.219–21.

12. That is, even in women.

13. I Corinthians 1:19–21.

14. *Philo* Philo of Larissa (d. 84 or 83 BC). A Greek philosopher, Philo was a student of Clitomachus and a late leader of the Platonic Academy. An academic skeptic, he influenced the skeptical writings of Cicero.

15. *One of the seven wise* one of the seven sages of ancient Greece. Most lists do not include Pherecydes (ca. 600–550 BC), who was an important pre-Socratic philosopher.

16. *The wisest that ever was* Socrates; see Plato, *Apology for Socrates*, and Cicero, *Academica*, IV.xxiii.74.

17. Cicero, *Academica*, I.xii.44.

18. *Ought* owed.

19. Cicero, *De divinatione*, II.iii.8

20. *Too much ado* Florio's translation is a little unclear. Montaigne has "*trop*

beau jeu" and suggests he would have it too easy—it would be too much of a game—if he were to consider human beings in their ordinary state.

21. Lucretius, *De rerum natura*, III.1048, 1046.

22. *Squared the same to all biases* found equanimity and balance.

23. *Stead* provide advantage to.

24. *Holdfast* firm or sure grip or grasp. The contrast is between movement and stasis, between moving forward and being stopped.

25. *College* assembly, fellowship, esteemed group.

26. *His* his own.

27. *Sciences* systems of knowledge. Throughout the essay, "science" means "knowledge."

28. *Pyrrho* Pyrrho of Elis (ca. 360–ca. 270 BC), a Greek philosopher and the founder of Pyrrhonian skepticism, kept alive by the writings of Sextus Empiricus (ca. AD 160–210), whose main work, the *Pyrrhonian Hypotyposes*, was published in Henri Estienne's Greek edition of 1562. Montaigne probably knew the Latin translation, published with the second edition of 1567.

29. *Epechists* from the Greek for "I abstain."

30. Lucretius, *De rerum natura*, IV.469–70.

31. *Concupiscible* appetitive.

32. *Discipline* doctrine, philosophy.

33. *But to* only to.

34. *Conceipt* conception, belief.

35. Cicero, *Academica*, II.iii.8.

36. Ibid., II.iii.8.

37. *Quarrelous* quarrelsome.

38. *A hundred and a hundred* hundreds of.

39. *Interdicted* forbidden.

40. *Wots* knows.

41. Cicero, *Academica*, I.xii.45.

42. *Burdens* refrains.

43. *Straggering* staggering, wavering.

44. *Fantazie* idea, notion.

45. Cicero, *De divinatione*, I.xviii.35.

46. *Downfalls* precipices, cliffs.

47. *Endearing of his discipline* making too much of his philosophy, making it too dear.

48. *Her wise Secter in chief* the sage of the sect.

49. *Comprized* comprehended, understood.

50. *Take shipping* goes out to sea.

51. *A mind warranted from prejudice hath a marvellous preferment to tranquility* an unprejudiced mind has a much better chance of reaching tranquillity.

52. *Nice-wits* schoolmasters, pedagogues, pedants.

53. As there is in Pyrrhonism.

54. *Disciplinable* teachable.

55. That is, the Pyrrhonist is a blank sheet of paper, a blank slate.

56. Psalms 94:11, 93:11 (in Vulgate).

57. *Conceit* feign.

58. Livy, *The History of Rome*, XXVI.xxii.14.

59. One of the most famous promulgators of this theory was Florio's friend Giordano Bruno.

60. Lucretius, *De rerum natura*, II.1085–86.

61. Ibid., II.1077–78.

62. Ibid., II.1064–66.

63. *It* the earth.

64. *Happily* haply, perchance.

65. *They had never knowledge nor of Bacchus nor of Ceres* they knew the cultivation neither of wine nor of wheat and grain; see also "Of the Cannibals."

66. The Blemmyi, see Shakespeare, *Othello*, I.ii.143–44.

67. *Women are brought a bed at five years of age* women give birth at age five.

68. *He is no more risible, nor perhaps capable of reason and society* If mankind is no longer capable of laughter, nor perhaps of reason or society, then our notions of the inner states of a man would be irrelevant.

69. *Hidden proprieties and quintessences* occult properties and essential qualities.

70. *Word* speech, language.

71. *Hoc* The debate over transubstantiation—the extent to which communion involves a literal or symbolic ingestion of Christ's body—centered around the interpretation of Matthew XXVI.26: "*Hoc est corpus meum* (This is my body)."

72. Montaigne invokes the famous "liar's paradox."

73. *Ours* our (philosophical) language.

74. *Physic* medicine.

75. *Conceit* attitude, humor.

76. *Impresa* heraldic device, typically containing a motto and an image.

77. *That ancient scoffer* The "*moqueur ancien*" is Pliny the Elder; see Pliny's *The Natural History*, II.vii.

78. Horace, *Odes*, III.xxix.43–48.

79. *Searce* sieve, filter (of judgment and perception).

80. Pliny, *The Natural History*, II.xxiii.

81. *Our times* the Christian era. This "man" is usually thought to refer to Tertullian (ca. 160–ca. 225), an early father of the Christian church.

82. Cicero *De natura deorum*, II.lxvi.167, III.xxxv.86.

83. Saint Augustine, *City of God*, XI.22.

84. A difficult passage. Montaigne suggests that Nature maintains order and balance in the world and thus keeps human beings from having the burden of being afraid of divine judgment.

85. Cicero, *De natura deorum*, I.xvii.45.

86. See Shakespeare, *All's Well That Ends Well*: "The mightiest space in fortune nature brings / To join like likes and kiss like native things" (I.i.205–6).

87. *Sans* without; see Shakespeare, *As You Like It*: "Last scene of all, / That ends this strange, eventful history, / Is second childishness and mere oblivion, / Sans teeth, sans eyes, sans taste, sans everything" (II.vii.162–65).

88. *Epistle to the Romans* Romans I:22–23.

89. *Juggling* hocus-pocus, fraudulence, deception.

90. *Cock-horse* toy horse, rocking horse.

91. Lucan, *Pharsalia*, I.486.

92. *Domineere* mastery; see Saint Augustine, *City of God*, VIII.23.

93. *Trismegistus* Hermes Trismegistus, the name given to the Egyptian god Thoth, was believed in Montaigne's day to have been the author of ancient mystical writings.

94. Saint Augustine, *City of God*, VIII.24.

95. Lucan, *Pharsalia*, I.452–53.

96. *Hath sense* is a sentient being.

97. *Is not this brave?* Is not this a triumph (of bogus argumentation)?

98. *Sottish* foolish.

99. *Lacedemonia* Sparta.

100. Ovid, *Metamorphoses*, X.331–33.

101. *The communication with women* the sharing of wives.

102. Cicero, *De finibus*, V.xxi.59–60.

103. *Quick* living.

104. *Bartolus and Baldus* fourteenth-century Italian legal authorities.

105. *Advises* (noun) opinions.

106. *Without peradventure* without doubt.

107. Lucretius, *De rerum natura*, V.102–3.

108. *Science* knowledge.

109. Lucretius, *De rerum natura*, IV.478–79, 482–83.

110. *Senses subject* subject of the senses.

111. *Want* lack.

112. Lucretius, *De rerum natura*, IV.486–88.

113. Ibid., IV.489–90.

114. *Naturally blind* blind from birth.

115. *Prospect* view.

116. *Shooting at buts* shooting at targets.

117. *In a fair champian ground* in a fine open ground.

118. *Streekes* strikes or strokes.

119. *In a piece* with a harquebus or small rifle.

120. *Virtues, either binding or restrictive* properties such as desiccating or shrinking.

121. *Proprieties* properties.

122. *As in the adamant to draw iron* as in the (occult, secret) property of a magnet to attract iron.

123. *Happily* by chance.

124. *Quarrelous* quarrelsome.

125. *Emmets* ants.

126. *Simples* medicinal herbs.

127. *Sects* philosophical schools.

128. Lucretius, *De rerum natura*, V.577–78.

129. Ibid., IV.379, 386.

130. Ibid., IV.499–510.

131. *Whether* if.

132. *Kenning* visual cognition, sight.

133. Lucretius, *De rerum natura*, IV.397, 389–90, 420–23.

134. *Our discourse* our reason.

135. *Re-enverse* overthrow.

136. *Demisse* downcast, lowly.

137. *Vastity* vastness.

138. *Chilnesse* a chill, a frisson.

139. *Chirurgion* surgeon.

140. *Ruby-red* ruby-red complexion.

141. *Its* her, the lady's; perhaps her beauty.

142. Ovid, *De remedia amoris*, I.343–46.

143. Ovid, *Metamorphoses*, III.424–26.

144. Ibid., X.256–58.

145. *Our Lady's church steeple in Paris* Notre Dame cathedral in Paris.

146. *Tilers or thatchers* those who work on roofs and would be used to the heights involved (unlike the philosopher).

147. Livy, *The History of Rome*, XLIV.6.

148. Cicero, *De divinatione*, I.xxxvi.80.

149. *Wound* bent around, shaped.

150. *Coyle* noisy disturbance, row, turmoil.

151. *Goodly piece* human judgment.

152. *They* the senses and judgment ("understanding," "mind"); *Avie* in emulation.

153. Virgil, *Aeneid*, IV.470.

154. Lucretius, *De rerum natura*, IV.1155–56.

155. Ibid., IV.811–13. The mangled translation obscures the point: even visible things need constant attention, or they can seem remote or even disappear.

156. *Amuseth* draw in, (pre)occupy; see *Cotgrave*: "*amuser*: to stay, hold, or delay from going forward by discourse, questions, or any other amusements."

157. *Cimmerian* refers to a people famous for living in perpetual darkness. The phrase was proverbial.

158. *Spittle* saliva.

159. Lucretius, *De rerum natura*, IV.636–39.

160. *Jandise* jaundice.

161. Lucretius, *De rerum natura*, IV.332–33.

162. Ibid., IV.450, 452.

163. Montaigne is more relativistic than Florio, claiming that these animals receive the sound differently ("*reçoivent le son autre*" [*Céard*, 924]) than we do. Florio suggests that there is a right way, and the animals hear the sound "other than it is."

164. Lucretius, *De rerum natura*, IV.75–80.

165. *Impreses* heraldric devices.

166. *Luxury* lust.

167. *Members* penises.

168. Lucretius, *De rerum natura*, III. 703–4.

169. *Distasted* jaded, lacking the ability to taste.

170. *Wallowishness* tastelessness, insipidness.

171. Lucretius, *De rerum natura*, IV.513–21.

172. *Subjects* somewhat strangely, Montaigne's "*sujet*" is closer to the modern English "object" than to "subject."

173. *Fantasy* faculty of perception.

174. What follows—until "sans ending"—is taken almost word for word from Jacques Amyot's French translation of one of Plutarch's *Moralia*, "On the Meaning of *Ei*."

175. *Poyson* a Florio mistranslation: Montaigne's "*empoigner*" means "grasp" or "seize."

176. *Self* same.

177. *Stripling* youth, adolescent.

178. Lucretius, *De rerum natura*, V.828–31.

179. *Sottishness* foolishness.

180. *Declinations* declinings.

181. At this point Montaigne's long citation of Plutarch ends.

182. Seneca, *Naturales Quaestiones*, I, preface, 5.

183. *Mere* purely.

WE TASTE NOTHING PURELY

1. *Empared* furnished, adorned.

2. *Composition* mixture, blending.

3. *Cyrenaic sensuality or Aristippian voluptuousness* Aristippus (ca. 435–356 BC) was a follower of Socrates and the founder of the Cyrenaic school of philosophy. The end of philosophy—for Aristippus and his followers—was pleasure.

4. *Incommodity* hindrance, trouble, hurt, injury.

5. Lucretius, *De rerum natura*, IV.1133–34.

6. *Our exceeding voluptuousness* our engaging in sexual intercourse.

7. *Morbidezza* see *WW*: "wantonnesse, ranknesse" (232).

8. *A great testimony of their consanguinity and consubtantiality* the deep connection between the "excellency" and the "sickish and dolorous qualities" of the sexual act. Montaigne is continuing his thesis about the blendedness—the lack of "purity"—of things of the world.

9. Seneca, *Epistulae morales*, LXXIV.18.

10. *Travell* travail, toil.

11. *Complexions* constitutions, natures.

12. For an example, see Shakespeare's Jaques in *As You Like It*.

13. Ovid, *Tristia*, IV.iii.37.

14. *Last friends* almost certainly a typo for "lost friends"; Montaigne has "*nos amis perdu*" (*Céard*, 1041).

15. Catullus, *Epigrams*, XXVII.1–2.

16. Seneca, *Epistulae morales*, LXIX.4.

17. In the climax of sexual pleasure, "man" is unable to bear his ecstatic joy.

18. *Upon the nick* at the critical moment; the moment of climax.

19. See the First Lord in Shakespeare, *All's Well That Ends Well*: "The web of our life is of a mingled yarn, good and ill together. Our virtues would be proud if our faults whipped them not, and our crimes would despair if they were not cherished by our virtues" (IV.iii.69–72). See also Feste's quotation in the next note.

20. *Botching and parti-coloured work* a work that is patched and of more than one color; see Feste, the "parti-coloured," motley fool in Shakespeare, *Twelfth Night*: "bid the dishonest man mend himself: if he mend, he is no longer dishonest; if he cannot, let the botcher mend him. Anything that's mended is but patched. Virtue that transgresses is but patched with sin, and sin that amends is but patched with virtue" (I.v.38–45).

21. Tacitus, *Annals*, XIV.44.

22. *less-wire-drawn wits* those with less taut, tight, firm wits.

23. *Volubility* versatility; see *Cotgrave*: "*voluble*: variable, wauering, often flitting, or changing; and, glib, nimble, rolling, always running, euer turning."

24. Livy, *The History of Rome*, XXXII.20.2.

25. The question was "What is the being and nature of God?"; see Cicero, *De natura deorum*, I.xxii.60.

26. *A mean engine* a modest talent or intelligence.

27. *Husbands* managers.

28. *Arithmeticians* Montaigne has "*conteurs*," which can mean either "counters"—as Florio takes it—or "tale-tellers."

29. *Pratler* talker.

30. *Blazoner* proclaimer.

OF A MONSTROUS CHILD

1. *This discourse shall pass single* this will be a simple tale.

2. *Went* walked.

3. *Puling* whining.

4. *Paps* breasts.

5. *Conduit of his back* spinal canal.

6. *This double body* the previous description is of conjoined twins (sometimes called Siamese twins).

7. So-called monsters were thought to demonstrate the will of God. Interesting in this essay is the conclusion that monsters can reveal the limitations of our access to God's will; they can demonstrate how little we know.

8. Montaigne hopes that this particular "monster"—possessing both a "double body and these different members" and "one only head"—will be a favorable omen of the king's ability to unify the religious and political divisions of post-Reformation France under his single rule.

9. That is, found to have been prophesied; see Cicero, *De divinatione*, II.xxxi.66.

10. *Divined contrary* prophesied backward.

11. *Genitorie* genital.

12. Cicero, *De divinatione*, II.xxii.49.

13. *There is nothing, whatsoever it be, that is not according to her* there is nothing that goes contrary to Nature.

OF REPENTING

1. *The public and their own motion* general, universal motion and particular motion.

2. *Counter-roule* catalog.

3. *Gainsay* contradict (more than "deny").

4. Although this is a later piece, Montaigne's use of *essay* is especially compelling here, suggesting the restless attempts to portray himself by testing—and tasting—the world. He essays and cannot resolve. See Frampton, 221–43.

5. *Prentise* apprentice.

6. *Conceits* fancies, imaginings.

7. *Hap* chance.

8. *Sottishness* foolishness.

9. *Munite* to fortify, strengthen, provide with munitions.

10. *Without reward* without rewarding him for his labor.

11. Seneca, *Epistulae morales*, XXXIX.6.

12. *Office* service, duty.

13. *Demisse* lowly, downcast, cowardly.

14. Cicero, *Tusculanae disputationes*, II.xxvi.63, and *De natura deorum*, III. xxxv.85.

15. *Nearly* closely.

16. Horace, *Odes*, IV.x.7–8.

17. *Play the juggler* play his part.

18. *Byas* Bias of Priene (sixth century BCE), one of the seven sages of ancient Greece.

19. *Familiars* domestic servants.

20. *Even so in things of nought* likewise in things of no significance. Montaigne goes on to talk about one of these "things of nought": the lack of appreciation afforded his writing in his own region of Gascony.

21. *Climate of Gascoigne* region of Gascony.

22. *Guienne* a region of southwestern France.

23. A difficult passage in which Montaigne suggests that some people keep themselves removed from the world while alive so that they will be more appreciated after they have died.

24. *Less* less favor, less fame.

25. *Ambassage* embassy.

26. *Remarkable* noticeable.

27. *Serve virtue more hardly* perform more difficult service to virtue.

28. *Exercitation* activity.

29. *Oughly* ugly.

30. *Bruite* (noisy) fame.

31. *Artificer* artisan, skilled manual laborer.

32. *Close stool* toilet seat.

33. *Institution* education.

34. Lucan, *Pharsalia*, IV.237–42.

35. *Grubbed* rooted, dug.

36. *Fashions* Montaigne has "*moeurs*": mores, even morals.

37. *Good-cheap* at little cost or expense.

38. *Intestine* internal, internecine.

39. *Swaying* ruling. This is an interesting moment, when Montaigne posits at least part of the self that is stable, governs, "sways."

40. *Institution* education.

41. *Retreat* retirement.

42. *Burthenous* burdensome.

43. *Happily* perhaps.

44. In this difficult passage, Montaigne imagines pleasure overwhelming the vice associated with it, as in theft, where there is a separation between pleasure and the vice, and sex, where pleasure is completely linked to the "sin."

45. *Pinching want* poverty.

46. *Of complexion* constitutional, inherent, natural.

47. *Courage* individual heart, person.

48. *He* the sinner.

49. That is, he has neither the meta-human soul of the angels or the elevated human soul of Cato.

50. *Respect* consider.

51. *Presage* predict.

52. *Success* outcome.

53. *Moathes* motes, atoms.

54. *Where leaving me* by leaving me alone.

55. *Impuissance* sexual impotence.

56. Quintilian, *Institutio oratoria*, V.xii.19.

57. *Sacietie* satiety.

58. *They* reason, rational powers.

59. *Amendment* convalescence, remedy.

60. *Preposterously* monstrously.

61. *Varlet* here—as often in Shakespeare—a worthless, dissipated man; Montaigne has "*un homme perdu*" ("a lost man").

62. *Discretion* wisdom.

63. Florio gets this one wrong. Montaigne says that our conscience must amend itself through reinforcement of reason and not the weakening of appetites. Florio adds an extra negative.

64. *Affect* love, practice.

65. *Catars* catarrh, discharge of mucus in the nose and throat.

66. That is, when I was taunted in my youth for my beardless chin.

67. *Frowardness* difficulty, contrary behavior.

68. *Tattle* prattle, useless speech.

69. *Carking for* anxiety about.

70. *Mustily* with a musty taste.

71. *Of purpose* on purpose, purposely.

72. *It* old age.

73. *Entrenchings* retrenchments.

74. *It* old age.

OF THREE COMMERCES OR SOCIETIES

1. *Commerces or Societies* associations or social relationships. This essay includes Montaigne's clearest description of the layout of his tower.

2. Livy, *The History of Rome*, XXXIX.xl.5.

3. *Wire-draws* stretches, elongates.

4. Seneca, *Epistulae morales*, LVI.9.

5. *It* the mind.

6. *Vacation* vocation.

7. Cicero, *Tusculanae disputationes*, V.xxxviii.111.

8. *Conceit* reason, thinking.

9. *Entertainments* conversations.

10. *Discourses of countenance* conversations for appearance's sake.

11. *Complexion* disposition.

12. *Nice* fastidious, difficult to please.

13. *For the nonce* for the purpose.

14. *Insipience* folly, silliness.

15. *Forsake* Montaigne uses the verb "*desmeler*," which *Cotgrave* defines as "to performe a businesse iointly with." Montaigne, in fact, is warning *against* forsaking common people.

16. *Wrested* strained, tense.

17. *Squareth according to* adjusts to.

18. *Science* knowledge.

19. *Burden* refrain.

20. *Amities* friendships.

21. *Vulgar worldly friendships* ordinary friendships (as opposed to the "rare amities" mentioned above).

22. *If not unresisted and with hoised-full sails* friendship is best when it is all out, with wind in its full and fully hoisted sails.

23. *It is a beast sociable and for company, and not of troupe* friendship works better in small groups and not in a herd.

24. *Quarrel* legal dispute.

25. *Sance* sans, without.

26. *Indifferent* equitable.

27. *But in extension* except when the mind reaches beyond itself, its normal limits.

28. Horace, *Odes*, III.xix.3–8.

29. *Lacedemonian* Spartan.

30. *Spirit* the mind.

31. *Mincingly* in an affected or effete manner. The Italian is proverbial.

32. *Books* book learning.

33. *Closets* private chambers.

34. *Their* the books'.

35. *Countenance* appearance.

36. Juvenal, *Satires*, VI.189–91.

37. *Well-born* well-born women.

38. Seneca, *Epistulae morales*, CXV.2. There is a criticism here of those whose lives derive completely from their clothes; all things, then, come out of a box. See Lafeu's description of Parolles, in Shakespeare, *All's Well That Ends Well*: "the soul of this man is his clothes" (II.v.40).

39. *Them* Montaigne is still talking about well-born women.

40. *Frowardness* harshness, unfavorableness.

41. *Both regents and schools* both schoolmasters and schools.

42. *Servant* attendant, suitor, lover.

43. *Local solitariness* solitude of place.

44. *Court* in Montaigne, it is "*la Louvre.*"

45. *Of mine own complexion* by my own nature.

46. *By intermission* at intervals.

47. *Envitings* escortings.

48. *Demeaneth* behaves.

49. *Conference, and frequentation* conversation and frequent gathering.

50. *Vouchsafe* is pleased to, desires to.

51. *Check-roll* roster of names.

52. Good minds are intrinsically great. Art merely records the productions of such minds.

53. Cicero, *Paradoxica stoicorum*, V.ii.38. See Shakespeare's Biron in *Love's Labour's Lost*: "From women's eyes this doctrine I derive. / They sparkle still the right Promethean fire. / They are the books, the arts, the academes / That show, contain, and nourish all the world" (IV.iii.324–27).

54. *It* sexual desire, lust.

55. My punishment for such acts in the past has taught me a lesson.

56. Ovid, *Tristia*, I.i.83–84.

57. *Comedians* actors.

58. *Ought* aught, anything.

59. *Bare-conned* merely memorized, not felt or believed.

60. *Brachmanian* Brahmans, high-caste Hindus.

61. *Intercourse* negotiation, business, sexual intercourse.

62. Tacitus, *Annals*, XIII.xlv.

63. Love and sexual desire go together like motherhood and babies.

64. *Inter-lend and inter-owe one another* lend and owe to each other.

65. *She* the beauty.

66. *Brutal* brutish.

67. *Mercenary and common acquaintances* encounters with prostitutes.

68. Montaigne has "*la courtisane Flora*."

69. *Cue* disposition, frame of mind, mood.

70. Masculine beauty approaches feminine beauty only when it looks most like it: childlike and beardless.

71. The two previously discussed: interactions with friends and engagements with women.

72. *Them . . . them* books . . . troubling thoughts (of "importunate imagination" and "insinuating conceit").

73. *Skreene* a seat with a high back to protect against the wind.

74. *His health* a cure.

75. *Sentence* maxim, proverb, sententia.

76. *Peregrination* life journey, pilgrimage.

77. *Want* lack.

78. *Indite and enregister* dictate and write down.

79. *Cabinet* little room.

80. *A walk* a place to walk.

81. My mind does not go along unless my legs move it.

82. *In the same case* in the same boat.

83. *Unresisted prospect* unrestricted view.

84. *Void* of free space.

85. *Importeth* suggests. His house (and family name), Montaigne, means "a Mountaine, a great hill" (see *Cotgrave*).

86. *Particularly court* pay court to himself.

87. Seneca, *Consolatio ad Polybium*, VI.4.

88. *So much as at their privy* even on the toilet.

89. *Churchmen* monks.

90. *This kind of stuff* books.

OF DIVERTING OR DIVERSION

1. *Their* women's.

2. Juvenal, *Satires*, VI.273–45.

3. *Froward* grumpy, churlish.

4. *Gull the assistants* trick the attendants or bystanders.

5. *Their mischief* the trouble caused by the woman's grief.

6. *Want* lack.

7. *Make a load of all this mass* arm myself with a pile of rhetorical cures.

8. *Wedge* ax.

9. *Amuse* satisfy, calm.

10. *Semblable* similar.

11. *Intercessors* mediators.

12. *Predicament* kind, category.

13. *Protectress of all amorous delights* Venus.

14. *As at unawares* as if inadvertently.

15. Ovid, *Metamorphoses*, X.666–67.

16. *Receite* remedy.

17. Cicero, *Tusculanae disputationes*, IV.xxxv.74–75.

18. *Wishly* intently, fixedly.

19. *And that so thick* and so abundantly and completely (killed themselves).

20. *Ruth-moving* pity-inducing, pitiful.

21. *Exigent* extremity, emergency.

22. *Let them blood* let their blood.

23. *Cogitations* thoughts.

24. *Down-fall* precipice, cliff.

25. Virgil, *Aeneid*, IV.382–84, 387.

26. Cicero, *Tusculanae disputationes*, II.xxvi.62.

27. *At each clap* all the time.

28. *The white* the bull's-eye, the target.

29. *Young prince* almost certainly Henri de Navarre, eventually King Henri IV.

30. Persius, *Satires*, VI.72; Lucretius, *De rerum natura*, IV.1065.

31. Lucretius, *De rerum natura*, IV.1070–71.

32. *Displeasure* grief.

33. *Complexion* disposition, nature.

34. *Buckle with* do battle with, combat.

35. *Fraughting* supplying, furnishing.

36. *Corrupteth* broke up, dissipated.

37. Almost certainly an allusion to the death of Montaigne's dear friend La Boétie, twenty-five years earlier.

38. *Foresight* anticipation.

39. See Quintilian, *Institutio oratoria*, I.xi, and Ben Jonson, "Timber: or, Discoveries," in *Works of Ben Jonson, Volume VIII: The Poems; The Prose Works*, edited by C.H. Herford, Percy Simpson, and Evelyn Simpson (Oxford: Clarendon Press, 1947), 597.

40. *Believe* believe me that.

41. *Vain rinds which rebound from subjects* empty husks fall off of the things themselves.

42. Lucretius, *De rerum natura*, V.803–4.

43. *Gingleth* jingle, ring.

44. *Auditory* auditors, audience.

45. Just as preachers' exclamations move their audiences more than their arguments do.

46. *Poising* balancing, weighing, keeping in equipoise.

47. *Massy* of mass, solid, substantial.

48. Lucan, *Pharsalia*, II.42.

49. *Stone* kidney stone.

50. *Yard* penis.

51. *Emperor* Tiberius (42 BC–AD 37; emperor of Rome AD 14–37).

52. *Sottishly* foolishly.

53. *Proules* robs, pilfers, makes a prey of.

54. Montaigne is saying that, in general (wholesale, "in great"), death can be held in contempt. In its minute details ("retail"), however, it affects him deeply.

55. *Lackey* servant.

56. *Cast suits* old clothes.

57. *Entender me* make me sad.

58. *Passionate* impassion.

59. *Indurate* obdurate, obstinate.

60. Florio is confusing. Montaigne's point is that one cannot know another's pain, only one's own, when "presence" affects the "eyes and ears," which cannot be affected except by direct experience.

61. *Blockishness* stupidity.

62. *Juggling* sleight of hand.

63. *Comedians* actors.

64. This entire section is influenced by Quintilian, *Institutio oratoria*, VI.ii, especially sections 32–36. Montaigne has already alluded to the phenomenon earlier when discussing women who become what they play. See note 39. See also Hamlet's advice to the Players in Shakespeare, *Hamlet*, III.ii.1–40. Perhaps even more relevant is Hamlet's speech on seeming, which, like this passage from Montaigne, is negotiating the boundaries between real and feigned grief: "Seems, madam? Nay, it *is*. I know not 'seems.' / 'Tis not alone my inky cloak, good-mother, / Nor customary suits of solemn black, / Nor windy suspiration of forced breath, / No, nor the fruitful river in the eye, / Nor the dejected haviour of the visage, / Together with all forms, moods, shows of grief, / That can denote me truly. These indeed 'seem,' / For they are actions that a man might play; / But I have that within which passeth show— / These but the trappings and suits of woe" (I.ii.76–86).

65. *As Martin the Priest* performed their roles like Prester Martin, a priest who famously recited both parts of the Mass—responses as well as questions.

66. *Waymentings* lamentations.

67. *Instructing party* instructive thing.

68. *Flearing* grimacing, grinning.

69. *Mumps and mows* grimaces, frowns.

70. *Skippings* fits and starts.

71. *Presage* omen.

72. Montaigne sardonically notes that we value life perfectly in being willing to abandon it for a dream.

73. *It* the body.

74. *Mark* target.

75. Propertius, *Elegies*, III.v.7–10.

UPON SOME VERSES OF *VIRGIL*

1. *Cupping-glasses* devices used for drawing blood.

2. *Heedy* heedful, wary.

3. *Distaste them of it* disgust them with sex.

4. *Excuse* permit.

5. *Forwardest* most passionate.

6. *Slow* physically immature.

7. *Obscene word* named in Montaigne, "*fouteau*" meant both "beech tree" and, with its proximity to *foutre*, "to fuck" or, as *Cotgrave* has it, "to leacher."

8. *Step over* skip over, omit.

9. Horace, *Odes*, III.vi.21–24.

10. See Plato, *Timaeus*, 42b and 90e.

11. Ovid, *Ars amatoria*, III.93; *Priapea*, III.2.

12. *That* jealousy.

13. *Fondest* most foolish.

14. *Adulter* adulterer.

15. Johannes Secundus, *Elegiae*, I.vii.71–72.

16. Catullus, *Epigrams*, XV.17–19.

NOTES TO "UPON SOME VERSES OF *VIRGIL*" · 399

17. Vulcan, in Ovid (see next note).

18. Ovid, *Metamorphoses*, IV.187–88.

19. Virgil, *Aeneid*, VIII.395–96.

20. Ibid., VIII.383.

21. Ibid., VIII.441.

22. Catullus, *Epigrams*, LVIIIb.141.

23. *Confusion of children* children raised in common.

24. Women don't mind the sharing of child-raising, which is interesting to Montaigne because, he says, they are constitutionally more jealous.

25. Catullus, *Epigrams*, LVIIIb.138–39.

26. Propertius, *Elegies*, II.viii.3.

27. See Shakespeare, *The Comedy of Errors*, in which the Abbess criticizes Adriana in similar terms (V.i.69–87).

28. Virgil, *Aeneid*, V.6.

29. A difficult passage in which Montaigne imagines how quickly men would be unchaste if—without fear of being seen or reported—they could fly like a bird from nest to nest of every woman who would have them.

30. *Colour of heat* pretext of passion, ardor.

31. *My universal form* my general nature.

32. *Fond* stupid, silly.

33. *In my room* in my place.

34. *Tisicke* phthisic, coughing and wheezing.

35. *Insufficiency* impotence.

36. Catullus, *Epigrams*, LXVII.21–22. Florio leaves this passage untranslated; see *Frame*: "Whose member, feebler than a beet, / Never rose even up to middle height" (659).

37. *To justify himself* to assert his masculinity.

38. *Performed twenty courses* had sex with his wife twenty times.

39. *Convince* convict.

40. *Against the wool* the wrong way.

41. *Infantine* childlike.

42. *Postern* back door, back entrance.

43. Martial, *Epigrams*, VII.lxii.6.

44. Ibid., VI.vii.6.

45. *Pudicity* chastity.

46. *Playing with it* engaging in sport, especially riding; perhaps engaging in masturbation.

47. *Felt* noticed, smelled.

48. *Knot of the judgement of this duty* the crux of judging this duty.

49. *This accident* cuckoldry.

50. *Brokage* mediation, sale.

51. *His* his wife.

52. *He avouched as prettily* he admitted gracefully.

53. *Careful vexation* painful anxiety.

54. Whether there is any profit in being agitated by jealousy.

55. *Ring them* to shackle or enchain women.

56. Juvenal, *Satires*, VI.347–48.

57. *Intelligencer* spy.

58. *Bewrayeth* betrayeth.

59. *Blazon* to proclaim or trumpet.

60. *Moaned* pitied.

61. Lucretius, *De rerum natura*, III.1028, 1026.

62. Catullus, *Epigrams*, LXIV.170.

63. *Curst pate* Florio misreads slightly: Montaigne has "*la mauvaise teste*," which means something like "bad temper" or "bad disposition." Florio reads this more literally as "bad head," thus "cursed pate." In Florio's defense, "*teste*" was the common French spelling for "head" in the sixteenth and seventeenth century.

64. *Massie* copious, abundant.

65. *They are not Bee-busied about rhetoric flowers* they are not preoccupied with rhetorical figures.

66. *Gallant* brave.

67. *Quaintness* clever, linguistically skilled.

68. Here, as often in Montaigne, "subject" is closer to what we think of as "object," so love is primarily a desire for a desired *object*.

69. *Semenary* seminal.

70. *Intermission* mediation.

71. Zeno (490–430 BC) was a pre-Socratic philosopher famous for his paradoxes, and Cratippus (first century BC) was a philosopher who supposedly taught Cicero's son. Both wrote about the terrifying power of emotions.

72. *Pell-mell* haphazardly, without order.

73. *Plaineth* cause (us) to complain.

74. Claudius Claudianus, *In Eutropium*, I.24–25.

75. *No barrel better hearing* nothing to choose between them.

76. In the sexual act.

77. Horace, *Satires*, I.i.24–25.

78. *This* the sexual act.

79. *Each other* every other.

80. *That* the sexual act.

81. *Esseniens* Essenes—a Jewish sect of the second century BCE; the others were the Pharisees and the Sadducees.

82. *Consume* consume itself (by refusing to procreate).

83. *As close* as secretly, privately.

84. *Bonifie* to do good.

85. Terence, *Phormio*, I.iii.20.

86. Virgil, *Georgics*, II.511.

87. Pseudo-Gallus, *Elegies*, I.180.

88. Lucretius and Virgil, cited previously.

89. *Networke* lacework.

90. Ovid, *Amores*, I.v.24.

91. *Baffles* gelds, castrates.

92. *Love* lovemaking.

93. *Nicely close . . . closely nice* timid and less open.

94. *A beck is as good as a dew guard* a mute signal or nod is as valuable as a *dieu vous garde* ("God preserve you").

95. *Febricitant* feverish.

96. *Wiredrawing* drawing out or prolonging to a great length.

97. *Their* the ladies'.

98. *Each one* each man.

99. *List's end* narrow strip, scrap.

402 · NOTES TO "UPON SOME VERSES OF *VIRGIL*"

100. *Jouissance* sexual pleasure, joy.

101. *At rack and manger* surrounded by abundance and plenty.

102. *Snatches and away* quick sexual encounters and departures.

103. *Reke* fear.

104. Catullus, *Epigrams*, LXIV.147–48.

105. *Viands* meats.

106. Martial, *Epigrams*, VII.xcv.10–11, 15. Florio gets embarrassed and does not translate the last line, using "&c." instead. Martial's line reads, "I would a hundred times rather lick his ass."

107. *Surpay* surpass, outweigh.

108. *Imagine mine* imagine being my possession.

109. *Moon* luna.

110. *Ethicke* meager (the French word is "*étique*").

111. *To work* to perform sexually.

112. Martial, *Epigrams*, XI.civ.12, XI.lx.8.

113. *Impart not themselves but that way* to communicate only in a sexual way.

114. Catullus, *Epigrams*, LXVIIIb.147–48.

115. Tibullus, *Elegies*, I.vi.35.

116. *Regent* teacher.

117. *Luxury* lust.

118. Livy, *The History of Rome*, XXXIV.iv.19.

119. *Resty* resisting control, refractory.

120. Ovid, *Amores*, III.iv.13–14.

121. *No right but by the ears* no right to noble women except as a listener or a counselor.

122. *Seld* seldom, rare.

123. Montaigne is meditating on the external evidence of desire in men—the erection—and the absence of such in women.

124. *Lances* a synecdoche for "warriors."

125. *Ione* Joanna.

126. *Andreosse* Andreasso.

127. *That action* sexual intercourse.

128. Florio is confusing. Montaigne is clearly stating that male desire is much more easily satisfied in copulation than is female desire.

129. *Happily* perhaps.

130. Martial, *Epigrams*, VII.lviii.3–5. Florio presumably finds these lines too crude to translate. *Frame*'s fairly tame translation follows: "Having explored his body, found his member limp, / As a wet thong, impossible by hand to primp, / She leaves the dastard bed" (676).

131. Catullus, *Epigrams*, LXVII.27–28. Again, Florio does not translate. *Frame* translates as: "A stronger lover elsewhere must be found / By whom her virgin zone may be unbound" (676).

132. Virgil, *Georgics*, III.127.

133. Horace, *Epodes*, XII.15–16.

134. Horace, *Odes*, II.iv.22–24.

135. *Lubberly* clumsy, lazy, stupid.

136. *It* old age.

137. *Guirle* This is a strange one, for Montaigne's word is "*enfance.*" He is talking about a youth, but a male youth, a boy, who can use the older man's ardor to help him with his sexual exploits.

138. Virgil, *Aeneid*, XII.67–69.

139. *Faintness* limpness, flaccidity.

140. *Dastardise* base cowardice.

141. Ovid, *Amores*, I.vii.21.

142. *Priapeia*, LXXX.1, VIII.4–5.

143. *Essence* reality.

144. *Seemliness* propriety, decorum.

145. Quintus Cicero, *Commentariolum petitionis*, XIV.54.

146. *Cocket* cocky, cocksure, proud.

147. Theodore Beza, *Poemata*, epigram LXXIV.10; Beza was a Reformer and successor to Calvin.

148. Mellin de Saint-Gelais, "Rondeau sur la dispute des vits par quatre dames" (14). Saint-Gelais was a Roman Catholic cleric and court poet.

149. Catullus, *Epigrams*, LXVIIIb.147.

150. In the world of voluntary acts, there are no prescriptive rights.

151. *Appointments* assignations.

152. *Impertinently genital* not a typo for "genial": Montaigne is asserting his physicality as a wooer and lover.

153. Horace, *Odes*, I.v.13–16.

154. Terence, *The Eunuch*, I.i.16–18.

155. Seneca, *Epistulae morales*, XCV.33.

156. *And blood wipes as well as dry-blows* cutting blows as well as bloodless ones.

157. Seneca, *Epistulae morales*, CXVI.5.

158. *Receipt* recipe, prescription.

159. Juvenal, *Satires*, I.iii.26–28.

160. *It* pain.

161. *Avie* in rivalry or emulation (*OED*).

162. *Entrained* constrained.

163. *She...them* the mind...bodily pleasures.

164. *Domage* damage, detriment.

165. *Carking* burdening, distressing.

166. *Comber* encumber.

167. *Sinnowes* sinews, tendons.

168. *Lives-blitheness* joys.

169. *Such a commodity* love.

170. Horace, *Epodes*, XII.19–20. Florio does not translate these lines, which tell us that the phallus of the young man is firmer than a young tree.

171. Horace, *Odes*, IV.xiii.26–28.

172. We (the older generation) no longer have any hold or control.

173. The old are not able to attract ("hook") young lovers ("fresh cheese").

174. Florio's translation obscures the paradox and makes no sense. Montaigne has "*Qui s'aymera, si me suive*": he who loves himself, let him follow me.

175. *Composition* combination, mix.

176. Martial, *Epigrams*, X.xc.10–11.

177. Ovid, *Ex Ponto*, I.iv.49–51.

178. Horace, *Odes*, II.v.21–24.

179. See *Screech*: "Conspirators who freed Athens from the tyranny of the Pisistratids. Similarly, a sprouting beard freed youths from the 'tyranny' of homosexual advances" (1014n177).

180. *Importune* disdainful.

181. Horace, *Odes*, IV.xiii.9–10.

182. *It* love.

183. *Princock* saucy, insolent. This "princock boy" is Cupid.

184. *Garb* from Montaigne's "*galbe*": gracefulness, comeliness, style.

185. *Them* women.

186. *Preoccupate* gain before or ahead of.

187. *Handy-gripes* firm, amorous grasps.

188. *Amain* violently, at full force.

189. Virgil, *Georgics*, III.98–100 (of an old stallion).

190. *Plast* placed.

191. Catullus, *Epigrams*, LXV.19–24.

192. *Ill may the kiln call the oven burnt-tail* the kiln should not call the oven burned-ass. Something like "the pot calling the kettle black" is meant. Montaigne has "*le fourgon se moque de la pelle*" (III:112)—the oven fork mocks the fire shovel.

OF COACHES

1. *Eftsoons* moreover.

2. Lucretius, *De rerum natura*, VI.703–4.

3. *Gourmandise* gluttony.

4. Seneca, *Epistulae morales*, LIII.3.

5. *Astonie* astonish.

6. *It* sense of fear.

7. *Represent flight* give us examples of flights from fear and danger.

8. *In respect of* in comparison with.

9. Livy, *The History of Rome*, XXII.v.1.

10. *Impetuosity* violent passion.

11. *Ward* position, preparation.

12. *I encounter not two* I cannot take a second attack.

13. *Litter* an enclosed vehicle containing a couch, often used to transport the sick.

14. *Display* describe.

15. *Availefully* usefully.

16. *Targeteer* soldier with a shield.

17. *Harquebuses or calivers* types of guns.

18. *Pavesado* a screen or wall of shields.

19. *Galliote* a small galley or boat.

20. *Disroute* uproot, dislodge.

21. *Embarricado* to make a barricade.

22. *The last kings of our first race* the Merovingien dynasty (481–751).

23. *Movables and household-stuff* tableware and furniture.

24. *Communality* common people.

25. *Aye-lasting* everlasting.

26. *Queen Catherine* Catherine de' Medici (1519–1589).

27. The Pont Neuf—construction on which began in 1578, was interrupted in 1588–1589, and was resumed in 1599—opened in 1603 and was christened by Henri IV in 1607.

28. *Casket* chest, money box.

29. Authority, like art, has an end outside of itself.

30. Cicero, *De finibus*, V.vi.16.

31. *Governours* tutors.

32. *Puissant* powerful.

33. Justus Lipsius, *De amphitheatro*, VII.

34. *Heedy* heedful, attentive, cautious.

35. *Intermission* intermediary, intervention.

36. *Fond* foolish.

37. Cicero, *De officiis*, II.xv.52–53, 54.

38. *Overplus* surplus.

39. *Behoof* benefit.

40. *Wound and oppress* Florio mistranslates Montaigne's *"assenoit"*; here it means "hand out, apportion, measure." Cyrus is being praised for his generosity.

41. *Croesus upbraided him* Croesus reproached Cyrus.[1]

42. *Him* Cyrus.

43. *Venter* venture, risk.

44. *Con-citizens* private citizens.

45. Cicero, *De officiis*, I.xiv.43. The Latin says that the passing of money to strangers should *not* seem a liberality.

46. *Coffers* chest of money and valuables.

47. In the amphitheater.

48. *Three hundred huge bears to be baited and tugged in pieces* the sport of bearbaiting, popular in Shakespeare's day. Florio embellishes Montaigne to give the text a more contemporary English flavor.

49. *Emperour Probus* Roman emperor from 276 to 282.

50. *Enchased* ornamented.

51. Calpurnius, *Bucolica*, VII.47, cited in Justus Lipsius, *De amphitheatro*, XIII.

52. Juvenal, *Satires*, III.153–55, cited in Justus Lipsius, *De amphitheatro*, XIII.

53. *Acted* played.

54. *Chap* crack open (into pieces).

55. *Cranishes* crevices, crannies.

56. *Storax* a fragrant resin.

57. *Banket* banquet.

58. *Only* single.

59. *Oresaffron'd* covered with saffron.

60. *Horse* refers to the hippopotamus.

61. Calpurnius, *Bucolica*, VII.64–71, cited in Justus Lipsius, *De amphitheatro*, X.

62. *Purling* rippling, swirling, murmuring.

63. *Streaks and purlings* streams and ripples.

64. Martial, *Epigrams*, XII.xxix.15–16, cited in Justus Lipsius, *De amphitheatro*, XVII. The English translation seems to make little sense but is deeply erudite. Martial's Hermogenes—"sprung of Hermes," the thief of the gods—steals napkins. Cloth of all kinds, the epigram suggests, is vulnerable when he is around—even that used to make awnings to cover the amphitheater stage. So when Hermogenes (one of the "linenthieves") is present, spectators hide their awnings or "sails" and bake in the sun rather than lose them to the thief.

65. Calpurnius, *Bucolica*, VII.53–54, cited in Justus Lipsius, *De amphitheatro*, XII.

66. *Admiration* wonder, amazement.

67. *We go our own pace* we retrace our steps.

68. Horace, *Odes*, IV.ix.25–28.

69. Lucretius, *De rerum natura*, V.326–27.

70. Cicero, *De natura deorum*, I.xx.54.

71. *Keep a coyle* make a fuss about.

72. Lucretius, *De rerum natura*, II.1150.

73. Ibid., V.330–34.

74. *Infantine* infantile.

75. *Convultion of sinnowes* convulsion of sinews or tendons.

76. *His* the New World's.

77. *Cony-catch* trick, deceive.

78. *Bucklers* small round shields.

79. *Topsy-turvied* turned upside down.

80. *Entreated* treated.

81. *Behoof* benefit, advantage.

82. *Minatory* threatening.

83. See his "Of the Cannibals" (1.31; 1.30 in Florio).

84. *Weights* ounces.

85. *Redeem the torment of being burned alive by the baptism* bought his way out of being burned alive by agreeing to be baptized before his execution.

86. *Pusillanimity* cowardice.

87. *Silly* "simple" more than "foolish" (as often with this word in Florio).

88. Montaigne gets this material from Francisco Lopez de Gomara, *L'histoire générale des Indes*, translated by Fumée (1578 and 1587), II.lxxv. Montaigne also may have read Bartolomé de Las Casas's attacks on the conquistadores. See *Screech*, 1034n33.

89. *Seld-seen* seldom seen.

90. *Intestine* internecine, internal.

91. King Phillip II of Spain.

92. *Moveable* movable goods.

93. *Encivilized* civilized.

94. *Munkeis* monkeys. Montaigne's word is "*magot*," which means "baboon."

95. *Cawcie* causeway.

96. *Battaile* army, battalion.

97. *Avie* in emulation.

OF THE LAME OR CRIPPLE

1. The Gregorian calendar—named after Pope Gregory XIII—was introduced in France in December 1582. It actually moved the date forward eleven days.

2. *Bissextile* "Containing the bissextus or extra day which the Julian calendar inserts in leap-year" (*OED*).

3. *Arrearages* arrears, debts.

4. *Limit* determine.

5. *Well holp-up* well accommodated, in fine position. Montaigne is being ironic.

6. *Plodding* musing, thinking.

7. *Gadding* wandering, flitting.

8. *First faculties* primary properties. For the gap between knowledge and experiential learning and enjoyment, compare Shakespeare's Berowne, in *Love's Labour's Lost*, I.1.72–93.

9. The body and the mind disrupt their enjoyment of the world by mixing it with the pretensions of learning.

10. *Let us reassume our custom* let us return to (an examination of) this custom of ours.

11. Persius, *Satires*, V.20.

12. *Defeature* ruin, defeat in battle; see *WW*: "*Soffratto*, a defeature or ouerthrow."

13. *Juggle* play the showman or fool.

14. *Quarelous* quarrelsome.

15. *Miss* fail.

16. *Descanted* tossed about (an idea).

17. Cicero, *Academica*, II.xxi.68.

18. *Port* bearing.

19. *Semblable* the same, alike.

20. We gravitate toward vanity because it is similar in form to our own being.

21. *End of the clue* Montaigne has "*le bout du fil*," which means "end of the thread" and makes the unwinding metaphor work.

22. *Wind off* unwind.

23. *Embrued* steeped in, imbued with (an idea).

24. *Botch up* to repair.

25. Livy, *The History of Rome*, XXVIII.xxiv.1.

26. Montaigne is noting that—in the world of rumors—people add interest to the loan that they receive. That is, they add their own fabrications to (false) reports.

27. *Furthest-abiding* remotest, farthest away.

28. *Earnested* heated, "fired up."

29. *Earnestness* excitement.

30. Cicero, *De divinatione*, II.xxxix.81.

31. Saint Augustine, *City of God*, VI.x.

32. *Composition* disposition.

33. Seneca, *Epistulae morales*, CXVIII.vii.

34. Quintus Curtius, IX.ii.14. The translation is especially obscure here. "Rumor never stops with the crystal clear" (that is, evidence).

35. *Heedy* attentive, cautious, heedful.

36. *Preoccupated* prejudiced, biased.

37. *Astonieth* astonishes.

38. *Country thereabout* neighborhood.

39. *Qualities* social classes.

40. *Seely* foolish, simple, silly.

41. *Sottishness* foolishness.

42. *Cheverell* pliable, like the leather of a kid goat. See Feste in Shakespeare's *Twelfth Night*: "A sentence is but a cheverel glove to a good wit, how quickly the wrong side may be turned outward" (III.i.10–12).

43. *His* his foolishness.

44. We should be as hesitant to reject marvelous stories as we are hesitant to receive them.

45. *Stile* the legal style.

46. *Thaumantis* Thaumas, or wonder.

47. *Admiration* wonder. That wonder is the beginning of the philosophy is an axiom derived from Plato, *Theaetetus*, 155D.

48. It takes as much learning to yield wise ignorance (which Montaigne is celebrating here) as it does to yield true knowledge.

49. See Natalie Zemon Davis, *The Return of Martin Guerre* (Cambridge, MA: Harvard University Press, 1983).

50. *Country* neighborhood.

51. *Author* authority.

52. *A body* substance and credibility.

53. *Irrefragable* undisputed, irrefutable.

54. *Most-mighty testimony* God's testimony in the Bible.

55. *Are of them* are proper miracles.

56. Whether he uses this amazing narration to testify against others or against himself.

57. Author unknown.

58. Tacitus, *Historiae*, I.xxii.

59. *Doubt of it* doubt the existence of witches.

60. *Mine* those who challenge my opinions; my detractors.

61. *They have as much appearance as their contradictors* they apparently have as good an argument as their detractors.

62. Cicero, *Academica*, II.xxvii.87.

63. *A bright-shining and clear light* clear and obvious evidence.

64. Our life is too real and fundamental to be used to prove these supernatural and imagined events.

65. Even those who have confessed to using drugs and potions should not always be believed, for they have been known to claim to have killed people who turn out to be alive and well.

66. *A supernatural approbation hath authorized him* a supernatural authority has confirmed his claim.

67. *Domestical* homegrown.

68. *Preoccupation* preconception.

69. Montaigne would rather give them hellebore, to purge madness, than hemlock, to poison them as criminals.

70. *Captivate* captivated, insane.

71. Livy, *The History of Rome*, VIII.xviii.

72. An allusion to the Gordian knot, which Alexander untied and, in so doing—according to prophecy—would make him the king of Asia. See Shakespeare, *Henry V*: "Turn him to any cause of policy, / The Gordian knot of it he will unloose, / Familiar as his garter" (I.1.46–48).

73. *For a sumpter-horse* as a packhorse would serve men.

74. *Gape for* guarantee, vouch for.

75. Cicero, *Tusculanae disputationes*, I.xxv.60.

76. *Malapert* presumptuous, saucy.

77. *Complexions* propensities, tendencies.

78. *To distaste them* to find them distasteful.

79. *Commodious for* suitable to.

80. Erasmus, *Adages*, II.ix.49.

81. *Unassayed* untried, untasted.

82. *Earnestly-luxurious* lusty.

83. *To a not-being* to something that does not exist.

84. Montaigne alludes to the adage cited in note 74.

85. *Torquato Tasso* an Italian epic poet (1544–1595), whom Montaigne must have visited in a Ferrara madhouse while on his Italian travels in 1580–1581. He does not mention the visit in his *Travel Journal* but does mention it in *Sebond* (2.12).

86. Theramenes was a Greek rhetorician and supposedly a teacher of Isocrates (436–338 BC), who was famous for arguing on both sides of a question.

87. Virgil, *Georgics*, I.89–93.

88. More precisely, "Every medal has its reverse" (Italian proverb).

89. *Exacted consent from men* torn away from men the habit of assent.

90. *Fantasia* opinion, judgment.

91. *Self-overweening* excessive arrogance.

92. *Set to sale* put on sale.

93. *Chapman* a buyer.

94. Montaigne reiterates his thesis that human beings do nothing in moderation. In the history of philosophy, this tendency has led both to rash claims that human beings can know everything and to equally rash claims they can know nothing.

95. *Impuissance* inability.

96. The human lack of moderation will be stopped only when the necessity of infirmity makes it impossible to go any further.

OF EXPERIENCE

1. Manilius, *Astronomica*, I.v.62–63.

2. *Dissemblable* dissimilar, various.

3. *Perozet* a manufacturer of playing cards in Montaigne's day.

4. *Cutting out their morsels* regulating their procedure, their judicial freedom.

5. *In their fashion* in their creation.

6. *To gloss* to provide commentary on.

7. *Epicurus* a Greek philosopher (341–269 BC) who posited multiple worlds and influenced the poet Lucretius (99–55 BC), who in turn, in this regard, influenced Giordano Bruno.

8. Tacitus, *Annals*, III.xxv.

9. *Them* laws.

10. *No other* no other laws.

11. *Quiddity* the essential nature of a person or thing (mostly a legal term); see Shakespeare, *Hamlet*, V.i.91.

12. Seneca, *Epistulae morales*, LXXXIX.3.

13. *Retailing* Montaigne's "*retaillant*" means "shredding," "paring," "clipping."

14. Quintilian, *Institutio oratoria*, X.iii.16.

15. Ulpian was a second-century AD "jurisconsult." Bartolus and Baldus were medieval legal commentators.

16. *Put in her head* cramming and clogging the mind of posterity with useless opinions.

17. *Distempering* diluting.

18. *Peddling* trifling, quibbling.

19. *Arrests* final decisions, decrees, sentences.

20. *Barres* railings that separate the judge from the criminal in a law court.

21. *Firret* ferret out, dig for the answer.

22. Erasmus, *Adages*, II.iii.68. Pitch is a thick tarlike substance used as a trap or snare. Iago famously boasted that he would turn Desdemona's "virtue into pitch" (Shakespeare, *Othello*, II.3.334).

23. *Lets* obstacles.

24. *Stifled* choked.

25. *More ways to the wood than one* a proverbial phrase inserted by Florio.

26. *Pretendeth* aspires.

27. *Admiration* wonder, inquiry.

28. Étienne de La Boétie, *A Marguerite de Carle*, 109–16.

29. *We do but inter-gloss ourselves* we do nothing but write commentaries on each other.

30. *Stock* trunk, source of a line of descent.

31. *Sereine or night-calm* nighttime mist or dew believed to have poisonous properties.

32. *Distemper* to cause disequilibrium, a loss of balanced humors.

33. *Swizzers* Swiss.

34. *Augusta* Augsburg; visited by Montaigne in October 1580 on his way to Italy.

35. *Without* outside, out of doors.

36. We do not like wine from the bottom of the cask, the Portuguese, however, consider this part of the wine to be the best.

37. *Scholastical* scholarly, textbook-based.

38. *Vascosane or Plantin* two major printing houses in Montaigne's day.

39. *Hoyting* romping.

40. *Tintimare* confused noise, hubbub.

41. *Rumours* noises, tumults, loud voices.

42. *Fain* glad, delighted.

43. *And easy to take snuff in the nose or to be transported* Montaigne has "*facile à prendre l'essor*" (*Céard*, 1685), which means "easily takes flight." Florio's "transported" makes sense in this context, but the "take snuff in the nose" is a cryptic idiomatic addition of Florio's. For a possible answer, see *WW*: "*Pigilare ombra*, to take snuffe or pepper in the nose, to mistrust" (277). The link could be that Montaigne's mind is capable of distraction—either with mistrust and doubt or flights of fancy and wonder. Thanks to Saul Frampton for this suggestion.

44. *Sextius* Sextius Niger (first century AD), a Roman philosopher.

45. *Attalus* Stoic philosopher (first century AD).

46. *Rudeness* austerity.

47. *Wantonness* softness, effeminacy.

48. *Common sink* dump heap.

49. Once again, Florio adds the proverb (in italics).

50. *Apprentisages* teachings.

51. *Corporal complexions* bodily qualities.

52. *Opiniative* opinionated, stubborn.

53. *Reasty* rancid.

54. *Art* the art of medicine.

55. *Sallets* salads.

56. *Friand* fond (of delicate food).

57. *Shroving* festive, carnival, connected to Shrovetide.

58. Just as it goes against my conscience to eat meat on a fish day, so it goes against my taste to eat fish and meat together.

59. It is as unwise to utterly shun physical pleasures as it is to be obsessed with them.

60. *Ninny-hammer* nitwit, idiot.

61. *Spirit* mind.

62. *He* the mind.

63. Horace, *Epistles*, I.ii.54.

64. The scale of Critolaus (ca. 200–118 BC) always gave greater weight to matters of the soul.

65. *She* imagination, the mind.

66. *Cyrenaic philosophers* those fourth-century BC ancient Greek philosophers who were devoted to hedonism.

67. *Them* bodily pleasures.

68. Let them live on War (Mars), Wisdom (Pallas), or Persuasion (Mercury) rather than Corn/Harvest (Ceres), Sex (Venus), or Wine (Bacchus).

69. *Quadrature* squaring.

70. *Even upon their wives* even while having sex with their wives.

71. *Mediocrity* mean, balance.

72. *Voluptuous* pleasurable.

73. *That . . . this* everyday bodily pleasures . . . violent actions and thoughts of war.

74. *Without . . . welt or guard* without ornamentation or trimming (*OED*).

75. *Appendixes* appendages.

76. Horace, *Odes*, I.vii.30–32.

77. *Gaudy* luxurious, ornate.

78. Whether it is true or merely a joke that the Faculty of Theology at the Sorbonne was characterized by wine-drenched feasts, it was acceptable that, after a morning of difficult study, professors engaged in drinking at lunch.

79. *Devoires* obligations, duties.

80. Cicero, *De finibus*, II.viii.24. Florio's translation is strange. The Latin stresses wisdom: "A wise palate should go with a wise heart."

81. *Play at cob-castle* clearly a game, but one not found in the *OED*. Montaigne has "*jouer à cornichon-va-devant*" (*Céard*, 1729). *Cotgrave* links "*cornichon*," or "little Horne," to games of "Quoites" and "Bowles."

82. *Continency* chastity.

83. *She may assist and favour him* the soul may assist and favor the body.

84. *Continually* Montaigne has "*conjugalement*," "conjugally."

85. Eudoxus (ca. 400 BC) was a follower of Plato and was famous as an astronomer and mathematician. In his *Nicomachaean Ethics*, Aristotle mentioned him as a proponent of hedonism.

86. *Who thereon established his chief felicity* he who made pleasure his principal good.

87. *Voluptuousness* pleasure.

88. Cicero, *Tusculanae disputationes*, IV.xxxi.66.

89. *Evitable* avoidable.

90. *Physic* medicine.

91. *Dictionary* lexicon, vocabulary.

92. *Severally* separately, uniquely.

93. *Bawk* shirk, avoid, pass over.

94. *Priseable* worth prizing.

95. Seneca, *Epistulae morales*, XV.9.

96. *Jouissance* enjoyment, pleasure.

97. *Promptitude of my hold-fast by it* the speed with which I can grip or grasp it.

98. *Custom* use of it.

99. *Him* God; *condign* proper, well-earned.

100. *Her part* the soul's part.

101. *Intestine* inner.

102. *Availful* beneficial.

103. Virgil, *Aeneid*, X.641–42.

104. Lucan, *Pharsalia*, II.657.

105. There is nothing wrong with our needing to eat and drink. In fact, these elemental functions are to be appreciated and embraced.

106. Seneca, *Epistulae morales*, CXIX.5.

107. *Insensibly* without sensation and pleasure.

108. Cicero, *De finibus*, III.vi.20.

109. *She* Philosophy.

110. There is irony here; the child is not really "well-pleasing." Montaigne is criticizing Philosophy for being childish when she rants against the "barbarous alliance" of the "divine" and the "terrestrial."

111. *His followers...his lessons* Florio confuses matters with the masculine pronouns here. Montaigne is still talking about Philosophy's anti-corporal strictures, and the feminine pronouns should be used.

112. *His* Philosophy's.

113. *Moderatrix* moderator.

114. *Sensualities* pleasures.

115. Cicero, *De finibus*, V.xvi.44.

116. *Academical and Peripatetical* following those of Plato's academy and those of Aristotle.

117. *Cousin-german to* cousin to, related to.

118. Saint Augustine, *City of God*, XIV.5.

119. *Frowardly* rebelliously, cheekily.

120. Seneca, *Epistulae morales*, LXXIV.32.

121. Montaigne praises true Christian ascetics who renounce the earthly for the spiritual; they engage in "privileged study." For the rest of us, though, hypocrisy reigns, and spiritual chatter ("Super-celestial opinions") tends to be essentially linked to subhuman behavior ("under-terrestrial manners").

122. *&c.* Florio's prudishness ruins the joke. Montaigne has "*chier*," or "shit."

123. *They will be exempted from them and escape man* human beings want to escape the human parts of themselves.

124. *He...him...he* Philotas...Alexander...Philotas.

125. Horace, *Odes*, III.vi.5.

126. From Jacques Amyot's translation of Plutarch's *Life of Pompey the Great*, 42.

127. *Blithe and social* happy and sociable wisdom. Apollo was the god of healing and music, and was in charge of the Muses.

128. Horace, *Odes*, I.xxxi.17–20.

TITLES IN SERIES

For a complete list of titles, visit www.nyrb.com or write to:
Catalog Requests, NYRB, 435 Hudson Street, New York, NY 10014

* *Also available as an electronic book.*

WILLIAM ROUGHEAD Classic Crimes

CONSTANCE ROURKE American Humor: A Study of the National Character

SAKI The Unrest-Cure and Other Stories; illustrated by Edward Gorey

TAYEB SALIH Season of Migration to the North

TAYEB SALIH The Wedding of Zein*

JEAN-PAUL SARTRE We Have Only This Life to Live: Selected Essays. 1939–1975

GERSHOM SCHOLEM Walter Benjamin: The Story of a Friendship*

DANIEL PAUL SCHREBER Memoirs of My Nervous Illness

JAMES SCHUYLER Alfred and Guinevere

JAMES SCHUYLER What's for Dinner?*

SIMONE SCHWARZ-BART The Bridge of Beyond*

LEONARDO SCIASCIA The Day of the Owl

LEONARDO SCIASCIA Equal Danger

LEONARDO SCIASCIA The Moro Affair

LEONARDO SCIASCIA To Each His Own

LEONARDO SCIASCIA The Wine-Dark Sea

VICTOR SEGALEN René Leys*

ANNA SEGHERS Transit*

PHILIPE-PAUL DE SÉGUR Defeat: Napoleon's Russian Campaign

GILBERT SELDES The Stammering Century*

VICTOR SERGE The Case of Comrade Tulayev*

VICTOR SERGE Conquered City*

VICTOR SERGE Memoirs of a Revolutionary

VICTOR SERGE Unforgiving Years

SHCHEDRIN The Golovlyov Family

ROBERT SHECKLEY The Store of the Worlds: The Stories of Robert Sheckley*

GEORGES SIMENON Act of Passion*

GEORGES SIMENON Dirty Snow*

GEORGES SIMENON The Engagement

GEORGES SIMENON Monsieur Monde Vanishes*

GEORGES SIMENON Pedigree*

GEORGES SIMENON Red Lights

GEORGES SIMENON The Strangers in the House

GEORGES SIMENON Three Bedrooms in Manhattan*

GEORGES SIMENON Tropic Moon*

GEORGES SIMENON The Widow*

CHARLES SIMIC Dime-Store Alchemy: The Art of Joseph Cornell

MAY SINCLAIR Mary Olivier: A Life*

TESS SLESINGER The Unpossessed: A Novel of the Thirties*

VLADIMIR SOROKIN Ice Trilogy*

VLADIMIR SOROKIN The Queue

NATSUME SŌSEKI The Gate*

DAVID STACTON The Judges of the Secret Court*

JEAN STAFFORD The Mountain Lion

CHRISTINA STEAD Letty Fox: Her Luck

GEORGE R. STEWART Names on the Land

STENDHAL The Life of Henry Brulard

ADALBERT STIFTER Rock Crystal

THEODOR STORM The Rider on the White Horse

JEAN STROUSE Alice James: A Biography*

HOWARD STURGIS Belchamber

ITALO SVEVO As a Man Grows Older